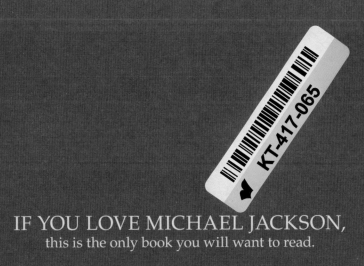

IF YOU LOVE MICHAEL JACKSON,
this is the only book you will want to read.

IF YOU THINK YOU KNOW THE
MICHAEL JACKSON STORY,
it's time to think again.

You Are Not Alone is an intimate, no-holds-barred portrait
of Michael – the man, not the legend.

Here, for the first time, we are shown Michael's
private world through personal stories and intimate
memories that have never before been shared.

To the rest of the world, Michael was an icon. To
Jermaine, he was a little brother with whom he shared
a bunk-bed, a room, a stage, dreams, laughter and tears.

You Are Not Alone is an epic story of brotherhood, family,
love and one extraordinary life.

YOU ARE NOT ALONE

MICHAEL

THROUGH A BROTHER'S EYES

YOU ARE NOT ALONE

MICHAEL

THROUGH A BROTHER'S EYES

JERMAINE JACKSON

HarperCollins*Publishers*

HarperCollins*Publishers*
77–85 Fulham Palace Road,
Hammersmith, London W6 8JB

www.harpercollins.co.uk

First published by HarperCollins*Publishers* 2011

1 3 5 7 9 10 8 6 4 2

A catalogue record of this book
is available from the British Library

ISBN 978-0-00-743566-1

Printed and bound in Great Britain by
Clays Ltd, St Ives plc

MIX
Paper from
responsible sources
FSC
www.fsc.org **FSC® C007454**

While every effort has been made to trace the owners of copyright material reproduced herein
and secure permissions, the publishers would like to apologise for any omissions and will be
pleased to incorporate missing acknowledgements in any future edition of this book.

The following images © their respective owners: plate p.1 (bottom right) UK Press / Press Association Images,
p.5 (top) and p.7 (bottom), Michael Ochs Archives / Getty Images, p.6 (top left) Erik Skipsey, (top right)
Olson / Time & Life Pictures / Getty Images, p.8 (bottom) Richard E. Aaron / Getty Images, p.9 (top right)
PA / Press Association Images, p.14 (top left) Eric Ryan / Getty Images, (top right) K. Mazur / Wire Image /
Getty Images, (middle) Retna / Photoshot, (bottom right) AFP / Getty Images, p.15 (top left) Press Association
Images, (top right) NPG.com, uncredited, p.5 (bottom), p.6 (bottom), p.14 (bottom left)

The following images © Harrison Funk: plate p.9 (top left, middle left, middle right, bottom),
p.11 (top and bottom), p.12 (top right, middle, bottom left, bottom right), p.13 (first row left, first row right,
third row right, fourth row left), p.15 (middle left, bottom)

All other images © Jackson family collection

'Billie Jean': © 1987 Mijac Music (BMI)
Words and music by Michael Joe Jackson; All rights administered by Warner / Chappell North America Ltd.

'Smooth Criminal': © 1982 Mijac Music (BMI)
Words and music by Michael Joe Jackson; All rights administered by Warner / Chappell North America Ltd.

'Word to the Badd': © 1991 Sony / ATV Music Publishing LLC, Ecaf Music, Green Skirt Music Inc, Black Stallion
Music, Pebbitone Music, Warner Tamerlane Publishing Corp. All rights on behalf of Sony / ATV Music
Publishing LLC and Ecaf Music administered by Sony / ATV Music Publishing LLC.
All rights reserved. Used by permission.

CONTENTS

THE END – THE NEVERLAND YEARS

I have built a monument more lasting than bronze and higher than the royal palace of the Pyramids. I shall not totally die, and a great part of me will live beyond death. I will keep growing, fresh with the praise of posterity.

– Horace, 23 BC

PROLOGUE

2005

THE BATHROOM MIRROR AT A LITTLE hotel in Santa Maria, California, is fogged with condensation, and there is so much steam from my morning shower that my reflection is rendered invisible. As I stand at the sink, dripping wet and wrapped in a towel, the opaque glass is now nothing but an inviting canvas of mist on which to log a thought I have been repeating in my head.

'MICHAEL JACKSON 1,000% INNOCENT', I daub with my finger, ending with a full-stop that I convert into a smiley-face. Believe in the happy ending.

I stare at this message and focus on a visualised outcome: victory, justice and vindication. It is 10 March 2005: day 11 of the courthouse circus that sees my brother accused of child molestation.

'MICHAEL JACKSON 1,000% INNOCENT', I read again. I continue to stare at the top left corner of the mirror, watching the smiley-face start to run. Transfixed, I flash back to Michael's bathroom at the Hayvenhurst estate in Encino, outside Los Angeles – his home prior to Neverland – and know that I am mimicking in 2005 what he did in 1982. Back then, in the top left corner of *his* mirror, he took a black felt permanent marker – to match the black marble – and scrawled: 'THRILLER! 100 MILLION SALES … SELL OUT STADIUMS'.

Think it, see it, believe it, make it happen. Will it into reality, as taught to us in childhood by our mother, Katherine, and father, Joseph. 'You can do this … you can do this,' I can hear Joseph insisting during early, scratchy rehearsals as the Jackson 5, 'we're doing this over and over until you get it right. Think about it, say it, see yourself doing it, visualise it happening … and it will happen.' Plant it in your head and focus with all your heart, Mother added, more gently. This was drilled into our young minds decades before positive-thinking became fashionable. Our minds are pre-programmed not to entertain doubt or half-heartedness.

Michael knew the scale of the breakthrough, innovation and success he desired as a solo artist with the *Thriller* album, so that one thought transcribed on his mirror was his positive starting point. Years after his move to Neverland, the permanence of the pen's marker had flaked and the message appeared to have disappeared to the naked eye, yet it had left its imprint embedded in the glass, because each time that mirror fogged, the faintest outline of his words could still be seen, as if it were one of those secret codes written by a magic pen. Condensation and misted glass always remind me of Michael's written ambition.

From the eighties, nobody knew about a lot of what he created until its execution, but the idea or concept was written down somewhere he could see it daily, or recited into a voice recorder as a visualisation he could see or hear. He didn't share ideas because he didn't want anyone to interfere; he relied on mental strength for his focus. Between November 2003 – when he was arrested and charged – and this day in March 2005, he's needed that strength.

Awake at 4.30am each day of the trial, he's bracing himself, getting prepared, psyching himself up to withstand another day of ritual humiliation.

Yesterday, 9 March, Gavin Arvizo, the 15-year-old boy being showcased as 'the victim', began his incredulous testimony, going into graphic detail. I was seated behind Michael the whole time, as I have been since the start.

Outwardly, my brother projects a hardened image: detached, expressionless, almost cold. Inwardly, the bolted brackets that had been holding him together are snapping violently under pressure, one by one.

I look at my mirrored message now fading as the air rushes in, but the intent remains stark: *Michael will be found innocent.* I would carve it into my grandmother's gravestone if I could. *Think it, see it, believe it, make it happen.*

But whatever intent I put out there is not enough to remove the ache and worry we feel as a family. I find myself constantly reflecting, going back to a time when we believed Hollywood to be only a magical place; when we believed in the Yellow Brick Road.

I watch the local news on the television in my room, looking ahead to day 11 of the trial. I think of Michael at Neverland. The cars will be pulling up in the courtyard. He will have been up four hours, eaten breakfast on a silver tray in his room, alone – stealing time on his own – before coming downstairs, giving himself 45 minutes between departure and arrival. His routine is clockwork, organised like some back-stage itinerary.

I think of all he has achieved, and all he is now being put through.

How has something so beautiful turned so twisted and ugly? Did fame do it? Is this the end-game in the American Dream when a black man achieves success on this magnitude? Is this what happens when an artist becomes bigger than his record label? Is this about publishing rights? Ruin the man, keep the money-machine?

These are the questions that race through my mind.

Are his Hollywood friends and one-time attorneys, allies and producers staying away because they regard him as nuclear – treating friendship like a sponsorship deal? What about those divisive people who whispered into a malleable ear that we, his family, should be kept at a distance, not trusted. Why aren't they alongside him now, whispering encouragement and support?

Michael is fast realising who his friends aren't, and what family means. But now his liberty is at stake, and everything he has built up is in danger of collapsing. I want to turn back time: lift the needle off the record and return us to the first track as the Jackson 5 – a time of togetherness, unity and brotherhood. 'All for one, and one for all,' as Mother used to say.

I play this eternal game of 'What If?' in my head and can't help but think that we could have – *should* have – handled things differently, especially with Michael. We stood off him too much when he wanted his space and that allowed vultures into the vacuum. We allowed outsiders in. I should have done more. Stood my ground. Barged down the gates of Neverland when the people around him never let me in. I should have seen this coming and been there to protect him. I feel a dereliction of duty in the promise of brotherhood we always had.

The cell-phone rings. It's Mother, sounding alarmed. 'Michael is at the hospital … We're here with him … He's slipped and fallen. It's his back.'

'I'm on my way,' I say, already out the door.

The hotel is equidistant from the Santa Maria courthouse and Neverland, and the hospital is a short detour. I'm met at a side entrance by a hospital manager to avoid any fuss out front.

On the hospital's second-floor corridor, I see an unusual number of nurses and patients hanging around and an audible fuss dies down as I approach. A presidential-style phalanx of familiar dark-suited bodyguards is clustered around a closed door to a private room. They step aside to allow me to enter.

Inside, the curtains are drawn.

In the half-light, Michael is standing, wearing patterned blue pyjama pants and a black jacket. 'Hi, Erms,' he says, in almost a whisper.

'Are you okay?' I ask.

'I just hurt my back.' He forces a smile.

The fall at the ranch, when getting out of the shower, has left him in miserable pain and it appears to be the final punch at a time when life keeps pounding him. But he's a child molester, right? He deserves this, right? The police *must* have some hard evidence, or he wouldn't be on trial, right? People have a lot to learn about how wrong this trial is.

Mother and Joseph are the only other people here, sitting against the wall to my right; they are like me in not knowing what to do but be present and appear strong. Michael winces with the pain in his rib-cage and lower back, but I sense his mental pain is far greater.

In the past week, I have witnessed his physical disintegration. At 46 years old, his lean dancer's body has withered to a fragile frame; his walk has become a pained, faltering gait; his dazzle is reduced to that forced smile; he looks gaunt, haggard.

I hate what it's doing to him and I want it to stop. I want to scream for the scream that Michael has never had in him.

As he stands, he talks about the court testimony yesterday. 'They are putting me through this to finish me … to turn everyone against me. It's their plan … it's a plan,' he says.

Our father has never been one for deep emotional examination and, as Michael talks, I can see him itching to divert the conversation towards other plans: a concert in China.

'Your sense of timing is not good, Joe!' Mother tells him in admonishment.

'What better time is there than now?' he says. That's Joseph. Very direct, and interpreting this time away from court as a small window to discuss something other than the trial. 'It'll take his mind off things,' he adds.

It doesn't surprise or sidetrack Michael. Like the rest of us, he's used to it and understands that this is Joseph's way. I interpret it as a father's ploy to deflect his own worry about events he can't control; to look beyond the trial to a time when Michael is free and able to perform again. Indicate light at the end of the tunnel. But it doesn't feel like a distraction, it feels inappropriate. Anyway, my brother keeps talking. 'What have I done but good? I don't understand …'

I know what he's thinking: he's done nothing but create music to entertain and spread the message of hope, love and humanity, and awareness of how we should be with one another – especially with children – yet he is accused of harming a child. It's akin to putting Santa Claus on trial for entering the bedrooms of children.

There is not one shred of evidence to justify this trial. The FBI knows it. The police know it. Sony knows it. (This irrefutable truth would be confirmed by an FBI statement in 2009, making it clear after my brother's death that there was never any evidence to support any allegation in 16 years of investigations.) The authorities are just making something fit in 2005. Think it, see it, believe it, make it happen. The negative version.

Michael lifts his eyes from the floor. He looks the saddest I have ever seen him, but I can tell he just wants to talk. Up until now, he has rarely released his emotions in front of us. He has been controlled and resolute, speaking about his faith, how he trusts the judge of God, not the judge in a robe. But his controlled demeanour is now undone, no doubt triggered by yesterday's testimony, and compounded by the frustration of this back injury.

It's all becoming too much.

'Everything they say about me is untrue. Why are they saying these things?'

'Oh, baby ...' says Mother, but Michael's hand rises. He's still talking.

'They're saying all these horrible things about me. I'm this. I'm that. I'm bleaching my skin. I'm hurting kids. I would never ... It's untrue, it's all untrue,' he says, his voice quiet, quivering.

He starts pulling at his jacket, like an exasperated child wanting out of a costume, shifting on to both his feet, ignoring his back pain.

'Michael ...' Mother starts.

But the tears are coming now. 'They can accuse me and make the world think they're so right, but they are so wrong ... they are so wrong.'

Joseph is paralysed by this show of emotion. Mother's hands are to her face. Michael pulls at his jacket buttons and starts struggling out of its sleeves. It falls off his shoulders and hangs backwards from his upper arms, revealing his bare chest.

He is sobbing. 'Look at me! … Look at me! I'm the most misunderstood person in the world!' He breaks down.

He stands in front of us, head bowed, as if he feels shame. It is the first time I have seen the true extent of his skin condition and it shocks me. His self-consciousness is such that he has kept his body hidden from even his family until now. His torso is light brown, splashed with vast areas and blotches of white, spreading across his upper chest; one patch of white covers his ribs and stomach, another runs down his side, and blotches cover one shoulder and upper arm. There is more white than brown, his natural skin colour: he looks like a white man splashed with coffee. This is the skin condition – the vitiligo – that a cynical world says he doesn't have, preferring to believe that he bleaches his skin.

'I've tried to inspire … I've tried to teach …' and his voice trails off as Mother goes to comfort him.

'God knows the truth. God knows the truth,' she keeps repeating.

We all surround him, unable to hug him tight due to his back, but it is comfort nonetheless. I help put his jacket back on. 'Just be strong, Michael,' I said. 'Everything's going to be all right.'

It doesn't take him long to compose himself and he apologises. 'I'm strong. I'm okay,' he says.

I leave him with my parents, vowing to return to the trial after a visit overseas. The brothers are taking it in shifts to provide support and I'll be back in a few days.

After I leave, the bodyguards convey a message relayed from his attorney, Tom Mesereau, at the courthouse. The judge is not happy that Michael is late, and if he's not in court within the hour, his bail will be revoked. Even his genuine pain is not honoured or believed.

At the hotel, I finish packing and watch my brother's delayed arrival at court on television. Shielded by an umbrella to protect his skin from the sun, he shuffles along just as I left him: in his pyjama bottoms and black jacket, now wearing a white undershirt. Joseph and a bodyguard stand either side, holding him steady.

Michael had always wanted to appear pristine and dignified for his trial, choosing his wardrobe carefully. To enter like this, in his pyjamas, will be making him cringe inwardly. This whole circus seems to be careening out of control … and we are only ten days in.

I grab the hotel phone and make a call. The person on the other end of the line provides the reassurance that I needed to hear one more time: Yes, the private jet is still available. Yes, it can be at Van Nuys airport. Yes, everything has been arranged. Yes, we are ready to go whenever you are. All that is required is a day's notice, and this DC-8 with four engines will have Michael up in the air and heading east – to Bahrain – to start a new life away from the scam of American justice. After this charade, I'm happy to disown my citizenship and take Michael, and his family, to a place where they can't touch him. We have the backer – a dear friend. We have the pilot. Everything is prepared. There is no way my brother – an innocent man – is going to jail for this. He wouldn't survive, and I cannot sit back and even contemplate the possibility, let alone the reality.

We've arranged 'Plan B' without his knowledge, but when I had told him not to worry because every scenario is covered, he will have suspected something, without wishing to know. He doesn't need to. Not yet.

I have negotiated with myself that the moment Tom Meserau starts to suggest that the scales of justice are tilting against us, I will action the plan and move him to the airport in the San Fernando Valley, outside L.A. We'll sneak him out of Neverland under a blanket, during the night. Or something. In the meantime, I resolve to play it hour by hour because, so far, Tom has said nothing other than 'yes, that was a good day for us', even when the testimony *sounded* horrible. He knows the evidential nuances, and when the prosecution is swinging with its punches and missing. We've quickly learned not to judge the trial by its truncated media coverage. So, I bide my time, but this trust takes all my power and has me writing messages on bathroom mirrors.

As I hit the road and drive south on auto-pilot, I start to wonder where Michael resources the strength and belief that is pulling him through this. I feel immense pride in him – at a time when he is presumed guilty until proven innocent by a media coverage that is unbalanced. It trumpets the weird and titillating testimony, leaving valid defence points as a postscript. I remember what Michael said at the start of these proceedings in 2003: 'Lies run in sprints, but the truth runs in marathons ... and the truth will win.' The truest lyric he never sang.

I start to visualise him walking free from the criminal court. I picture it like a scene in a movie. When this is over, I will do everything I can to clear his name in the public arena. The worst will be behind us. There will be nothing else they can throw at him. And I will defend him because I know what makes him tick – his heart, his soul, his spirit, his purpose. I know the boy inside the superstar's costume. I know the brother from 2300 Jackson Street. We have been in sync since infancy, throughout everything: the dream, the Jackson 5, the fame, the separate paths, the rifts, the sorrows, the scandals, and the impossible pressure. He has cried with me. I have shouted in his face. He has refused to see me. He has begged me to be with him. We have known each other's loyalty and each other's unintended betrayal. And it is because of everything contained within this history – this brotherhood – that I know his character and mind like only true blood can.

One day, I tell myself – when 2005 is behind us – people will give him a break and attempt understanding, not judgement. They'll treat him with the same gentleness and compassion he extended to everyone else. They'll cast aside their preconceived ideas and view him not just through his music but as a human being: imperfect, complex, fallible. Someone very different from his external image.

One day, the truth will win the marathon ...

THE BEGINNING
THE EARLY YEARS

CHAPTER ONE
Eternal Child

MICHAEL WAS STANDING BESIDE ME – I was about eight, he was barely four – with his elbows on the sill and his chin resting in his hands. We were looking into the dark from our bedroom window as the snow fell on Christmas Eve, leaving us both in awe. It was coming down so thick and fast that our neighbourhood seemed beneath some heavenly pillow fight, each floating feather captured in the clear haze of one streetlight. The three homes opposite were bedecked in mostly multicoloured bulbs, but one particular family, the Whites, had decorated their whole place with clear lights, complete with a Santa on the lawn and glowing-nosed reindeers. They had white lights trimming the roof, lining the pathway and festooned in the windows, blinking on and off, framing the fullest tree we had seen.

We observed all this from inside a home with no tree, no lights, no nothing. Our tiny house, on the corner of Jackson Street with 23rd Avenue, was the only one without decoration. We felt it was the only one in Gary, Indiana, but Mother assured us that, no, there were other homes and other Jehovah's Witnesses who did not celebrate Christmas, like Mrs Macon's family two streets up. But that knowledge did nothing to clear our confusion: we could see something that made us feel good, yet we were told it wasn't good for us. Christmas wasn't God's will: it was commercialism. In the run-up to 25 December we felt as if we were witnessing an event to which we were not invited, and yet we still felt its forbidden spirit.

At our window, we viewed everything from a cold, grey world, looking into a shop where everything was alive, vibrant and sparkling with colour; where children played in the street with their new toys, rode new bikes or pulled new sleds in the snow. We could only imagine what it was to know the joy we saw on their faces. Michael and I played our own game at that window: pick a snowflake under the streetlight, track its descent and see which one was the first to 'stick'. We observed the flakes tumble, separated in the air, united on the ground, dissolved into one. That night we must have watched and counted dozens of them before we fell quiet.

Michael looked sad – and I can see myself now, looking down on him from an eight-year-old's height, feeling that same sadness. Then he started to sing:

'Jingle bells, jingle bells, jingle all the way
Oh what fun it is to ride,
On a one-horse open sleigh …'

It is my first memory of hearing his voice, an angelic sound. He sang softly so that Mother wouldn't hear. I joined in and we started making harmony. We sang verses of 'Silent Night' and 'Little Drummer Boy'. Two boys carol-singing on the doorstep of our exclusion, songs we'd heard at school, not knowing that singing would be our profession.

As we sang, the grin on Michael's face was pure joy because we had stolen a piece of magic. We were happy briefly. But then we stopped, because this temporary sensation only reminded us that we were pretending to participate and the next morning would be

4

like any other. I've read many times that Michael did not like Christmas, based on our family's lack of celebration. This was not true. It had not been true since that moment as a four-year-old when he said, staring at the Whites' house: 'When I'm older, I'll have lights. Lots of lights. It will be Christmas every day.'

'GO FASTER! GO FASTER!' MICHAEL SHRIEKED, hitting an early high note. He was sitting tucked up in the front of a shopping cart – knees to chin – while Tito, Marlon and I were running and pushing it down 23rd Avenue, me with both hands on the handlebar, and my two brothers either side as the wheels wobbled and bounced off the road on a summer's day. We built up speed and powered forward like a bobsleigh team. Except this, in our minds, was a train. We'd find two, sometimes three, shopping carts from the nearby Giants supermarket and couple them together. Giants was about three blocks away, located across the sports field at the back of our home, but its carts were often abandoned and strewn about the streets, so they were easy to commandeer. Michael was 'the driver'.

He was mad about Lionel toy trains – small, but weighty model steam engines and locomotives, packaged in orange boxes. Whenever Mother took us shopping for clothes at the Salvation Army, he always darted upstairs to the toy section to see if anyone had donated a second-hand Lionel train set. So, in his imagination, our shopping carts became two or three carriages, and 23rd Avenue was the straight section of track. It was a train that went too fast to pick up other passengers, thundering along, as Michael provided the sound effects. We hit the buffers when 23rd Avenue ran into a dead-end, about 50 yards from the back of our house.

If Michael wasn't on the street playing trains, he was on the carpet in our shared bedroom with his prized Lionel engine. Our parents couldn't afford to buy him a new one, or invest in an electric-train set, complete with full length track, station, and signal boxes. That is why the dream of owning a train set was in his head long before the dream of performing.

SPEED. I'M CONVINCED OUR EXCITEMENT AS kids was built on the thrill of speed. Whatever we did involved going faster, trying to outgun one another. Had our father known the extent of our thirst for speed, he would have banned it for sure: the potential for injury was always considered a grave risk to our career.

Once we grew bored of the shopping-cart trains, we built 'go-karts', constructed from boxes, stroller wheels and planks of wood from a nearby junkyard. Tito was the 'engineer' of the brotherhood and he had the know-how in putting everything together. He was forever dismantling clocks and radios, and re-assembling them on the kitchen table, or watching Joseph under the hood of his Buick parked at the side of the house, so he knew where our father's tool box was. We hammered together three planks to form an I-shaped chassis and axle. We nailed the open cockpit – a square wooden box – on top, and took cord from a clothes line for our steering mechanism, looping it through the front wheels, held like reins. In truth, our turning circle was about as tight as an oil tanker's, so we only ever travelled in straight lines.

The wide open alleyway at the back of our house – with a row of grassy backyards on one side and a chain-link fence on the other – was our race-track, and it was all about the 'race'. We often patched together two go-karts, with Tito pushing Marlon, and me pushing Michael in a 50-yard dash. There was always that sense of competition between us: who could go faster, who would be the winner.

'Go, go, go, GO!' yelled Michael, leaning forward, urging us into the lead. Marlon hated losing, too, so Michael always had fierce competition. Marlon was the boy who never understood why he couldn't out-run his own shadow. I can picture him now: sprinting through the street, looking down to his side, with a fierce determination on his face that turned to exasperation when he couldn't put space between himself and his clinging shadow.

We pushed those go-karts until the metal brackets were scraping along the street, and the wheels buckled or fell off, with Michael tipped up on his side and me laughing so hard I couldn't stand.

The merry-go-round in the local school field was another thrill-ride. Crouch down in the centre of its metal base, hold on tight to the iron stanchions, and get the brothers to spin it as fast as they could. 'Faster! Faster! Faster!' Michael squealed, eyes tight shut, giggling hard. He used to straddle the stanchions, like he was on a horse, going round and round and round. Eyes closed. Wind in the face.

We all dreamed of riding the train, racing the go-karts and spinning on a proper carousel at Disney.

WE KNEW MR LONG WAY BEFORE we had heard of Roald Dahl. To us, he was the original African-American Willy Wonka; this magical man – white hair, wizened features, leathery dark skin – dished out candy from his house the next avenue up, on 22nd, *en route* to our elementary school at the far end of Jackson Street.

Many kids beat a path to Mr Long's door because his younger brother went to our school. Knowing Timothy meant we got a good deal, two to five cents being good value for a little brown bag full of liquorice, shoe strings, Lemonheads, Banana Splits – you name it, he had them all neatly spread out on a single bed in a front room. Mr Long didn't smile or say very much, but we looked forward to seeing him on school mornings. We grasped at our orders and he dutifully filled the bags. Michael *loved* candy and that morning ritual brightened the start of each day. How we got the money is a whole other story that I will reserve for later.

We each protected our brown paper bags of candy like gold and back at the house, inside our bedroom, we all had different hiding places which each brother would try and figure out. My hide-out was under the bed or mattress, and I always got busted, but Michael squirreled his away somewhere good because we never did find it. As adults, whenever I reminded him of this, he chuckled at the memory. That is how Michael laughed throughout his life: a mesh-up of a chuckle, a snicker, a giggle; always shy, often self-conscious. Michael loved playing shop: he'd create his counter by laying a board across a pile of books, then a tablecloth, and then he'd spread out his candy. This 'shop' was set up in the doorway to our bedroom, or on the lowest bunk-bed, with him kneeling behind, awaiting orders. We traded with each other, swapping or using change kept from Mr Long, or from a nickel found in the street.

But Michael was destined to be an entertainer, not a savvy businessman. That seemed obvious when our father challenged him about getting home late from school one afternoon. 'Where were you?' asked Joseph.

'I went to get some candy,' said Michael.

'How much you pay for it?'

'Five cents.'

'How much you going to re-sell it for?'

'Five cents.'

Joseph clipped him around the head. 'You don't re-sell something for the same price you bought it!'

Typical Michael: always too fair, never ruthless enough. 'Why can't I give it for five cents?' he said, in the bedroom. The logic was lost on him and he was upset over the undeserved whack on the head. I left him on the bed, muttering under his breath as he sorted his candy into piles, no doubt still playing shop in his head.

Days later, Joseph found him in the backyard, giving out candy from across the chain-link fence to other kids from the street. The kids who were less fortunate than us – and he was mobbed. 'How much you sell 'em for?' Joseph asked.

'I didn't. I gave them away for free.'

EIGHTEEN HUNDRED MILES AWAY, AND MORE than 20 years later, I visited Michael at his ranch, Neverland Valley, in the Santa Ynez region of California. He had spent time and money turning his vast acres into a theme park and the family went to check out his completed world. Neverland has always been portrayed as the outlandish creation of 'a wild imagination' with the suggestion that a love of Disney was its sole inspiration. Elements of this may be correct, but the truth runs much deeper, and this was something I knew immediately when I saw with my own eyes what he had built.

Childhood memories were brought to life in a giant flashback: white Christmas lights trimming the sidewalk, the pathway, the trees, the frame and guttering of his English Tudor mansion. He had them turned on all year round to ensure that 'it was Christmas every day.' A huge steam train with carriages ran between the shops and the movie theatre, and a miniature train toured the circumference of the estate, via the zoo. In the main house – through the doors, passed the welcoming, model life-size butler with tray, up the wide stairway and down the hallway – was the playroom. Inside, beyond the full-size Superman and Darth Vader at the door, was the biggest table dominating the room. On it, a vintage Lionel train set was always running: two or three trains travelling the tracks with lights on, around a model landscape of hills, valleys, towns and waterfalls. Inside the house and out, Michael had built himself the biggest electric train set you could ever imagine.

Back outside, there was a full-on professional go-kart track with chicanes and tight bends, and the merry-go-round was spinning to music, a beautiful carousel of ornate horses. There was a candy store too, where everything was free, and a Christmas tree lit up all year round. In 2003, Michael said he developed the ranch 'to create everything that I never had as a child.' But it was also about re-creating what he *had* enjoyed for too short a time, rebuilding it in an exaggerated version. He called himself a 'fantasy fanatic' and this was his eternal fantasy.

Neverland brought back our lost days because that is how he perceived his childhood – as a missing person; an inner child wandering around his past looking to somehow reconnect with him in the future. It wasn't a refusal to grow up because if you asked him, he never felt like he was a boy in the first place. Michael was expected to be an adult when he was a kid, and he regressed into a kid when he was expected to be an adult. He was more Benjamin Button than the Peter Pan comparison he made himself. However much I might remember laughter in our childhood, he struggled to recall it, which probably had a lot to do with the fact that I am four years older.

A friend, a nephew and I took quad bikes to explore Neverland's 2,700 acres, which seemed endless, rolling beyond every green horizon, scattered with oak trees. One dusty fire road took us climbing to the highest peak, far away from the developed area, and a plateau, providing a 360-degree vista. My eyes scanned it all – the property, the theme park, the lake, the ferris wheel, the trains, the greenery – and it filled me with awe and pride. *Look at what you've created*, I said to my brother in my head, and repeated to him later.

'A place of ultimate happiness,' he told me.

The later warped perception of Neverland shows how Michael was judged on the face value of his world and, in many cases, on the claims of others. There only ever seemed to be lurid judgements about him and his ranch without any attempt to figure out the more complex 'why?'. As with everyone, his background shaped him. But fame – especially the iconic status attached to my brother – built a public barrier as big as a dam in front of his need to be understood. But to understand him, we need to walk in his shoes and see life from *his* perspective. As Michael said in 2003, in a message to his fans via Ed Bradley at CBS: 'If you really want to know about me, there's a song I wrote. It's called "Childhood". That's the one song people should listen to ...'

Michael's honest awareness that he was a grown man with a kid's mind shows in the lyrics: 'People say I'm strange that way because I love such elementary things ... but have you seen my childhood?' His way of saying, this is the way I've been made. This is who I am.

Many people have attempted to look through the window of our childhood, and see past the smears of media coverage and the persona of a pop icon. But I feel that you need to have lived it, and shared it, to truly know and understand it. Because ours was a unique world, as brothers and sisters under the roof of one big family. It was in a small house at 2300 Jackson Street – named after

President Andrew Jackson, not us – that we shared memories, music and a dream. It is here that our stories and his lyrics begin, and where, I hope, a better understanding of just who Michael was can be found.

CHAPTER TWO

2300 Jackson Street

IT ALL STARTED ONE DAY WHEN we found our voices around the kitchen sink.

It was more assembly line than kitchen sink, the wash-dry-stack-put away ritual after dinner. We divided the chore into weekly shifts as pairs – two children drying, two others putting away, our mother standing in the middle, an apron over her gown, hands deep in soap suds. She always whistled or sang some tune, but the song that first enticed us into joining her was 'Cotton Fields', an old slave number by blues musician Lead Belly. This hit resonated with her, for her roots were in Eufaula, Alabama, where she was born Katie Scruse in May 1930.

Her grandparents had been cotton farmers in what was then named 'the Cotton State' and her great-grandfather was a slave to an Alabama family called Scruse. This forefather could sing, too – 'You could hear his voice from church ring out through the valley' – and so could Papa Prince, her father. She swears that the voice we heard in our kitchen was channelled from her ancestors and developed in a church choir; she was raised a Baptist. Fine voices ran in the family, we were told. My father's father, Samuel Jackson, was a teacher and school director who always gave a near-perfect rendition of 'Swing Low, Sweet Chariot' but he also had 'a beautiful high voice' that graced a church chorus. Our mother played the clarinet and piano at high school, and Joseph the guitar.

When our parents met in 1949, their individual DNA must have combined to create some kind of super-gene for our musical inheritance. It was no accident of birth, Mother assured us: it was God's gift. Or, as Michael later put it, 'the divine union of song and dance.'

We each loved the sound of Mother's voice. Standing at the sink singing, she was lost in those fields of Alabama, and she sent a shiver down my spine with a voice that was never flat and always on pitch. Her voice singing was like her voice talking: warm, soft and soothing. We began singing at the sink for entertainment when our black-and-white television was sent for repair, and one day I started making harmonies with Mother. I must have been about five, but I was keeping it high and staying on note. She looked down at me, still singing but beaming with surprise. Before she knew it, my brothers, Tito and Jackie, and sister Rebbie had joined the chorus. Michael was a baby, still stumbling into a walk with diapers on, but when the dishes were put away and the surfaces wiped *spotlessly* clean, Mother sat down, cradled him and sang him to sleep. 'Cotton Fields' was my vocal initiation and Michael's lullaby.

Michael in his diapers is my first memory of him. I don't remember his birth, or Mother walking through the door with him. New arrivals were no big event in our family. I was five when I started changing his diapers. I did what we all did – helping Mother where we could, providing an extra pair of hands for what would become a family of nine children.

Michael was born hyper, with boundless energy and curiosity. If any of us took our eyes off him for a second, he'd have crawled under the table or under the bed. When Mother turned on our excuse for a washing-machine, he jigged and bounced on the spot in time to its vibrations. Changing his mushy diaper on the sofa was like trying to hold a wet fish – wriggling, kicking and turning. The art of putting on a diaper with safety-pins was a test for any adult, let alone five-year-old me, and more often than not, Rebbie or Jackie came to my rescue. Michael had these extraordinarily long, thin fingers that used to grab my thumb, and he had wide, doe-eyes that said: 'I'm having fun giving you a hard time, buddy.' In my eyes, though, he was the kid brother who needed looking after. Caring for one another was instilled in all of us, but I felt protective of him from day one. Maybe it was because all I heard being shouted was 'Where's Michael?' … 'Is Michael okay?' … 'Is Michael changed?'

'Yes, Mother … We got it … he's here,' one of us shouted.

Don't worry. Michael's okay. Michael's okay.

OUR MOTHER'S MOTHER, MAMA MARTHA, USED to bathe us as babies in a bucket-sized pan brimming with soapy water. I watched Michael, arms held high and face screwed up, standing inside this tiny chrome 'bath', washed with tedious thoroughness from the gaps between his toes to the backs of his ears. We *always* had to be clean and stay on top of germs. I think this was drilled into us before we could walk or talk. And nothing beat Castile soap, and its coarse lather, for staying clean. Lather up and scrub *hard*. Mother was fastidious about cleanliness, and about everything being neat and looking pristine. Everything didn't just have to *be* clean. It – and we – had to *look* pristine.

Germs were portrayed as invisible monsters. Germs lead to sickness, we were told. Germs are what other people carry. Germs are in the air, on the street, on the surfaces. We were constantly made to feel we were under threat of invasion. Whenever one of us sneezed or coughed, the castor oil came out: we all got a spoonful to keep infection at bay. I know I speak for Michael, La Toya, Janet and myself in saying that we grew up with an almost neurotic fear of germs, and it's not hard to understand why.

In the kitchen, before the singing started, came the first elementary lesson: 'We wash up only with clean water … CLEAN water!'

Then: 'Use the hottest water your hands can bear, and lots of suds.' Each plate was squeaked within a layer of its ceramic life. Each glass rinsed and dried, and held up to the light to make sure there was not a single watermark. If one was found, do it again.

After coming in from the street, we had to be virtually decontaminated. The first words out of Mother's mouth were 'Have you washed your hands? Go wash your hands.' If she didn't hear the tap running within seconds, there was trouble. On mornings before school, the hygiene inspection was always the same: 'Did you wash your face? Wash your feet? In between your toes? Your elbows?' Then came the acid test: a cotton swab dipped in alcohol rubbed across the back of the neck. If it turned grey, we weren't clean enough. 'Go back and wash yourself properly.' If we wanted chocolate cake or a cookie, our hands were up for inspection, too. 'But I washed them earlier!' I often protested. 'You been out touching door handles, boy – go wash them again!'

Clothes were never worn two days' running, and had to be clean and pressed. No one from our family walked into the street with a single crease or stain. By the age of six, we had all learned to pitch in with the laundry. This was all part and parcel of a *perfect* order that helped keep so many kids – and potential chaos – in check.

When I joined the UK's *Big Brother* house in 2007, everyone made fun of how I was always on guard against germs, asking house mates if they had washed their hands before preparing food. My wife, Halima, wasn't surprised. She calls me a 'germaphobe' and I can hardly deny it. To this day, I won't touch a door handle in a public restroom because I know how many men *don't* wash their hands. I won't touch the banister on public stairways or escalators. I'll use a handkerchief or tissue to hold the gas pump trigger when filling the car. I'll wash down with alcohol a hotel's TV remote control before using it. I'm alive to cross-contamination from every surface.

Michael was no different. He even worried about other people's pens when signing autographs, in the days when fans could get close enough. But his neurosis mainly centred on breathing in airborne germs. People mocked him for wearing surgical masks. There was speculation that he was hiding plastic surgery and I always laughed when I saw an article referencing the mask, saying it was 'sparking fears about Michael's health'. Because that was the point: it was all about fear – Michael's fear that he could get ill. At these times, he will have felt he was coming down with something, or his immune system was low. He was, like me, on guard against germs all his life. At least, that was the origins of his surgical mask wearing and then, after a while, I think it became something of a fashion accessory that allowed him to 'hide'; a mini shield for a man who wanted to grab whatever fraction of privacy that he could.

I DON'T REMEMBER A TIME WHEN Mother was *not* pregnant. I cannot recall her walking up the street with anything but a waddle, carrying in both hands two bags of shopping or second-hand clothes. Between 1950 and 1966, she produced nine children. That is some feat when measured against her and Joseph's initial plan: three children maximum.

My sister Rebbie (pronounced Ree-bie) came first, then Jackie (1951), Tito (1953), me (1954), La Toya (1956), Marlon (1957), Michael (1958), Randy (1961) and Janet (1966). We would have been 10 but our other brother, Brandon, died during his twin birth with Marlon. That was why, at Michael's memorial service in 2009, Marlon said, in his message to Michael: 'I would like for you to give our brother, my twin brother, Brandon, a hug for me.' A twin never loses that bond with his other half.

As kids, we received plenty of hugs from Mother. Contrary to the general depiction that we had some form of cold, unhappy childhood, our upbringing was full of love as Mother smothered us with kisses and affection. We still feel the strength of that love today. I was a real mama's boy – as was Michael – and our worship became a fight between me, him and La Toya as to who occupied the coveted spot by Mother's side, tight to her legs, gripping her skirt. La Toya did her best to unglue my attachment.

Whenever Mother was out and we brothers fought, we swore her into a pact. 'Promise you won't tell, La Toya. Promise!'

'Promise,' she said convincingly. 'I won't tell!' As soon as Mother was through the door, the promise was undone with a dramatic confession. 'Mother, Jermaine's been fighting.' We wanted to jack her up because she told on everyone. She always was the quiet observer, collecting her tales to spill later. It didn't even matter if she made stuff up; she just wanted to win favour with Mother while I was left with extra chores as punishment. But the joke in later years was that I must have won favour more times than most because I was 'always Mother's pet,' says Rebbie.

'The favoured one!' Michael said, which was a bit rich because he could do no wrong either.

I didn't feel like a favourite but if Mother ever over-compensated, it had everything to do with an event that happened when she was pregnant with Michael. Aged about three, I decided it was a good idea to eat a bag of salt and so I was hospitalised with near kidney failure. I remember nothing of this trauma. I was a strong kid, but that illness put me in hospital for three weeks. Mother and Joseph couldn't afford to visit me every day. When they did, the ward sister told them I had been screaming out my lungs for them. Every time they left, I stood on the bed, wailing. I'm kind of glad I don't remember the look on Mother's face as she was forced to walk away. She said it was 'the most awful feeling.'

Eventually I was allowed home, but that event might explain why I became such a cry-baby and overly clingy, desperate not to be left behind again. On my first day at school, I struggled free of the teacher's grip and sprinted down the corridor and out of the doors to find Mother. 'You have to be here, Jermaine … You have to be here,' she said, with the calmness that made everything okay again. Her compassion is rooted in a devout, unbreakable faith in God and she manages to strike a balance between the aura of a disciple and the authority of a Justice of the Peace. She has her breaking points, of course, but her calm made better any difficult situation.

She suffered for us, in being pregnant for 81 months of her life. She was beautiful, too, from the way she wore her wavy black hair to her pristine gowns, to the perfectly applied scarlet lipstick that left smudges on our cheeks. Mother was sunshine inside 2300 Jackson Street.

The moment she left for her part-time work at Sears department store, we couldn't wait for her return. I have this warm image of her arriving through the front door, having trudged through the deep snow of an Indiana winter. She stood there, stamping her feet on the mat and shaking her head to dust off the snow. Then Michael – growing into the fastest of the brood – ran up and wrapped his arms around one leg, followed by me, La Toya, Tito and Marlon. Before taking off her coat, she brought out her hands from inside her pockets – and there was our regular treat: two bags of hot Spanish peanuts.

Meanwhile, Jackie and Rebbie prepared the kitchen for Mother to start cooking, waiting for Joseph to come home. We grew up calling him Joseph. Not Father. Or Daddy. Or Papa. Just 'Joseph'. That was his request. In the interests of respect.

THERE IS A NURSERY RHYME ABOUT an old woman who lived in a shoe and 'had so many children, she didn't know what to do'. In terms of family size and cramped living quarters, it provides the best image of life inside the shoebox of 2300 Jackson Street. Nine children, two parents, two bedrooms, one bathroom, a kitchen and a living room were packed tight into a space about 30 feet wide and no more than 40 feet deep. From the outside, it looks like the kind of a house a child would sketch: a front door with a window either side and a chimney poking out the top. Our home was 1940s build, wood-framed, with a tiled pyramid lid that seemed so thin for a roof that we swore it would blow off during the first tornado. It faces on to Jackson Street on the corner of its T-junction with 23rd Avenue.

At the front, a short path from the sidewalk cut through grass to a black, solid door, which, when slammed, shook the whole house. One step inside and there was the living room – and the brown sofa-bed where the girls slept – with the kitchen and utility room to the left. Straight ahead was a hallway – about two strides long – leading to the boys' bedroom on the right, and our parents' room on the left, adjacent to the back bathroom.

Jackson Street was part of a quiet grid bounded by Interstate-80 to the south and a railroad to the north. Directions to our home were easy because of the landmark we backed on to: Theodore Roosevelt High School and a sports field. Its outer chain-link fence created 23rd Avenue's dead-end, providing an open view of the running track to the left and, just to the right, a baseball field with bleachers on the far side. Joseph said we were lucky to own our home. Others in the neighbourhood were not so fortunate. For this reason, we never officially classed ourselves as 'poor' because the people who lived in the Delaney Projects – across the field on the other side of the high school – were living in government tract housing, which we could see in the distance from our backyard. 'There is always somebody worse off, no matter how bad things might appear,' we were told. So, the best way of describing our situation was: not enough money to buy anything new, but we somehow scraped by and survived.

Mother learned how to make food last: a freezer was more essential than a car or a television in the black community. Make food in bulk, freeze it, thaw it, eat it. We often had the same meals over and over again: bowls of pinto beans and pinto soup, chicken, chicken and chicken, egg sandwiches, mackerel with rice, and we ate so much spaghetti that I can't stand pasta today. We made popsicles from Kool-Aid. We even grew our own vegetables because Joseph had a nearby allotment, producing potatoes, string beans, black-eyed peas, cabbage, beets … and peanuts. From an early age, we were taught how to plant seeds and peanuts, lining up enough space so they had room to grow. If we moaned – and we often did – about getting our hands and knees dirty, Joseph just reminded us that his first job as a teenager was working the cotton fields 'where I collected 300 pounds of the stuff each day.' He said Mother was 'the best damn cook in the city!' and dinner was always waiting for him as he walked through the door. She kept the house spotless, he said. Everything was always neat. This made her the perfect wife, he said.

He couldn't fault Rebbie either because she took on motherly duties – preparing the food, cooking, cleaning, overseeing chores – whenever Mother worked. Rebbie was the big sister turned nanny and was equally stern, gentle, methodical and controlled. If I have one abiding memory of Rebbie, it's of her standing in the kitchen, baking cookies and tea-cakes for us all. She was also the first child to show 'promise', according to Joseph, entering and winning local dance competitions. She and Jackie had some duet thing going on, and brought home prize certificates and trophies.

Mother worked weekdays, some Saturdays and some evenings as a cashier at Sears. She couldn't really afford to shop there. When she did, she chose items to 'put in Layaway', reserving something with a down payment, then making a series of small instalments before taking the item home. Sears was our Harrods, and we grew up hearing the words 'put it in Layaway'. We all hated seeing Mother handing over money and walking away empty-handed. That made no sense to us. Feeling hard done by, we kids regularly moaned about it, but not Mother. She just got on with life and trusted in God. If she ever had a moment to sit down, she spent it reading the Bible.

As a two-year-old, she had had polio, which led to partial paralysis; she had worn a wooden leg splint until she was 10. I don't know too much about her suffering except that she had several operations, missed a lot of school and was left with a permanent limp because one leg is shorter than the other but I've never once heard her complain about it. Instead, she always said how grateful she was to have survived a disease that killed many others. She had dreamed of becoming an actress, but she showed no resentment over a dream that illness had crushed. Her condition led to some merciless taunting from other children when she was a teenager, which left her painfully self-conscious and shy. On one early date with Joseph as a 19 year old, they were on the dance-floor at some party, moving cheek to cheek to a slow number, when Mother started trembling. 'What's the matter, Katie?' asked Joseph.

'Everyone is staring at us,' she said, head down, unable to look up.

He looked around and they were the only couple on the floor. He noticed people pointing and talking behind their hands, presumably about one of Mother's legs being shorter than the other, or that one of her heels was a wedge to correct her balance. She had grown up dreading parties and social gatherings, but Joseph ignored the stares and turned it into a positive. 'We have the floor to ourselves, Katie,' he said. 'Let's keep dancing.'

Mother had moved from Alabama to Indiana as a child when Papa Prince chased work in the steel industry. She had dreamed of one day meeting a musician so guitar-playing Joseph fitted the bill, and it took the length of one spring and one summer for their romance to turn into marriage. They had 'met' in the street. It's probably more accurate to say that Mother was in the street and Joseph was inside, sitting near his front window, when she rode by on a bicycle. They noticed each other and, for another week or two, she kept to the same route. One day, he plucked up the nerve to rush outside and introduce himself. That led to a date at the movies and then the party with the dance-floor. Katie Scruse, the golden-skinned girl so shy she struggled to look anyone in the face, fell in love with Joseph Jackson, the lean, brash, charismatic working man. They were wed by a Justice of the Peace in November 1949 and bought our childhood home in Gary for $8,500, using his savings and a loan from Mother's step-father.

As their plans for three children became four, then five and so on, they started saving what little money Mother could earn as she harboured a dream that Joseph would one day build an extension for an extra bedroom and more space. We grew up with a stack of bricks in the backyard – a constant reminder of our mother's hope for a bigger and better home.

Our little house comes with so many layers in my memory. Its compactness – huddling around Mother and living on top of one another – might not have made it the most comfortable home but it reflected our parents' continual talk of togetherness and staying close. Within this togetherness, there comes loyalty. With loyalty comes strength. This was instilled in us. It was why we became a unit, moving together as one. Few in Gary could claim such family cohesion. It was a working man's city built in 1906 by the muscle of African-American immigrants who helped turn a north-west Indiana landscape of sand dunes and scrub vegetation into a hub of the national steel industry.

Old men always spoke of a blood, sweat and toil work ethic back in the day. No man from Gary was ever afraid of putting in the hours and doing the grind. 'If you work real hard, you will achieve,' Joseph said. 'You get back what you put in.' In the eyes of his forefathers, getting a paid job and owning a house represented 'achievement', but he always wanted us to be more than he became. None of us grew up with a dream that ran into a father's resistance: 'You'll stop this day-dreaming and get yourself a real job!' No. Our father *wanted* us to have a dream, and hold on to it.

About 90 per cent of Gary's population, and most of Indiana, found employment at 'The Mill' of Inland Steel, located a half-hour drive away in neighbouring East Chicago. Joseph was a crane operator, moving steel beams back and forth. He worked real hard in a tough job with rough eight-to-10 hour shifts. While inside his glass bubble atop the crane, his mind wandered back to his beginnings in Durmott, south of Little Rock, Arkansas. As a young man, he used his pocket money to watch back-to-back silent movies at the cinema, telling himself that, one day, he would be the first black actor to star in one. Ending up at The Mill was not part of that dream. It was slavish work, echoing generations of black men before him. 'It's about getting on top, not staying at the bottom,' he said.

Before meeting Mother, and when he first arrived in Indiana, he had worked on the railroads. He then landed a job at a foundry, working a pneumatic jackhammer in the steel-melting heat of a blast furnace. 'Hot? Men fainted,' he said. 'We worked in

10-minute bursts, then got out of there because those floors were heated white.' He was skin and bone, apparently. No matter how much he ate, he couldn't put on an extra pound because the work kicked his butt. It is a metabolism that most of us inherited – especially Michael. Joseph's 'worst kind of work' continued when he had to collect dust from the furnace. This meant his skinny frame became useful when lowered by cord, in a bucket, into a deep flue, three feet in diameter. When I heard these stories, I thought a crane operator's job was glamorous by comparison.

Let no one say that Joseph doesn't know the meaning of hard work. I think it takes a certain type of man to do that kind of job – someone hardened and emotionally strong – and he worked his fingers to the bone to 'earn a life', as he put it. I think this is where his insistence on 'respect' comes from. Worked as a 'subordinate' for most of his young adult life, and with an ancestry rooted in the slave trade like Mother, he had *earned* respect so he expected it from his family. He knew his responsibilities, too. The more children he had, the more hours he worked to bring home extra pay. When Michael arrived, he got a second job and started juggling shifts at a canned-food factory.

As children, we sensed that struggle to make ends meet. Our parents' combined take-home pay was about 75 dollars a week. They were too proud to claim welfare, so in the winter, Tito and I shovelled snow from neighbours' driveways to put some extra money on the table. We always knew when Joseph had collected his pay packet because a new loaf of bread was on the kitchen worktop, with a packet of luncheon meat. On more than one occasion, Joseph was laid off and then hired again. During those lulls, he got work picking potatoes. We instantly knew when the steel shifts had dried up because all we ate was potatoes – baked, mashed, boiled, roasted.

Inland Steel was the end of the rainbow for generations of families. It was said there were only three outcomes to life in Gary: The Mill, prison or death. The last two options were related to the gang-life that was the flip-side to our community. But whatever destiny seemed laid out for us, Joseph was determined to change its course. Every hour he worked was with that in mind. Our escape was his escape, with Mother.

JOSEPH WAS ONE OF SIX CHILDREN: four boys, two girls. As the eldest, he was closest to the sister who followed him in order of birth: Verna Mae. Our sister Rebbie reminded him of her, he said – dutiful, kind, the proper little housewife, and wise beyond her years. Joseph loved how Verna Mae took care of the house and children. He remembers her, aged seven, reading bed-time stories to their brothers Lawrence, Luther and Timothy, by oil lamp. Then she fell ill and Joseph could do nothing to help her. The doctors couldn't even diagnose what was wrong with her. From her bed, Verna Mae was stoical. 'Everything is well. I will be healthy again,' she said. But Joseph watched his sister's deterioration from the bedroom door as the adults surrounded her bed. She succumbed to the illness and passed away. Joseph sobbed for days, unable to comprehend such a loss. As far as my understanding goes, that was the last time he shed a tear: he was 11.

As self-confessed cry-babies, Michael and I always hated how hardened our father was. None of us can remember a time when we saw him show any emotional vulnerability. Whenever we cried as kids – even after he had chastised us – he berated us: 'What you crying for?'

Joseph had spent his formative years mourning and missing his sister. At her funeral, after walking behind the horse-drawn cart that carried her coffin, he vowed he never wanted to lay eyes on anyone's tomb again. One loss in life sealed our father's emotions and Joseph kept his word: he never attended another funeral. Until 2009.

WHEN JOSEPH WAS A SCHOOLBOY, HE was terrified of one woman teacher. The 'respect thy teacher' decree carried extra force because his father, Samuel, was a high-school director and believed in strict discipline by corporal punishment. This fearsome woman apparently scared Joseph so much that he shivered whenever she called out his name. Once, so the story goes, he was called out to the front of the class to read from the chalkboard. He knew exactly what the words were, but fear left him mute. The teacher asked him again. When he couldn't answer a second time, the punishment was swift: a wooden paddle board across his bare behind. This thing had holes in it, too, for extra suction with each whack. As she paddled him, she reminded him why he was getting hit: he had disobeyed her when he didn't read. He hated her for it, but *respected* her too. 'Because of this, I listened to her and always did my best,' he said.

It was the same when Papa Jackson chastised him. That was how he was raised – on the old theory that in order to control some-one, you first need to shock fear into them. This was his lesson in life, marked out on his backside. In later weeks, that same woman teacher held a talent contest and pupils were invited to do anything they wished: art, poetry, craft, a short story, a dramatic presenta-tion. Joseph wasn't artistic; he wasn't good with words – he'd only ever watched silent movies. He knew only one thing: the sound of his father's voice, singing 'Swing Low, Sweet Chariot'. So he decided to sing, but when it came to his turn, he shook so much that his pitch was quivery and rushed – and the whole class burst out laughing. He returned to his desk 'humiliated' and expected another beating. When his teacher approached, he cowered. 'You sang very well,' she said. 'They are laughing because you were nervous, not because you were bad. Good try.'

On the walk home from school, Joseph says he made a vow to himself that 'I'll show 'em' and he started dreaming about 'a life in show-business'. I didn't know that story until recently. He exca-vated it from his past, trying to apply meaning after the event. I don't suppose any of us Jacksons have taken the trouble to under-stand our deepest history, or even talk about it too much. Michael once said he didn't truly know Joseph. 'That's sad for a son who hungers to understand his own father,' he wrote in 1988, in his autobiography, *Moonwalk*.

I think there is something unknowable about Joseph. It's difficult to reach him beyond his barriers, perhaps built by a fear of loss
and reinforced by his need for respect. None of us can remember
him holding or cuddling us, or telling us, 'I love you'. He never
play-wrestled with us, or tucked us into bed at night; there were no
heart-to-heart father-son discussions about life. We remember the
respect, the instructions, the chores and the commands, but no
affection. We knew our father as he was; someone who wanted to
be looked up to, and to provide for his family – a man's man.

Acceptance of this *was* to know him in its limited way, and as
much as Michael struggled to accept the way Joseph was, he always
had compassion for him, not judgement. The sad thing is that I
don't think he knew the back-story I have just shared. I guess many
people only know their parents as 'Mother' and 'Father' and not as
people prior to that role but if we understand more about our
parents when they were young, then maybe we have a better
chance of knowing who we become. I like to think that the stories
about Joseph's schooldays explain quite a lot.

JOSEPH DIDN'T NEED TO DAY-DREAM ABOUT a life in
California, like most working men in Indiana: he had already
whetted his appetite by living there. That was why his horizons
were set somewhere between the sunsets on the Pacific and dreams
of the Hollywood sign. Aged 13, he moved from Arkansas to
Oakland on San Francisco Bay, via Los Angeles, by train. He
moved with his father, who quit teaching for the shipyard after
discovering that Joseph's mother, Chrystal, had had an affair with
a soldier. Initially, Samuel Jackson went alone, leaving Joseph
behind. Three months later, after pleading letters from son to
father had gone back and forth, Joseph made the 'toughest of
choices' and moved west. More letters went back and forth, this
time between Joseph and his mother. Our father must have been
persuasive even as a kid because some months later, Chrystal
Jackson left her new man and returned to the husband she had
recently divorced.

The arrangement lasted a year before she headed back east to set up a new life with another man in Gary, Indiana. I suspect Joseph felt like the rope in a tug-of-war being pulled by both parents. For a man who has forever preached 'togetherness and family', I don't know how he stood it. All I know is that he first pitched up in Gary after taking the bus all the way from Oakland. On arrival, he thought the city 'small, dirty and ugly' but his mother was there and reading between the lines, I think he detected a small sense of 'celebrity' around him. Here was a kid not from Arkansas but from California, and his stories of West-Coast life brought a lot of attention from the local girls. So, aged 16, Joseph moved to be with his mother in Gary, Indiana but in his mind, he would one day return to California. 'We'll go out West. Wait till you see it out West,' he used to say to us – an explorer on stopover from some great adventure he had yet to resume.

Joseph's face was lined and furrowed by his years of hard work, and he had thick eyebrows that seemed to cement a permanent frown, hardening the hazel eyes that looked right through you. One glare was enough to make us wobble as children. But talk of California softened his features. He remembered 'the golden California sunshine', the palm trees, Hollywood and how the West coast 'was the place to be in life.' No crime, tidy streets, opportunities to get on top. We watched the television series *Maverick* and he pointed out streets he knew. Over the years, we constructed this city into a fictional paradise – a distant planet: when man could walk on the moon, we could also perhaps visit LA. Whenever the sun was setting in Indiana, we always said to each other, 'The sun will be setting in California soon': we always knew that there was some place, some life, that was better than what we had.

LONG BEFORE MICHAEL WAS BORN, AND while Mother was pregnant with me, Joseph first conceived a plan of 'making it'. As a guitarist, he formed a blues band named the Falcons with his brother, Luther, and a couple of friends. By the time I came along, they had built up a slick act, performing at local parties and venues to put some extra dollars in their pockets. While he was working the crane, Joseph composed songs, shifting steel beams on auto-pilot and conjuring lyrics as a singer-songwriter.

In 1954, the year I was born, he claims to have written a song called 'Tutti Frutti'. One year later, Little Richard released a same-titled hit. When we were growing up, the story of how Little Richard 'stole' our father's song became legendary. It was never true, of course. But all that was important was that a black man from the middle of nowhere had created a song that redefined music – 'the sound of the birth of rock 'n' roll'. It was *that* possibility that locked deep in our minds every time the story was told.

I don't remember vividly the Falcons rehearsing, certainly not when measured against what 'rehearsing' would come to mean for us! But I have a vague memory of Uncle Luther – always smiling – arriving with packs of beer and his guitar, then riffing with Joseph as we sat around, sucking it all in. Uncle Luther played the blues and Joseph switched between his guitar and the harmonica. Those were the sounds that sometimes helped us drift off to sleep.

Joseph's musical dream floundered when the Falcons disbanded after one of them, Pookie Hudson, quit to form a new group. But Joseph still came home and unwound by playing his guitar, then putting it away in its usual spot at the back of his bedroom closet. Tito, the first budding guitarist among us, eyed that closet like an unlocked safe containing gold but we all knew it was Joseph's pride and joy. As such, it was untouchable. 'And don't even think about getting out my guitar!' he warned us all before leaving for work.

WE FIVE BOYS SHARED ONE BEDROOM – the best dressing room we ever shared. Within this confinement, we grew up as best friends. Brotherhood grows stronger each year. We are the only ones who can ever say to one another, 'Remember how we were. Remember what we shared. Remember where and what we came from.'

Or, as Clive Davis would later tell me, 'Blood is thicker than mud.' We were inseparable in Gary, forever together, night and day.

We shared a metal-framed three-tiered bunk-bed. Its length was just big enough to fit against the back wall and its height meant that Tito and I slept head to toe, about four feet from the ceiling. In the middle were Michael and Marlon, and Jackie had the lowest bunk all to himself. Jackie was the only brother who didn't know what it was like to wake up with a foot in his eyes, ear or mouth. The girls, Rebbie and La Toya, slept on the sofa-bed in the living room (later joined by our brother Randy and baby sister Janet) so every room was crammed to its limit. Imagine being Rebbie – the eldest child – and never once having a bedroom to herself!

As brothers, we spent a lot of time in our bedroom, with its one window looking out on to 23rd Avenue. Every night felt like a sleepover. We went to bed at roughly the same time – 8.30 or 9pm – regardless of age and hurled pillows, wrestled and talked up a storm for a good hour before sleep, planning on what we'd be doing the next day.

'I got the skates, so I'm the one roller-skating!'

'I got the bat and ball, who's playing?'

'We're building a go-kart. Who's in?'

We ripped the sheets from the bed and threw the mattresses on the floor, and built Greek columns out of books, draping sheets over them to create a tented roof. We loved sleeping on the floor in our self-built 'dens'. We loved sleeping on the floor even when we hadn't built a den – it felt like camping out.

Come the morning we were each other's alarm clocks. 'You awake, Jermaine?' I'd hear Michael ask in a loud whisper. 'Jackie?' We'd wait for the reply that rarely came because he always liked his extra ZZZZ.

Then came the chaos of the '15-minute bathroom' rule. As one brother or sister darted out, another darted in and then we heard Mother shout: 'JERMAINE! Your 15 minutes is up!'

I loved mornings at home. I loved the chaos in the kitchen, and I loved making harmonies in bed when we woke. We didn't need to see each other's faces, we just lay there singing. We always sang, even during chores like painting the house, doing the laundry, cutting the grass, or ironing. Our self-entertainment eased the tedium and we 'covered' hits from sounds we heard at home: Ray Charles, Otis Redding, Smokey Robinson and the Miracles, and Major Lance (whose keyboardist was an unknown man called Reggie Dwight, nowadays better known as Sir Elton John).

Michael often recalled the 'joy' and 'fun' we shared in our tiny bedroom. I think he yearned to have those days back; to have brothers 'sleeping over'. He always said that he missed the company of brothers around him. As grown men, whenever we had a family meeting or a brotherly catch-up, we all convened in the smallest room. We did this unconsciously for years until it was pointed out that it was, perhaps, a bit strange to meet in the smallest room at places like Neverland or Hayvenhurst. Something within each of us obviously enjoyed feeling close and confined with the others. It felt natural; it always felt like 'home'.

Something else we didn't realise until adulthood was that Mother and Joseph had lain in their bedroom just across the way listening to us sing through the walls, from 3-year-old Michael to Jackie aged 11. 'We heard you singing all night, we heard you singing in the morning,' said Mother. But even then I don't think Joseph heard the distant drumbeat of his California dream. That didn't happen until the day Tito broke his prized guitar – and then we had to sing for our lives.

JOSEPH OWNED A DARK-BROWN BUICK THAT looked like an angry fish coming at you. The configuration of the headlights, the grille and the V-shaped rim of the hood was like one big scary face frowning and baring its teeth. I don't know if they made cars with engines that *purred* back then, but that car – just like Joseph himself – definitely did *not* purr.

It seems comical, looking back, that this 'angry fish' was our warning system that our father was minutes from home. We'd be out in the street playing when one of us would spot the cruising scowl in the distance and shout, 'Clean the house! Clean the house!'

We'd drop everything and bolt inside, cleaning up our room faster than Mary Poppins ever could. In the rush, we grabbed all our clothes and shoved them into one great pile in the closet or stuffed them into drawers, unfolded and out of place. We were brought up better than that, Mother always said, when she found clothes bundled into a bed-sheet and hidden away. But all we wanted to achieve was the *appearance* of neatness: so long as everything looked good on the surface, we were fine. We also knew that, while we were at school, Mother would go into our bedroom, pull out everything, refold our clothes, restore order and say nothing.

It was no surprise to her that Michael and I grew into the kind of men who left clothes on the floor where we stepped out of them but we cited the same defence: when you grow up as brothers in one tiny room, you get used to knowing where everything is in the chaos or clutter. We got away with a lot more things with Mother. Don't get me wrong, she was strict, too: if we misbehaved, she wasn't afraid to administer a firm slap around the ear with the palm of her hand. But where Mother had patience, Joseph had a short fuse trip-wired by another hard shift at The Mill. We heeded what Mother said: respect that your father is in the house, respect that he's had a hard day at work, respect that he doesn't want to hear noise.

When he arrived home, Respect walked through the door and the air in the house stiffened. His basic rule was simple: I'll tell you something once and if you have to be told again, you'll be punished. As kids within a growing family, we regularly had to be told again. Jackie, Tito and I knew from sore experience what the consequences were. Michael and Marlon, as infants, felt our fear vicariously – at first. When Joseph got angry, just one look on his face was enough – he didn't need to say a word. He had a mole the size of a dime on one cheek and I can still see it in my mind, close up: whenever he got really mad, it and his face crunched up – the storm clouds rolling in before the clap of thunder and the dreaded words 'WAIT FOR ME IN YOUR ROOM!' followed by the flash of lightning; the eye-watering sting of a leather belt against skin. We normally received 10 'whops'. I call them 'whops' because that was the exact sound the belt made as it whipped the air. I screamed out for God, for Mother, for mercy, and anyone else's name that I could think of, but Joseph just shouted louder, reminding us why we were being punished: the discipline followed by the reason, mimicking his lessons as a schoolboy.

Whenever we were punished, our screams were what Michael heard, and he saw the red marks and belt-buckle imprints on bare skin at bedtime. This made him fear something long before he actually felt it. In his mind, the mere thought of Joseph's discipline was traumatic. That is what exaggerated fear does: it builds something in the mind to a scale that, perhaps, it is not.

A WHITE MOUSE HAD BEEN RUNNING loose around the house and Joseph was desperate to catch it because it was driving the girls crazy. When we heard them scream, we knew this rodent had scurried in for a visit. An exasperated Joseph couldn't understand why we suddenly had this problem. What he didn't account for was the start of Michael's lifelong affinity with animals.

Unknown to any of us, he'd been treating this mouse like a pet, encouraging its visits with bits of lettuce and cheese. Looking back, it was obvious: whenever Mother screamed and Joseph cursed, Michael fell suspiciously quiet and slid away. He was only three: who was going to suspect his cunning? But it was only a matter of time before he was found out. That moment arrived when Joseph crept into the kitchen and caught him red-handed, kneeling on the floor, feeding the mouse behind the fridge.

The house shook when Joseph bellowed, 'WAIT FOR ME IN YOUR ROOM!'

What Michael did next surprised everyone.

He bolted.

He started running around the house like a terrified rabbit. Joseph chased him with the belt and grabbed the back of his shirt, but my brother was a flexible, agile little dynamo, and he wriggled and fought and pulled his arms out of the sleeves, and ran on. He darted into Joseph's room, up and over the bed, and pinned himself against the wall, tight into the corner, knowing the belt's arc couldn't reach him without first striking the walls.

I hadn't seen Joseph so angry. He dropped the belt, grabbed Michael and spanked him so hard that he screamed the house down.

I hated the awkward silence that hung in the air after one of these episodes, broken only by Mother's murmurs of disquiet and the quiet sobs into the pillow of whichever one of us had got hit.

Michael didn't help himself because he was the most defiant. Rebbie remembers the time when he was 18 months old and tossed his baby bottle at Joseph's head. That should have put our father on notice because when Michael was four, he threw a shoe at him in a temper tantrum – and that earned him a good spanking, too.

Michael's fear of a spanking always sent him running. Sometimes he'd do a sliding dive under our parents' bed and tuck himself against the back wall in the centre, gripping the bed springs. It was an effective tactic because after half an hour under there, Joseph was either too exhausted to care or had calmed down: Michael got away with a lot more than he ever let on.

TITO'S PASSION FOR THE GUITAR COULDN'T help itself.

As Jackie and I started learning songs from the radio, his talent blossomed through lessons at school. But when he was at home, he couldn't practise. So, despite all warnings from Joseph, he borrowed our father's guitar from the back of his closet. What he wouldn't know couldn't hurt him, right?

Whenever Joseph worked, Tito seized his moment. He started playing and we began making harmonies. On a couple of occasions, Mother walked in and found us out, but apart from a gasp that told us we were playing with fire, she turned a blind eye. She was *a lot* more lenient than our father. On one particular weekend, Tito started playing and we were singing some Four Tops' song. He was sitting there, plucking away, and Jackie and I were crooning when suddenly there was a twanging noise. Tito went white when he realised one of the strings had broken. 'Oooh, you're going to get it now!' squealed Jackie, part excitement, part fear.

We're all going to get it now, I thought.

We put the broken treasure back in its rightful place and were sitting in our bedrooms when we heard his car pull up. The bomb was primed. Each loud footstep on the linoleum matched what was going on inside our ribcages. One … two … three … 'WHO'S … BEEN MESSING … WITH MY GUITARRRR?' He hollered so loud I think they heard him in California. When he pounded into our room, Michael and Marlon scarpered, leaving Jackie, Tito and me standing by the bunk-beds already whimpering over what we knew was coming next. Mother tried intervening, claiming it was all her fault, but Joseph wasn't listening. We cried even louder when he told us we were all going to get it until one of us owned up.

'It was me,' Tito said, barely heard. 'I was playing it –' Joseph grabbed him '– but I know how to play. I KNOW HOW TO PLAY!' he screamed.

I've read accounts that say Joseph clobbered him there and then, but that's not what happened. Instead he stopped, scowled and said, 'Play, then. Let me see what you can do!' With a broken string, Tito started to play, and Jackie and I started to sing – even if our crying meant we could give only 50 per cent. 'Doing The Jerk' by the Larks became our plea for clemency and we started making harmonies, slightly off note, but it must have sounded good because Joseph visibly loosened. We kept on singing: we saw his head moving to the beat, and he did what would become a habit – he started lip-synching the lyrics, going through the motions with us. We became emboldened, stopped sniffling and pulled ourselves together. Our harmonies came good and we were snapping our fingers. Our audience's eyes widened and narrowed in both victory and defeat. When we stopped playing, he didn't say a word but we had been spared a major spanking and that was all that seemed to matter.

Two days later, Joseph arrived home from work with a red electric guitar for Tito and told him to start practising. He told Jackie and me to get ready for rehearsals. He told our mother that he was going 'to support these boys.' His focus switched from the Falcons to his sons. We had won his approval and he wanted to harness something we loved doing. It felt like recognition and it excited us. People have said that our father 'made them sing' or 'forced those boys into entertainment', but singing had come naturally to us and that passion was our choice. We had sung up a storm long before Joseph arrived with his rocket fuel. As a trio of brothers, we told ourselves that we were going to be the best group in Gary.

CHAPTER THREE
God's Gift

MICHAEL SAT ON THE CARPET WITH two empty, cardboard tubs of Quaker Oats sandwiched between his knees. He bound them together by sticking a pencil through their middle. This, he told everyone, was his set of bongos. Taking up his position as a spectator on the sidelines with Marlon, he was eager for rehearsals to start even though he wasn't involved since he'd been deemed 'too little'. But he had decided he was going to join in anyway and four fingers on each hand contributed his beat to whatever rhythm we played. He watched as a purposeful Joseph took Jackie, Tito and me by the shoulders and positioned us like chess pieces 'on the stage', which was our living room. Tito, on guitar, took centre position, with me to his right; the three of us stood around wondering what our next move was going to be.

In the kitchen, Mother stayed out of the way with Rebbie and La Toya, allowing us to do our thing. She knew what we'd soon find out: these sessions were not some dreamy pretence but a serious business in our father's eyes. A single microphone was hooked into its stand in the middle of the room. No hairbrushes or shampoo bottles for his sons. It was borrowed from the Falcons, a baton passed to the next generation. 'You've got to learn how to use it, not be afraid of it, hold it, play it,' said Joseph.

Play the microphone? I think our faces said it all.

He put on a James Brown LP, turned it up loud, grabbed the mic, dipped left, dipped right, then threw it forward so it bounced right back. *That* was 'playing' the mic. 'Hear that voice, Jermaine? Do it like that. Do it *just* like that.' He played classic 45s and LPs so that we could study, over and over, one song at a time, how it was sung, and how it should be performed. I remember the repetitiveness of 'Green Onions' by Booker T. & the MGs, and James Brown's version of 'Night Train'. As Joseph encouraged us to move, we started doing the cow-step, snapping our fingers, and self-consciously shuffling around. He wasn't impressed. 'Boys, you can't just sing and sway. You gotta *move* – put more feeling into it! Like this ...'

He stepped in, with James Brown as his dance track, and started getting down, bobbing his head. We couldn't help but giggle at his lack of grace. 'I can see you laughing,' he said, 'but I don't want *you* looking like amateurs.'

We went back to our 'marks', back to being choreographed. Back to the class where there was no motto above the door but if there had been, it would have read: 'The Right Way Becomes Habit'.

In the meantime, there was always Joseph's verbal handbook, which was seared into our memories. 'You have to entertain. Be dynamic. Be different. Take it to the audience!' We studied songs and learned moves for two, three, sometimes five hours a day for months on end. Whenever Joseph wasn't working or sleeping, we practised. 'Practice does not make perfect,' he *always* said. 'It makes consistency.' Practice made us remember. And yet we seemed to forget regularly. 'Let's do it again ... and again ... and again, until we get it right,' he said.

Meanwhile, Michael kept pounding those upturned oatmeal cartons. I lost count of how many he went through, but Joseph eventually found him a real set of second-hand bongos. And our lessons kept coming. 'Imagine the crowd … picture them … look out … feel them … and SMILE!'

We looked straight out of the window on to Jackson Street – always facing the light – and saw other kids running around playing tag-football or roller-skating. We heard fun and laughter. When school friends knocked on our door to ask if we wanted to play, Joseph refused. 'No, they're busy rehearsing,' he said. This, in turn, built an endless curiosity about the goings-on inside our house for the rest of the 1960s. On a few occasions, children came up to the window to see what was happening, mushing their noses against the glass. I guess that was the start of living in a goldfish bowl. Some kids banged on the window and made fun of us.

'You're locked up! You're locked up!' they chanted, and ran away laughing.

Joseph drew the curtains. No one got anywhere in life from playing in the street. 'Focus', he said. 'You'll always face distractions,' he added, 'but it's about keeping your minds on the job.' If *he* could take time out to work hard between his shifts, so could we. That was the unspoken message.

As we continued, he recognised our talents. But entertainment wasn't just about skill: it was *showmanship*, he said. We had to create 'the Jackson mystique'. As for those dance moves, never, ever start counting them. 'You must not do that. It can't be one, two, three … kick. That's dancing by numbers,' he said. 'You've got to know and feel what's coming up next. Take OUT the numbers, bring IN the feeling!'

In those early days, Joseph was patient and took his time shaping us. He knew we were green, so he was forgiving. When he witnessed our gradual improvement, this pleased him and in turn, made us dig deeper. Impressing him and winning *his* respect mattered. Family members like Uncle Luther and Mama Martha came over, and Joseph asked us to sing. He noted their enthusiastic reactions, but it was never good enough. 'You can give more. We can do better!' At least Joseph was kicking our butts with something we loved doing. At least he was spending time with us, unlike a lot of fathers in the neighbourhood. We felt driven, not pushed, guided into where we wanted to go.

'Blood, sweat and tears, boys – if you wanna be the best, blood, sweat and tears,' he said.

Tito had the guitar down, I was vocally strong, and Jackie's forte was honed by the dance contests he'd won with Rebbie. He led the moves Joseph wanted, and we mirrored him until we were in sync. We were light on our feet so it soon came easy. Outside these sessions, I was encouraged to sing ballads: 'Danny Boy' and 'Moon River' – Mother's favourites. I mastered them by putting on the LP and writing out the lyrics. The tough part was holding my notes with the lungs of a kid but Joseph noticed my initial struggle.

'You gotta sing from your stomach,' said our vocal coach, choreographer and manager. 'Imagine a balloon expanding as it sucked in air,' he said. 'That's breathing in. Releasing that air is how you sing, hold and control a note. Think bagpipes.' I compared my lungs to balloons and bagpipes for many years because knowing how to breathe – swelling the stomach – taught me how to sing.

'Master the melody before the lyrics. Know where the key change is. Know where the notes are,' he said. This was the strongest lesson inside 2300 Jackson Street: understanding our voice is the melody, and that the melody is everything. 'You should be able to sing a song without music.'

Even our 'ear' was being trained.

We knew it was all starting to click together when none of us looked down at Jackie's feet, or muttered a countdown under our breath. We just fell into it. Performing felt like the most natural thing in the world.

MAMA MARTHA WAS EVER-PRESENT IN OUR childhood, always visiting from her house in Hammond, East Chicago, about 20 minutes away. She arrived with pound cake and a big smacker of a kiss, which, when planted on the cheek with vigour, made one of those squelching sounds of puckered lips on skin. A real grandmother's 'mwah'!

After we had put in endless practice as a trio, Joseph was keen to show his mother-in-law what his micro man-management had created. What we didn't know was that Michael was also itching to get in on the action. As our all-female audience – Mother, Mama, Rebbie and La Toya (plus two-year-old Randy) – stood watching, Jackie, Tito and I lined up in formation, ready to do our father proud.

Michael was, as always, seated with his bongos on the floor. As we came out of the intro of some song I now forget, the girls started to clap with the rhythm and Michael stood. Then, sensing the song building, he started to sing spontaneously, coming in on a part. Distracted, I waved him away, trying to hush his mouth. As far as we were concerned, he was ruining our moment.

Before we knew it, Joseph had stopped the record.

'He's not supposed to be singing!' I said, protesting.

Mama Martha jumped to his defence. 'Leave him alone. Let the boy sing if he wants to sing! You want to sing, Michael?'

His face lit up. We stood to one side to let him have his moment in our grandmother's sun and Joseph begrudgingly turned on the music as our little brother started to sing. What he produced was no 'Jingle Bells' at a Christmas window. It was one hundred times better because it was an invited rendition, not a forbidden carol. This was Michael, shy but confident and knowing exactly what to do: he played the mic, worked the floor and sang beautifully, and we were, like, 'Damn – that's good!'

I didn't know where that voice came from.

'Heaven,' said Mother.

The wide-eyed look on Joseph's face was a picture.

All that time on the sidelines, Michael had been memorising everything we were doing. And then Talent emerged from its hiding place.

As everyone applauded, he felt as big as his brothers, and that's all a kid brother wants to feel.

Mama Martha and Mother nodded knowingly to one another, as if to say 'Always knew that one had it in him'.

I don't remember Joseph immediately installing him in the group because there were still reservations about his age: he had only just turned five on 29 August 1963. But a few weeks later that no longer mattered when Michael became the first brother to perform before a live audience – at a Parent Teacher Association gala at Garnett Elementary School. It was Michael's first term there, and a set of grey, oblong blocks became his first stage.

The gymnasium was filled with wooden foldaway chairs and it felt like the whole community had turned out to see local kids perform. I was sitting with Mother and Papa Samuel, and we knew Michael's class was due to sing and that he had been asked to do a solo. We sensed it was a big deal for him because he had left the house that morning in a blue shirt, buttoned up to the neck, and smart pants, not his usual T-shirt and jeans. His chosen song was 'Climb Ev'ry Mountain' from the 1959 Rodgers and Hammerstein musical *The Sound of Music* (which would become one of his all-time favourite movies).

Michael hadn't made a big fuss about this spot and I don't remember him rehearsing his solo at home but that probably speaks of a quiet confidence first being displayed; a boy getting on with something in his own head until the moment of execution. Something he'd do throughout his life.

When it came to his spot, the woman teacher on the piano nodded and Michael stepped forward. Mother squeezed the purse on her lap with both hands and I didn't know what I was going to do: die of embarrassment or claim him as my own.

I shouldn't have worried.

He did everything our father had taught us to do – and then came the unexpected 'wow' moment: the high note at the end, which soared and echoed around the gymnasium with acoustic perfection. It was like God had reached down into one moment and said: 'Kid, I'm going to give you a voice that is out of this world. Now use it!'

Michael was animated, wandering the stage with confidence. He didn't follow the lead of the teacher, like most kids: *she* followed *him*. What amazed everyone was that he sang it so high. On that end note everyone stood and applauded. Even the teacher at the piano was up, clapping faster than I had ever seen anyone clap.

That's my brother! I thought.

Mother was in tears. And even Papa Samuel was choked.

Damn, Michael – you've even made Papa Samuel cry!

I suspect that was the very moment Michael's soul locked into its purpose to entertain, upon feeling the buzz of applause and seeing the reaction *he* had created. I knew that I wanted to be alongside him, feeling the same thing.

After that day, our musical group became five. Michael was drafted in, and so too was Marlon. Not because he had demonstrated anything outstanding but because Mother wasn't having him be the odd one out. 'You'll crush him if you don't include him, Joe,' she said.

Over the years, it has been written that I was somehow hurt or jealous over Michael's inclusion but I was not: there was nothing to be jealous about. We were a group without a name that hadn't even broken out of our living room, so there was no limelight to steal. There was nothing but enthusiastic harmony between brothers. We used to lie awake in our bunk-beds, imagining being stars. Our morning singing now took on purpose. As we climbed out of bed, one brother would sing, another would jump in, then another and before we knew it, we had a three-part harmony going.

There were notes I couldn't hit and all of a sudden, Michael reached them with ease. That boy was like a bird. He found octaves that I didn't know existed and our father was blown away. You could tell he viewed Michael as the unexpected bonus to his game plan. The only thing missing now was the right name.

I HAVE OFTEN WONDERED HOW MANY names my parents went through before agreeing on the final nine. Not that it mattered in the end, because the choice of 'Sigmund Esco' for their first son morphed into 'Jackie' when Papa Samuel thought it easy to refer to him as 'Jackson boy', then laziness shortened it some more. And 'Tariano Adaryl' became 'Tito' because it was easier for us all. I was forever curious as a child about how two people's taste could go from the exotic-sounding 'Jermaine LaJuane' to 'Michael Joe'. From somewhere, and especially after Michael's death, a rumour began that his middle name was Joseph. Maybe this myth prefers the echo with our father's name because the crossover reads better about a father and son who struggled to see eye to eye. 'Joe' was his middle name, as recorded on his birth certificate. His first name was almost 'Ronald', at the suggestion of Mama Martha, but Mother quickly quashed that one. In the light of history, 'Ronald' doesn't have the same ring to it.

Michael was the seventh child with seven letters in his first name and '7' was his favourite number. So, numerically, his name is '777'. That's the Jackpot there. The Lucky 7s. A number that appears only once in the Bible. There's a lot that can be read into a name. That's the power of its sound and interpretation; the story it can tell, and the memories it can evoke. But '7' was central to his identity. He wore jackets with '7' sewn into the arm. When he doodled on paper, '7' was tagged all over. And what the world never saw were his pencil sketches in later life for a furniture range he had in his head. He drew throne-like upholstered chairs with '7' carved into the centre of the oak frame beneath the seat, set within an intricate, floral design.

I think about all the names we considered across the years: song titles, album titles and names for our own children, all in search of the one name that *sounds right*. That is one reason why biographers should always have known that 'The Ripples and the Waves' was not a name we would have chosen as a group. To our amusement, the rumour went around, and made it into print, that this was our first name. It started, no doubt, because a song titled 'Let Me Carry Your Schoolbooks' was released by the Ripples and the Waves + Michael on the Steeltown Records label – which would become our first label. I suspect the use of the name 'Michael' was a deliberate marketing ploy aimed at catching our coat-tails. But this Michael was a Michael Rogers, and the Ripples and the Waves was another group.

Our first name could actually have been a lot worse. One lady suggested we needed something fancy like the El Dorados. We were in danger of being made to sound like some damn Cadillac. Luckily, that idea was sunk when we discovered there was another band from Chicago of the same name. Joseph wanted 'Jackson' in the name, but it had to be catchy. Our parents talked about 'The Jackson Brothers 5' and that was the lead contender until Mother had a conversation with a local lady named Evelyn Lahaie, who said, 'It's too much of a mouthful. Why don't you just call them the Jackson 5?' Mrs Lahaie ran 'Evelyn's School of Charm' for local girls in Gary and seemed to know a thing or two about image, so that was how the Jackson 5 was born. On paper, at least.

JOHNNY RAY NELSON, THE KID WHO lived next door, was always good value for entertainment because his brother Roy would chase him out the front door with a crow-bar, Johnny running and giggling, Roy vowing to get him; playfighting, Gary style. When Johnny had stopped running and peace had returned, he'd overhear us singing through the open windows. He said he was always amazed by how we could harmonise so young.

Once, Michael was out front in the sunshine when Johnny said, 'Sing us a song and I'll get you some cookies.' On cue, Michael stood there and sang. Sure enough, we all caught on to this neighbourhood perk and before anyone knew it, five brothers were lined up at the fence, giving Johnny Ray Nelson a private performance for a plate of his cookies.

BETWEEN 1962 AND THE SUMMER OF 1965, Joseph kept honing our performance until he felt we were ready. He fixed us a rehearsal timetable: Monday, Wednesday and Friday evenings, starting at 4.30 after school, and running, non-stop, until seven or sometimes nine o'clock.

By the early sixties, the Temptations had broken through to become our newest role models. In Joseph's eyes, Dave Ruffin's mellow but raspy vocals, with his stage presence, set the bar for what he wanted us to achieve. But he didn't expect us to match him, he expected us to *better* him. The Temptations, for all their greatness, represented basement level in our father's standards. There were groups all over America trying to be the next Temptations, he said. 'You aren't going to be the next, you're going to be better!'

He illustrated his point with one hand in the air to show where we needed to aim. 'We don't want you *here*,' he said, jabbing a flat hand at waist level. 'We want you *here*' – top of the head – 'and when you're here, we want you here!' Two feet above his head. 'Reach higher … always go for more …' He didn't want the audience reaction to be 'Hey, they were good for a bunch of kids.' He wanted 'Wow – who *are* they?' We would achieve this by creating a performance that pulled on the audience's emotions, he said. 'When they watch you, you're controlling them and bringing them into your world. Sell the lyric. Make 'em stand and make 'em scream.'

Five boys, none of us yet teenagers, wondered privately how we would ever make people scream.

When she was doing the dishes, Mama Martha could squeeze every last drop of water out of a wet tea-towel. If it didn't think it had one more tear left in it, she would prove it wrong. Joseph was the same with us. And as we saw our performance coming together, we understood better – and then we embellished it some more, especially Michael. When he told us to slide a certain way, or fall to our knees, or show a certain expression, we added more. We watched and learned from Dave Ruffin's anguished performances and James Brown's pained soul.

When the Jackson 5 went live, many people said the body language and emotion Michael demonstrated belied his years. There was talk – then and now – that he was an old soul tapping into feelings he couldn't know, let alone understand, as a child. People even suggested that this showed how quickly he had been forced to grow up. The truth is simpler: it was nothing more than another child imitating adults. Michael was a master of imitation, as coached by Joseph – our drama teacher. Each time a song required heartache or pain, he told us, 'Show it in your face, let me feel it …' Michael dropped to his knees, pulled at his heart and looked … pained. 'No. NO!' said our harshest critic. 'It doesn't look real. I'm not *feeling* it.'

Michael studied human emotions on the faces of others in the same microscopic way he studied song and dance. Ask him then what he was doing and he would have parroted our father: 'I'm just selling the lyric …' His practice began to focus more on the required showmanship, so he played James Brown records, this time breaking down the music into steps and dance moves. Or he'd watch a Fred Astaire movie, lying on the living-room carpet in front of the television, chin on hands. He didn't make notes: he just watched awestruck and soaked it up like a sponge. If ever he was in bed, and Joseph was at work, and James Brown or Fred Astaire came on television, Mother would come into our bedroom. 'Michael,' she'd whisper, 'James Brown is on TV!'

Michael's world stopped for either James Brown or Fred Astaire. He idolised the very ground they danced on.

We had a black-and-white Zenith TV and its reception depended on a metal coat hanger. We tried to make the picture 'colour' by adding one of those transparent plastic sheets that could be fixed to the screen back in the day. It had a blue hue at the top for the sky, a yellow-bronze as the middle layer for people's skin, and green at the bottom for grass. We even had to use our imaginations when it came to watching television.

It became Michael's tool for memorising everything. If he saw someone doing a move, he channelled it, as if his brain sent an instant signal to his body. He watched James Brown and became James Brown junior. He moved with a finesse that was fluid from the start. From the very beginning, he was a man dancing in a kid's body. It was innate. He always knew his part, and never asked where he was supposed to be.

His confidence gave us confidence. Joseph restrung his old guitar and put me on bass. Like Tito, I had never read a sheet of music in my life but I listened, played and picked it up. None of us understood notes or chords, or anything like that. I still wouldn't know my way around a sheet of music if you put one in front of me. Notes on paper – a written instruction – do not carry feeling. A musical ear comes from the heart. Take Stevie Wonder – his blindness proves that it's all about playing from the heart.

Michael and I often shared lead vocals by alternating verses, but he was very much the group's frontman holding the mic. We lined up in the living room as we would line up on stage. Facing the audience, I was on the far left and bass, Michael to my right, then Jackie, Marlon – who was the same height as Michael – and Tito on the far right with his guitar. With Tito's and my height book-ending us, and Jackie as the tallest in the middle, we stood with the symmetry of five bars on an equaliser.

But we weren't the only group forming in Gary: dreams were being rehearsed in plenty of other houses because of the soul market sprouting in nearby Chicago. There were several barbershop quartets going down, and the genre was all about choreographed routines. But we always sensed there was something unique about us, in real terms, not just in Joseph's mind. Being brothers brought us an instant synchronicity and kinship that other groups didn't have. This unity was our edge and I doubt anyone across all of America had a coach as fiercely passionate as Joseph. People ask about the pressure and burden we must have felt, but we didn't. There was no such thing as fear of failure because Joseph made us imagine – and believe in – success: think it, see it, believe it, make it happen. As Michael said in an interview with *Ebony* magazine in 2007: 'My father was a genius when it comes to the way he taught us: staging, how to work an audience, anticipating what to do next, or never let the audience know if you are suffering, or if something's going wrong. He was amazing like that.'

One day, Joseph made us stand a few feet away from the wall and stick out our hands. As we stood in this position, our fingers fell a few inches short of the wall. 'You can touch it,' said Joseph.

'How can we? Our fingers aren't long enough … it's impossible,' we moaned.

'Get it in your head that you *can* touch that wall!' he insisted.

Here started yet another Joseph mental lesson: the mind is stronger than the physical. 'Believe that you can touch the wall,' he said. 'When you think you're at the limit of your reach, then reach more. Visualise reaching it. Picture yourself touching the wall.' Michael stood on tiptoe and strained to outreach us all. That made us giggle. He was the tiniest boy, yet he always wanted to be fastest and first.

If Joseph had any doubt of his influence on Michael's career, then that doubt will have gone when Michael put his stamp on Hayvenhurst in 1981. Nailed to an exterior wall of his old studio remains a sign with a pale blue background and big-lettered words: 'Those Who Reach Touch The Stars'.

IF WE COULDN'T WAIT FOR MOTHER to return home from work, we couldn't wait for Joseph to *leave*: with him out of the way, we could run around, act the fool, go outside and play. Rebbie, especially, couldn't wait for him to work a night shift because then she could sleep in a proper bed with Mother, not on the sofa-bed. The common perception of our youth seems to be framed by the use of Joseph's belt and the timetable for rehearsals, and it's true that our circumstances developed us more as artists than as boys. But, as much as I hear the voice of discipline and instruction in my memories, I also hear the distinct sound of fun, laughter and play. As brothers, we always had someone to hang around with and those memories have not been allowed to breathe in public. Anyone from a large family will tell you that we each remember things differently.

With Joseph at work, Mother made sure we didn't slacken off on the routines we were expected to know. 'Did you learn that song you're supposed to do? Did you learn those steps?' she would ask.

She was our father's eyes and ears, but she balanced that with our need to play. As well as the go-karts, the trains and the merry-go-round, we rode our bikes (again built by Tito out of junkyard frames and wheels) and went roller-skating (with those wheeled brackets that clamped on to sneakers, bought second-hand). We couldn't wait to get out and tear up and down Jackson Street – 'But go no further than Mr Pinsen's house!' He was our baseball coach and lived 10 doors down.

We enjoyed family camping holidays to the Wisconsin Dells, where we went fishing with Joseph and he taught Jackie, Tito and me how to bait the hook. We always stayed near old Indian towns and walked the trails in homage to our ancestry. We grew up knowing we have Native American blood in our veins, passed down from both the Choctaw and Blackfoot tribes. The inherited physical attributes were our high cheekbones, light skin and hair-less chests.

Back home, we watched lots of television and it was always a fight between Jackie wanting sports, Michael and Marlon wanting *Mighty Mouse* or *The Road Runner Show*, and me wanting *Maverick*, starring James Garner. The only programmes we all liked were *The Three Stooges*, *Flash Gordon* and any Western starring Randolph Scott. It's *The Three Stooges* we must thank for first teaching us the harmonies we took to Mother at the kitchen sink. We loved mimicking their introductory triad-harmony of 'Hello … Hello … Hello'.

We huddled around Mother on the sofa to watch TV. My abiding memory of this happy scene is of her seated in the middle and Michael lying across her lap, head facing the screen, me sitting on her other side, La Toya on the floor, against her legs, resting her back on the sofa, Marlon on the other side (with Janet when she entered the equation). Tito and Randy would lie on the floor, while Rebbie and Jackie took the armchair or a kitchen chair. In the window – opened during sultry summer evenings – we wedged one of those square fans that blew cold air into the room. Michael would stick his head in front of the fan, on its highest whirring speed, and hum – fascinated by how the blast of air made his voice waver.

In the winter, there was no shortage of cold air blowing through every crack of our poorly insulated home. The brutal winters of Indiana punched through the paper-thin walls and the walk to school sometimes felt like an expedition across Antarctica. On school mornings, Joseph ensured Mother cooked a pot of boiled potatoes before we set off from base camp into the deep snow. We couldn't afford gloves – and didn't wear hats because of our blow-out Afros – so we placed a hot potato in each pocket to keep our hands warm. Mother then covered our faces with Vaseline, rubbing it in like sun-lotion, from hairline to chin, ear to ear. In those severe winters, this stopped our skin getting dry but it also served another purpose in Mother's eyes: 'It makes you look all shiny, fresh, new and clean,' she said, making the greasy smears of Vaseline sound almost fashionable. We told her that other kids didn't have Vaseline faces; she told us that they didn't look as clean as we did.

MOTHER STILL WANTED JOSEPH TO BUILD an extra room on to the house and for as long as there was a stack of bricks in the back-yard, she was not going to relent. We were eight-strong now with the addition of Randy (Janet was still to come), but if one sentence was repeated in our house – apart from 'Let's do it again' – it was 'This place is falling to pieces', as expressed by our mother. Her savings, which had been building since Tito's birth, were now somewhere in the region of $300, but I don't think anyone dared point out that the money would be better spent on fixing the patched-up water-pipe or buying a new television: this was Mother's growing nest-egg for another room …

Until, that is, the day Joseph made a unilateral decision in the interests of our group. His VW van, which had replaced his old Buick, pulled up outside and he started unloading microphones, stands, amplifiers, tambourines, a keyboard, drum-set and speakers. It was like the Christmas we were never allowed. Mother was breathless with anger. 'Joseph!' she said, rushing outside as he pulled our new instruments out of the van. 'What have you done? What is all this stuff?' We were too excited to know which 'toy' to play with first. Mother trailed Joseph as he went back and forth between living room and van. 'I don't believe it!' she said. 'We can't dress our children in new clothes and Jackie has holes in his shoes, this place is falling to pieces, and you've gone and bought instruments?'

As with everything in our household, Joseph's decision was final. He said it was a necessary investment, 'if we are to support our boys.'

I had never really heard our parents fight before because Mother usually stepped down, but this time he had crossed the line. Not only had he failed to consult her, he had used most of her precious savings. 'You'll get your new room, Katie,' he said. 'We're going to move to California and then I'll buy you a bigger house, but our boys can't perform without instruments!' On several nights, we heard raised voices from their bedroom. Mother was worried that he was chasing a pipe-dream and building up our hopes, leading us towards disappointment. Joseph was adamant that he was doing the right thing, and he needed her support. This was how he expressed his love for us – by believing in our talent. Where Mother soaked us in love and affection, Joseph compensated with what she lacked: confidence and belief. In terms of what children should receive from two parents, these opposites weighed themselves out evenly. Mother tended to look pragmatically at life, whereas Joseph was more 'speculate to accumulate'. His tough love was expressed not in affection or being tactile, but in the focus and discipline he instilled and the respect he asked for. It was the love of a football coach, expressed with a heart that was all about winning the game. A slap on the back, a smile on his face, and an excited clap of the hands was his way of expressing admiration. It was his *only* way of knowing how to express his love.

There was tension in the house for a few weeks, but eventually Mother calmed down and agreed to trust Joseph's gamble. We just didn't see the chips being pushed on to the red square in our name.

THE RADIO CRACKLED INTO ITS BROADCAST and that night in 1964, the house was the quietest it had ever been. 'Good evening, sports fans across the land,' the boxing commentator announced, 'and now the questions will be answered. Liston in the white trunks with the black stripes. Clay – half an inch taller – in the white trunks and the red stripes …' It amazed me that this man could take us there, painting a picture so vivid that we could 'see', heightening Joseph's tension as he hunched forward in his kitchen chair, pulled up alongside the radio on the side cabinet. 'The Heavyweight Championship of the World,' the voice continued. 'If it goes past the first round, there will be surprises already …'

We heard the bell. The crowd roared. We pictured the contender, Cassius Clay, the man from Louisville, Kentucky, springing from his corner to take on the reigning champ, Sonny Liston. 'AND HERE THEY COME!'

Even before the 22-year-old Cassius Clay became known as Muhammad Ali, 'The Greatest', we were rooting for him because Joseph loved his boxing and said we should cheer the underdog who had the fire to take on the best. Joseph had boxed competitively as a teenager in Oakland and he always had Tito, Jackie and me on the front lawn with our red gloves on, teaching us 'never be afraid of no one'. He'd referee bouts with other kids from the street and Michael would sit on the front step shouting, 'Hit him! Hit him! Hit him!'

Joseph taught us technique and how to defend ourselves. 'No one beats a Jackson,' he said, and no one ever did. Joseph said he had trained using one of Papa Samuel's solid oak doors, not a punchbag – it strengthened the callouses and toughened the mind. He was the strongest, hardest, toughest man we knew and I'm sure he imagined himself in the ring as we gathered around the radio.

As we listened, he couldn't help making a link between entertainment and boxing. 'Float like a butterfly and sting like a bee – that's what you need to be doing onstage,' he said, using Clay's boast from a press conference earlier that week. Joseph found these convenient associations everywhere and disguised them as lessons. He did it with Jim Brown of the Cleveland Bears whenever we talked football. The No. 32 and the greatest running back of all time was an example of dedication: 'Never missed a game or a training session in nine years because he knows you've got to work at being the best.'

He even hid lessons in the chores he made us do. That pile of bricks in the backyard – the ones Mother now knew would never be built on to the house – still served a purpose. There must have been 100 of those real heavy cinder-block bricks sitting in a stack at the left of the house. Our job was to carry them, one by one, to the other side and build a new stack. It was a pointless exercise, but we didn't ask why; we just did as we were told. When Joseph returned home, he inspected our work. Every brick had to be flush, and every line must be straight, running down the pile. 'No ... do it again. I want them stacked evenly,' he said – and we moved them from right to left until we had it *just right*. We learned discipline and perfection through cuts, blisters and grazes. Work as a team. Do it right. No room for error. If one person is off, it messes up everyone else – and messes up 'the look'. Noted for choreographic reasons.

All this might explain why some of us turned into obsessive compulsives as adults. Whenever Michael walked into a room and saw a pillow 'out of place', he'd change it. 'This is bothering me,' he'd say with a smile. Same with me. Same with Rebbie. 'Remember the bricks?' we'd say, and then we'd fall about laughing.

So when Cassius Clay arrived on the boxing scene, he presented Joseph with the perfect new example to fold into his lectures. Because here was someone *new*, who was doubted by the experts yet supreme in his confidence. As we huddled around the radio, Michael and Marlon started shadow boxing to one side as the commentator took us through the first round. Sonny Liston was missing more punches than he landed. 'That's all about footwork,' Joseph said. Mother muttered something about not agreeing with a violent sport but Joseph wasn't listening – he was too busy translating the commentary. 'Sonny Liston is like your audience ... You've got to go out there, tear up the stage and lay 'em out flat!'

That night Cassius Clay won and became the youngest boxer ever to take the title from a reigning heavyweight champion. 'I shook up the world,' he told the media. Point made – both in the ring and in the minds of the kids he had no idea were rooting for him in Gary, Indiana.

ON THE GRASS BETWEEN OUR BEDROOM window and 23rd Avenue, there was a tree. During high winds and the tornado warnings that swept across Indiana, Michael and I watched from the window to see how strong that tree really was. It was endlessly fascinating to observe the bout between Mother Nature and the muscle of *our* tree. It bowed and bent, and ducked and dived like Ali, but it never snapped or uprooted. In my mind, the strongest trees represent family: the parents are the trunk – providing stability – and the branches are the children, sprouting new life in different directions. But everyone belongs to the same tree from the same seed: forever solid, whatever weathers it may face.

I once shared this analogy with Michael and he turned it into a plaque at Neverland. It had been inspired, no doubt, by Joseph telling us as children that our family's roots were as deep and entwined as a tree's. A solid family was important to our parents, both of whom came from broken homes. The tug-of-war between his own parents was something Joseph didn't wish to repeat. Mother's parents had divorced after moving from Alabama to Indiana: she went to live with her father – Papa Prince – and her sister Hattie with her mother, Mama Martha. Mother and Joseph had vowed to build a family and stick together, preaching to us that nothing and no one should ever come between us.

Before the Jackson 5 ever went public, Joseph took us outside the house one Fall to give us a final lesson to carry through life. He led us to *our* tree. There were broken twigs strewn all around it and he bent down to collect six, of more or less equal length. He asked us to gather round and pay attention.

He reminded us about togetherness and always looking out for one another. Then he separated one twig from the rest and snapped it in half. 'They can break one of you when you are separated …' he said, leaving five thick twigs in his hand. He bunched them tight, side by side, and tried breaking them between his hands and over his knee. Try as he might, with a mill worker's grip, he couldn't. '… but when you stick together, you are unbreakable,' he added.

CHAPTER FOUR

Just Kids With a Dream

IN TODAY'S LIGHT, I THINK IT apt that our first true public performance as the Jackson 5 was on 29 August 1965: Michael's seventh birthday. No one noticed it at the time. Birthdays were like Christmas: non-events that were not marked in the house of Jehovah. But at least Michael's seventh birthday was different in that it wasn't another ordinary, unremarkable day.

Evelyn Lahaie, the lady who first suggested our group name, invited us to take part in a child's fashion event she had organised at the Big Top shopping centre on Broadway and 53rd. She was the commentator on a 'Tiny Tots Jamboree' and we were billed as 'The Jackson Five Musical Group: Another Spectacular Little Folks Band'. All I remember is seeing a decent-sized crowd of young girls and Joseph telling us after the show to 'get down there and start selling your photos.'

In our eyes, the jamboree was just a warm-up for the proper stage at Jackie and Rebbie's school, Theodore Roosevelt High, a few months later in 1966. Mother had said at the mall that we'd get to perform at 'nicer places'. The school held an annual talent contest, featuring a variety of acts from around the city – Gary's equivalent to *The Ed Sullivan Show*. We were the youngest act by far and couldn't wait to get out there.

Backstage, Michael tapped the bongos he still played. Jackie rattled his Maracas and two band members joined us: local boys Earl Gault, our first drummer, and Raynard Jones, who played bass on a couple of occasions. The school hall was packed. It was a paying crowd, too – 25 cents a ticket. We also knew it would include some familiar faces, such as those who had been mushed-up against the living-room window, waiting to laugh at us.

When Tito went for our guitars – left leaning against a wall in the wings – he discovered someone had attempted sabotage by messing with the tuning pegs. Joseph's advice – 'Always check your tuning before going on' – came good in plenty of time. 'Someone doesn't want you to win,' he said, 'so go out there and show 'em!'

He stood with us in the wings, looking nowhere near as confident as we felt. He was always tense before a show, whether it was the talent-show days or record-label years. For the duration of a set, he had no input and no control. But we couldn't have been more ready. When we walked on, met by polite applause, we just switched to the auto-pilot of rehearsals. 'My Girl' by the Temptations was our opener. As everyone's quiet curiosity sat in that gap between applause ending and music starting, I looked across to Tito and behind him, in the shadows, to Joseph. Still pensive. Raynard, on bass, gave the song's intro that opening bounce … and in came Tito on guitar with the melody lick … and Jackie with his Maracas … and Michael poised with his bongos … and then I started to sing.

Our momentum built as I led the vocals into another Temptations number: the more up-tempo 'Get Ready'. And Jackie, Marlon and Michael killed it front of stage, revving them up for Michael's lead vocal finale – James Brown's 'I Got You (I Feel Good)'. By his first verse, the crowd was on its feet. I looked to my right, for Joseph's approval. Still pensive, arms by his sides. Only his lips were moving as he mouthed the lyrics, fixated on Michael. 'Eeeeeooowwww!' Michael screamed. 'I FEEEEL good …' With his high-pitched, hyena-like screech, the crowd's jaws opened as one and they screamed. Then, during our closer, 'I Got The Feeling', he made them feel it. He jumped out front of stage and started to dance; a choreographed whirling dervish. Aged seven.

We were not supposed to be this good, but Michael tore up the place. It didn't matter that this was only our local school. When you're kids, a screaming crowd is a screaming crowd.

Backstage, post-show, we jumped around, reliving it all. I guess it was like hitting a home-run or scoring a great goal. Joseph was … content. 'Overall, you did good,' he told us, 'but we've got some work to do.'

Next thing I remember is the MC announcing us as winners. We bounded on stage. More screaming. Funnily enough, one of the acts we beat was Deniece Williams. A few years later, she released her chart topper 'Let's Hear It For The Boy'. We didn't need Joseph's approval that night: we were winners first time out and that was good by anyone's standards.

We went home and celebrated with ice-cream all round. Joseph pointed to a proud corner of the living room – home to a small collection of baseball trophies, speaking to our other obsession in life. Those trophies stood as unintended props to support the one point he always made: being rewarded is about becoming the best.

FROM OUR BEDROOM WINDOW, WE HAD an open view of the baseball field where we played, next to Theodore Roosevelt High. Had you asked us back then to choose between the musical dream or the sporting dream, I think we'd have opted for baseball. Especially Jackie, the jock of the family. Whenever he was in trouble with Joseph and wanted to run, we always knew where to find him: the dug-out across the way, in front of the bleachers, tossing a ball between hand and glove.

We'd have opted for the baseball dream for the simple reason that it seemed more realistic and three of us were already decent juniors. The miniature gold players swinging a bat on the podium of our trophies were testament to the glory and championships won with the Katz Kittens – the team we played for in Gary's Little League baseball. We grew up watching the Chicago Cubs, aspiring to follow its stars: Ernie Banks, their first black player, and Ron Santo.

Jackie was so good he had people scouting him and he felt sure a contract was imminent. He was a great pitcher and batsman, hitting home run after home run. Baseball was where his heart was, more than any of us. At games, Michael was like our mini-mascot, sitting with Marlon and Joseph in the bleachers, wearing his mini green-and-white jersey, which came down to the knees of his jeans, chewing his red shoestring candy and cheering whenever one of us got the ball. One weekday evening, there was a 'big game' – a play-off or something – with some local rival. I was playing outfield, Tito was on second and Jackie was pitcher. We had started to earn a bit of a reputation as 'The Jackson Boys' and Jackie's pitching was key to that hard-earned kudos.

During the warm-up, the coach hit balls into the air as catch practice and he hit one fly-ball that bounced off the clouds before it came back down. We were always taught to call it, so I ran and kept my eye on the ball, yelling, 'MINE! I got it …' Wesley, our catcher who had torn off his mask, was running for the same ball, but he didn't call it and didn't hear me. He just kept his eye on the falling ball. Then BOOM! We collided. For the first time, I saw stars without feeling Joseph's belt on my behind. Wesley's forehead hit me across the right eye and split me wide open. He was out cold and blood was everywhere. I remember seeing concerned faces peering down but then they parted as Joseph's face came into full focus. His pained expression didn't leave me all the way to the hospital or even as a doctor sewed me up with 14 butterfly stitches. I was bruised, swollen and messed up – my 'image' as an entertainer had been put at risk. As Mother thanked God that my sight was not impaired, Joseph cursed himself for allowing such an injury to take place. Then he made the swiftest decision. 'No more baseball for you, Jermaine,' he announced. 'None of you. No more baseball! It's too dangerous.'

I don't remember much else about that night except Jackie's grief for the dream that had ended all because one boy didn't call the ball. 'One day you'll thank me,' Joseph told him unsympathetically. 'You're too young to understand.'

AS ROOSEVELT HIGH'S TALENT CONTEST CHAMPIONS, we entered another competition that pitched us against the winning finalists from other schools in the area. We won that, too, and the *Gary Post-Tribune*'s flashbulb captured our triumph and trophy for posterity in black-and-white. I remember that grainy photo because of the giant bandage still plastered over my right eyebrow. The importance of first place – *that* prestige and *that* trophy – became obvious on the one occasion we *didn't* win. It was at Horace Mann High and the reason it sticks in my mind is because of the prize we received for coming second: a brand new colour television.

The problem was that Joseph didn't take losing very well, so none of us knew how to behave in defeat. We knew there was nothing to gloat about, but there didn't seem any great reason to be disappointed either. It was Marlon who broke the ice as we packed our stuff and headed out. 'Least we won a colour TV!' he said, speaking for everyone as we sensed the end of watching programmes through the coloured hues of a plastic sheet.

But Joseph didn't see any consolation in the prize. 'There is only one winner, and winning is about being number one, not number two!' he said, sharing his stare equally among us. We didn't collect our colour TV that day: Joseph said we didn't deserve it. There is no reward for second place.

I WISH I HAD ARCHIVED THOSE precious times and kept a diary or maintained a scrapbook, especially now that Michael has gone. A deep loss makes you grasp at nostalgia, wanting to recall every last detail of every experience you once took for granted. Things happened and moved so fast that performances and years have merged into one. In my mind, those early years of the Jackson 5 are a bit like a high-speed rail journey: the places *en route* whizzed by, and it's only the departure, the destination, and certain memorable stations that remain vivid. Between 1966 and 1968, most weekends were spent on the road building our reputation. We played before a mix of audiences: the friendly, the enthusiastic, the drunken and the indifferent. Usually, just the sight of five kids walking on stage got people's attention and the 'cute' factor was on our side, especially with Michael and Marlon up front. It was the best feeling when our performances animated a reserved crowd.

Mr Lucky's, the main tavern in Gary, was where we spent many week-nights and where we earned our first performance fee: $11, split between us. Michael spent his on candy, which he shared with other kids in the neighbourhood. 'He earns his first wage and spends it on candy to give to other kids?' said Joseph, bemused. But when it came to 'share and share alike', Michael wore the shiniest halo; we were always encouraged by Mother to think of others and do the good deed.

Meanwhile, our parents backed our progress by investing in a 'wardrobe'. Our customary uniform was either a white shirt, black bell-bottomed pants and red cummerbund, or a forest-green shiny suit with crisp white shirt. Mother had made all the alterations to our suits on her sewing-machine and a lady named Mrs Roach sewed 'J5' into the jacket breast pockets. I remember that detail because she sewed them on crooked and something felt imperfect but, for once, uncorrectable.

If we weren't performing at Mr Lucky's, we were at the supper club Guys and Gals, or the High Chaparral on the south side of Chicago. Often, we didn't go on stage until 11.30pm on school nights and didn't arrive home until 2am with school the next day: five brothers always asleep as we pulled into the driveway of 2300 Jackson Street.

YOU ARE NOT ALONE

One show night, we arrived outside some hotel in Gary and soon understood our city's reputation as a rough place, infamous for crime. Folklore had it that if you dug deep enough you'd find the roots of the OGs – the original gangsters – before gang culture spread east to New York. I don't know about that. All I know is that we discovered being 'local' offered no immunity from violence. It was dusk and we were carrying our equipment inside via the back entrance when Joseph was stopped by five thuggish 20-something men. 'Do you want some help with that?' asked one, grabbing a mic stand.

Joseph thought he was being robbed so he refused to let go of the stand and pushed away the man. The next two or three minutes happened quickly as all of them turned on him and he hit the ground under a windmill of punches. Michael and Marlon screamed, 'JOSEPH! JOSEPH! No! No! *No!*' The gang started using our drumsticks and mic stands as weapons. Joseph curled into a ball, covered his face with his forearms and took the beating.

Meanwhile, Michael had sprinted to the nearest phone booth at the bottom of the street and called the police. 'I couldn't reach, so I had to jump up to drop the coin into the slot!' he said afterwards. By the time he ran back, the gang had fled and Joseph was being helped to his feet by hotel management. He got hurt real bad: his face was mashed up and had already started to swell. Someone ran inside to grab some ice and he used it to wrap the hand he had fractured. He had also suffered a broken jaw. Sitting on the bumper at the back of the van, he steadied himself. Then, through one-and-a-half eyes, he looked at us: 'I'm okay.' He told Michael and Marlon to wipe their tears. 'You can't perform in that state,' he said.

'You want us to go on?' asked Jackie, incredulous.

'People are here to see you – people are *expecting* to see you,' he said, gingerly getting to his feet. 'I'll go to the doctor in the morning.' That night, we had to pull ourselves together and focus on our performance. Joseph was ever-present, nursing his hand, with Band Aids on his face. He had taught us another hard, if unintentional lesson: whatever happens, the show must go on.

I DON'T REMEMBER DOING HOMEWORK ON school nights. We ate dinner and got ready to perform. Homework assignments were something we crammed in at weekends or scribbled in bed in the mornings. That was when our childhood started to become eclipsed by adult duties. There was always a new show to prepare for, a new routine to rehearse, or a new town to conquer.

Aged nine, Michael had to grow up fast. As we all did. We now had a profession where other kids had nothing to do but play all the time. But had it been any other way, we might never have broken through as the Jackson 5, and the world would never have known Michael's music. Things were as they were meant to be. We found real joy on stage: we looked forward to it in the same way that other kids looked forward to whatever pastime brought them enjoyment.

With Mr Lucky's and Guys and Gals offering us regular work, Joseph quit his canned-food-factory job and reduced his hours at The Mill to part-time day shifts. Our fees can't have been all that good, but he maintained his gamble on the great future he banked on. Mother fretted, obviously, but Joseph reassured her that the momentum was building. She nodded silently in agreement and then, knowing Mother, she probably worried herself to sleep and said countless prayers to Jehovah.

What she didn't immediately know was that some of the late-night acts that followed us included strippers. That was the variety of bar acts back then and we often came offstage to find half-naked ladies in fishnets and suspenders waiting in the wings. If Christmas and birthdays were a sin in the eyes of Jehovah, then sharing a venue with erotic strippers was tantamount to hanging with the Devil, so you can't blame Joseph for not detailing our exact itinerary to Mother. But the game was up one night when a stray lacy accessory found its way into one of our bags. Mother marched out of our bedroom holding an elaborate nipple tassel between her fingers. 'WHERE did THIS come from?' For once in his life, Joseph was speechless. 'You have our children up all night when they have school in the morning and you have them peeking at NAKED women? WHAT kind of people do you have our sons mixing with? This is QUITE the life you are showing them, Joseph!'

We brothers viewed such incidents differently. In my mind, a woman's body is hypnotic and beautiful, but Michael saw these women as degrading themselves to tease men, and men treating them like sex objects. Yes, he gawped and giggled like the rest of us, but his lasting impression formed differently. He always remembered one regular stripper – her name was Rosie – tossing her panties into the crowd and jiggling her bits as men tried to touch her. Michael always hid his eyes. 'Awww, man! That's awful. Why she do that?'

Mother has said that she didn't realise there were strippers until she read Michael's autobiography. I think that's the 'official' line for the sake of the Kingdom Hall. Not that her objections had anything to do with being a Jehovah's Witness. As she says, what mother of any faith would want her young sons mixing in such an environment so late at night? I think that was where the crucial difference lay between Mother and Joseph. She viewed us as her sons and often worried about the impact of all the performing and travelling, and to Joseph, perhaps, we were performers first and sons second; he regarded anything and everything as a necessary step in the right direction.

PERFORMING MIDWEEK WASN'T ENOUGH FOR JOSEPH. Every weekend, he booked us anywhere he could find an opening, helped by two Chicago DJs, Pervis Spann and E. Rodney Jones. They acted as our club promoters and were also bookers for B.B. King and Curtis Mayfield, but their main job was on-air at Chicago-based WVON Radio, the most listened-to station in Gary. With Purvis working the graveyard shift and E. Rodney on days, they pushed soul music heavily, so our promotion was in good hands: black radio was the route-one approach to getting noticed back then. If you were 'in' with WVON, you were on the local recording industry's radar.

Pervis, who always wore a grey-and-black fedora-type hat, had an Otis Redding look about him and he hyped us up by telling people, 'Just wait till you see these kids perform!' Joseph cursed about Pervis's cheques occasionally bouncing, but what Pervis lacked in financial reliability, he compensated for by spreading the word. He and E. Rodney Jones waved our flag like no one else.

As a result, we five piled ourselves – and our instruments – into Joseph's VW camper van while Mother and Rebbie stayed at home with La Toya, Randy and baby Janet. For a while we saw more of school and the insides of clubs and theatres than we did of the four walls of our own home. Our VW 'tour bus' had two seats up front, with the middle seats removed to make room for the amps, guitars, drum-kit and other equipment. There was a bench seat at the rear but we would sit and sleep wherever we could prop our bodies, using the drum as a head rest. We couldn't have been more tightly packed, but the journeys were full of jokes, laughter and song. As Joseph drove, we brothers went over the whole show in our heads, unprompted.

'On this part, don't forget we turn on this word ...' Jackie would say.

Or Tito: 'At the beginning of the bridge, remember, throw your hands in the air.'

Or Michael: 'Jackie, you'll go one end of the stage, I'll be in the middle. Marlon, you go the other side ...'

This was how we prepared *en route*: verbally walking through every routine. It didn't matter that we were aged between seven and 17: there was no superiority in rank.

We each chipped in as equals and Michael, the youngest, was probably the most vociferous and creative. It wasn't just the way he walked the walk that made him seem older than his years, it was the way he talked the talk, too. Due to Joseph's conditioning, our focus was intense, but even as a boy Michael had something extra. He added dynamics that gave our choreography that extra punch and then, mid-performance, threw in his own freestyle section that took things to another level before falling seamlessly back into line.

I knew when he was about to bring it because just as the music started, he'd turn to me and wink.

Michael also emerged as a prankster. If one of us fell asleep with our mouth open, he tore off a piece of paper, wrote something silly like 'My breath smells', dabbed it with a wet finger and affixed it to the sleeper's bottom lip. He found this stunt endlessly hilarious. If it wasn't notes on lips, it was itching powder down the pants or a whoopie cushion placed on a seat. Michael was carving out his role as the principal jester of the pack.

In the summer of 1966, we drove the 1,500 miles to Arizona – stopping only for gas – to perform a set at the Old Arcadia Hall in Winslow, near Phoenix, because Papa Samuel lived nearby and wanted to show us off to his home crowd. It meant driving through Friday night and into Saturday, performing that night, then heading back to arrive home beyond midnight on Sunday for school the next day. Michael didn't laugh much on that torturously long journey. What I vividly remember is sitting upfront with Joseph and at one point, he pulled over, put his hands over his face and started vigorously rubbing his cheeks. His eyes were watering. He caught me staring. 'Just tired,' he said. He took five minutes and we hit the road again.

By this time, we had a newly installed drummer named Johnny Jackson and despite what the marketing hype would later claim, he was no cousin and no distant relation. His surname was just a happy coincidence that future publicists would exploit. We found him because he attended Theodore Roosevelt High with Jackie and a local music teacher recommended him. Aged about 14, he was a bubbly, animated little guy with a cheeky smile. He was the best young drummer around for miles, as confident with his skill as Michael was with his dance. Johnny had a great back-beat and a strong-foot, and his timing was exquisite. He used to hit the drums so hard that we could feel the rhythm coming through our feet from the stage. Johnny Jackson helped make our sound.

Another addition to the 'family' was the nicest man – Jack Richardson, a friend of Joseph's. He arrived as designated driver because the endless miles became too much for our father. Jack would stick with us for years and become an integral part of the team. His hours behind the wheel without complaint told us how much he also believed in us. Wherever we were booked – Kansas City, Missouri, Ohio – Jack jumped up with enthusiasm.

Our marathon road trips were important, said Joseph, because 'You need to appeal to white audiences as well as black audiences.' He was determined to build for us an interracial fan base at a time when the civil rights movement was at its height. As kids, the racial nuances went over our heads. It didn't matter to us if the faces in the crowd were black or white and it didn't affect how we performed. The audience reaction was always the same – they loved us.

ALL BUSINESS TALK WENT OVER OUR heads, too: we just jumped into the van, showed up and performed. That was all we were interested in. As we hung around post-show in different venues and hotels, Joseph was busy hustling on our behalf, shaking hands and making connections. All we wanted was to go home but then he'd bring over some new 'contact' and we'd have to stop kicking our heels, reapply our show faces and smile. During our struggle for recognition, Joseph forever seemed to battle other people's anxiety that a bunch of 'minors' could cut it. Typically, he was undeterred. He said that if Stevie Wonder could make it, then so could his kids.

And then came hope, in the face of a guitarist named Phil Upchurch, whom we met after some show in Chicago. Joseph told us enthusiastically how this artist had already worked with the likes of Woody Herman, Curtis Mayfield and Dee Clark. In 1961, he had released a single, 'You Can't Sit Down', that sold more than one million copies. 'Now, he's going to work with you on a demo tape,' announced Joseph. This was a big deal because Phil was an influential player on the scene in Detroit and we jumped around as if Jackie had just hit a forbidden home run.

Michael broke free from our elated huddle and hugged Phil around his legs. 'Can I please have your autograph?' Phil, no more than a fresh-faced 25-year-old, took out a scrap of paper from his jacket and scrawled a quick signature. Michael clutched it like a prize all the way home. What I love about this story is its postscript: decades later, Phil wrote to Michael and asked for *his* autograph. But he got more than that – he was invited to play guitar on 'Working Day & Night' from Michael's first solo album, *Off the Wall*.

Back in Gary, 1967, Mother was more concerned about who was paying for the studio and copies of the tapes. 'I am,' said Joseph. 'The momentum is just starting,' he told her again.

I DON'T REMEMBER THE TRUE ORDER of how everything happened next, but the facts are these: Phil Upchurch shared the same manager as R&B artist Jan Bradley. In 1963, she released her hit 'Mama Didn't Lie'. The man behind that song's core arrangement was saxophonist and songwriter Eddie Silvers, formerly of Fats Domino and musical director at a fledgling label, One-derful Records. Within the six degrees of separation, Eddie wrote the song for our demo tape, 'Big Boy'.

I suspect that Pervis Spann also played a role in this set-up but my memory betrays me. I have no idea why the One-derful label wasn't interested in us, but the next thing we knew was that Steeltown Records were at the door in the shape of songwriter and founding partner Gordon Keith. When he turned up, Joseph wasn't overly excited because he was a fellow steel-worker who had established this mini label with a businessman named Ben Brown the previous year. It hardly represented the great dream. But Keith was keen to sign us. Or, as Mother tells it, 'He wanted you locked into a long-term thing, but Joseph said, "No, we've got lots of interest, I'm not doing it." He was that desperate to sign you that they agreed to the shortest contract – six months.'

Joseph never viewed Steeltown as capable players in the big game, but he saw the value of a recording contract: it would lead to local-radio air time. 'Big Boy' was our first single released in

1967. According to Keith, it sold an estimated 50,000 copies throughout the Midwest and New York. We even made the Best Top 20 Singles in *Jet* magazine. But the greatest moment was when WVON Radio played it for the first time. We huddled around the radio, hardly believing our voices were coming out of that box. It was like the times when you're handed a group photo and the first thing you do is find yourself and see how you look. It was the same with the radio – we listened for our own voices within the harmonies and background oohs. We had worked damn hard in that living room and suddenly we were being broadcast to most of Gary and Chicago: we were ecstatic.

WITH OUR HEARTS SET ON PERFORMANCE, our academic education seemed almost irrelevant. It was hard to knuckle down when we knew our foundation in life was going to be the stage – and we knew Joseph knew it, too.

School actually made me feel sad because it divided us. It sent us our separate ways into different classrooms or, in Jackie and Tito's case, different schools. I felt anxious without the brothers around me. I say 'the brothers' because we weren't just siblings, we were a team. I found myself clock-watching, looking forward to the break when Marlon, Michael and I could get together again. Teachers mistook my listlessness for good behaviour so I became a teacher's pet by default. I was one of those lucky students who didn't have to try too hard to get B grades. As a result, I was trusted to go on errands – take this or carry that.

I used these 'office-runs' as an excuse to take a detour via Michael's class, just to make sure he was okay. I'd stand in the corridor – with a clear view into his class through the open door, in a position where the teacher couldn't spot me – and he was always concentrating intensely, head down writing or eyes fixed on the chalkboard. The kid sitting next to him would see me first and nudge him. His eyes darted between me and the teacher – he never liked getting into trouble. When her back was turned, he flashed a quick wave.

Mother found it curious that I checked up on him but, in my mind, I was just the older brother checking up on the younger brother. Doing my duty.

Michael applied himself better than I did at school. His thirst for knowledge was far greater than any of the rest of us. He was *that* curious kid who asked, 'Why? Why? Why?' and he listened to and logged every detail. I'm sure his head had an in-built recording chip for data, facts, figures, lyrics and dance moves.

I always walked Michael to school; he always ran home. The walk home from school mirrored the dynamics of our childhood, showing who was tightest with whom. Michael and Marlon ran around like Batman and Robin. In the street or on the athletics track, Michael always challenged Marlon to races – and always out-sprinted him. Marlon *hated* being beaten … and then he'd accuse Michael of cheating and they'd start fighting, and Jackie had to break them up. It always puzzled Michael why things had to turn nasty. 'I won fair and square!' he'd say, sulking.

Their combined energy was relentless, running around the house, inside and out, screaming, laughing, shouting. That double-act often drove Mother to distraction as she tried to prepare dinner. She'd spin around, grab them in mid-run by both arms and drill her middle knuckle into their temples.

'Ow!'

'You boys need to calm down!' she'd say.

And they did. For about 20 minutes. Then, they would be at the bedroom window playing 'Army' – two broomsticks poking out the window, 'shooting' at passers-by.

Tito and I were each other's shadows, too, and Mother dressed us alike, leaving our clothes as the hand-me-down wardrobe for our younger brothers. We used to boss Michael and Marlon, telling them to go get stuff for us, do this and do that, but we tended to give Jackie his space because he was older and crankier, and Randy was the baby brother still curious about everyone and anything.

Out of all of us, people outside the family found Michael hard to figure out because he only came alive in two certain places: in the privacy of our own home, and onstage. He had all this energy and focus when it came to the Jackson 5; no other child could have looked so sure and commanding as he. To watch him on stage was to witness a supreme, precocious confidence but in the school play-ground he seemed withdrawn until spoken to.

One of Michael's closest buddies was a boy named Bernard Gross. He was close to both of us, really, but Michael liked him a lot. He thought 'he was like a little teddy bear' – all chubby-faced and round, someone who blushed when he laughed. He was the same age as me, but the same height as Michael, and I think Michael liked the fact that an older kid wanted to be *his* friend. Bernard was the nicest kid. We all felt for him because he was raised by a single mum and we struggled to understand how that could ever feel: the loneliness of being an only child. I think that's why we embraced him as a rare friend; the one outsider given honorary membership to the Jackson brothers' club.

Michael hated it when Bernard cried. He *hated* seeing him get upset over anything and if he did, Michael cried with him. My brother developed empathy and sensitivity at an early age. But Bernard felt for us, too. Once, Joseph told me to go out into the snow to buy some Kool-Aid from the store and I refused. He banged me across the head with a wooden spoon several times. I cried all the way there and all the way back, and Bernard walked with me to make me feel better. 'Joseph scares me,' he said.

'Could be worse.' I sniffled.

Could be worse. Might not have a father at all, I thought.

ONE OF THE BIGGEST EDUCATIONAL FORCES musically in Michael's life was the emergence of Sly and the Family Stone. We were inspired to listen to them by Ronny Rancifer, our newly recruited keyboardist from Hammond, East Chicago, an extra-tall body to squeeze into the back of the VW camper van. His lively spirit added to the jovial atmosphere on the road, and he, Michael and I would dream about one day writing songs together. Which was why he made us take a look at the brothers Sly and Freddie

Stone, keyboardist sister Rose and the rest of the seven-strong group that blew up in 1966/7 as their posters found their place into our bedroom alongside those featuring James Brown and the Temptations. With tight pants, loud shirts, psychedelic patterns and big Afros, this new group represented a visual explosion and we loved everything about their songs, the lyrics inspired by themes of love, harmony, peace and understanding, as epitomised by their 1968 hit 'Everyday People'. They brought to the world music that was ahead of its time: R&B fused with Rock fused with Motown.

Michael thought Sly was the ultimate performer and described him as 'a musical genius.' 'Their sound is different, and each one of them is different,' he said. 'They're together, but also strong independently. I like that!'

Like the rest of us, Michael had started to sense that we could match Joseph's belief. We released one more single on the Steeltown label, 'We Don't Have To Be 21 To Fall In Love', but we wanted more than regional success.

IN THE SUMMER, WE ALWAYS SLEPT with our bedroom window open to feel the cooling night breeze, but this worried Joseph because we lived in a high-crime area. What he didn't know until we were older was that the chief reason we left it open was for daytime access when we wanted to skip school. Michael was far too well-behaved to take part in such a thing, but when I didn't feel like class, I'd walk out the front door, peel away from the crowd, hide and return home via the window. I hid in the closet – the den-like hideout space we used – and sat there, or slept, with my stash of candy or salami sandwiches. Tito and I used this space as our hideout for years. Come home time, I'd jump outside and return through the front door.

Eventually Joseph grew tired of yelling about the open window. One night, he waited until we were all asleep, went outside and crept in through the window, wearing an ugly, scary mask. As this large silhouette clambered into our bedroom legs first, five boys woke and screamed the house down. Michael and Marlon apparently just held on to one another, scared witless. Joseph turned on the lights and removed his mask: 'I could have been someone else. Now, keep the window closed!'

There were a few nightmares in that bedroom afterwards, mainly in the middle bunk, but to suggest – as some have – that Michael was deeply traumatised and scarred by this event is laughable. Joseph *always* used to wear masks and get his thrills from jumping out of the shadows, creeping up behind us or placing a fake spider or rubber snake in the bed, especially at Hallowe'en. Ninety-nine per cent of the time, Michael found it hilarious, revelling in the scary thrill. If anyone was harmed by the new policy to close the window, it was me: it forced an improvement in my school attendance record.

JOSEPH ENTERED US IN A TALENT contest at the Regal Theatre, Chicago, and we won hands down. We kept returning and kept winning, taking the honours for three consecutive Sundays. In those days, the reward for such a hat-trick was to be invited back for a *paid* evening performance and that was how we found ourselves sharing a bill with Gladys Knight & the Pips, newly signed by Motown Records.

At rehearsals, we were midway through our routine when I looked to the wings to find the usual sight of Joseph accompanied by the unusual sight of Gladys Knight. As she tells it, she 'heard some performance, jumped up and said, "Who is that?"' When we came offstage, Joseph told us that she wanted to meet us in her dressing room. It was a big deal because she and the Pips were all the rage, having broken into the charts the previous year with their No. 2 hit 'I Heard It Through The Grapevine'.

We shuffled into her room, led by Joseph. I don't know what she must have thought when five shy brothers walked in, considering the performance that had grabbed her attention. Michael was so small that when he sat down on the sofa, his legs dangled off the end.

'Your father tells me that you boys have big futures ahead of you,' she said.

We nodded.

Gladys looked at Michael. 'You enjoy singing?'

'Yeah,' said Michael.

She glanced at the other four of us. We all nodded. 'You boys should be at Motown!'

That was the night Joseph asked Gladys if she could get someone from Motown to watch one of our performances. She promised she'd make that call, and she couldn't have been more sincere.

Back home, Joseph told Mother that it was only a matter of time before the phone rang. But it never did.

As it turned out, Gladys was as good as her word because we later learned she had called Taylor Cox, an executive at Motown, but there was no interest higher up the ladder. Berry Gordy, the founder of the label, wasn't looking for a kid group. He'd been there, done that with Stevie Wonder, and he didn't want the headache of hiring tutors or the Board of Education's restrictions on working hours.

Meanwhile, Joseph kept us on the road and we kept plugging away at the Regal and places like the Uptown Theater, Philadelphia, and the Howard Theater, Washington DC. Our road led towards 'The Chitlin' Circuit' – the collective name given to a host of venues in the south and east of the country, showcasing predominantly new African-American acts. These were our 'roughing-it years', when the professional stage educated us in the dos and don'ts of live performance. And all the time, we just kept performing and pushing our Steeltown 45s.

CHAPTER FIVE

Cry Freedom

'IF THEY LIKE YOU HERE, THEY'LL like you anywhere,' Joseph said, in the van *en route* to New York City. Destination: the world-famous Apollo Theater in Harlem – a place 'where stars are made'.

All the way from Indiana, he talked up a storm about what this venue meant and the singers who had triumphed here: Ella Fitzgerald, Lena Horne, tap-dancer Bill 'Bo Jangles' Robinson … and James Brown. In an era when black faces on television were still relatively rare, the Apollo was *the* platform for African-American acts. 'But if you get it wrong, make a mistake, this audience will turn on you. Tonight, you have to be on your game,' he continued.

We honestly weren't intimidated: we knew that winning over the crowd meant we'd be walking through a door towards bigger things, so what greater motivation could there be for young boys with a dream? Sometimes there were benefits to being lambs in the entertainment industry – our innocence made us blind to the enormity of certain occasions. We pulled up beneath the Apollo sign, which hung vertically, lit sunset orange at night.

When we first went in, the walls were lined with the photographs of legends. We walked the corridors and then noticed the shabby carpet. Joseph asked us to imagine the feet that had worn it away; to imagine the kind of shoes we were walking in. We had our own dressing room with a mirror surrounded by light-bulbs and a chrome clothes rack on wheels. And the microphones popped up electronically from beneath the stage, all space age.

Inside our dressing room, Michael stepped up on a seat with Jackie and pushed up the window to look out. 'There's a basketball court!' shouted Jackie. That brought a new burst of excitement. We wanted to get outside and shoot some baskets, but then Joseph walked in. Everyone jumped into line and pretended to be focused again. Time to get serious. I don't know if Joseph ever realised how nonchalant we were on the inside about performing, but he knew Harlem wasn't Chicago. The Apollo crowd was well versed in entertainment: it knew its music. If things went badly, disgruntled murmurs grew into boos, followed by missiles of tin cans, fruit and popcorn. When things went well, they were up on their feet, singing, clapping and dancing. No one walked off the Apollo stage and asked, 'How did I do?'

Before going on, we sensed the buzz of a full house. Michael and Marlon stood in front of Tito, Jackie, Johnny and me in the shadows and whoever was on before us wasn't getting the greatest reaction. The boos were loud and unforgiving. Then a can landed onstage, followed by an apple core. Marlon, startled, turned to us. 'They're throwin' stuff!'

Joseph looked at us as if to say, 'I'm telling you ...'

Between the curtains, backstage and hidden from public view, there was a section of tree trunk. It was the Apollo's 'Tree of Hope' chopped from a felled tree that had once stood in the Boulevard of Dreams, otherwise known as Seventh Avenue, between the old Lafayette Theater and Connie's Inn. In an ancient superstition, black performers touched that tree, or basked beneath its branches, for good luck. It had come to symbolise hope for African-American acts in the same way that the tree outside our home symbolised unity. Michael and Marlon duly stroked the 'Tree of Hope', but I don't think Lady Luck had anything to do with the performance we gave that night.

We rocked the Apollo and the crowd was soon on its feet. I don't think we brought a finer performance to any venue in our pre-Motown days and we ended up winning the Superdog Amateur Finals Night. We must have impressed management because we were invited back ... this time as paid performers. That May of 1968, we were on the same bill for an Apollo night with Etta James, the Coasters and the Vibrations. We knew we'd done good at the highest level. What we didn't know was that a television producer had been sitting in the audience, taking notes and developing a keen interest.

A SHORT JEWISH LAWYER WHO ALWAYS wore suits arrived on the scene. Apparently Richard Aarons had knocked on Joseph's hotel-room door in New York and sold his services. We were introduced to the debonair and playful Richard as the man 'who is helping us get to where you need to be.' As the son of the chairman of a musicians' union in New York, Richard had useful connections.

Straightaway, Richard put together a professional pitch-package that contained our Steeltown hits, newspaper cuttings of rave reviews, promotional material and a letter explaining why the Jackson 5 should be given a chance. It was dispatched to labels such as Atlantic, CBS, Warner and Capitol. In addition, Joseph personally mailed a package to Motown Records in Detroit, addressed to Mr Berry Gordy, hoping to follow up on Gladys Knight's recommendation. Apparently he used to tell Mother: 'I'm going to take the boys to Motown if it's the last thing I do!'

Many weeks later, and with us still technically attached to Steeltown Records, Joseph brought in an envelope, opened it and our demo tape slid out on to the table ... Returned and rejected by Motown.

THE BEST THING ABOUT JOURNEYING THE Chitlin' Circuit was the feeling that we were always tiptoeing in the shadows of the greats. We had already found ourselves in the dressing room of Gladys Knight and on the same stage as the Delfonics, the Coasters, the Four Tops and the Impressions but two thrilling 'meets' were golden and both at the Regal in Chicago.

On the first occasion, we were either waiting for Smokey Robinson to head to rehearsal or go onstage to perform. I can't remember which. But Joseph reassured us that if we hung around and behaved ourselves, we'd get to meet the greatest songwriter of all time. That was one of the few times we'd ever feel butterflies in the stomach: getting ready to meet one of our heroes was more nerve-racking than performing.

When Smokey walked up to us and stopped to talk, we couldn't believe he was actually taking time out for us. But there he stood, in a black turtleneck and pants, smiling broadly and shaking our hands, asking who we were and what we did. Michael was always intrigued by another artist's way of doing things. He peppered Smokey with questions. How did you write all those songs? When do the songs come to you? I don't remember the answers but I'll guarantee that Michael did. Smokey gave us a good five minutes – and when he walked away, you know what we talked about? His hands. 'Did you feel how *soft* his hands were?' whispered Michael.

'No wonder,' I said. 'He ain't done nothing but write songs.'

'They were softer than Mother's!' Michael added.

When we burst through the door in Gary, it was the first thing we told Mother, too. 'MOTHER! We met Smokey Robinson – and you know how soft his hands were?'

That's what people forget. We were fans long before we became anything else.

The day we met Jackie Wilson we advanced one stage further with our VIP access: we were invited into his hallowed dressing room. It was 'hallowed' because, to us, he was the black Elvis before the white Elvis had come along, one of those once-in-every-generation entertainers. Jackie and his revue were regular headliners at the Regal so our sole focus that day was to meet him. After Joseph had had a word with someone, we got the 'Okay, five minutes' privilege that our boyhood cuteness often bought. I'll say this about our father: he knew how to open doors.

This big-name door opened and we entered single file from the darkness of the corridor into the brightness cast by the light-bulbs arcing around the dressing-table mirror, where Jackie was seated with his back to us. He had a towel wrapped into a thick collar to protect his white shirt from the foundation and eye-liner he was self-applying.

It was Michael who spoke up first, politely wondering if he could ask him some questions.

'Sure, go ahead, kid,' said Jackie, speaking to our reflections in his mirror.

He then bombarded him with questions. How does it feel when you go on stage? How much do you rehearse? How young were you when you started? My brother was relentless in his quest for knowledge.

But it was Joseph who handed us the biggest piece of information to take away that night: he told us that some of Jackie Wilson's songs had been written by none other than Mr Gordy, the founder of Motown. ('Lonely Teardrops' had been Mr Gordy's first No. 1.)

In meeting both Smokey Robinson and Jackie Wilson, we all knew theirs was the level where we needed to be. Maybe that was what Joseph had been doing all along: introducing us to the kings so that we, too, would want to rule. It was almost like he was saying, 'This can be you – but you've got to keep working at it.'

I wish I could remember the pearls of show-business wisdom that each man left us with – because each one had 'sound advice', according to Joseph – but those words are now buried treasure somewhere deep in my mind. Michael hoarded these influences, absorbing every last detail: the way they talked, moved, spoke – and how their skin looked and felt. He watched them on stage with the scrutiny of a young director, focusing on Smokey's words, focusing on Jackie's feet. Then, in the van going home afterwards, he became the most vocal and animated out of all of us: 'Did you hear when he said ...' or 'Did you notice that ...' or 'Did you see Jackie do that move ...' My brother was a master studier of people and never forgot a thing, filing it away in a mental folder he might well have called 'Greatest Inspirations & Influences'.

WE WERE NOW EARNING ABOUT 500 dollars a show and our father worked us harder than ever, with an unremitting expectation of precision. 'We've done this over and over. WHY are you forgetting what to do?' he shouted, when a song or a move broke down – and then reminded us that James Brown used to fine his Famous Flames whenever they made a mistake.

But fines weren't Joseph's choice of sanction. Whippings were. Marlon got it the most because he was singled out as the weak link in the chain. It's true that he wasn't the most co-ordinated, and he had to work 10 times harder than the rest of us, but none of us saw anything in him that hampered our performance. But Marlon became the excuse for Joseph to cram in extra rehearsal time and keep us indoors more. It would turn out there was a deeper reason behind all this, but that would dawn later.

One time there was a step Marlon just couldn't master and Joseph's patience snapped. He ordered him outside to get a 'switch' – a skinny branch – from the tree outside. We watched as Marlon chose the stick with which we knew Joseph was going to beat him – from the very tree he had used to symbolise family and unity. 'When you forget,' Joseph barked, 'it's the difference between winning and losing!' As he struck Marlon on the back of the legs, Michael ran away in tears, unable to watch.

The sight of that switch made us all dig deeper in rehearsals but time and again, Marlon messed up. 'BOY! Go out there and get a switch!' Marlon tried to get clever – taking his time to find the skinniest, weakest branch to lessen the impact. 'NO! You go back out there and get a bigger one!' said Joseph. Marlon learned to scream louder than it actually hurt. That way, the beating stopped sooner.

What Marlon didn't hear was the talk about turning the Jackson 5 into the Jackson 4.

'He can't do it, he's out of step and out of tune, and he's ruining our chances!' Joseph told Mother. But over her dead body was Marlon going to be kicked out and scarred for life: Mother picked her battles, and Marlon stayed in the group.

I'll say this about Marlon: he's the most tenacious of us all. He knew his limits but never stopped trying to push beyond them. Whenever we took a break, he kept on practising. He even used the walk to school to rehearse. There we were, a group of brothers ambling to school, and Marlon broke out, dancing on the sidewalk, going through his steps, moving sideways.

From the middle bunk at bedtime, we heard Michael reassuring Marlon – 'You're doing good, you'll get there, keep at it.' At school, Michael would use break-time to show Marlon spins and different moves. As lovers of Bruce Lee movies, we had our own nunchucks – martial-art sticks – and Michael used to take them to school (rules were more lenient in the days when kids didn't use weapons to harm one another). Michael and Marlon were like poetry in motion, using the *nunchaku* techniques to practise fluidity, flexibility and grace in movement. I think this was why Marlon eventually became an accomplished dancer, too – because he put in the extra hours. But Michael hated Joseph using his own excellence as the measure by which he judged his brother. He hated the way that such unforgiving scrutiny always planted doubt: 'Was that good enough? Was that what he wanted? Did I make a mistake?' – the early whisperings of a rabid self-doubt that would compel each one of us to worry if our best was our best.

Maybe the resentment this stoked was what lay behind Michael's rebellion. During rehearsals, if Joseph asked him to do a certain new step, or try a new move, Michael, whose developing freestyle required no instruction, refused. At the age of nine, he had turned from a compliant, ask-me-to-do-anything child into the stubborn kid with attitude. 'Do it, Michael,' said Joseph, glaring, 'or there'll be trouble!'

'NO!'

'I'm not going to ask you again.'

'NO – I wanna go outside and play!'

Michael became one of those kids who strained against imposed order, pushing his luck more than we ever dared. Inevitably, he received the switch. Time and again, he stood at the tree, crying, trying to choose his branch. Buying time. I remember getting the switch once – for not doing some chore – but Marlon (for errors) and Michael (for blatant disobedience) received it the most.

There were times when Mother felt Joseph was administering his punishment too hard. 'Stop, Joseph! Stop!' she begged, trying to make him see through his red mist.

In time, Joseph would learn that the switch was not the most effective man-management tool because it made Michael recoil so far. He barricaded himself in the bedroom, or hid under the bed, refusing to come out – and that ate into precious rehearsal time. Once he screamed in Joseph's face that he would never sing again if he laid another hand on him. It was left to us, the older brothers, to talk Michael down and coax him with candy: it was amazing what the prospect of a Jawbreaker could do.

Let's also not forget that Michael was a big tease and it wasn't all tears and tantrums. If watching *The Three Stooges* taught him anything, it was how to be silly and he *loved* to tease. He'd make this face where he opened his eyes real wide, puffed out his cheeks and pursed his lips – and he did this whenever someone was talking all serious. Once, Joseph was lecturing me about a missed chore. It wasn't serious enough for a spanking, but I had to stand there while he gave me a good talking-to. As he stood across from me – his face thunderous – I spotted Michael behind him, making *that* face. I tried to focus on Joseph but Michael stuck his fingers in both ears, knowing he'd got me. I started smirking. 'BOY! Are you laughing at me?' yelled Joseph. By which time, Michael had darted into our bedroom, out of sight.

He and Marlon even dreamed up a new nickname for Joseph behind his back: 'Buckethead'. They would say it behind his back, or whisper it when he was near and crack into fits of giggles. We also called him 'The Hawk' – because Joseph liked to think he saw and knew everything. That was the one nickname we told him about. He liked it – it sounded respectful.

JOSEPH'S TEMPER AND DISCIPLINARIAN UPBRINGING ARE never going to win much support today, but as I moved through my teenage years, I began to understand the thinking behind the beatings. We didn't know it at the time, but our parents worried about the growing influence of gang violence in the mid-sixties, which led to a crop of youth gangs. The Indiana Police Department set up its own Gang Intelligence Unit and there was talk at school of automatic weapons and FBI surveillance in the neighbourhood. In Chicago 16 youths were shot in one week, two fatally.

At the Regal Theater, the management went to the extreme of hiring uniformed police officers to patrol the lobby and ticket booths because gangs were terrorising the region. It was this unease and local talk that spread to the ears of fathers at the steel mill. Joseph wasn't just determined to save us from a life of struggle at The Mill but to keep us from gang involvement – and wrecking our, and his, dream. As he would tell newspaper reporters in 1970: 'In our neighbourhood, all of the kids got into trouble and we felt that it was very important for the family to involve themselves in activities which would keep them off the streets and away from the temptations of the modern age.'

Gang-bangers preyed on the impressionable (which we all were) and, in a city where the divorce rate was high and kids had little respect for their fathers, gang recruitment brought many kids a sense of belonging, of family, and a chance to earn the love of 'brothers'. That, and the prospect of something terrible happening to us, was what Joseph dreaded. His dread was heightened when Tito was ambushed on his way home from school and held at gunpoint for his lunch money. The first we knew was when Tito burst through the front door, screaming that some kid had tried to kill him.

Joseph responded by doing two things. He ensured we had a purpose: we had constant rehearsals, which meant we had to come home and couldn't go out to play. He then turned himself into a greater force of fear. In becoming the tyrant at home, he prevented us submitting to the tyrants on the street. It worked: we were more scared of him than we were of any gang member. Michael noted that Joseph had more patience with us at the beginning, but then his discipline hardened. The timing coincided with the increase in gang violence. Throughout our childhood, we had only ever been encouraged to play with one another and sleepovers with friends were *never* allowed. Apart from Bernard Gross and next-door neighbour Johnny Ray Nelson, we didn't really get to know other children.

'Letting the outside in', as Mother put it, was fraught with risk because none of us could know what a child from another family might bring in terms of bad thoughts, bad habits and domestic troubles. 'Your best friends are your brothers,' she said.

In our minds, 'outsiders' were people to be wary of and when you're raised like that, it can only go two ways: you either become extremely guarded and mistrusting of anyone who isn't family, or you bounce to the opposite extreme and let anyone in, reacting to the restrictions of the past.

Once the gang threat had become an issue, we were kept indoors more and even kept back from school on the last day of the year because that was thought to be when kids settled scores. Joseph even considered moving us to Seattle 'because it's safer there.' At his hands, we may have seen stars as he beat our asses with a leather belt, the switch and sometimes the broken cord from the iron, but we never saw a knife, a gun, a knuckle-duster, a police cell or a hospital emergency room. I guess Joseph did what he felt was right at the time, in that era, in those circumstances.

TITO AND I REGULARLY WALKED THE fields that led from our house to the Delaney Projects where all the gangs congregated. This was our back route to our new school, Beckman Middle. One day, we saw a police officer standing by a big patch of blood in the snow. We asked him what had happened. He told us we didn't want to know. But, kids being kids, we pressed him for the answer. He used a long word to make it sound less gory. We took this word home for translation: 'decapitated'. Someone had been 'decapitated'. The horror on Mother's face was matched in the following weeks when I told her that my walk to school wasn't so bad: the gang-bangers were real friendly and waved, giving us credit for being the Jackson 5. 'Those boys are not good, Jermaine. You heard what your father said – steer clear of them.' So the walk to school, through the Projects, with the clothes-lines, abandoned toys and junk wrecks parked up, became a constant head-down-don't-look-at-anyone exercise.

But then the gangs, and their fights, started encroaching nearer our street. From our front window, we witnessed about three bad rumbles between rival gangs. As the gangs moved in – one coming down 23rd Avenue, the other from the far end of Jackson Street – Mother screamed for us to get inside and shut all doors and windows. Our five little heads must have looked like a row of Afro wigs as we lined up at the window, spying the action.

One time, things got out of hand. Two gangs decided to rendez-vous on our corner and school had been abuzz with talk of this showdown. When the day came, we were locked indoors. We knew trouble was near when we heard shouting. And then the pop of a gunshot. That was when we hit the deck. 'Get down! Everyone down!' Joseph yelled. Inside the house, the family kissed the carpet. Rebbie, La Toya, Michael and Randy screamed and cried, and Joseph's face was pinned to the floor, side on, eyes wide. There must have been about two other shots that rang out and we were lying there for about 15 minutes before Joseph checked to see if the coast was clear. 'Now do you see what we've been telling you?' he said.

From that story, you now know the inspiration behind Michael's 1985 hit 'Beat It' – and the video that begins with two gangs approaching from different ends of the street before he jumps into the middle and unites them with dance.

In an interview in 2010, Oprah Winfrey asked our father if he regretted his 'treatment' of us – as if he had been a waterboarding jailer at Guantánamo Bay. It is a question that is easy to ask with a condemnatory subtext in a different age, but had Oprah asked that question in 1965 before a black community pitched into the middle of gangland warfare, she would have been treated as the oddity, not Joseph. It was the way of the world back then. Joseph was a hard man with better managerial skills than fatherly ones, with a heart encased in steel but a dedication driven by good. The only expressed regret was Michael's. He wished we had known more of the absent father than the ever-present manager. But here's one irrefutable fact: our father raised nine kids in a high-crime, drug-using, gangland environment and steered them towards success without one of them falling off the rails.

Until I was researching this book, I hadn't understood the extent of the nonsense written about Joseph's discipline: that he had once cocked an empty pistol to Michael's head; that he had locked him, terrified, in a closet; that he had jumped out of the shadows with kitchen knives because he 'enjoyed terrifying his children'; that he had violently shoved Michael into a stack of instruments; that Michael had had to step over La Toya on the bathroom floor – and then brushed his teeth – after Joseph had laid her out cold. It's a sad truth of celebrity that when something isn't officially denied or legally contested, outside commentators feel free to push the boundaries of fantasy until myth is cemented as fact. Whenever I have attempted to place Joseph's behaviour into a true context, I am accused of being a sympathiser or an apologist, and yet I was there. I saw what really happened – and it doesn't line up with the portrayal of him as a monster.

People cite to me Michael's televised Oprah interview of 1993 or the Martin Bashir documentary of 2003. They have heard how the thought of Joseph made Michael feel sick or faint; how Joseph used to 'tear me up' and give him 'a whipping' or 'a beating' and be 'cruel' or 'mean', and it was 'bad … real bad'. All of which is true. There is no denying that Michael was terrified of our father and his fear grew into dislike. As late as 1984, he turned to me one day and asked, 'Would you cry if Joseph died?'

'Yeah!' I told him, and he seemed surprised by my certainty.

'I don't know if I would,' he said.

Michael was the most sensitive of brothers, the most fragile, and the most alien to Joseph's ways. In his young mind, what Joseph did wasn't discipline, it was unloving. This was reinforced when, after moving to California, new friends (both young and old) reacted in horror when Michael openly told them about Joseph's actions. 'That's abuse, Michael!' they said. 'He can't do that to you. You can report him to the police for that!' If Michael didn't think it was abuse before, he did now. Joseph had a big problem in controlling his temper and none of us would raise our children the same way today. But had he truly abused us we wouldn't still be speaking to him, as Michael was until the rehearsals for the 'This Is It' concert of 2009. He had forgiven Joseph and didn't subscribe to the notion that any of us had been 'abused'.

In 2001, Michael gave a speech to students at Oxford University about parents and children. The words he used then still stand today: 'I have begun to see how my father's harshness was a kind of love, an imperfect one, but love nonetheless. With time, I now feel a blessing. In the place of anger, I have found absolution ... reconciliation ... and forgiveness. Almost a decade ago, I founded a charity called Heal the World. To heal the world, we first need to heal ourselves. And to heal the kids, we first have to heal the child within each and every one of us. That is why I want to forgive my father and stop judging him. I want to be free to step into a new relationship with my father for the rest of my life, unhindered by the goblins of the past ...'

HOWEVER MUCH MICHAEL SPOKE ABOUT HIS fear of Joseph, he liked taking it to the edge. Between the ages of six and 10, his love of candy propelled him into a mission that, for him, was akin to crawling into the big bad bear's cave as it slept. Each morning before school, and with Joseph in bed after working a swing shift, we'd send Michael to grab change from inside the pockets of the pants left lying on the bedroom floor.

Jackie, Tito, Marlon and I stood against the wall, shushing one another and trying not to giggle as Michael slithered slowly on the floor and through the partially open door into darkness. I stood as lookout – checking for movement from the big bundle under the sheets. Next thing we knew, Michael was backing out with some change and we'd run out of the house, yelping with delight that we had pulled off another successful mission. Sometimes our candy-heist yielded a disappointing haul of cents and nickels, but some-times we struck gold with dimes and quarters.

Throughout our childhood, we thought we were the bravest kids until Mother told us in later years that she and Joseph would lie there in bed, eyes open, looking at one another, raising their eye-brows and smiling as they heard Michael shuffling in.

MICHAEL'S SWEET TOOTH WAS BEHIND THE one moment in his life when he said time stood still. It was winter and thick snow was on the ground. He hadn't wanted to venture out into the cold so he'd begged Marlon to go and buy him some bubble gum.

Some time later, we were all playing inside and Mother was in the kitchen when a kid pounded on the door, shouting, 'Marlon's dead!' He had been hit by a car.

Mother ran outside, yelling, 'WHERE? WHERE?'

I stood on the pathway, watching her hurry through the snow up the street. Behind me, Michael was rooted by guilt to the door-step. 'Oh, Lord, what have I done? I sent him for some gum … Erms, it's all my fault.'

Marlon had suffered a head injury after a car slid in the snow and slewed into him. Mother found him knocked out under the front bumper, being tended by people in the street. He was taken to hospital, where he stayed for a few days. When Mother came home and said he was going to be okay, Michael burst into tears of relief. He had convinced himself that his brother was dead all because of him and that his punishment would be exclusion from God's paradise.

That was because, in our home, the lessons of the Kingdom Hall held equal weight to the lessons in entertainment. The irony was lost on us. We never questioned things as kids: I don't think we ever *learned* how to question things. We just followed instructions and did as we were told. Michael believed it when the elders preached that only 144,000 people would be saved by Jehovah and transported to a new paradise when Armageddon happened. Why only 144,000 out of the four million practising Witnesses across America? We never did ask. Jehovah's influence was one aspect of life at 2300 Jackson Street that people perhaps haven't properly weighed: those doctrines conditioned Michael and pinned us to the straight and narrow, just as much as Joseph's discipline.

GOD WAS ALWAYS RESIDENT IN OUR house, but Jehovah moved in before Mother fell pregnant with Randy, when Michael was two. She had been raised a Christian with devoted family links to the Baptist Church, but two things happened in 1960: a local pastor she respected at Gary's Lutheran church turned out to be having an affair and therefore broke his covenant with God; and a practising Jehovah's Witness, a friend named Beverly Brown, knocked on our door at the exact time of Mother's spiritual disillusionment. That was when Christmas and birthdays moved out of our home. Mother says that I 'must' remember having a Christmas tree and presents until I was six, but I honestly can't.

After her conversion the only 'special occasion' was the obligatory visit with Mother to the local Kingdom Hall. It was her responsibility to show us the love of God: Joseph rarely joined us as we dressed up in our second-hand smart pants, jacket and tie to sit in the chairs and get shushed for fidgeting, moaning or rocking our feet. Only the hymns brought things to life.

Mother ensured we made time for Bible study. The Old and New Testaments and the faith's main publications, the *Watchtower* and *Paradise Lost* magazines, were always on the living-room table. A fellow Witness joined Mother to read over the scriptures as Jackie, Tito, Marlon, Michael and I sat squashed up on the sofa, with the girls at our feet, Bibles in our laps and pencils in hand to underline certain passages to be discussed at the next sermon. Rebbie couldn't wait to join Mother on 'field service' – going from door to door to spread Jehovah's message. The times we trailed after Mother, up and down people's pathways, were a lesson in determination if nothing else.

I watched curtains twitching and used to count how many seconds it would be before the door was slammed in Mother's face. Rejection didn't faze her – she was serving Jehovah. Bless her, she's still blazing a trail in His name in California to this day. The one lesson imprinted on our minds from our own Bible study was that we'd take a fast trip to Hell if we didn't serve Jehovah and attend the Kingdom Hall. Our Judgement Day was Armageddon, when all evil life would be destroyed and a new world created for the chosen 144,000. Salvation hinged on our devotion to Jehovah.

Just in case our young minds were not imaginative enough, the *Watchtower* illustrated what Armageddon would look like. I remember reading it with Michael, scanning vivid illustrations of buildings imploding and people falling into cavernous cracks in the earth, arms reaching out to be saved. The anxiety spread as we pondered the questions that would decide our fate. Do we honour Jehovah enough? Are we good enough for eternal life? Will we survive Armageddon? If we get into trouble with Joseph, does that mean we're in trouble with Jehovah, too?

'I want to go to Paradise!' I said, more out of fear than enthusiasm.

'Mother, are we going to be saved?' asked Michael.

The most important thing in life, she said, was to be good and be good to others: salvation is granted to those who keep the faith, do field service and live according to the scriptures. As an adult, Michael would later accept the *Watchtower* illustrations as 'symbolism', but as boys, it was still scary to wonder how Jehovah noticed the difference between us being good and, say, the mailman. What about the times Michael gave kids in the neighbourhood candy and I didn't? Mother's stock answer was the same: Don't worry, He sees everything.

And then there was the proximity of Armageddon. When was it going to happen? Next week? How long have we got? An inquisitive mind like Michael's never could stop thinking about it. I can see him now looking up to an elder to ask some earnest question, only to be patted on the head and humoured. But witnesses seemed forever braced for the end of the world. The first Armageddon was estimated to be 1914. When that didn't happen, it was changed to 1915 ... And they're still waiting.

I distinctly remember when the Jackson family was convinced it was coming: 1963. The Russians seemed sure to bomb the US, JFK was assassinated, and then the suspected gunman, Lee Harvey Oswald, was shot – an event we watched on our black-and-white TV. Our household was sure all this was a prelude to the end of the world – and we brothers had never been so keen to get to the Kingdom Hall to honour Jehovah.

Michael always said he was raised biblically. In fact, he was the only one of the Jackson 5 to be baptised. Michael prayed, I did not. Michael learned the Bible, I did not. I didn't appreciate that Jehovah was the ultimate Father because we were made to believe that He can disown you if you don't behave. The threat of abandonment – of being 'de-fellowshipped' – was ever-present. Michael would learn all about Jehovah's threat of banishment in later life but in his childhood, the threat of it was a whip in itself.

When the Jackson 5 took off, I would say his faith became his bedrock; something solid to hang on to, a place to which he could retreat and be regarded not as famous but as equal and normal. Witnesses never made a fuss of Michael because they were only allowed to make a fuss of Jehovah. The Kingdom Hall brought him a sense of normality that, in the outside world, dwindled year upon year. Michael was dedicated to walking the higher path. I know that he confided in God and felt He was a presence you could never fool or hide anything from. In later life, he once told me he still felt a twinge of guilt for celebrating Christmas and birthdays.

Collectively speaking, the ever-watchful Jehovah, combined with our parents' determination to ring-fence us from the threat of gang violence, ensured that we didn't learn how to integrate socially except with each other. Even then, there was no real sense of *coming together* because of the lack of family occasions such as Christmas, birthdays and Thanksgiving. In our childhood we walked the line between Joseph's strict expectations and Jehovah's salvation. The stage was the only place where there were no rules; it became our one area of freedom.

WE DIDN'T THINK STAGES GOT ANY bigger than the one that talk-show host David Frost offered us. One of his producers had been in the audience that night at the Apollo and he called Richard Aarons, saying he wanted us to perform on *The David Frost Show* from New York, to be broadcast to the whole of America. For nights afterwards, we climbed into our bunk-beds, unable to sleep through excitement. We told everyone at school that we were going to be on the TV and teachers made announcements in class.

David Frost was the Englishman with a talk-show in America: he was part of 'the British invasion'. There were the Beatles, the Rolling Stones and David Frost – and we were on his radar.

What we didn't know was that Joseph had been simultaneously thrown into a dilemma. We had performed again at the Regal on 17 July 1968, where we shared a bill with Bobby Taylor and the Vancouvers. Bobby was so impressed that he got on the phone to a lady who had recently moved into the Detroit apartment block where he lived. Suzanne de Passe was a 19-year-old who had just started work in town as creative assistant to Berry Gordy at Motown and we ended up auditioning for her in Bobby's living room. As Suzanne remembers it, she rang Mr Gordy about 'these amazing kids', but he wasn't impressed.

'Kids? I don't want more kids! I've got enough on with Stevie Wonder!' To him, of course, kids were a headache, with tutors and all. Apparently, he had been the same with Diana Ross and the Supremes at first, dismissing them as 'too young'.

Mr Gordy clearly needed persuading, and Suzanne persuaded him. This was where Joseph had his dilemma: our invitation to audition at Motown clashed with the David Frost booking. It was dream national-television exposure versus one golden opportunity. Michael and Marlon were initially devastated when Joseph chose to audition. Instead of performing to an audience of millions from New York, we found ourselves at Motown's headquarters – Hitsville USA – performing to a handful of people, including Mr Gordy. Joseph was smart in not grasping at the instant celebrity of television: David Frost wouldn't bring us closer to a record deal – but the audition did.

On 23 July 1968, that audition took place before a selected group of people. We couldn't see them because they were gathered in the dark on the other side of the glass in the sound studio; we only saw a camera on a tripod, capturing our 'screen test', as was standard. We sang the aptly titled 'Ain't Too Proud To Beg' and 'I Wish It Would Rain' by the Temptations, before ending with 'Who's Lovin' You?' by Smokey Robinson. The weirdest thing was the pregnant pause that greeted our final note: no one said a word.

Michael couldn't stand it. 'So? How was that?' he chirped.

'*Michael!*' I said in a loud whisper, embarrassed by his rudeness.

'That was great … very good,' said some voice. But that was all we got. We had to wait a few years before we learned the truth of the reaction when Mr Gordy wrote about it in his Foreword to Michael's reissued autobiography, *Moonwalk,* in 2009: 'Michael sang "Who's Lovin' You" with the sadness and passion of a man who had been living with the blues and heartbreak his whole life … As great as Smokey sang it, Michael sang it better. I told Smokey, "Hey, man, I think he gotcha on that one!"'

Two days later, we got the call back: Motown wanted to sign us.

CHAPTER SIX
Motown University

'THE BOSTON HOUSE' WAS ANOTHER WORLD, with a size and opulence beyond our comprehension. We'd thought only kings and queens lived so grandly, but Mr Gordy's mock-Tudor mansion in Detroit was something else. It was also our venue for the night, to perform at one of his annual parties. One thing was certain: there would be no midnight strip-teases or fruit thrown on stage. This was no Mr Lucky's or amateur night at the Apollo. It wasn't a home, either. It was a residence – and one that music had provided. Michael wandered around, ever-curious, looking up at the great ceilings, shimmering chandeliers, the grand oil portraits of Mr Gordy himself.

Outside, there was an ornamental fountain and marble Greek statues. Inside, there were butlers and white people working as household staff. Everything was so ornate, immaculate and clean. We arrived as newly-signed Motown artists, even if our signed contracts had got snagged due to some legal issues we didn't ask about, but it was 'nothing to worry about' and our host didn't seem too concerned. It was his first time showcasing us so the night was a big deal. It was the winter of 1968 and we had no idea what to expect.

The bearded, effusive Mr Gordy greeted us, his sole performers for the night, at the door with a golf club in his hand. (He had a putting green out back.) Our 'dressing room' was the pool house just outside the indoor swimming pool and the 'stage' was an area set aside at the far end of the pool, with just enough room for Johnny's drums and Ronny's keyboard. Guests would face us from the opposite end and down the flanks, between the Greek columns.

As men in suits and women wearing diamonds started to gather, Michael and Marlon kept running outside from the pool-house to take a peep through the windows to see who was out front. Jackie, Tito, Johnny, Ronny and I got changed and sat around, going over the performance in our heads. Suddenly Marlon darted in. 'Smokey Robinson is here!' He dashed back out.

Then Michael's head appeared at the door. 'Whoa! I've just seen some of the Temptations!'

Then Marlon: 'Gladys Knight is here!'

Then Michael again, shrieking: 'DIANA ROSS! I'VE JUST SEEN DIANA ROSS!'

Tito and I jumped up and raced outside to make sure it wasn't another of his pranks. But it was true. Mr Gordy had gathered the *crème de la crème* of his Motown family – and who knew how many other movers and shakers from the music industry? Ever since July, we had kept pinching ourselves that we were actually Motown artists – grouped with the Temptations, the Marvelettes, Martha & the Vandellas, Smokey, Gladys, Bobby Taylor, Diana Ross, Marvin Gaye and the Four Tops. For so long, they were who we wanted to be and where we wanted to be. And we were about to perform for half of them.

Jackie grew agitated. 'Guys, we need to concentrate. Come on. Do y'all know what you're supposed to do?' The occasion was clearly getting to him, and Michael and Marlon's regular news updates weren't helping. Funnily enough, it was the one occasion when Joseph wasn't backstage. He was busy rubbing shoulders with the big names and maybe that was why Jackie had the jitters. 'C'mon, y'all ... we must get this right. Let's focus,' he said. After Joseph, Jackie was the one who most used that word.

Michael and Marlon settled down and we gathered in a huddle and told one another that we should 'go out there and tear this place up'. That was how we spoke before a show over the years: 'Tear 'em up'; 'Let's knock 'em out'; 'Let's kill 'em'; or 'Let's go out there and hurt 'em'. Michael carried forward these phrases into his work as a solo artist. Anyone who worked with him will recognise that vernacular. Fighting talk, borrowed from Joseph.

As kids, we knew the calibre of talent waiting to watch us and yet we didn't for a second feel out of our depth or inferior. As Motown's first child group, we couldn't wait to do our set: 'My Girl', 'Tobacco Road' and a James Brown number. The big question in our mind was: how would they react? What were these Motown folk like in a private setting? In an audience?

If there were two absent people we wanted out there, it was Mother and Rebbie. Mother had waited in the wings for so long on our behalf, taken a back seat, sacrificed her own dreams and missed her boys most weekends. And when Motown first exploded, Rebbie was the one going to the local record store, buying the newly-released 45s and dancing the 'sock hops' with Jackie. She was all about what Mr Gordy had invented – 'the sound of young America'. Or, as another Motown motto would go, 'It's what's in the groove that counts'.

Once we were poolside, with mics and instruments in hand, we looked out across the lit water and kept spotting the faces of the greats who were watching. It took one wink from Michael and then we started killing it. The energy of that performance was incredible and we could tell our VIP audience was into it. They weren't just gracious, they *loved* it. By the second verse of 'My Girl', they were clapping and dancing and cheering, even whooping when Michael turned on his moves and set fire to the place. As we took our bows, we spotted Mr Gordy front-centre of the standing crowd, clapping the loudest, smiling the widest alongside Joseph, puffing out his chest. Always a good sign.

When Smokey Robinson and Marvin Gaye came over and expressed their enthusiasm, we started to feel that we *must* be good. Everyone talked about 'the little fella' – Michael – and Diana Ross made a beeline for him. She said a few words and grabbed his cheeks like an auntie meeting her favourite nephew. I was talking to someone else at the time, but I saw how starry-eyed he was. That was actually the first time we met Diana, which puts to bed the Motown folklore that insisted it was she who discovered us. That marketing myth was invented because, we were told, it was stardom by association, so we memorised it as 'fact' to tell journalists.

That night, we stayed at Bobby Taylor's apartment in Detroit and rang Mother in Gary, each one of us taking turns on the phone to tell her how brilliantly the night had gone. 'Did they really like it? Did they really? I'm so proud of you boys.'

PEOPLE HAVE ALWAYS ASKED, 'WHAT *EXACTLY* is the Motown Sound?' In 1983, Smokey – the label's first artist – tried answering that question: 'The Motown Sound is the bottom, you know. They got the foot working and you can hear the bass real good.' In his 1994 autobiography, Mr Gordy defines it as 'rats, roaches, struggle, talent, guts and love'. I'd go further: its uptown-downtown mix is part funky, part melodic, with a distinct pop sound thrown in. And then there's the feel-good mood it evokes, tapping into universal human emotion, elevating happiness, remembering desire, soothing heartbreak, as inspired by Mr Gordy's early days with Jackie Wilson. It's a catharsis that touches you; a force that compels you to move. It's that blend of beats, bass lines, drums, keyboards, tambourines, hand-claps and the interplay of harmonies that create an instantly knowable sound, and one on which we built our live performances and musical education. And even then I don't feel I've done it justice.

Our first Motown tutor was Bobby Taylor and we spent a lot of time with him in the months before Mr Gordy's party, working at weekends and when school was out for summer. He didn't have much room in his apartment so we threw down mattresses and sleeping-bags on his carpet. It felt like the sleepover we were never allowed to have. Bobby, a tremendous singer himself, spent those summer weeks producing us and cutting tracks like 'Can You Remember?', 'Who's Lovin' You', 'Chained' and 'La-La-La-La-La Means I Love You' and 'Standing In The Shadows Of Love', songs that would feature on our first album. We must have cut more than a dozen covers from the likes of the Delfonics, Smokey Robinson, the Temptations and Marvin Gaye, and that work allowed us to ease into the recording process as a team prepared our original material.

Bobby knew how to inspire us, and he taught Michael and me how to use a mic properly in the studio. 'Guys, you're not on stage any more,' he'd say. 'The mic will give you the volume, so don't worry about projecting your voices.' That was when Michael's imitation came into its own. Bobby first sang a song, then Michael repeated it, note for note. If Bobby liked what he saw on stage, his judgement was validated in the studio.

We first recorded at Motown's headquarters, using a four-track board. The studio was in a cellar of the old house that Mr Gordy had converted into Hitsville USA in West Grand Boulevard, Detroit. It wasn't fancy and looked nothing like an empire, but it was the epicentre of the Motown Sound so it felt instantly magical. The pre-taped arrangements were the work of the in-house rhythm section, known as the Funk Brothers – the unsung heroes behind the Motown Sound, the dynamic team of musicians who created everything we had ever heard from the label. We couldn't believe they were our collaborators. It was as though we had jumped into the radio on the side cabinet.

After a summer and early fall of recording, life returned to normal and we turned into a new year. Between August 1968 and March 1969, progress seemed to stall so we kept rehearsing, performing and revisiting our usual haunts – the Apollo, Guys and Gals, and the High Chaparral – to maintain our regional exposure, if nothing else.

Ironically, it was Mother who first got restless. 'Are you sure these Motown people are going to come through, Joe?'

He told her to be patient – to trust the agreement. Legal loose ends were still being tied up with Steeltown Records and Motown was in the process of setting up a division in Los Angeles. All major record labels had started to head west in the late sixties and Joseph could almost smell success.'We're going to Hollywood, boys. I just know it,' he said, winking.

But we'd be going without Rebbie. In November 1968, she married a fellow Witness named Nathaniel Brown and announced she was moving to Kentucky. Joseph was furious; Mother heartbroken. Neither found it easy to accept that she was leaving the family: their plan to keep everyone together was coming undone and there was nothing they could do. Rebbie couldn't understand why they were not overjoyed for her happiness, but I suspect Joseph felt his control unravelling. Or maybe Rebbie's departure was a painful reminder of losing his sister Verna-Mae? Either way, he refused to give her away on her wedding day. That duty fell, instead, to Papa Samuel.

What upset Rebbie most was that Joseph didn't arrange for us to be there either. A performance at the Regal was deemed more important. I never did understand how that fitted with Joseph always saying that family came first.

Meanwhile, Randy – then six or seven – started wanting *his* talents to be noticed. He had watched the five of us go out most nights and weekends, leaving him as the only boy at home. He says it inspired him. Like Marlon, he had his own determination, so when Joseph handed him a pair of bongos, he practised day and night. 'Listen, Joseph! Listen to this,' he said, whenever we arrived home.

'You keep at it,' Joseph said, 'and when you're ready, I'll let you know.'

Randy never stopped thinking he was ready. At school, he started learning the guitar and the piano. One day, he told himself, he, too, would become a member of the Jackson 5. Janet was three years old, as cute and doe-eyed as Michael; she always wore a braided pigtail and played hopscotch in the alley, or sat cross-legged and clapped 'patty-cakes' with Randy. But that's the extent of my memories of my little sister from our days in Indiana: she would make her presence felt when life eventually moved us to new pastures in southern California.

After Motown contracts were finally resolved and a new recording contract signed, the long-awaited call came from Mr Gordy, asking us to move to Los Angeles. It was time to claim our dream ticket out of Gary and truly enter the business for which we were destined.

Mother, Randy, La Toya and Janet stayed in Gary, packing boxes and preparing to rent out our home to a relative. But we headed west. Leaving our home-town wasn't hard because we were leaving it for our dream. The only hard part was leaving Mother behind, but we knew she'd be following two months later so we felt okay to go.

JOSEPH TREATED US TO OUR FIRST colour television in 1969. I think he felt we had earned it this time. And that was how the move out West felt – like someone had turned the contrast dial, taking us from the bleak black-and-white of Gary to the vivid, vibrant colour of California. The drive from Los Angeles airport to Hollywood was a discovery in itself. For the first time we saw the towering, verdant palm trees, a cloudless blue sky, the bronzed people in tight T-shirts and flared jeans, and we smelt pines and freshness. It contrasted sharply with Gary. All we had ever known was the foul air of steel mill smoke with its smell of sulphur dioxide and polluting red-hazes.

At street level, Los Angeles felt alive. We had arrived in the land of milk and honey, and Michael and I hung out of the car windows either side, a cooling breeze in our Afros. We drove around Hollywood and saw homes barely hanging on to hills, and mountain ranges in the distance.

In those first few days of July 1969, we watched sunsets and went to the beach – all Michael wanted to do was ride the

Hippodrome carousel on Santa Monica Pier – and we toured inland to find the best spot to see the Hollywood sign. We visited Disneyland and LA Zoo, and Michael fell in love with Mickey Mouse and the animals. We even managed a road trip to San Francisco.

Our first base was a playground for the music industry – the Tropicana Motel in West Hollywood. In those days, if you were music royalty, you checked into Chateau Marmont but if you were new in town, you stayed at the Tropicana – a white-painted, two-storey motor lodge built into a squared horseshoe, off Santa Monica Boulevard. It had a few bungalows in its grounds and a swimming pool, and the T on its front sign was a palm tree. We got excited about that. Palm trees were everywhere: there were almost as many palm trees as there were hippies.

We had a view of the Hollywood Hills from our room and all we did was swim. The motel was built into a slope, which meant the roof was only about 10 feet higher than the pool deck out back. Johnny Jackson fancied himself as an Olympic diver and was the first to climb up on to the tiles and show off: 'Watch me! Watch me! I'm going to do a double somersault!' We watched as – *smack!* – he belly-flopped with a splash. Johnny's humiliation was our signal to join in and we took running jumps from the roof and dive-bombed, ass first.

Meanwhile, as the search continued for a rented family home in LA – paid for by Motown as part of our deal – we found ourselves moving to new temporary accommodation: the home of the boss, Mr Gordy, whose next-door neighbour happened to be Diana Ross.

BACK THEN, DIANA WAS A 25-YEAR-OLD hit-maker, whose star was outgrowing – and was soon to be detached from – her fellow Supremes. She lived in the Hollywood Hills in a home that was all white and bright, with sumptuous cushions, billowing curtains and shag-pile carpets that we would do our best to ruin. Wide floor-to-ceiling sliding doors led to the pool deck and the balcony overlooked a grid of distant rooftops set within LA's basin. It was built into a hill directly beneath Mr Gordy's home, where he lived with his children. He called it The Curzon House.

It was a big wooden ranch-style property that managed to sprawl on its lot. Its most impressive feature was at basement level, where a window looked into the swimming-pool, like an aquarium. Michael and I would sit down there, looking up at people swimming on the surface, and imagine we were staring through a port-hole of our own submarine. There was a basketball court, too, so Jackie was happy, but Michael developed an annoying gift for scoring baskets with the most audacious shots. He'd throw the ball from afar, using both hands, and it was in without touching the sides. What he lacked in height, he made up for in accuracy.

We lived at Mr Gordy's for a week or two, but spent some afternoons and evenings at Diana's, walking the winding street between the two. I say we lived 'between two homes' because that was how it felt. But it wasn't true that any of us, including Michael, lived with Diana. This was another of those marketing myths – upheld by Michael in his book in 1988 – for the sake of image. That's not to say we didn't spend good times there. Diana taught me to swim, coaching me in her pool, holding me afloat as I held on to the sides and kicked my legs while Michael and Marlon played ball in the deep end.

It helped that Diana's brother Chico, who was my age, 14, was a ready-made playmate. He was a boy version of his older sister – the mouth, the wide eyes, the big smile – and we grew close. He ensured that we found pockets of time to play pool, table tennis and basketball with Mr Gordy's boys, Berry Junior, Terry, Kerry and Kennedy – the son who would, much further down the line, also become a Motown artist known as Rockwell. (In 1984, he would release the smash hit 'Somebody's Watching Me' featuring Michael and me on backing vocals.) Sports always turned into a Jacksons versus Gordys event, with Chico as their ringer – and we *always* kicked their butts, especially at baseball and football. The Gordys were sports-mad and I don't think they expected the brothers from Gary to be any good.

The benefit of these victories was that I shone in front of his daughter, Hazel, standing on the sidelines. Hazel was 14, and she had beautiful eyes, skin like honey, and was beyond sweet. I liked her when Suzanne de Passe first introduced us in an elevator at Motown but she was the boss's daughter so I had to behave myself. It was hard to resist the one amazing thing we had in common: we both loved Bazooka Joe bubble gum. In my book this was a meeting of minds and I couldn't hide it, especially from Michael. Younger brothers are embarrassingly perceptive and he couldn't wait to taunt me: 'Erms is in love! Erms is in love!'

What I liked about Hazel was that she was always honest, sincere and devoid of snobbery despite her well-to-do background. I was also in awe when she happened to drop into conversation that she'd often played hide-and-seek with Stevie Wonder and her brothers at Hitsville. That made her the coolest girl in LA. 'Wait,' I said, as the one obvious question dawned. 'How do you play hide and seek with Stevie? I mean, how does he find you?'

'Easy,' said Hazel. 'He takes off his belt and starts swinging it around the room. When he hears someone go, "Ow!", he says, "Found you!"' That was the day Stevie climbed even higher in my estimation.

Michael loved playing hide and seek. If he wasn't swimming, that was the game he always wanted to play, revelling in the suspense of being found or not. And then there was his other pastime: learning to paint, courtesy of Diana. She had set up easels and canvases in her living room and bought us paints, which was probably not the wisest decision with five boys in an all-white pristine environment: paint equalled fun, and fun meant going wild. When she was out, we decided to splash each other with our brushes. After a few mad minutes, we stopped – and saw multicoloured blotches all over her carpet. Michael was mortified. 'She's going to kill us! What are we going to do?' In Gary, it would definitely have been an offence punishable with the belt or switch.

Thankfully, Diana was a lot more forgiving. It was a mistake, we must clean it up, but it was never mentioned again.

She passed on her appreciation of art to Michael. He had an 'eye', as well as a voice, she said. We brothers had watched on the odd occasions when Joseph painted in our living room in Gary. Michael yearned to paint even then, but Joseph never invited him to get involved and he was too afraid to ask. He painted fruit and birds with Diana. Sometimes we didn't see him for days because he was immersed in his 'art lessons' or books on Michelangelo, Picasso and Degas. I think he learned a lot from being in Diana's company. She coaxed him out of his shell because he was the shyest of the brothers and yet, as our front man, he needed the biggest personality.

Today's artists could learn a thing or two from Diana's wisdom, style and class. Lots of modern-day performers emerge from nowhere and jump onstage without going through any kind of charm-school process. Motown trained artists to be stars: it groomed, prepared and educated them for the big-time. The likes of Diana Ross & the Supremes or the Temptations weren't born with silver spoons in their mouths, but when you saw them on TV, you thought they were kings and queens. There was no need for headline-grabbing stunts. It was all about the class, finesse and elegance of a performing artist and Diana epitomised the true superstar.

She was the perfect mentor for Michael because he instantly adored her. It was obvious from the way he looked up to her and hung around her – and she mirrored it back. She was special to each of us, but there was a unique bond between her and Michael. She was sister, best friend and mentor rolled into one, and they shared one of those inexplicable but natural understandings. Diana always said Michael had 'a great vibration and an aura of nothing but love.'

We learned a lot from her professionally, too. Her softness carried a forceful edge because she knew what she wanted, and wouldn't have it any other way. One time she warned us about Hollywood and said we needed thick skins and wise people around us but, as kids, it was hard to see how such a fun town could hurt anyone. In fact, in one 1970 interview, Michael told a reporter: 'Diana Ross has told me that people in show business can get hurt. I don't see how, to tell the truth. Maybe one day I will ... but I doubt it.'

By the end of August, Motown had rented our new home at 1601 Queens Road, sitting on the corner of one of those climbing, winding roads in the Hollywood Hills. This was our base as we set to work on our first album for Motown.

I DON'T THINK ANYONE CAN SAY they knew the scale of the fame and success that awaited us, but Mr Gordy certainly had a precise strategy. 'I'm going to make each one of you a star,' he promised, one afternoon in his living room, with us sitting on the sofa and him in an armchair, surrounded by some of his creative team. He then outlined his vision. It was characteristically bold, aggressive and confident: we'll release three back-to-back No. 1 singles, stay hidden, make people wait, let the mystique build ... then go on tour. *Three No. 1s? Wow, you believe in us that much?* Our eyes must have widened because Mr Gordy laughed. 'Trust me, you're going to be sensational' – he used that word all the time – 'and when you finally get out there, there will be pandemonium.'

The faces around him smiled and agreed, but let's face it, we had the easy part (performing) and the executives got the hard part (making it happen). We would come to know that the 'release-only-No.1s' was not a hope but an edict for his songwriters to heed. No. 1 was the level where he traded. There was a reason why he called the Motown headquarters 'Hitsville USA'. We also understood the subtle lesson in keeping us hidden – the strategy of wait-and-reveal: release the music to get people talking ... but don't let them see you. Give 'em nothing. Leave 'em in suspense, like a movie. Get them curious and when they're hooked, get them over-excited. Then, when the mood is right, 'reveal' the great spectacle, album, appearance or concert.

Michael would later compare this build-up to a magician's act – the unseen sleight-of-hand behind the music to whip up the magic of the actual performance. We'd heard the great stories from Joseph about how Mr Gordy – whose ancestors were slaves – had walked away from a job on the car assembly lines of Detroit and started his label in 1959 with 800 dollars, five employees and a natural ear for music. (Mr Gordy would sell Motown to MCA for $61 million in 1988.) He could write songs, play the piano, produce, manage and inspire; he had even been to London and produced a track for the Beatles. He launched black music in a decade of race riots and the civil rights movement; a time of shocking violence when black people were treated as second-class citizens and beaten for exercising democracy. One year before our arrival in LA, Dr Martin Luther King was assassinated in Memphis. Yet Mr Gordy stood up to be counted and heard, as he first employed an equal number of blacks and whites, then invented a black sound that was embraced by white America and the rest of the world. *That* was the real triumph in Joseph's eyes, and it mirrored what he had always wanted for us: to appeal to black or white, man or woman.

Mr Gordy was humble, too. To us, over the years, he actually became the biggest star at Motown because he chose to pour his time and vision into others. When he could have been the cover story of *Time* or *Life*, he said, 'No, it's not about me, it's about my artists.' He was a small man, yet imposing with his presence; he was a power-house who commanded your attention and everyone jumped when he walked into a room. When he looked at us, he did so studiously, as if eyeing something we couldn't see, something he wanted to extract and maximise.

Mr Gordy was much more than the president of Motown Records. If Diana Ross was a surrogate mother to us, he became a second father. At his house, he always took time to play with us: backgammon, pool, chess, swimming, and on the mini-bikes. Michael observed that Mr Gordy spent time with us in a way that Joseph never did. Quality time, not rehearsal time. Michael had yearned for our father to communicate in this way but I guess Mr Gordy was a lot freer in himself; a gentle family man as well as a mighty businessman, deftly balancing the two. The best example was one night when he turned in early, leaving us downstairs. 'I don't care what you all eat or what you do,' he said, 'just clean up behind yourselves.' *Do what you like. I'm trusting you – feel free.* We looked at each other disbelievingly, waited till the door closed, raided the fridge, then jumped in front of the TV. Hollywood seemed like an unrestricted heaven.

I've heard the stories that Mr Gordy was unfair, ruthless and mean, but that's alien to me because we only experienced someone loving. I think those who have criticised him have been non-business-minded folk or former artists who felt they should have got this or that, and forgot he had made them household names. Those who went elsewhere and signed new, improved record deals also forgot that he had done all the hard work, groomed them and built them a world platform that had made them attractive to rivals – which would become relevant to us further down the line.

IF AMERICA'S BRAINS WENT TO HARVARD, America's talent went to Motown – and artists graduated with a lifetime's knowledge. 'You're entering the finest finishing school in the business,' Mr Gordy told us. Our education was fast-track: every song should be a three-minute story with a beginning, a middle and an end. Music is story-telling and that linear thread makes it universal, we learned.

The chorus must summarise the story arc – you should be able to sing it and know what the song is about ('Billie Jean is not my lover/She's just a girl that says that I am the one/But the kid is not my son'); the lyrical content should be catchy and commercial *with a message*; each song's dynamics should keep building and, at the vamp, go through the roof.

And then there were Mr Gordy's tell-tale signatures. Go out with the hook so that the last thing people remember is the title. Like the final fade of 'I Want You Back' or 'I'll Be There'.

The packaging and trappings of being an artist were an education, too. We went from a VW camper van to limousines; from carrying our own stuff to having roadies; from Joseph juggling everything to a management team and A&Rs; from shopping for second-hand clothes to a professional wardrobe. We even had lessons in etiquette, PR and how to hold ourselves in public.

We learned 'going on the record': how not to put a foot wrong with the media, how to be courteous, how to answer questions in an interview, what to say, what *not* to say. There were a few marketing myths we rolled with because we were told to: 'Michael, you lived with Diana Ross'; 'Boys, remember – you were discovered by Diana Ross'; 'Michael, we're saying you're eight, not 10 – makes you cuter.'

We adopted 'the look': elaborate pencil sketches were presented to us on designer boards, depicting us in formation wearing different costumes, complete with big Afros; a wardrobe of Argyle tank-tops, flowery shirts, elaborately embroidered bell-bottomed pants and psychedelic waistcoats with tasselled fringes. Our look was very Sly and the Family Stone meets Mod Squad. Motown then handed us our separate marketable identities so that the pre-teen market could decide who was their favourite: Jackie was now officially the 'athletic' one, Tito 'the mechanic', Marlon 'the dancer', Michael 'the super-talented baby' and I was 'the heart-throb'. Motown packaged me as one of music's first teen idols, and the PR revolved around 'Love Gift Ideas for Jermaine' and 'Jermaine's Love Wishes'. Michael couldn't stop giggling – he said it made us sound like the Seven Dwarfs. We performed under a new logo, too: 'J5' – lipstick red set in a yellow heart, with the bottom curls of the letter and number licking up into two bubble hearts. It would cover our stages and backdrops, and also adorn the canvas on Johnny's drum-kit.

The Motown machine was like something out of the Willie Wonka factory that we would see at the theatres two years later: five boys from Gary squeezed through some magic machine and coming out the other end all shiny, new and repackaged. Nothing was our choice and everything was dictated; that was just the way it was. Our sound was 'bubble-gum soul' – not too much soul, not too much pop – and it was plain, but catchy family entertainment, straddling decades. We didn't really have to be marketed as anything more than we actually were: innocents, wholesome and well-behaved. Yet we found ourselves in this wonderland of Hollywood and music where we were given the best in life.

But within everything, we were always brothers. Brotherhood stopped us feeling disoriented throughout the whole metamorphosis. Whenever we looked at each other – in motels, new homes, recording studios and on the stage – we always felt 'home'. In our minds, we never left the confines of our bedroom in Gary.

Within that inseparableness, Michael always knew which brother he could turn to for different things and that was how he viewed each one of us back then: Jackie – the pair of sensible shoulders, armed with the facts of life; Tito – with the technical know-how and the ability to answer Michael's endless whys; Marlon – the playful competitor and fellow jester, always pulling Michael's arm to show him a dance step one more time; and me – the brother who always talked songs, creativity, 'mushy stuff' and girls. It would be some years before I understood the extent of my positive influence on Michael. He always told me, of course, how he loved and admired me, but he said it most succinctly to someone else, the writer and family friend David Ritz. It was during a conversation they shared in the 1970s that Michael said, 'Growing up, it was Jermaine I focused on. He'd walk me to school. I'd get his hand-me-down clothes. It was his voice that I first imitated. I loved his sound. He showed me the way.'

Every older brother likes to hear something like that, I think.

OUR DAY-TO-DAY MANAGER WAS Suzanne de Passe. She oversaw everything we did and played a pivotal role in keeping what Joseph had cultivated, but framing it within Motown's vision. She, with Tony Jones and Shelly Berger, worked all hours to make our operation run like clockwork under Mr Gordy's command. Suzanne was a tall, beautiful New Yorker with blonde hair and she had amazing skin. After Diana Ross, she was the most beautiful woman we had ever seen.

Beauty is a whip that makes you fall into line, we discovered. Whatever Suzanne wanted us to do, we would do. She nicknamed Michael 'Caspar Milquetoast' (a cartoon character known for being timid) and me 'Maine' – two terms of endearment that stuck throughout the Jackson 5 years. Suzanne had the patience of a saint and must have felt like our babysitter as well as manager. Onstage, we were wild and energetic and knew our professional job but offstage, we were just kids, messy, wild, crazy and clowning around. There'd be tantrums and fights and silliness; we were a handful. Or, as she said, 'You were *two* handfuls!' In many ways, she was as green as we were – but that was what made the adventure so much fun. She had lots of energy and ideas, and made us feel comfortable in a world unknown to us.

But within the whirlwind, Mr Gordy didn't want us getting carried away. 'As much as you have the ability to become enormous stars and make a lot of money, the most important thing is to be a good, decent human being,' he said. He was a businessman, and signed us to make a mint, but his personal interest and emotional investment were such that he looked out for us throughout the whole process. His philosophy echoed our upbringing: stick together, work hard, be loyal.

I suspect most of Hollywood will laugh as it reads that line today. But it was a different age and it shaped Michael's expectations. I think he honestly expected everyone to be as kind, affable, fun and accommodating as Berry Gordy and Diana Ross. Because it wasn't only Motown University, it was the Motown Family.

EVERY WEEKDAY WAS A STUDIO DAY, but before the serious business of recording could begin, we had to get school out of the way. Our first focus was music, then education and we had to go through the motions of normal school days but when most kids went home to play, we set to work as recording artists. We ran out of the school gates around 3.30pm, grabbed something to eat at home and then went off to the studio for around 5.30pm, and sometimes stayed there till 10.30pm. Some people say this sounds exhausting but we were too excited to notice because we loved being 'at work'.

The West-Coast Motown studio, the Sound Factory, was in Vine Street, just north of Hollywood Boulevard. Inside were the master-minds behind our creation: a songwriter-producer team named 'The Corporation', which comprised Mr Gordy, Freddie Perren, Deke Richards and 'Fonce' Mizell. We also worked with indepen-dents such as Hal Davis, Willie Hutch, Bob West and the Marsilino Brothers – we had a new bunch of musicians because the Funk Brothers had stayed in Detroit. This set-up meant that Tito, Johnny, Ronny and I were instrumentally redundant during studio sessions, but it was like Joseph said: we had to pay even closer attention to what the in-house musicians were doing because we'd need to repeat everything on tour.

Usually, the first time we'd hear a song was when we walked into the studio. We'd sometimes record two new songs, which had been instrumentally fine-tuned for us to lay down our vocals. We worked hard on improving our song presentation, but there was nothing we couldn't do because Michael had an incredible range in his voice. It was part Marvin Gaye and Smokey Robinson, with the heights of Diana Ross and the accents of James Brown, all mixed into one to become the beginnings of his own unmistakable sound. As ever, Michael emulated his idols and then created his own style. The only thing out of reach for him was the non-adjustable micro-phone hanging from the ceiling. He had to stand on an apple box before we could be cheek-to-cheek, Afro-to-Afro around the mic, doing the backgrounds.

Hal Davis was the one producer who always wanted us to huddle closer and he'd sit in his chair, behind the glass, raising his arms into an arch above his head, like a ballerina, mouthing, 'Get closer, get closer.' Seeing this thick-set producer with big arms strike what we saw as a ballerina pose always made us laugh and Hal had the least patience. He'd push record, we'd start singing, Hal would arc his arms ... and Michael would be chuckling. 'Come on, guys! Concentrate! We've got a lot of work to do,' said Hal. But the more serious he got, the more Michael laughed. And once he got the giggles, he couldn't stop, and once he couldn't stop, it became infectious. 'Come on, guys – you've got to take this seriously!'

Previously, there hadn't been much laughter in rehearsals. I guess we were letting it all out after holding it back while we were working under Joseph. But no one could seriously complain about our work ethic: we always stepped up and were eager to learn from a team who knew how to write and arrange a hit. More importantly, it knew what a hit *felt* like. It was all about the *feeeeeling* – just as Joseph first taught us. Fans of Michael would hear this echoed in future interviews: 'I'm feeling the music ... It's all about the spirit ... I'm feeling it in my heart.'

The best feeling we had was when we cut our first original Jackson 5 song: 'I Want You Back'. It was originally titled 'I Want To Be Free' and written for Gladys Knight by Freddie Perren, who had joined Motown as a producer after being with Jerry Butler's band. In fact, there's a certain serendipity to this song's back-story because Freddie played with Jerry at the Regal one night and we opened for him. Now we were recording our first song together. We were convinced we had done a great job when we first listened back to that recording, but most of all we were excited because it was the birthing moment of *our own sound*, not a cover. It was something for us to own, not borrow – and we loved its beat.

But when Mr Gordy heard it, he wasn't impressed. 'Sorry, not good enough ... I'm not *feeling* it ... Let's start over,' he said. Looking back, I can't say who had more of an exacting standard: Joseph or Mr Gordy. But we were used to repetition so there were no groans.

For Michael, it was his first real lesson in dissecting and understanding a song's anatomy. Mr Gordy would hear something, find everything wrong with it and strip it away until the song was wearing nothing but its drumbeat. 'Less is more ... less is more,' he said, tinkering with the lyric sheet, scribbling his changes with a pen. If he felt the drums needed something extra, he added it; if the bass was too busy or not busy enough, he changed it; if the keyboards needed less impact, he softened them; if the strings wailed too much, he'd pare them down. He put a song under a microscope and peeled away every element. He listened to its playback and instantly knew where the kinks were and what note needed fixing.

And his painstaking attention to detail was worthwhile because when we heard the finished product of 'I Want You Back', it sounded incredible; the difference between a song sounding 'sensational' or like it contained everything but the kitchen sink. 'Less is more, boys ... less is more.' He winked.

Musicians who would work with Michael in the future would see this stringent perfectionism mirrored in his song production, too. 'I'll make musicians do something several hundred to a thousand times till it is what I want it to be,' he once said. As taught at Motown.

Everyone who ever came into Michael's life during his musical journey was there to hone and enhance what was innate within him. When you have worked with the greatest writers and musicians of all time, the acquired knowledge enables your ear to listen to any song from anyone else, pick it apart and know what is wrong or missing, and your soul can't rest until the feeling hits home. Mr Gordy was the first to teach us that music is a mosaic and every single piece matters. That is why, at the end of all my future solo albums, I wrote on the sleeve: 'Thank you, Mr Gordy – you've taught me well.'

WE GAVE 'I WANT YOU BACK' its first run out before a select, invited crowd at the Daisy Disco nightclub in Beverly Hills. It was some PR night and we were introduced by 'the woman who discovered us', Diana Ross. Days later, we opened for her and the Supremes at LA's main venue, the Inglewood Forum, home of the LA Lakers. We were being teased gradually into the outside world, but the *Los Angeles Times* seemed indifferent to our inclusion on the bill with the Eddie Hawkins Singers and young soul singer Edward Starr: 'Unfortunately, the supporting line-up was not nearly as interesting as the time they were given,' it said. Not everyone could see the diamond in the rough at the start.

We made our television début as musical guests at the telecast of the Miss Black America Pageant in Madison Square Garden, New York, and then we hit prime-time on ABC's Saturday-night *The Hollywood Palace Show*, where guest host Diana Ross introduced us. In newspapers, there were articles with headlines like 'JACKSON 5 – THE NEW DIANA ROSS GROUP'. In *Variety* magazine, the show was hyped with a full-page ad that read: 'Pick up on Diana's discovery ... everyone will be picking up this red-hot single.' Later, publicity photos from the show placed Diana at our centre, applying makeup to Michael's face and lowering his microphone. Publicly, it must have seemed like we were joined at the hip to her and that was by design: she was already huge so Mr Gordy wanted to deflect some of her shine on to us. It's like, if Michael Jordan presents a new basketball player, everyone is going to listen up and pay attention. And so it was with the whole 'Diana Presents the Jackson 5' vibe. That was why it became the name of our début album. She had the most juice in Motown, she liked us, we hung out at her house – and she was soon going solo. It was a perfect fit.

Come the broadcast, we knew Mother would be watching with Randy, La Toya, Janet and whoever else could cram into our living room in Gary. She'd later tell us that she held her breath for those two minutes 44 seconds, with tears running down her face. Diana introduced us twice that night as 'Michael Jackson and the Jackson 5', which made Joseph frown, because we were the Jackson 5 and no one should get singled out, but the semantics were lost on us. After all, in our earlier days, club promoters had given special billing to Johnny. We had been 'The Jackson 5 with Johnny Jackson' for a few shows, and it said so on the front of his bass drum. So, special billing for Michael seemed no different. Besides, at the end of our song, she made amends in Joseph's eyes when she came over to us to lead the applause: 'YAY! The Jackson 5, ladies and gentlemen!'

That was the night we first met the great Sammy Davis Junior. When Sammy saw what Michael could do, he referred to him as 'the little midget', which wasn't usually appreciated but somehow sounded fine from the mouth of a legend. Sammy always rocked back on his feet in mock-astonishment when he saw Michael because he couldn't believe how well he knew his movements and delivered a song. 'This kid's not supposed to know so much at his age!'

Michael couldn't watch enough of his movies and performances because Sammy was the ultimate all-round entertainer – song, dance, music, comedy, acting – as well as the first black cowboy we had followed on TV. And all that Michael could talk about was how Sammy played Vegas. 'That's where we need to perform – that's where everyone performs!' he said. 'That's what Sammy does and that's what we should be doing – giving 'em a show they'll never forget!' This is why Michael became who he became, because of the greats we rubbed shoulders with. They were around to look up to. There were so many genuine greats back then and he took elements from that collective to mix into his own pot and create something even greater.

WE HAPPILY SURVIVED ANOTHER LIVE TELEVISION performance, this time on *The Ed Sullivan Show*. Just before air-time, we were standing alongside the host as he took several rapid draws on his cigarette. *What's that? Nerves?* He caught me staring at him. 'Do you do that each time before you go on?' I asked.

He threw the stub on the floor and squashed it like a fly, grinding it with his foot. 'Sure do!' He skipped out to start the show, all smiles.

I remember this occasion for another image, too – Michael wearing a wide-brimmed pink hat with his blue waistcoat and brown-patterned shirt. It's become a classic image over the years, but what people never saw was the panic behind that clashing costume choice. We had arrived at the studios and, by now, Michael had developed as great a love for hats as drummer Johnny. Headgear was now part of the look, especially for Jackie, Marlon and Michael. The problem was that someone had forgotten the hats for *The Ed Sullivan Show*. Poor Suzanne de Passe had to dash out and grab what she could from Greenwich Village Market – and pink for Michael was all that she could find. Michael stared at himself in the mirror – all pink, blue and brown – and said, 'I like it!' He never was afraid of standing out in a crowd when it came to fashion.

FIVE BROTHERS, JOSEPH, HIS BROTHER LAWRENCE and Jack Richardson formed a welcome party at Los Angeles airport for Mother, La Toya, Randy and Janet. It had been almost three months since we'd seen them. When Mother came around the corner at Arrivals, it was like she had walked in the door with a pocketful of hot Spanish peanuts. We smothered her. We couldn't wait to show her our new home: a three-storey, detached house with a front path that zigzagged its way to the front door, about 15 feet higher than the road. Below us was Sunset Boulevard. Behind us were different homes, stacked around the hills. But the main thing was that it was 10 times the size of 2300 Jackson Street.

As Mother went on her disbelieving tour of the house, we followed her everywhere. When she reached her new master bedroom with a near-panoramic view of Los Angeles, she almost cried. It was night-time so the city was bejewelled with lights. 'That is the most beautiful sight I have ever seen,' she said.

We all remembered the bricks in our old backyard. 'I told you I'd get you a bigger house, didn't I?' said Joseph.

QUEENS ROAD MARKED THE BEGINNING OF our fondness for wild and exotic animals. Michael acquired some pet rats, finally earning reluctant parental approval nine years after his beating for feeding the rodent behind the fridge in Gary. And Hazel Gordy, knowing I loved reptiles, turned up on my sixteenth birthday with a wooden box housing a boa constrictor we called Rosie – coincidence, or a deliberate reminder of the stripper we met? I honestly can't remember …

Michael preferred the faster pace of rats. He allowed one to hang from his back, digging its claws into his shoulder-blades, then scurrying up and over his arms, neck and head. His pets soothed him. In 1972, he sang the Oscar-nominated title song for the movie *Ben* – a story about a lonely boy whose best friend is his pet rat, Ben: art was accidentally imitating his life because our house was soon overrun with rats. Michael – unknown to anyone – had started breeding his pets with the wild rats outside, so a cage of two or three soon became a small colony and there must have been eight or 10 of them, running through the closets, over our shoes, in our clothes. Mother was furious and told him to stop breeding them or he'd lose them all.

That was when we started feeding them to Rosie. We figured she needed to grow, and Michael needed to control his rat population. Plus it honoured the natural food chain. 'We're getting ready to feed Rosie!' Michael shouted, and a dozen footsteps pounded up the stairs to watch the great event. We opened the front lid of the aquarium and let the rat scurry from the palm of his hand, leaving us all eating our clenched fists, barely able to observe Rosie's first banquet. 'Poor rat,' said Michael. From that day on, we fed the rats to her until they'd all gone.

We didn't tell our neighbours about the pets we kept – we didn't wish to alarm anyone. Anyway, we had enough complaints about the noise we made in rehearsals. It became so bad that Motown had to transfer us to a new rented home north of Beverly Hills in Bowmont Drive. It was a 12-roomed, one-level house built on stilts, which meant we had to drive under it to get inside. But I liked it because the actor James Cagney was our closest neighbour. In my mind, this meant we really had arrived in Hollywood.

OUR LIFE IN LOS ANGELES WAS soon a repetitive loop of school, studio, sleep, school, studio, sleep. We just kept on working with new songs, building material for our début album, *Diana Ross Presents the Jackson 5*. Its prospects looked good because our single releases had gone through the roof. 'I Want You Back' went to No.

1 not just in the R&B charts but in the Billboard Hot 100, selling two million copies in six weeks in America, then catching fire in the UK, the rest of Europe, Australia, New Zealand, Japan and Israel. In February 1970, we followed up with 'ABC' which also went No. 1, selling two million copies in three weeks. Three months later 'The Love You Save' sealed our hat-trick of No. 1s with another two million copies sold – and all three 45s would keep on selling. Mr Gordy's forecast had come good: three back-to-back No. 1s. We couldn't have felt more on top of the world. And now Motown was ready to take our music on tour across America – and that was when the madness started.

CHAPTER SEVEN

Jackson-mania

IT WAS LIKE THE BEGINNING OF a small earthquake: a first tremor felt in the balls of the feet. We must have been five numbers into a 15-song set at our first official Motown concert at the Spectrum arena in Philadelphia and we knew something wasn't right. *What was that? Did you feel that?* Michael kept singing. All I could see was his back as he bobbed and danced and clicked his fingers on the stage's edge. In front of him – almost within touching distance – a mass of fans was pulling at their own hair, screaming hysterically and crying; a wailing wall of teens and pre-teens, and outstretched arms.

Hundreds of fans from a 16,000 crowd had left their assigned seats and poured down the aisles, getting the most from their $5.50 tickets and pushing their combined weight against a stage not designed for a crush. That was when the tremors started; the first hint of trouble. Michael looked back at me as he sang. Now the stage was slanting as its underneath supports started to buckle. Behind me, my bass amp fell, Johnny's cymbals crashed down and five mic stands were swaying.

This wasn't the curtain raiser we'd had in mind. We looked to the wings – Joseph, Suzanne de Passe and Bill Bray, our new security man, were waving us off, yelling, 'GET OFF THE STAGE! GET OFF THE STAGE!'

A fire marshal marched out front, waving his arms. 'SHUT IT DOWN! SHUT IT DOWN!' The lights came up and the screams reached breaking-glass decibels as fans realised the concert was ending abruptly – at which point the fun and games really started. I hurriedly unhooked the strap across my shoulder and dumped my bass – leaving it there – and we brothers ran for the wings. 'GO! GO! GO!' Michael and Marlon were always the quickest, running up front. We were shepherded by someone, leaping down the side steps and sprinting backstage, through the corridors and into the belly of the arena. We knew fans had swarmed the stage and given chase.

'DON'T STOP! KEEP RUNNING! KEEP RUNNING!' someone shouted. From backstage, a crowd's roar always sounded like a constantly crashing wave, and that wave was coming down the corridors. In those days there was no such thing as crowd barriers or tight security. Not at first, anyway. So, we bolted for the up-ramp of the loading zone, leading outside from beneath the arena, where our limo was waiting, engine idling, doors open. Ahead of us, girls were running down the ramp. Behind us, girls were closing the gap. With seven running jumps, we bundled into the limo, ending up in a heap on top of one another as the doors slammed shut, back in the relative safety of our leather seats and blackened windows, breathless, shaking, exhilarated and bewildered.

'You all okay?' asked Bill Bray, leaning back from the front seat. *Yeah, we're okay.* As the limo crawled up the ramp into daylight, the fans surrounded us, throwing themselves on the hood, running alongside the vehicle, banging on the windows, crying for us not to leave. From stage to stadium exit, it was crazy, and somewhere in that kinetic bond between group and fans, people had lost it. Michael had one word for it: 'wild' – 'We sent 'em wild, huh?' – and then he bemoaned the fact we never got to finish the song.

As our limo disentangled itself and managed to pull away from the arena, he knelt on the back seat and looked out from the narrow rear window. That was when we discovered how determined our fans were. 'BILL! THEY'RE STILL COMING! THEY'RE RUNNING! THEY'RE RUNNING!' yelled Michael. A bunch of girls were sprinting after us as if their lives depended on it.

'Look at how fast that girl is running!' one of us said, as the pack receded into the distance. Michael was already chuckling. 'LOOK at that girl's titties wobbling!' he added, and we giggled all the way back to the hotel, mainly out of relief.

NOTHING COULD HAVE MADE US READY for what they called 'Jackson-mania'. The scale of our popularity had been invisible to us before Philadelphia. Sure, it had registered in record sales, chart positions, newspaper articles and sacks of fan mail, and we had jumped around in celebration as the first child group to sell more than a million records. But there was nothing tangible because we had been 'hidden away', confined to our Motown cocoon, the windowless walls of the recording studio and the sleepy, late-night limo rides home. In the television studios, we only ever received sedate applause. Even at school, nothing hinted towards the crazy days ahead. At Bancroft Middle, which Marlon, La Toya and I attended, we had kids asking for autographs and everyone wanted to befriend us. Suddenly we became the 'cool kids' from Indiana and the increased attention was something we laughed about when we arrived home at the end of the day: Jackie and Tito from Fairfax High, and Michael from Gardner Elementary, where his main buddy was Mr Gordy's son, Kerry. It was only when we stepped onstage that the reality of Motown's making truly hit us. 'You boys better get used to it!' said Mr Gordy, 'I told you there'd be pandemonium!'

Sure enough, the craziness continued at the Cow Palace in San Francisco and the Inglewood Forum back in LA, where two things happened: we set a new record for the highest attendance at an entertainment venue (18,675) and we caused 'a near riot' among the fans, according to the newspapers. Chaos would become a regular event at every venue around the world. Someone in the camp tried to explain the fans' reaction to us, saying that they 'own your music, love your music, and think they own you – that's what they're plugging into every time you perform.'

The beginning of this communion felt peculiar at first because we weren't stars, we were five brothers from Indiana. With that initial mind-set, we looked at girls and thought, what's gotten into you? or why you crying like that? Why are you falling to pieces? We had met our idols – Smokey Robinson, the Temptations, Jackie Wilson – and had maintained our composure. Don't get me wrong, we soon got used to it because when something becomes an everyday occurrence, it loses its strangeness. The very thing that had bewildered us turned into a thrill we thrived on. This was the beginning of fame and we had never considered 'fame' before. Or adulation. We had only ever thought about success and being the best. The change was swift and dizzying.

At the Forum, Papa Samuel and Mother, holding Janet asleep in a blanket, sat in the front row. I think Janet, then four, was the only person in America who could ever claim to have slept through a Jackson 5 concert.

Mother said she couldn't believe her eyes. 'All I could see was my babies being chased and running for cover, and I worried for you.' Rebbie came to see us in Kentucky, but spent half her time watching the fans, not us. 'How can they hear the music if they scream like that?' she asked.

Even Joseph was intrigued. 'The last time I saw people wail and faint like that was when I was a kid at the Baptist church,' he joked. It was mass approval that he couldn't argue with.

From state to state, the craziness and record sales kept escalating, heightened by the June 1970 release of our fourth single, 'I'll Be There', which topped the charts – making us the first group to come out of the gates with four straight No. 1s. In our first year, we sold 10 million singles worldwide. It was unbelievable then, it's unbelievable to me now.

By the time of our fourth concert at Boston Gardens, Boston, Motown had installed increased security, so we had police protection at arenas and motorcades to sweep us through each city. Venues ensured that police were posted to the front and side of the stage. We rehearsed our 'exit strategy' during sound checks, running through our evacuation like it was a dance routine. The roadies told me never to dump my bass again, so Tito and I learned to run with our guitars (which turned running to the limo into a fine art, let me tell you). As brothers, we also made a time-saving pact: 'When it's time to run, it's every man for himself. Don't hang around, just keep running and head for the car.' Ultimately, we had our mad-dash exit – at the end of a finished show or an interrupted one – down to a personal best of 30 seconds from stage to limo.

We savoured the build-up and beginning of a concert: backstage, standing in a huddle, stacking our hands in the middle, vowing to go out there and 'hurt 'em'. Then the arena was plunged into darkness, triggering the roar. In that pitch-black, we took our positions at our microphones, heads down, feeling the energy emitted by the crowd. Feeling everything, seeing nothing. Johnny played the opening drum-beat of 'Stand!'. Then Ronny on the keyboards. The lights beamed on and everything went wild.

From the stage, the sight of fans rushing forward was one unforgettable spectacle. At its worst, if you happened to be sitting in a row in the path of this stampede, it was time to run or be trampled. From Michael's front-of-stage perspective, he said it was an optical illusion – 'like the walls are falling in as everyone funnels down the middle.' We saw girls fight and climb over one another to reach the front. They wept. They fainted. They were carried away on stretchers.

One thing Michael *never* understood was why teenage girls took off their bras and panties and threw them onstage. 'Ugh! Why do they do that?' he said. It probably reminded him too much of Rosie from the striptease nights, but the rest of the brothers didn't mind. I lost count of the nights I had underwear hanging from the neck of my bass as I played. Many times, girls ran onstage and the police often seemed stretched to keep order. We learned to expect fans to appear out of nowhere mid-song, grabbing or hugging us until they were bundled away.

Often, we had to retreat offstage. I remember being in Detroit and our one-time promoter E. Rodney Jones took the mic to appeal for calm: 'The Jackson 5 want to finish the show, but you must go back to your seats … Go back to your seats otherwise the show will be cancelled for safety reasons,' he warned.

After three futile warnings, the fire marshal ran out and the lights went up. 'SHUT IT DOWN! SHUT IT DOWN!' It was a joke among us that being a fire marshal almost guaranteed a walk-on part in most cities.

Ironically, the times when we *really* had to run for our lives were at the end of a completed concert, because fans left early and bolted for the venue's exit to mob our car. Those were the scariest times because it was as comfortable as running through a giant rosebush. Once inside the vehicle, we could never see out of the windows because the mass of bodies eclipsed daylight. When that limo rocked on its wheels, it was one unnerving experience. Once we tried to calm the situation by rolling down the window to slip out an autograph: 10 hands grabbed at the piece of paper, tearing it to shreds, piranha-style. Bill Bray yelled, '*Never* do that again! They'll pull your arms off!'

He didn't seem to appreciate that we already knew what it felt like to almost lose a limb, because getting through the mob – at venues or airports, or when out and about – was a bruising experience. Everyone pulled on our arms, hands, shoulders, faces, heads and hair. For me, there was only one way to negotiate the mêlée: take running jumps, because the bouncing momentum kept me going without getting snared. Michael just stayed low, hands covering his face, and ducked through like a little dynamo.

Back at the hotels, we compared the cuts, scratches and bruises that became souvenirs from different cities, and Wardrobe assessed the damage to our ripped shirts. None of the fans intended to hurt us, we knew that much, but we still had to talk it through and get it out of our systems, especially about those girls who ran on stage.

Michael: 'Did you see the way she just flew at me? Didn't see her coming!'

Tito: 'I was thinking, damn, he better start running.'

Michael: 'Did you see how she was acting? Kiss me, kiss me – she was stuck to me!'

Me: 'And she did that thing – went all limp to make herself heavier.' And I'd do the play-dead impression that girls used to do and we'd die laughing.

Management's concern was always *our* welfare and one day, someone came up with the idea of a decoy strategy: use a VW as our getaway car and let the fans follow the empty limo. Which they did. Unfortunately, the brains that ordered the Volkswagen hadn't reckoned on enough space for seven boys, Joseph and Bill Bray. We had no choice – and no time – but to cram in. We were all legs and feet, kissing the car's roof, the windows and each other, but we got away. Back then, that was all that mattered.

But the fans tried to outsmart us, too, by trying to catch us unawares. Instead of rushing the stage (which we expected) they started rushing the planes. This trend started in Detroit in about 1971. We landed, the plane was taxiing and we prepared to disembark when Jackie glanced out of the window and shouted, 'THEY'RE COMING!' In the days when airport security was as tight as it was at a supermarket car-parking lot, this mob of fans had broken free from a police cordon in the distance and was wheeling towards us. We couldn't hang around for the plane's steps to arrive: the stewardesses opened the door and we jumped to the ground, piled into the limo and got away in the nick of time.

Undeterred, other fans waited in cars at the airport exits to follow us, girls tracked us down to our hotels, and some hid in the bushes in the hotel grounds to sneak inside later as 'hotel guests'. They followed us to sound checks and shopping malls, and the chase was back on, causing chaos on the occasions when we dared go sightseeing in different cities. If a counter or shelf was in the way, the fans just bulldozed through as we ran and ran.

I'll never forget the time we managed to blend unnoticed into a massive crowd – there must have been 50,000 people – when we went to the Grambling–Cal State Fullerton Classic at the LA Coliseum to catch some football. Jackie was in heaven, and all was going so well until the announcer got overexcited and revealed to the crowd that (a) we were inside the stadium and (b) where we were seated. We looked at each other, we watched all these people stand and turn, and we knew what was coming next. As the *Los Angeles Sentinel* said: 'The Jackson 5 had to literally run for their lives when they were introduced …'

The weirdest thing was ringing home to check in with Mother and being told that fans were camped outside the house, having made the trek from Sunset Boulevard.

'Are you okay?' we asked her.

'Oh, yes, I'm fine,' she said. 'I just invited them in and gave them some drinks.'

'Why did you have to invite them in, Mother?'

'Well, I couldn't be impolite and turn them away, could I?'

Janet would tell us that different posses of girls would sit around the kitchen table for hours, staying until about eleven o'clock at night because Mother couldn't bring herself to be 'rude' and ask them to leave. We all took a while to adjust to fame back in those days. It was a different age of 'celebrity'.

Back then, the hunt wasn't led by the paparazzi looking for a photo but by the fans wanting a piece of us, tracking us down to hotels, and camping outside our house. It didn't upset us, and previous suggestions that Michael was reduced to constant tears after a mobbing are not true. We all found the mad pursuits scary at times, but Michael thrived on the adulation, as we all did: it told him we were doing good; it told him we were loved. His only frustration was that the finale was ruined or cut short most nights, but he accepted early on that the craziness was part of the transaction made with the fans. 'They're the ones buying the records and coming to the concerts,' he said. 'They're making this happen, not Joseph, not Motown, not us.'

He never lost his respect for the fans: he regarded them as a second family and he, like the rest of us, would share a unique relationship with them in an age when accessibility was far greater than it is today. He always viewed his fan base as peripheral friends, people he truly cared about and loved.

Of course, there are always extremes, and some fans would make an impact in strange ways. But it would be a little longer before the 'Billie Jean' type showed up.

POST-SHOW, POST-GREAT ESCAPE, WE'D TURN ON the television in our hotel room and catch the local news. It was the strangest thing, watching ourselves – and all that mania – on TV. Michael watching Michael was a sight to see, because he studied himself in the concert snippets as closely as he had previously examined James Brown or Sammy Davis Junior. It was the one time of day when he was quiet, critiquing himself, watching every move, finding room for improvement. He didn't know how good he was. People rave about Michael Jackson the artist who erupted in the eighties, but he had it back then in the seventies, too. Take it from someone who was alongside him for every show: he was electrifying as a boy and he knew how to get the crowd going. His personality, delivery and sheer vocal authority bossed it, and he spoke like a leader, not our 12-year-old brother. 'Are ya READY, fellas?' he said, counting us in, or, when a song had gone really well, he yelled, 'Right on!' – taking a phrase from Marvin Gaye – and the audience cheered. '*Riiiight ooon!*' he said, louder, and the place went nuts.

And Jackie stoked the hype by goading everyone's emotions: 'Do you want to take it higher? YOU WANT IT HIGHER?'

Performing provided a sense of euphoria that is hard to describe. Imagine being Clark Kent turning into Superman and every city believing in your power. I guess that's pretty much how it felt.

During press junkets, reporters were always fascinated by Michael's precocious talent and they tried to extract the great, grand answer by asking the most unoriginal question: 'Michael, how do you do it? Where does it come from?' Michael, usually flipping the pages of a magazine that was his defence barrier, looked up and practised the device taught at Motown: repeat the question to give yourself time to think about your answer, 'How do I do it?'

'Yes ... everyone wants to know.'

Then came the great, grand answer: 'Most of the time, I don't know what I'm doing. I'm just doing my best – I'm just performing.'

It was like asking a bird how it flies: it doesn't know, it just flaps its wings and takes off.

With all that adrenalin in our systems, it was almost impossible to get to sleep and it wasn't as if we could release it with a quick sprint around the local park or a brisk walk in the fresh air because the fans not only laid siege to our hotel, they roamed the corridors to find us, looking for the one man they recognised – our security guy, Bill Bray. Find Bill, and you had the Jackson 5. He was always sitting on a chair outside our rooms or in the room directly opposite, door open, watching the television. Bill's job description was, he told us, 'to make sure no girls come up and none of you go down to get girls.'

Once – I think it was in Chicago – three girls turned up at the exact moment he'd thought it was safe to take a toilet break. Michael, Marlon and I had just ordered room service when we heard an over-keen knock on the door – Bill was neither keen nor a knocker. He'd always say, 'Open the door, jokers.'

We looked through the peep-hole and saw three young concave faces holding their mouths, trying not to scream. Until they heard Michael ask, 'Who is it?'

Then they couldn't help themselves. They started hammering on the door, screaming to be let in. 'MICHAEL! MICHAEL! Just let us see you ... just let us in ... one minute ...' On one side, three fans hammering for their lives on a door. On the other, three brothers with their backs pressed against it, heels dug into the carpet, just in case the girls tried to barge through. That sounds crazy, but trust me, when you've seen a mob of girls tear up a stage, there's no question which is the stronger sex.

Because the fans were *everywhere*, our enforced confinement didn't provide too many options to relax and breathe, which meant seven boys were bouncing off the walls with pent-up energy. We had to release it somehow so, with Bill's approval, we used to hold sprints in the corridor, or see who could walk to one end and back fastest. We had the wildest pillow fights and I don't know how many mattresses we wrecked by using them as trampolines.

Within our own unconstrained craziness, Michael was in his element. As chief prankster, he had a hoard of itching powder, whoopie cushions, stink bombs and water balloons. Dropping water balloons on to strangers' heads from hotel windows, letting off stink bombs in elevators, and leaving plastic ice buckets of water balanced on a door left a little way open were among his favourite tricks and booby-traps. He'd get us all doing it, mainly dousing Suzanne de Passe, Bill Bray, Jack Richardson and Motown's PR man, Bob Jones. Suzanne always knew we had something up our sleeves and entered with extra-caution, but Bob walked into it every time.

Those nights in hotels were probably hardest for Jackie, then 20 going on 21, and Tito, 17. They knew that roadies not much older than them were going to nightclubs and blues cafés, and yet they remained under curfew; Jackie on his bed, watching sports on the TV, Tito at his desk, gluing Airfix models of planes and battleships.

I think Bill Bray felt sorry for us, because he saw how hard we travelled, rehearsed, performed and ran, yet there was no real down-time on the road. We did about 15 dates in 1970 before our first major national tour in '71, when we did approximately 46 dates, east to west, plus numerous television shows, media interviews and appearances. Bill was an ex-detective assigned to us by Motown, an avuncular figure. Broad, light-skinned, with thinning hair and a salt-and-pepper beard, he was hard of hearing so we always had to yell. We nicknamed him 'Shack Pappy' and respected him enormously, mainly because he could take a joke. Sometimes the pace of our schedule got to him and he fell asleep backstage or at the hotel before a performance. Michael, lightest on his feet, would creep up and tie his shoelaces together and retreat to the door. Then we'd scream in pretend panic, 'BILL! BILL! HELP!' He'd jump up and fall flat on his face.

Our rapport with Bill was special and it meant he was more forgiving if, beyond eleven o'clock, he spotted us trying to tiptoe by his station. 'I see you, joker! I see you!' he'd shout.

'Bill!' I'd say. 'I just want a midnight feast!' There was always a vending machine down by the icebox at the end of any corridor and it became the focus of many late-night sorties to get extra cookies, chips and Coke.

'Now get yourself to bed before Joseph comes back,' he'd say.

MICHAEL VIEWED MUSIC AS A 'SCIENCE' as well as a feeling. From the moment we moved into Bowmont Drive, he started to study composition. He strove to understand the make-up of someone's song in the same way a scientist set out to understand a person's DNA. Together we tuned into any classical station we could find on the radio, listening to the structure of a piece of music and 'seeing' what colour, mood and emotion each instrument would create. 'It's about seeing the music, not just hearing it,' he said. Hear a tinkling piano, see rainfall. Hear the English horn, see the sun rise or set. Hear the cello played with the bow, see mystery or sadness. Hear the song, see the story.

Michael's favourite composition was *The Nutcracker Suite* by Tchaikovsky but he loved so many classical pieces, how they started slowly with the strings, swelled into something dramatic or racing, then calmed again. This structure – the A-B-A form – was something we constantly dissected. And this classical inspiration runs as a thread through so much of his music because his forte was being able to combine a melodic structure and great lyrical content with a beat that gave it the pop feel. Next time you listen to 'Heartbreak Hotel' or 'Dirty Diana', for example, you'll better detect the classical thread running through them: the instrumentation he used to enhance the story. Listen to the cello in both those songs and the set-up it provides. Or listen to the opening chord progressions of 'Thriller' and the suspense they build, the dread you feel. Michael always wanted you to listen to his music, close your eyes and visualise.

AS CO-LEAD VOCALS, MICHAEL AND I shared a bedroom on the road. From a bunk-bed for five, we progressed to the luxury of a twin bed each. On occasions, Marlon would share with us, too, but he usually doubled up with Tito, then it was Johnny and Ronny, and Jackie had a room to himself. Different bedrooms didn't really affect our togetherness because we still went everywhere as one unit. It infuriated Michael that Joseph always insisted on an adjoining room to keep an eye on us, probably because he knew Michael was the prankster and that my interest in girls had awakened. As Motown's designated 'heart-throb', that was my role!

Joseph could walk into our room whenever he liked via his connecting door, which Michael hated: it made him feel policed. Unable to be free outside the hotel, he was also unable to escape our father's scrutiny inside. If we ever laughed beyond eleven o'clock, Joseph thumped the wall several times: 'GO TO SLEEP, YOU TWO! REST THOSE VOICES.' Michael rolled his eyes. 'IF YOUR VOICES GO, THERE'S NO SHOW, AND IF THERE'S NO SHOW ...' The unspoken end to that sentence always hung in the air. We understood. 'The Hawk' never missed a thing.

But Michael was no better. Whenever he heard our father's booming voice on some telephone call, he would grab a glass, cup it to his ear and listen at the wall. He did this whenever we were asked to leave the room at Motown, too: he was fascinated by what was being said, especially when he heard his name mentioned. Michael was born nosy, a trait inherited from our father's mother, Mama Chrystal. He said the best gadget to have would be a hearing aid to amplify people's distant conversations and whispers, allowing him to eavesdrop. 'Can you imagine how cool that would be?' he mused. 'Then we'd know everything Joseph was planning!' His need to know what was being said would extend to label executives and attorneys, but that came later, in his solo career.

He was curious as to what the fans talked about, too. In many cities, we turned out the lights and knelt at the window to look down on the courtyard or parking lot to watch car loads of fans arrive. At times, it looked as busy as a drive-in theatre, with clusters of people around many pairs of headlights. They chanted our names and blared their horns, oblivious that we were watching them silently. It was a spectacle to us, and kept us fascinated for many an hour. This window was no more than a grander version of the one in our bedroom at 2300 Jackson Street. We had advanced from wannabe rehearsals to dreamy stardom but it had done nothing to alter the sense of 'them and us'. Now we looked out from the dream and the other kids looked into it. And the grass, at times, looked greener from both sides. Especially to Michael.

We knew one thing was certain, though: other kids didn't wake up to find two or three pretty chambermaids standing at the foot of their bed, taking photos and giggling ... with a laughing Joseph standing alongside, endorsing it. Our father was an early bird; we liked to sleep in. With his access via our connecting door, we'd hear him in our half-sleep brightly offering to introduce his sons. 'Do you wanna see the boys?' Next thing we knew the bedclothes were being pulled off us, leaving us lying there in our pyjamas with squinting eyes and smashed-up Afros. For a man who was all about us presenting the right image, it seemed an odd thing to do. But that was Joseph's joke – catching us unawares.

On the occasions when Michael got wise and locked the door, we'd be woken by an angry Joseph. 'OPEN THIS DOOR NOW, BOY!' He didn't stop yelling until we did. When he brought the maids in, we got mad internally but we couldn't speak up because we had to respect him. That was just how it was.

Michael and I seemed to spend all our down-time together in those days and the bond between us was sealed tight. I cannot remember an argument or a fight in our childhood. In fact, there was rarely any friction between any of the brothers. I had no reason to fight with Michael or Marlon because they were too little. My rumbles were always with Tito when play-fights got out of hand, instigated by Jackie. But we had too much of a team spirit among brothers to get real mad at one another. Michael looked up to me; I looked out for him. Onstage, he was always to my right. In hotels, he was always in the bed to the left. If I couldn't see Michael, and know he was okay, I didn't feel at ease. At night, either on the road or back in LA, his bedtime reading was either *The Jungle Book* or *The Guinness Book of Records*. 'I want to be the entertainer that sells the most records,' he said one night. 'I want my name to appear in this book!'

We talked ourselves to sleep about anything and everything, and we shared each other's fan mail – the racy, romantic, mushy stuff to me from 16-year-olds, and the cutesy, you're-adorable stuff to him from 10-year-olds.

He laughed at the marriage proposals I received and teased me about how 'coooool' I thought I was. We even introduced this to an onstage skit he did during a talk spot between songs. 'Ladies, Jermaine thinks he's *sooooo cooool* on his gueee-tar ...' the arena roared '... but, ya know, we gonna change all that ...' cue more hysteria '... because we gonna do our own thing and be just like Jermaine!' And we launched into a performance of 'It's Your Thing'.

The only thing Michael and I fought over was the bathroom mirror. Each brother had a blown-out Afro and we were always picking and patting our hair, using a hair pick to fluff it out, then patting it down with our hands to create that perfectly round shape before we added the Afro Sheen for shine. We were proud of our voluminous hair: they were our Afro crowns. On planes, we learned to sleep with our heads dropped forward to avoid crushing the Afro. Not good for the neck, but it maintained the shape! Michael's time spent in front of the mirror was almost as long as mine, so it was always a chase to pole position first thing each morning. I argued that I had the biggest and thickest hair, and he argued that he was front of stage and had the hair the girls most wanted to grab. Every detail about our hair – and skin – had to be *just right*.

ON THE ROAD, MICHAEL'S OTHER HABIT was room service; the most decadent perk of the music industry in his eyes. When he felt particularly mischievous at night, he'd ring up as someone else's child and place the biggest bogus order to a different room. But his funniest ruse was calling one of the roadies and using his high voice to impersonate a girl fan. Jack Nance, our road manager and Jack Richardson, our driver-come-right hand man, were always our favourite targets. When they picked up their room phone Michael spoke into the receiver and introduced himself as a girl fan: 'I saw you tonight ... I love the way you looked,' he squeaked, and then detailed what Jack had been wearing that day for added authenticity, '... and I was a fan of Michael's but you stole my eye ...'

I was laughing so hard that I had to go into the bathroom, but Michael kept it going with a straight face: 'What do I look like?' (cue the shy giggle) 'Well, I'm tall, slim and very pretty ... all my girls tell me so ... How old am I? I'm almost sixteen,' he'd say. He kept this going for a good ten minutes, teasing them and pumping their egos, but we never once let on it was us. We just let them believe that they, too, had adoring fans. The next morning, when we saw either Jack in the hotel lobby, looking all dour and serious, Michael nudged me and whispered: 'Old dogs – they dirrrrty.'

IF THERE WAS ONE CITY THAT didn't totally put out the Jackson-mania welcome mat, it was Mobile, Alabama. We had looked forward to this date because it returned us to Mother's roots, but there was no warm home-coming. The fan reaction wasn't the problem – that was typically raucous. It was the reception outside the arena that provided a sober lesson in the rich diversity of America. Our parents had warned us about the infamous preju-dices of the Deep South and how black communities were still awakening after the Montgomery bus boycotts of the 1950s, and the civil rights stand that had brought violence from the white supremacists of the Ku Klux Klan. We had seen images of grown men walking around with sheets on their heads, and we had seen them burning crosses, but our knowledge of history was scant until our first-hand experience in Alabama, in January 1971.

The first difference we noted was when the white driver of our limousine was cold and abrupt, not talkative like other drivers we'd had. At our hotel, he refused to get out of the car and open our doors, and no staff came out to help us with our bags either. This wasn't a spoiled-kid expectation, it was just an observation of a sharp difference in our treatment. It was as we pulled our bags out of the trunk that one of us noticed some KKK parapher-nalia, clearly intended for our eyes. We froze. It was like one of those moments in a thriller movie when you realise your driver has been the killer the whole time; it felt that sinister. We stayed quiet and kept our heads down. At the hotel reception, we faced the same cold awkwardness. 'We don't seem to have got any rooms booked for you,' said the man at the front desk, all curt and stern. Suzanne de Passe, or someone, argued that this was a long-standing booking; we were the Jackson 5 and there must be a mistake.

'No mistake. We have no rooms booked,' he repeated.

We effectively begged for a room, which we were eventually given – facing an alley and trash-cans. Michael was, typically, the first to question what had happened when we got to the basic quar-ters of our second-rate room. 'Why would someone treat us like that because of our skin colour?' he asked. It confused him because he knew our fans were both black and white, and it was the first time we had been made to feel unwanted, let alone unpopular.

It made us more determined to kick some butt onstage, because we soon recognised the importance of being black kids performing for black fans who could now identify with us. We were carrying the torch for our forefathers, winning respect for every black kid with a dream. The screams and cheers that night felt like a lot more than just Jackson-mania: they felt like defiance and victory. As

Sammy Davis Junior had said in 1965: 'Being a star has made it possible for me to get insulted in places where the average Negro could never hope to go and get insulted.'

Michael's memories of Alabama were not the greatest back then, because when we left Mobile our 727 plane hit bad weather and severe turbulence. I think we were all nervous flyers to begin with and preferred touring in the VW camper van, but we seemed to have a concert every few days so we had no choice but to take to the skies. But this flight left Michael – and me – petrified when it abruptly dropped and started shaking violently. Sitting together, we gripped the armrests tightly. When I looked to my left, Michael was crying, his eyes screwed tight. Armageddon must have flashed through both our minds, and it didn't help that the skies were dark and the cabin lights kept flickering. When the conditions calmed, a stewardess came over and crouched beside Michael to reassure us both of how normal such an event was. That calmed us – until the pilot ruined it after we landed: 'The airplane was hard to control but we got through it, didn't we?'

Our fears increased in 1972 when we saw news footage of some Eastern Airlines passenger plane going down in the Everglades, dropping from 2,000 feet during its descent into Miami.

Some time later, when it came time to leave the hotel for the airport in a city I can't remember, we couldn't find Michael. One minute he was with us, the next he was not. Bill and Joseph started to worry until instinct reminded us of a habit Michael had adopted when he was in trouble at 2300 Jackson Street. Sure enough, Bill found him hiding under the hotel bed, crying and refusing to come out. 'I'm not getting back on that airplane – I'm not! I'm *not!*' Outside, there was stormy weather and heavy rain.

Everyone tried the gentle art of negotiation – Bill, Suzanne and Jack Richardson – but the next memory I have is of seeing Bill walking from the limo to the plane steps, carrying a kicking and screaming Michael over his shoulders. Such tantrums happened a few times when Michael didn't feel safe and he usually screamed for Mother. Joseph was there, of course, but he didn't provide – or was incapable of providing – the love and comfort when needed. Instead, we brothers and a stewardess often pulled him through. And, yes, plenty of candy helped, too.

The J5 juggernaut kept trail-blazing across America and demand for us spread across the rest of the world. We had calls to perform in every major city and it was hard to understand that we were big in Australia and Japan. They seemed like other planets, but Joseph said we were 'going to conquer the world.' Our fifth single, 'Mama's Pearl', became our first song *not* to reach top spot. The same happened with 'Never Can Say Goodbye' a few months later, and we had to settle for the No. 2 position on both occasions, but neither Joseph nor Mr Gordy complained.

Whatever we had started had grown bigger than anyone imagined and seemed unstoppable. Life was coming at us so fast and none of us brothers knew where it was leading or how much better it might become. But we understood that the day the fans stopped screaming was the day we stopped playing, so we rolled out second and third albums, lined up more tour dates, and kept the profile rolling with interviews to *Teen* magazine, *Soul*, *Time*, *Life*, *Ebony* and *Rolling Stone*, the latter calling us 'THE BIGGEST THING SINCE THE STONES'. And somewhere within all of this, we managed to squeeze in school. Somehow. In Japan, we were declared 'The Most Promising Vocal Group', which followed our 1970 accolade in America – Billboard's Top Singles Recording Artists and NAACP's Image Award for Best Singing Group 1970. Motown hired Fred Rice, who had worked with the Beatles and the Monkees, to begin franchising us around the world with dolls, clothes … and hairspray. He even started talking to New York animators Rankin & Bass, the makers of ABC's *The King Kong Show*, about turning us into cartoon characters. 'I'm going to have your faces everywhere,' he said. 'You're the black Beatles.'

In our hotel room, Michael and I always expressed our dislike of that comparison. Why did everything white and great need a black equivalent? We were not the black Beatles, we were the black Jackson 5. Outwardly, when the press made the same comparison, we smiled graciously and took the compliment but this comparison ignored one fact: two of our songs – 'I'll Be There' and 'ABC' – had knocked Britain's finest from the No. 1 spot and that felt as good as anything to us. That was how fiercely proud we were, carrying forward our competitiveness from the talent-contest days. We were winners. We had to be the best. And the talent of others always forced us to raise our bar the highest.

THE ONE PLACE WE WERE GUARANTEED a warm welcome was Gary, Indiana, when we returned home to perform two concerts at Westside High School in early 1971 – our first visit 'home' in 14 months. Something like 6,000 people turned out each night, and it was all captured on camera for a television special called *Goin' Back to Indiana*.

We had landed by helicopter in the school parking lot, in the snow, and there was a real carnival vibe. Even our helicopter joined the home-coming with a banner along its tail saying: 'WELCOME HOME JACKSON 5'. We walked from the helicopter to a waiting limousine and the locals didn't so much as mob us as ogle us, fascinated by the boys who had returned from their Motown makeover. We weren't a distant fantasy on a bedroom wall to these people, we were one of them.

As we pulled around the corner and our old home came into view, we saw one difference straightaway: the new, if temporary, street sign – 'Jackson 5 Boulevard'. Everyone held up duplicates and behind them, on the snow-covered lawn in front of our house, there was a bigger sign: 'WELCOME HOME JACKSON 5 – KEEPERS OF THE DREAM'.

The street was swamped, and kids started shouting out memories.

'Remember me? We went to elementary school together!'

'You know me! I met you one time at ...'

'Michael! I was there when you sang "Climb Ev'ry Mountain"!'

And then we found the one face in the crowd we had been looking for: our old buddy Bernard Gross. We pinched his chubby cheeks and he laughed. 'You out in the sunshine making all that money now!' he said. 'Congratulations, guys, you deserve it.'

'We're still the same – not changed!' we said, which was internally true. But we noticed how most people, except Bernard, looked at us differently – looking *into us* curiously. Outwardly, the changes were obvious. We had a wardrobe department now, and we sparkled without using Vaseline. But we didn't feel better than anyone else: we just felt lucky and privileged. And we'd never thought we'd ever stand outside our house and feel privileged. It was hard going back because the taste of California had broadened our horizons. Life had moved us on, and being in Gary felt like trying on a pair of shoes you've outgrown but don't want to throw away.

Even our house seemed reduced somehow. Outside, everything appeared the same, right down to the bricks stacked in the backyard. But as soon as we stepped inside, we all said the same thing: 'How did we fit in here, let alone live here?' We brothers went to our old bedroom where our bunk-beds were no more.

Michael and I stood around, looking at the crowds in the street. 'Can you believe they've done all this for us?' he said. Then nostalgia rewrote history: 'We left behind a lot of friends, didn't we?' he said.

'Left a lot of folk behind, but gained fans around the world,' I said. 'We've got friends everywhere now.' It was optimism, which made the reality seem rosier at the time.

Outside, Mother and Joseph basked in their deserved glory. Colleagues from 'The Mill' turned up and Mother's friends from the street and Sears were there. Everyone seemed sincerely happy for us. At an official reception at the school, Gary's mayor, Richard Hatcher, said we had put the city on the world map (which was probably also why they renamed the Palace Theater the Jackson 5 Theater) and he presented us with the 'key to the city'. That was a huge honour for our family. We seemed to have the keys to the best things in life at this time, but there was something *earned* in the symbolic freedom that Gary offered; it officially recognised the struggle before the achievement.

The house still stands today, looking no different from the outside. It is occupied and still in the ownership of our parents. I'm not sure they will ever truly let go of our roots. In 1989, we came together as siblings – all nine of us – to release the song '2300 Jackson Street'. Those lyrics, which include Michael in the first verse, said more back then than I can convey without music now. It is the song of home and family, but Michael and I particularly liked the line that runs 'My friends, I won't forget your name, I'm still the same …' And that was all Michael was ever really trying to say throughout his life.

THE EARLY YEARS: (Clockwise from top left) Me as a boy; Bathtime for Michael (left) and Marlon; Joseph's pride and joy – his guitar, before Tito broke it; 2300 Jackson Street; Mother as the young woman who caught our father's eye.

HOPEFUL BEGINNINGS: (Clockwise from top left) Our first performance as the Jackson 5 was hyped as part of the 'Tiny Tots' "Jamboree'"; Our 'discovery by Diana Ross' was also big news; As this family photo shows, it was all about smiling for the cameras from an early age; Notice the bandage over my eye in this publicity photo – I was still nursing my Katz Kittens collision wound!

LEARNING CURVES: (From top to bottom) A weathered photo of Michael, Marlon, Randy and Janet standing outside our Queens Road home in Hollywood; Michael went on to score good grades at Montclair School; He made our tutor, Rose Fine, proud.

THE JACKSON 5 YEARS:
We always seemed to be
posing, rehearsing or going
to fancy places.

LIFE'S A BEACH: Michael leads the way as our front man during a TV performance on *Soul Train*; When we had down-time, we loved nothing more than hitting the beach in Santa Monica or Malibu.

(Turn To Page 56)

HEADLINERS: Front covers and inside
spreads; we were always making news
somewhere!

BACKSTAGE: One of the greatest moments in our careers – meeting Queen Elizabeth II at the Royal Variety Show, London; Michael and me relaxing backstage somewhere.

HOMECOMING: Goin' Back to Indiana in 1971 where it seemed that half of Gary turned out, re-naming our street 'Jackson 5 Blvd' for the day; And then we started growing up before the onset of teenage years changed everything.

THE MIDDLE
THE HAYVENHURST YEARS

CHAPTER EIGHT
Life Lessons

WHEN MICHAEL, AGED 13, SAW THE swimming-pool with two dolphins set into its bottom tiles, there was no question about it: Hayvenhurst was the dream house – which music had provided. It was May 1971, and Mother and Joseph put down our California roots in the LA suburb of Encino in the San Fernando Valley. Today the house is very different: then it was a bland one-storey ranch-style property, devoid of Michael's later redesign. But there was still a lot going for it because it had previously been owned by Earle Hagen, the Emmy-award-winning composer of television scores, so its walls were already charmed with music and it had its own studio. It came with six bedrooms, the pool, a basketball court and two acres of land screened by trees, set back from a main road.

We could swim till dusk and have breakfast under the morning sun, sitting on the flagstoned patio, looking out over the gardens, with lemon and orange trees. Suddenly, for the first time in our lives, we had space – although we had sacrificed views of Hollywood for the suburban practicalities of large-family living.

Our family had now grown to 13 members, with the addition of Jack Richardson and Johnny, so we needed every inch of the 8,000 square feet the house offered.

Back then, Hayvenhurst sat behind the wrought-iron rails of an electric gate – the start of life lived behind gates. The house had classic seventies décor: lots of sliding doors, plastic seating, gaudy colours and wood panelling, and we felt we'd hit the big-time with a spiral staircase that twisted its way out of the sunken living room with its wraparound couch. The sleeping arrangements now meant twin rooms for Marlon and me, Tito and Johnny, Michael and Randy, La Toya and Janet, Jackie and Ronny (with Michael and me still sharing on the road). I read somewhere that Hayvenhurst was so big that we started 'losing touch' and 'had to make plans in advance to see each other', but that wasn't true: it was a house, not a castle. Thirteen people can make 8,000 square feet feel compact.

The new house was a sure sign that we were making serious money, and we each received an allowance of five dollars a week. Michael spent his on art materials. He also developed a fascination with magical tricks – he loved the process of illusion. The more surprised Mother looked – as he turned an umbrella into a flower or when a coin disappeared from his hand – the happier he was. Mother bought new furniture for the first time and treated herself to a new wardrobe. Joseph bought a new Ford Kombi and Jackie had his own pride and joy: an orange Datsun 240Z (until the day he reached for some gum while driving and totalled it north of Ventura Boulevard).

Despite our new wealth, our parents never spoiled us. The work ethic remained in place: they didn't want us thinking that money was no object – Joseph even installed a pay-phone. And we were still given chores. Had anyone visited us on any random weekend, they would have found Tito and me doing vacuuming and laundry, Michael, Randy and Janet washing the windows, and Jackie and La Toya mopping floors and raking leaves.

Joseph still ruled. It eased from its worst excesses, but that's not to say he didn't still have a short fuse. There was a time when

Michael was dressed and ready to join Mother at the Kingdom Hall and Joseph wanted him to rehearse for a national tour. But it was a Sunday, and Michael clung to Mother. Joseph ended up smashing a window in his fury, while mother and son left to pray with Jehovah. Over time, Randy and Janet got to know what the belt felt like, mainly for disobedience, and our pre-tour rehearsals at home were still administered under the threat of a beating. We were on the world stage now; nothing could go wrong. We had 'made it' and the media endearingly referred to Joseph as 'Papa Joe', but that didn't mean he could change his character and way of being overnight.

MICHAEL RECEIVED SOME KIND OF DEATH threat. I don't remember the details, but it was enough for us to be pulled out of public school in favour of private. Nobody was taking chances, especially after one of the Supremes, Cindy Birdsong – Diana Ross's replacement – was kidnapped after being attacked in her home in the year we moved West. She was being driven to Long Beach when she managed to unlock the car door and throw herself from the moving vehicle on to the highway. Maybe that was the reason behind two new additions to the household: Lobo and Heavy, the German Shepherds. Lobo snarled to such a degree that whenever a journalist visited our house he always warranted a mention in the interview. (Fans of Janet may remember she wore a key as an earring – that was for Lobo's cage because she, as the chief dog lover of the family, ended up taking care of him.)

There was also Johnny's Dobermann. With characteristic mischief, he named him 'Hitler', but we didn't mention that to the press.

Tito, Marlon, Michael and I now attended the Walton School in Panorama City. Its liberal attitude better suited our touring requirements and we were treated as equal with everyone else. Michael still had to audition for the part he landed in a school production of *Guys and Dolls*.

One day, we brothers were hovering around the school gates when everyone's attention was caught by a hearse parking at the kerb. *Who arrives at school in a hearse? That's not cool.*

Out stepped this tall, good-looking dude with an Afro that was almost as impressive as ours. He was engaged in a full-on sulk with an adult – I think it was his mother – about not wanting to go to this lousy school, he didn't like it, and it was too far from home (he lived in Hancock Park).

Then, he turned and spotted Tito. 'Wait … You all at this school?'

'Yeah – except Jackie,' said Tito.

I have never seen a kid switch so fast from sulks to smiles. Before we knew it, John McClain, the funeral director's son, was standing on the pavement waving off his mother, thinking he had arrived at the coolest school in the world. He became a friend for life and his constant presence at our house meant that we regarded him almost as an adopted brother. As a teenager, it was clear he had musical ambitions of his own as a guitarist/songwriter/composer, and he and Tito often jammed together. John shared Michael's hunger to learn and he was fascinated by our Motown education. Whatever Mr Gordy taught us, I passed on to him. He had a mischievous side like Michael, so when those two got together, it was always double trouble.

I was standing with them in the playground one afternoon when we saw this kid called George having a great time on the swings, about 50 yards away. 'I bet you can't throw this peach and hit him on top of the head!' said Michael, daring me, forgetting my outfield accuracy.

'How much?'

Michael knew he'd hooked me. 'Two bucks.'

Game on. He handed me the peach. I adjusted my eyes to the arcs of the pendulum called George and I took aim. The peach flew and … BOOM! George swung right into it.

Michael jumped up and down – like he used to during Katz Kittens games – then ran off as George wondered who and what had hit him.

Their biggest joke was on a mouthy kid called Sean and they decided he needed teaching a lesson. John, no doubt relying on skills learned in the funeral trade, dug a hole in the school grounds, about four feet deep. I didn't witness how they got him in there, but Sean – all blond hair and Beatles cut – somehow ended up knelt in the hole as Michael and John kicked in the soil, burying him to his chest. Then, a teacher marched out.

'Who did this? Get him out of there right now!'

It was one of those rare times when I heard a teacher use the admonishing words: 'I'm surprised at you, Michael Jackson!'

Michael stuck to me like glue outside class. Wherever I looked, he was there, wearing his black velour hat, hanging in my shadow. There was one time when I thought I'd shaken him off. It was after a photography class and I'd disappeared with a girl who had invited me into the dark room because she said she wanted to kiss me. With the door shut, we were awkwardly overcoming our teenage shyness in the red luminescence, reaching the point where our lips were about to touch, when – 'I CAUGHT YA! I CAUGHT YA!' Michael burst in.

He caused such a commotion that a teacher arrived to find out what all the noise was about. As I explained my way out of being with a girl in the dark room, I heard Michael running down the hallway, laughing.

THERE WERE SO MANY GIRLS COMING at me back then, and my teenage self found the attention impossible to resist, but sneaking a girl by Bill Bray's door, and knowing when Joseph was not around, was a skill in itself. Because it was also 'forbidden', it felt like a home run every time I managed to get a girl beyond checkpoints and beyond the threshold of the bedroom door. I had never been so grateful for exterior fire exits and back stairways. The awkward problem, of course, was sharing a room with Michael. What made this worse was that if he knew I was pursuing a certain girl, he'd deliberately attach himself to my hip. But once – one golden once – Michael was nowhere to be seen and I managed to sneak away from some hotel gathering to hook up with the prettiest of girls.

Back home, I had been seeing a lot of Hazel Gordy, but while we liked each other – and sent endless love letters – puppy love had not advanced into anything serious, leaving me free to build my experience on the road. We older brothers had a way of describing how far we got with a girl: from 'first base' (the kiss) to 'second base' (touching / clothes off) to 'third base' (the sex) and, in my hotel room that night, I was an LA Dodger running wild; eyes closed, on top of this girl, kissing and touching with a freedom I didn't think possible. 'That feels really good …' she said. I was getting serious, she was groaning. Third base was in sight. I had one hand stroking her face, and the other on the mattress beside her head.

'I love how you stroke my thighs,' she continued, '… you're real gentle …' *I'm not stroking your thighs.* '… it feels good,' she whispered. I peeked open my eyes and manoeuvred my head to take a sly look down the bed, and that's when I saw it – Michael's arm, reaching up and over from underneath the bed, his hand circling her thigh.

'MICHAEL!' I jumped up, the poor girl was mortified and Michael, chuckling, was already scrambling for the door. I could have killed him, not only because he was hiding there the whole time, but because he heard me whispering all these sensual, sweet nothings that he would tease me with for weeks after. I refused to speak to him that night. When we turned out the lights and he wished me goodnight, I said nothing. He waited a few minutes in the dark and then brokered the peace. 'She got some real creamy thighs!' he said. And we both burst out laughing.

GIRLFRIENDS WERE TECHNICALLY BANNED, SO JACKIE'S and my illicit conquests were kept on the down-low. First, Motown wasn't keen on promoting us as anything other than boys-without-girlfriends-and-looking-for-love. We understood that our appeal was contained in the hope that we could one day become our fans' boyfriends. Second, outside the bubble of Motown PR, Joseph's equally image-conscious rules didn't allow girlfriends, and this came across loud and clear. Girlfriends are bad for you. Girls will distract you. Girls will wreck record sales. You will lose fans. They will stop screaming for you – and so forth. We older brothers rolled our eyes. It was an extension of 'never let the outside in'.

But I'm not sure Michael fully understood. If anything, it confused him. For the longest time, he was expected to play the public role of available boyfriend, but was then told girls were career poison and would stop him becoming the best. If he ever doubted the seriousness of this unwritten rule, he saw its truth rammed home one day when Joseph caught Tito with Dee Dee, his childhood sweetheart and future wife.

Tito was at the school gates waiting to be picked up when our father pulled up with Jack and saw him kissing Dee Dee. It opened a big can of whoop-ass. When Tito got in the van, Joseph really gave it to him. Tito protested, screaming how much he loved this girl, but Joseph kept hitting him, yelling that his selfish actions were going to split up the group. I know it upset Michael because when we stayed up late on the road, talking about girls, he spoke all hush. He asked me about how to treat a girl, wondering when was the right time to make the first move on a date. 'I always want to be a gentleman,' he said, 14 going on 42.

Not that Michael was *completely* green. At certain venues or functions, Jackie and I used him as our wing-man when Joseph wasn't looking. Our father never suspected the young ones of hitting on older girls, so Michael's adorability became our secret weapon. 'You see that cute one over there,' we'd say, 'go over and ask for her number.'

When an approach didn't concern him personally, he was devoid of shyness. He'd walk right on over and start talking. We'd see the girls coo and, nine times out of ten, he returned with a piece of paper, mission nonchalantly accomplished. 'Here's her number. She's real nice!' he'd say.

But we had different tastes back then. Where I was looking for easy girls, he idealised a young lady. Where I dreamed of getting them back to my room, he dreamed of taking them for ice-cream and watching cartoons. He was fussy; I was not. In fact, when it came to girls – and women in later life – he studied them in the same way he studied great artists. He looked out for every delicate detail: mannerisms, hair, smile and the way she walked. And his ideal chick 'needs to be honest and kind.' He always said that. As a boy, he wondered aloud if 'honesty' was too much to ask. 'Will they want us for who we are, or want us because we're the Jackson 5?'

I always gave realistic advice: 'Michael, take these girls for what they are – great admirers of what we do, but they don't really know us.'

'But they love us … and they'd do anything for us!'

Big brothers shouldn't have to dash little brothers' hopes, and it was hard for me then to explain the distinction between the fans I brought back to the room and the true love he romanced about. 'You don't need to worry about any of this stuff yet,' was my cop-out.

Michael just kept on nurturing his growing crush on Diana Ross – his idea of the perfect woman. 'A girl has to be as dignified and beautiful as Diana,' he said, and it was a view he would carry into adulthood. One day, at the house, he started teasing a teenage La Toya and Janet, and told them: 'you aren't pretty until you start looking like Diana!'

OUR EDUCATION TRAVELLED WITH US ON tour in the form of a private tutor, Rose Fine, who would also teach Janet. On first impression, you would have thought she was the strictest, most unforgiving principal, all stiff-backed, prim, proper and enunciating her words with clipped perfection, yet she was the warmest, most loving of ladies and we adored her. Rose was our educational shadow wherever we went, and it was always a strange sight seeing her endure the insanity of Jackson-mania, trotting behind us, trying to keep up.

One of *her* missions was to ensure we didn't forget our Ps and Qs as she continually attempted to improve our eloquence. 'You sing beautifully and you can learn to speak beautifully, too,' she said. She was determined that five boys in the spotlight should speak 'proper English'. Every time one of us said something like 'We ain't gonna do that!' she corrected us. 'You are speaking incorrectly. What you say is "We are not going to do it." Repeat after me. We – are – not – going – to – do – it.'

'But that's not how we talk, Rose!' Michael said. 'We gotta be us.'

'No, Michael – you say, "We have got to be ourselves."'

Bless her, she kept fighting Mission Impossible.

In our hotel room at night, Michael and I talked about how 'nobody black and hip is prim and proper'.

'Rose don't understand cooool,' Michael laughed.

As much as we played with Rose, and probably exaggerated our dialect in front of her, we used to say she was the most powerful person around, even beyond Mr Gordy. Power invested by the Board of Education. If one of us so much as yawned onstage, or looked like he needed rest, or if media interviews ate into our four hours of daily education, she could shut us down faster than a fire marshal. It was a discretion she never used but it meant that she earned instant respect from everyone, especially Motown.

We respected her role in our lives and her positive influence on Michael cannot be overestimated. Whenever we dropped her off at home in Studio City, she invited us in and her husband Sid took the opportunity to play a song. It was usually old-fashioned 1940s fare – something from the Ink Spots or the Mills Brothers – but we clapped along politely. But it was when we first laid eyes on her library that Michael started to become the voracious reader that he was. Rose handled each book like a precious artefact, and she was always on at us to read, read, read – and Michael heeded this advice. Few people know that my brother was a bookish nerd, always swotting up on some random subject to better his vocabulary, knowledge or understanding of life. 'I love reading. There is a wonderful world to be discovered in books,' he said. Michael's early reading material concerned Fred Astaire or Elvis, or child stars Shirley Temple or Sammy Davis Junior. In later years, his reading extended from Steven Spielberg to Alfred Hitchcock, President Reagan to President Roosevelt, Malcolm X to Dr Martin Luther King, and Mussolini to Hitler. I doubt many people would have given him credit for the general knowledge he amassed. Except Rose. She always taught us that we can learn from the best by following history's lessons; that it has left the footprints for us to follow. That is why Michael's autobiography, *Moonwalk*, starts with a quote from Thomas Edison:

> *When I want to discover something, I begin by reading up everything that has been done along that line in the past – that's what all the books in the library are for. I see what has been accomplished at great labour and expense in the past. I gather the data of many thousands of experiments as a starting point and then I make thousands more. The three essentials to achieving anything worthwhile are, first, hard work; second, stick-to-it-iveness; third, common sense.*

That quote still stands as the truest reflection of Michael's approach to his own mastery, and they were the words he actually posted in gold letters to the cloth, coffee-brown walls of his sound studio at Hayvenhurst. Rose Fine opened the doors to his mind. 'I wouldn't be the same person if it wasn't for her,' he later acknowledged. Without her, I doubt his final grades would have been so good, either.

By the end of 1972 the Walton School had closed, so Michael spent ninth grade at Montclair School in Van Nuys where, that June, he received a school report he was so proud of that it became the only one he pinned up at the house. In History, English Grammar, Math and Study Methods, he received A grades. In French, he received a B minus and in English 9, he earned a B plus with the comment from the teacher: 'Greater effort I have never seen.' Teachers also marked 'work habits' and 'co-operation' and gave him E-marks pretty much across the board. An 'E' = 'does assigned work, responds to instruction well'. All this is not bad for a pupil who, biographers claimed, 'was a terrible student' and 'didn't have a clue what was going on'.

Michael created one of his most telling pieces of school work during an art class at Walton. He had regularly asked Rose about the Vietnam War. Newspaper photos of wounded and screaming children always distressed him. His interpretation of what he saw became the subject of a drawing. I had forgotten it existed until it showed up on-line from the school's yearbook. He drew a soldier standing in the foreground of a battle, beneath skies filled with fighter planes; he was unguarded, arms outstretched, machine-gun surrendered. The caption read, 'STOP THE WAR'. With the charity he pioneered, Heal the World, and then his smash hit 'Earth Song' – its video and stage performance had him blocking the path of a military tank with his arms outstretched – you see the humanitarian spirit that had long existed within the sensitive boy.

Michael ended his school years at Cal Prep, where, in art classes he sketched version after version of Charlie Chaplin. One of his classmates was a girl called Lori Shapiro: she quietly observed my brother immersed in his drawings, then scrunching them up and throwing them away. 'Michael,' she said one day, 'that drawing of Charlie Chaplin? Before you ball it up, can I have it?'

'Sure,' he said, signing his name in black felt tip and handing it over.

But Michael knew that a favour deserves its return. He hated algebra and he knew Lori was 'the brains'. So, sitting near her desk, he swapped math books with her when the teacher wasn't looking and she worked out his x + y = z. I reckon Lori was the chief reason he got an A grade in math!

Come graduation year, Cal Prep published its own roll of honour, where its pupils nominated the winners in a 'Who's Who' roll call. Michael emerged with his first clutch of awards: 'Best Dressed', 'Shyest', 'Most Creative', 'Most Artistic' and 'Most

Likely to Succeed'. So, who won 'Biggest Smile'? That honour went to Marlon.

MICHAEL TALKED A LOT ABOUT GOD with Rose. He was the only brother still attending the local Kingdom Hall and doing field service with Mother, La Toya and Janet, tour dates permitting. But different faiths and others' relationship with God fascinated him, and Rose was Jewish. Michael learned – and loved – that the Jewish Sabbath was all about family, and that everything came to a halt on that day 'so that humanity may make the ordinary extraordinary and the natural miraculous,' as he wrote in 2000, in an essay on a website called 'beliefnet'. Michael was intrigued that there was one guaranteed day each week to celebrate life and each other. But it also became much more than that to him. As he wrote: 'In my world, the Sabbath was the day I was able to step away from my unique life and glimpse the everyday.'

Increasingly, Michael stayed true to the only sanctuary he knew, the Kingdom Hall, and the only inner balance he could find by 'staying in happy fellowship with the Lord,' as he put it.

THE COMMODORES, A SIX-MAN GROUP FROM Alabama, joined the Motown family in 1972 and came with us on the road as an opening act. Back then, Lionel Richie was mainly the saxophonist and Clyde Orange was lead vocals, and we enjoyed the best of times with them. Our camaraderie was special – must have been the southern thing. One time, at the Hollywood Bowl, they actually received more screams than we did ... because their wardrobe didn't show up and they had to play in their undershorts! Their legs stole the show.

By now, Joseph had decided Randy was worthy of a run-out with the group, playing the bongos. He was more of a suck-it-and-see-how-it-works addition than a permanent fixture – for now – but he would grow into a capable performer and an incredible songwriter. If only he had played tennis and not the bongos: offstage, the Commodores kicked our butts on the courts. They called out our competitiveness and it was no contest – we later discovered they had each had tennis scholarships. I swear Lionel Richie was Arthur Ashe in disguise. He was *that* good.

In the hotels, we spent time in their rooms, jamming and writing songs. They brought out the keyboards and worked on ideas, which fascinated us: we were a group who had material written for us. I can still see Michael lying back on the bed, having his hair braided by Lionel's girlfriend (and future wife) Brenda, as we watched Lionel inspire the songwriting process. The Commodores were still six years away from releasing their smash, 'Three Times A Lady', but seeing how they built a song, from city to city, was inspiring.

At this time, Michael already had ideas of his own fermenting. 'I feel there are so many songs in my head,' he used to say. In fact, prior to the tour with the Commodores, he had started finding his creative voice at Motown, deciding to speak up for himself. That artistic watershed moment came with the recording of a song called 'Lookin' Through The Windows'. Michael had suggested his own take on a certain delivery, but when the idea faced resistance from the Corporation, he got upset and phoned Mr Gordy direct. Five minutes later, he returned with the boss's approval. That day, he began to develop the confidence to trust in his own creative instincts. Everyone sat back and allowed him free rein. He pretty much improvised, feeling his way through the song, but they must have liked it because his interpretation was kept on the final cut. So, when Michael, at 13, witnessed the Commodores' songwriting autonomy, it strengthened his creative resolve.

In later life, he looked back on our constant touring and said it denied us the chance to form lasting friendships with anyone. Schedules and living out of suitcases meant we couldn't nurture true friendships on the road. Yet those touring days with the Commodores created a bond between him and Lionel Richie that lasted throughout his life. It was the genesis of their collaboration on the USA for Africa charity, 'We Are The World' – it won

Grammys in 1986 for Song of the Year and Record of the Year – and showcased Michael's true humanitarian heart on a global scale.

'WHAT DID THE CAPTAIN JUST SAY?' I asked, as we flew over the Atlantic, bound for our first European tour of France, Germany, Italy, Holland, Spain and our first destination: London.

'He said there are 10,000 fans waiting at Heathrow airport,' said Joseph.

On our arrival in London we all wondered how big this thing was getting. We seemed to be locked into something that was forever mutating: from the Chitlin' Circuit to Motown, from Motown to Hollywood, from a record deal to four back-to-back No. 1s, and from conquering America to selling records on different continents. We had to pinch ourselves to believe that our records had reached as far as the flight was taking us.

London represented the ultimate disbelief: we were there to appear at the Royal Variety Show at the London Palladium in a performance for Queen Elizabeth II. This huge honour was appreciated by everyone but drummer Johnny, it seemed. He'd always had a sharp wit, but that could sometimes come across as cockiness and, we soon learned, no one should try to be funny with a British Customs officer. As we showed our passports, Suzanne de Passe politely explained that we were arriving to do a Royal Command Performance 'as guests of the Queen.' One by one, we were asked how long we intended to stay in the country. We all stepped up, answered politely and expected Johnny to do the same. 'And how long are you intending to stay in the country, young man?' asked the stern-looking Customs man. The moment I saw Johnny smirk, I knew we were in trouble.

'Just long enough to f*** your Queen,' he said.

I swear the world stopped spinning at that precise moment. It wasn't only his temerity that shocked: it was the fact that a member of the Jackson 5 had uttered a swear word. It was akin to hearing a pastor swear on a Sunday. Well, that was it. All officialdom hell broke loose and the indignant Customs officer was sending Johnny back to America on the first plane. As the adults scrambled around the passport desk, we stared at Johnny and said things that mirrored his remark about the Queen. Somehow, the combined desperate diplomacy of Suzanne and Joseph managed to persuade the Customs guy to relent, but Johnny got a real rocket afterwards. 'That stupidity nearly cost us the entire performance!' said Suzanne.

We opened the Royal show with a 10-minute spot, including our new release 'Rockin' Robin', sharing a bill that included Elton John, Liberace, Carol Channing and some names we didn't know: Rod Hull and Emu (a comedian with a blue-feathered emu puppet), Arthur Askey, Danny La Rue and Ken Dodd with his 'Diddymen'. Elton John wished us luck backstage. We had last known him as Major Lance's keyboardist, but he'd since changed his name. But it was his flamboyant style that made the most noise that night: all outrageous shaded spectacles and colourful zany costumes, with big buttons and shiny pieces. In fact, when we saw a crew wheeling by his wardrobe and the even more substantial one of Liberace, ours felt minuscule and dull by comparison – and that was saying something.

After our three-part harmony dedicated to the Queen – our fan song 'We Thank You For The Joy You Have Given Us' – we were presented to Her Majesty backstage. Michael said for many years afterwards that it was 'one of the greatest nights of my life' – and it probably was until it was eclipsed when he met Princess Diana much further down the road. But shaking the gloved hand of the Queen wasn't our only treat in 1972.

Earlier, while kicking our heels in the dressing room, Marlon noticed a small hole in the wall, reached by standing on a chair. We knew this was an exciting 'find' because his face was doing one of those screams without emitting noise. Clearly delirious, he waved us over, jabbing at this hole in the wall and keeping his hand over his mouth. One by one, we fought for our turn to place our eye to it … giving us direct sight into the neighbouring dressing room. There, sitting on the toilet, was a lady whose name shall remain nameless, but Michael was beside himself, pointing to his ass to confirm that, yes, we had all seen her naked butt. Man, she would have killed us had she known, but on a night performing in front of the Queen, this one woman had provided us with our biggest thrill of the tour without even realising it. Even performing at the Liverpool Empire the following week and breaking all attendance records in the Beatles' home city couldn't beat that for a bunch of Indiana boys.

WHEN WE PLAYED THE MID-SOUTH COLISEUM in Memphis, we were excited because it meant that we'd not only be reunited with Rebbie, but we'd get to meet her daughter, our new niece Stacee, then about 10 months old. As we flew in from another state, Rebbie drove from Kentucky to our hotel for the night and management arranged for a crib to be set up in a side room of one suite. No one was more excited than Michael when our eldest sister arrived and he was the perfect, doting uncle. He spent more time with Stacee, pulling faces to make her coo and laugh, than he did with anyone else. In fact, I don't know who was entertaining whom as they crawled around on hands and knees. We left them alone, with Michael dangling a red, white and black transistor radio, shaped like a globe, over her crib. We must have been catching up with Rebbie in the adjoining room for about an hour when we wondered, 'Is Michael still in there?'

Rebbie went to check. Seconds later, she popped her head around the door, waved us over, but put a finger to her lips. We all crept to the doorway and saw the funniest, cutest sight – Michael had climbed into the crib, cuddled up next to Stacee and fallen fast asleep. It was an angelic picture. Michael was 13 – a good two decades away from that horrible period in his life when some would suggest his pure love of children was sinister and perverted. And yet his empathy, gentleness and connection with children was always an intrinsic and innocent part of him.

The clues to his pure heart were not only evident in private, they were there to be seen in public, too. Of all the journalists who interviewed him over the years, his favourite was a lady called Lisa Robinson. She was the one reporter he trusted, knowing she wouldn't twist what he said. After his death in 2009, she wrote up a compilation in *Vanity Fair* of her numerous taped interviews. In one segment, she republished a Q&A session she had done with Michael.

How many children would you like to have? *20. Adopted. All races.*

What is your most prized possession? *A child ...*

It dated from 1977. Michael was 17 years old.

AUSTRALIA FELT LIKE ANOTHER PLANET, AND with each new frontier we conquered, Rose Fine had us reading about different histories, cultures and peoples. Wherever we went, she scheduled the odd afternoon of sightseeing. To her, touring with the Jackson 5 was a grand version of a school field trip. Australia greeted us like royalty and rolled out the red carpet. At one place, there was a reception with a fancy buffet fit for a king. I can't pinpoint the exact city, but the Aussie hospitality was so legendary that everywhere seemed the same. Anyway, we were by now so slick with the social pleasantries that any official event was part of the routine and we worked the room, smiling away the jet-lag.

As we mingled, Joseph wandered off and approached a crowd of about a 100 black teenagers, standing behind a fence. They were Aboriginals. Rose had told us how Sydney Opera House sits on Bennelong Point, a camp taken from the Aboriginal people by the British in pre-colonial days. We were starting to wonder what Joseph was doing when he marched over and said he wanted to invite this group inside. The organisers told him that wouldn't be permitted 'because they are Aboriginal.' To someone who had striven for respect and equality as a black man, this was a red rag to a bull. Next thing we knew, he was back at the fence, taking a young Aboriginal girl by the hand and pulling her through a small gap. She looked scared and bewildered at first, but her friends started to follow and squeezed through, one by one. You could have heard a pin drop as the white guests watched our father trample over social etiquette and protocol.

'Boys! Come on over and meet your new fans!' said Joseph. The joy on the faces of the Aboriginal teenagers was something to behold and Joseph was laughing, making his point. No one asked them to leave and after an awkward transition, the night continued to be a success as whites and Aboriginals mixed at the Jackson 5 party.

Some days later, we received an invitation from the Aboriginal community to visit them at a remote reserve. 'We wouldn't advise going there, Mr Jackson,' said some official. 'We cannot guarantee your safety.'

Joseph ignored that advice, and Michael said it simply, 'We can have Aboriginal fans, too, can't we? They are no different.'

With a translator in tow, we ended up having a memorable time at the Aboriginal reserve, feeling like overdressed aliens among the bare-chested tribe. Yet we faced no wariness or judgement. What struck us was how spiritual the whole place felt. We watched people carve tree bark, and we learned the simple joys of the boomerang and how to play the didgeridoo – Tito still has one as a treasured souvenir.

It was in Senegal that we encountered our first African baobab tree – one of Mother Nature's marvels, thousands of years old, with a trunk that can grow to anything between 15 and 40 metres in girth. The tree at the front of 2300 Jackson Street was a twig by comparison. 'This is one of the strongest trees you will ever see,' said Rose Fine, 'and there was a time in the 1880s when the baobab's hollow trunk was used as a prison.' In Western Australia. For the Aboriginals.

Michael was perplexed. How could something so naturally beautiful – a creation of Mother Earth – be twisted and used to incarcerate people? Trees were family, not prisons. Light and dark. Good and evil. These were the contradictions of life that we had yet to understand.

MICHAEL HAD SEEN MOST OF THE world before he turned 18, and it was an incredible experience to share as brothers, filling our passports on Motown's dime and moving beyond Europe to Australia, New Zealand and Japan. Out of all our travels, the most insane episode happened in the Brazilian city of São Paolo. Just when we thought we had seen it all, when it came to mania, our South American tour surprised us.

We flew into São Paolo, and our equipment – instruments and wardrobe – followed us on the next flight. Come the evening of the concert, we discovered this hadn't been such a great idea. The second flight was delayed or cancelled, and no one was sure if it would arrive in time for the show. The optimists in the camp kept saying things like 'Maybe it will still show up – there's plenty of time yet,' but everyone could hear the concert hall filling up. Within an hour, it was full to capacity and we were empty-handed.

That was when someone thought it would be a good idea to go out there, 'talk to your fans and explain the situation.' With no fanfare, the house lights on full beam, we brothers – plus a promoter – walked onstage wearing the T-shirts and jeans we had flown in. The crowd went crazy. Jackie raised his hands for quiet and attempted an explanation. I'm not sure how our English was received by the Portuguese-speaking crowd, but they must have understood the basic facts – no wardrobe, no equipment, no concert – because the boos and heckles started. The mic passed to me. Maybe the 'heart-throb' could calm things. But the boos got louder. So we passed it to Michael. Maybe the cute front man could kill it. But nothing was working. Beneath the rising boos, we heard a chant growing in Portuguese which, we were later told, was the equivalent of 'BULLSHIT! BULLSHIT! BULLSHIT!' We were lost, looking at each other, wondering what to do. A bottle bounced on to the stage. Then it was raining cans and coins. All the time, we stood there, putting our arms up, ducking and stepping back to dodge whatever was thrown, trying to get them to understand. But it was futile and growing increasingly hostile. Jackie ordered us offstage. As we turned away, it sounded like the whole of Brazil was booing us back to America.

'We need to get out of here,' said Bill Bray, backstage.

A handful of angry fans jumped on to the stage, and we ran for the bus outside. By now, a sizeable crowd had anticipated our exit, with more and more spilling out of the gates. We each made it on to the bus and the doors closed. 'GO, DRIVER, GO!'

As he started to pull away, fans were hammering on the sides, venting their anger. Everything had turned ugly so we were glad to be getting out of there. On a seat two rows behind me, Michael looked as white as a ghost, curled up in his seat.

'WAIT!' screamed Marlon. 'There's ROSE!'

We looked out of the window and there, fighting her way through the crowd, with her clutch held aloft in both hands, was our tutor. In the rush to get out of there, we had left her behind, reading a magazine in the dressing room. Rose had one of those seventies hairstyles that flopped at the fringe and hung in one neat style, but she looked now as if she had been dragged backwards through a rosebush. As she banged on the door, the driver opened it, let her in and snapped it shut again, leaving our dishevelled tutor – all breathless and red-faced – standing at the front, in the aisle.

'Well! I can't *believe* there is not one *gentleman* in the whole *bunch*!' she said, pronouncing every word precisely.

Thankfully, there was no time for a discussion about it. At that very moment, the driver put his foot down, jolting Rose into the front seat. Then – CRASH! – a brick shattered a side window. CRASH! Another. We all hit the deck. It was a terrifying experience to be under attack. I was crying. Michael was crying. Randy was crying. We couldn't comfort each other because we were too busy lying low, covering our heads. As we pulled away, the bus kept receiving hits from God knew what, and the ambush seemed to go on for ever. By the time we reached the comparative safety of the hotel, it had three shattered windows and countless dents. Michael and I were quivering wrecks, pleading with Joseph that he mustn't make us go back and perform there. Thankfully, he announced we were leaving on the first flight the next morning.

Come daylight, we were up and ready, and took a replacement bus to the airport. As Jack and Bill started organising the unload, we walked into the terminal to check in and realised our drama was not over: we were met by a group of soldiers, each holding machine guns across their chests, and some official was forcefully explaining that we were not allowed to leave until we had honoured our contractual commitment. There was a lot of serious talk we didn't hear, but the symbolic muscle of the army was a deliberate reminder that we were going nowhere. The upshot of this madness was that we had no option but to return to our hotel and wait another 24 hours for our equipment to show up.

It felt kind of strange doing a show that we were made to do, and it put a real dampener on our spirits. It was probably the one concert we didn't feel excited to perform, but we still got into show-mode and turned it on. And you know what the crazy thing was? The fans had a wild time: they screamed and sang, and fainted – and told us how much they loved us.

WE ACTED THE FOOL ALL THE time so when Motown's collaboration with Rankin & Bass came good, we found it apt that we morphed into cartoon characters in ABC's animated series, *The Jackson 5*. For Michael, the reality that our life had been turned into a cartoon had him more excited than he was over any album or concert. He was in front of that television each Saturday morning, at home or in hotels, like it was the only thing to watch in the world. Each episode featured our songs but they used actors for our voices, so we didn't even have to work for it. That made Motown's Fred Rice a magician in my book. For Michael, the cartoon was a C.S. Lewis fantasy turned real. In that Narnia-like space, the make-believe version of our lives came without the rough and tumble of Jackson-mania. In his eyes, we were now on a par with Mickey Mouse and, as a Disney nut, he *loved* that. As he grew older, he was torn about the cartoon's success. On one hand, he loved 'being' a cartoon character that belonged in another world. On the other, those re-runs threatened to keep us forever perceived as the child group and Michael was by now itching to break out from the restrictions of bubblegum soul. If he didn't necessarily want to grow up as a person, he wanted to develop as an artist.

CHAPTER NINE

Growing Pains

PUBERTY IS ALWAYS A POTENTIAL THIEF for a child star: it threatens to take away the image your dream is built on. Michael and I both struggled with acne; mine still stubborn and raging as an 18-year-old, his rabid and new at 14. A liking for fried food and soda in dressing rooms had caught up with us. Like me, Marlon – who also suffered – accepted the break-outs without too much angst, and I didn't think Michael would be any different. I didn't appreciate *how much* he worried about the threat his acne posed to his image because he never really spoke about it. We didn't talk about that sort of thing. What 'cool' teenage boy does? We Jackson brothers were especially bound that way. We had been taught so much about pride, respect and performance that we had never learned the art of easy communication. We didn't check in with one another unless it was album talk, tour madness, choreography ideas, basketball plans or girls. So Michael suffered quietly as his features changed and his skin flared up with pimples. Indeed he locked it deep inside, except for the odd worry he expressed to Mother.

As things turned out, his voice changed to his advantage: it kept its pitch and he learned how to use other voices, giving him an infinite range, with the ethereal timbre that was uniquely his. There were ridiculous rumours that he received hormone injections to keep that sweet high sound. Even when his voice coach Seth Riggs vouched for its natural range, people doubted it. But his voice was the least of his concerns. Michael's acne was a confusion he wasn't expecting. And then there was his nose. It widened noticeably and he hated it. In fact, he hated his skin and his nose so much that he found it hard to look at himself in the mirror. This wasn't just typical teenage self-consciousness: it became a full-blown inferiority complex. The more he looked at himself, the unhappier he felt. In fact, he was painfully brittle during conversations with anyone, always looking down to avoid eye contact.

His comfort zone, as always, was the stage or the 'platform' of press interviews when reporters spoke of how 'energised', 'inquisitive' and 'ebullient' he was. In performance mode, Michael's teenage woes were well concealed behind makeup or the performer's personality he projected. Offstage, our merciless teasing only made matters worse, but teasing is what brothers do, and we all had to go through it. When my acne first kicked in, they – including Michael – called me 'Bumpy Face' or 'Map Face' and Marlon was 'Liver Lips'. I even received a second label, 'Big Head', because my head was, apparently, too big for my body. So when Michael was called 'Big Nose', it was just part of the common initiation into manhood – but he struggled with it. Not that we knew so until much later.

Michael always recalled Joseph using the tease, and that was what hurt him most – hearing it from an adult's lips and from the man who had driven home the importance of image all our lives. 'Hey, Big Nose, come over here,' said Joseph. Michael said nothing and cringed each time.

I woke up one morning concerned by a discoloured area that had appeared on the inside of my left thigh, a white blemish – the size of a spot. It bothered me so I had it checked out. The doc said it was tiny area of vitiligo and was nothing to worry about unless it started to spread. And there were bigger issues to tackle – like the acne. Michael and I spent mornings busting those bumps together, standing side by side in front of the mirror, and we used the skin-bleaching cream Nadinola, because Michael soon learned that, for black kids, busting and picking leaves a mark darker than the natural skin colour. We viewed Nadinola as a magic potion: one tiny dab could fade a little area of discoloration, keeping our skin tone even.

As I write this, I am fully aware that this one fact – if taken out of context – is in danger of fanning the myth that Michael bleached his skin so that he would appeal to a wider audience: nonsensical when you think how vast our Jackson 5 fan base already was. Anyway, over-the-counter Nadinola is used for acne and skin discoloration. Its three per cent hydroquinone is nowhere near strong enough to transform anyone's actual pigmentation. So I'll be clear: Michael never bleached any part of his face or body, save for the dark spots on bad-skin days. In later life, other measures would be necessary to treat more serious skin conditions. Suggestions that he was trying to stop being a black man hurt him greatly, especially when his pigmentation was like La Toya's – she was always that paler shade when younger. Michael was proud of his roots as a black man and proud to be a record-breaking black artist – but learning how headlines started was all part of growing up.

I don't think any of us anticipated growing pains as a group. On paper, our hit records, cohesion, synergy and public demand made us the least likely group to split. But we hadn't reckoned on the impact of becoming young men who would want to move out, have wives and raise children. Michael, especially, didn't see the realities of adulthood coming.

MR GORDY ANNOUNCED SOLO PROJECTS FOR Michael and me, deciding to showcase our diversity from under the umbrella of the Jackson 5 as Motown capitalised on our separate fan bases. Within this opportunity, we never forgot that the group came first: the Jackson 5 was our security, the solo projects were our experimental adventures. We felt that any independent success could only strengthen the brand. Michael went first with 'Got To Be There', which charted at No. 4 in the Billboard Hot 100, followed up with 'Rockin' Robin' at No. 2 and then his first solo No. 1 'Ben', which sold 1.5 million copies. My LP *Jermaine* spawned the single 'Daddy's Home' – a cover of the Shep & the Limelites hit – and it reached No. 3, selling around one million copies. We would both release other solo singles until 1975 but none of them worried the Top 10.

But in the wake of our charted successes, I suddenly faced a press that was curious to find rivalry. 'What's it like being your brother's rival?'; 'Jermaine, Michael went No. 1, do you wish you had, too?' They were questions from an old script, as yellowed as a newspaper left in the window too long. Journalists forgot that we were brothers first, artists second. Michael cheered me like he had on the baseball field. I had his back like I'd had it in Gary, at school and onstage. Our upbringing was about pushing each other to raise the bar. That is healthy competition, and that was what we shared. Music didn't usher in rivalry, but we saw how the outside perspective betrayed what we were as brothers. I've always said that when you're looking into the goldfish bowl it's impossible to know what the fish are thinking – yet people still try. During our transition into adults, the 'rivalry' and 'jealousy' between Michael and me would stick to our media portrayal. It was like everything else that left its mark in childhood – an emotion, a feeling, a scar, an experience: it never goes away.

As a group, we would release four more albums: *Skywriter, Get It Together, Dancing Machine* and *Moving Violation*. We moved away from bubble-gum soul into a sound that was more funk with a pop edge. But while our average worldwide album sales hovered around the two million mark, our chart success wasn't through the roof any more. We were no longer permanent residents of the Top 10 and found ourselves struggling to make the Top 50 albums. Measured against our early successes, it was a decline that we struggled to understand. Somewhere between albums – say mid-1973 – I started to hear the first murmurings of worry that Motown's team wasn't bringing it any more. Michael – believing more and more in his creativity – spoke about how we needed more freedom to write our own material, and I could see Joseph paying attention. Their view was that we were hit-makers not releasing enough hits, and that Motown wasn't promoting us as vigorously.

I couldn't understand the complaint. Why are you getting so hung up on one or two records going nowhere when we've had so many hits? I thought. The juggernaut wasn't stopping, the touring demand was still there, and the crowds were still screaming. It was hardly a crisis. Anyway, I had bigger things on my mind. After a succession of teenage conquests, I realised there was no one in the world quite like Hazel Gordy, so I proposed when she joined up with us on an East-Coast leg on tour, and she said yes.

Ever since we'd arrived in LA., the Jacksons and the Gordys had been one. Now we were cementing that bond. We were both ecstatic. Back then, I believed in the 'forever' and the happy ending; I believed that nothing good would ever end.

I KNEW IT WASN'T GOING TO be easy breaking my happy news to the family. That was why I left it for a few days, to think over my approach. I dreaded telling Joseph, because – ever since Tito had married Dee Dee the previous year – he thought he was losing us, and he didn't handle it very well. His reaction was always going to be unpredictable. I worried about telling Michael because we were so close that I knew he'd feel the wrench of me moving out. Bottom line in our house: marriage wasn't celebrated as the joy of two people coming together, it was initially viewed as a wedge driving apart a winning team of brothers.

I remember rehearsing the conversations in my head but all I could visualise was Joseph's angry face and Michael's sad eyes. Maybe that was why I chose to break the news first to Joseph from a phone booth when our tour passed through Boston, with Hazel by my side. (By now, Joseph didn't accompany us all the time. He dropped off on occasion to rest up, trusting the Motown operation.)

When I phoned Encino, Mother answered. I told her the news. She was delighted. 'Joseph always said that girl was crazy about you,' she said. 'Let me go get him. He's out in the garden.'

Joseph was either blowing the leaves or cutting the grass, and I seemed to be waiting an age, pushing dimes into the coin slot. Mother came back to the phone. 'I'm sorry, Jermaine … he can't come to the phone. He's busy in the garden.' The resignation in her voice told me everything, and it crushed me. Mr Gordy backed me. My own father didn't – and that hurt.

That same night, I plucked up the courage to tell the rest of the brothers. 'We already know,' said Michael. 'I love Hazel. I'm really happy for you.' He was all smiles, and would refer to this new addition to the family as 'Mrs G'.

What he didn't say was that he saw his brothers' marriages (Jackie would soon marry his girl, Enid) as events that left him behind. I learned all this from Mother later. 'He's not feeling good about it, Jermaine,' she said. 'He feels everything has changed and everyone is leaving him. Marlon and Randy will be next. He's sad. He's scared of being lonely.'

Michael never did say anything, then or later. Instead he hid his true feelings, not wishing to ruin my happiness or spoil the big day.

WITH MR GORDY AS THE BRIDE'S father, it was always going to be a 'wedding of the century', as *Ebony* magazine billed it. I didn't have much say in its theme or decadence. It was like creating a new album: I'd just show up, do my thing and everything would fall into place. The guest list was a Who's Who of the music industry and the grand theme a Winter Wonderland at the Beverly Hills Hotel with 175 white doves, artificial snow and Smokey Robinson singing 'Starting Here & Now' written especially for us. Hazel and I found ourselves on the cover of *Soul* and *Life* for an 'inside the wedding exclusive'.

Come the big day on 15 December – one day after my nine-teenth birthday – Mr Gordy handed over his beautiful daughter at the end of the aisle by pinching my upper arm and winking, as if to say, 'She's yours now, you take care of her.'

The day went like a dream, and I was so carried away that I didn't see Michael, dressed in his groomsman suit, sitting alone at a table, all glum. I remained oblivious to the separation he felt. Anyway, Hazel and I had found a house in Bel Air so I was only going to be a 15-to-20 minute drive away, and we'd still be recording and touring together. If anything, the positive consequence was that our marriage tied us to the heart of Motown. I couldn't see the down-side; I just presumed everyone was happy for me.

But some days later, Hazel told me that her father had received a letter from Tito. The gist of it was that he felt it unfair that Hazel and I had received such a lavish wedding when he and Dee Dee had had to settle for something more sedate. Or words to that effect. This complaint overlooked one fact: the wedding was provided by Mr Gordy in his capacity as a father of the bride, not as president of Motown. But that didn't stop me being viewed as the brother receiving special treatment from the boss.

I didn't believe for a second that Tito was behind that missive. Men don't get jealous about the trappings of a wedding – wives do – but he had signed it and that made me wince. Not that I said anything. I brushed the letter's contents under the same carpet where Michael kept his feelings about the splintering effects of marriage. We didn't like confrontation. Big elephants have sat in our rooms all our lives and been ignored for the sake of avoiding conflict. Better to have peace (Mother's way) than cause upset (Joseph's way).

It seemed Hazel's and my wedding caused ripples in the Gordy and Motown families, too. It would also transpire that Marvin Gaye – a genius riddled by his own insecurity, and Hazel's uncle by his marriage to Mr Gordy's sister, Anna – was concerned too. I later learned (as confirmed by his confidant and collaborator on 'Sexual Healing', David Ritz) that he worried about 'the new singer walking into the family', saying, 'It's all part of Berry's plan to

YOU ARE NOT ALONE

replace me.' It was crazy talk from an incredible artist in a class of his own, but Marvin had irrationally convinced himself that I would now become the favourite son of the Motown family.

Looking back, it's hard to believe that my love for Hazel caused such ructions. Thankfully, I was too wrapped up in my own happiness to care.

IF THERE WAS ONE SIGHT OF himself that Michael did like in the mirror, it was when he was dancing. For our 1974 single 'Dancing Machine' – which went to No. 2 in the charts – he wanted to try something 'different' and perfect a dance he'd seen in street theatre: 'The Robot'. He used every spare minute to practise in front of the mirror at Hayvenhurst or in the studio, and probably before he went to bed. When I saw his first attempt, it seemed scratchy and disjointed, but when he finally showed us the polished version, it was incredible. He glided like he had wheels on the balls of his feet and electric wires running through each joint. He became remote-controlled. 'The Robot' was his first real signature move long before the Moonwalk moment, but none of us knew how it would go down when he first performed it during 'Dancing Machine' on the *Soul Train* show. All I can say is, go YouTube it, because you'll see how electric it was when Michael first threw his hat into the ring to announce that one of the most poetic dancers of our generation had arrived. Kids all over Los Angeles were busting 'The Robot', and the song put us back in the Top 10. That was the power of dance and television, we said. Noted for the future.

IN 1974, MICHAEL GOT HIS CHANCE to play Las Vegas and dance in the footsteps of Sammy Davis Junior – and we did it in true Vegas style with a full-on variety show. Showcased as 'The Jacksons', we introduced La Toya, Janet and Rebbie into the fold for a two-week run at the MGM Grand.

It was a rare treat being in the same city and at the same venue for 14 days straight and for once, we had a chance to unpack our suitcases. What also made it special was that it was solely a Jackson production, nothing to do with Motown. Organised and managed by Joseph, devised by the brothers, we brought a vaudeville feel to the show, with music, tap dancing, acting and comedy skits, with strings, brass and band in support. All nine brothers and sisters entertained a different crowd – sit-down tourists, not the screaming fan-base. We had packaged the mad energy from 2300 Jackson Street and found a stage to unleash it. It was especially nice having the first wanderer, Rebbie, sharing the show-time experience and there was something proud about walking onstage to a packed house every night *as a family*, not just five brothers. Those revue nights also benefited Michael because they gave him an ideal opportunity to work with his post-puberty voice and to experiment with his repertoire of talents and creative ideas.

It was his idea for Janet to incorporate her impression of Mae West during a part-skit, part-medley of songs performed with Randy, she playing a grown woman, he playing the man. During their rendition of 'Love Is Strange', there was a part where she ignored Randy calling out to her and he'd get mad, yell her name, and then the music would stop. In that pause, she turned and walked over to him, throwing her hips to a drum-beat with each strut. And then Janet, the cutest little thing, put a hand on a hip and purred, 'Why don't you come up and see me some time?' She brought the house down at every single show.

The name Janet Jackson stayed on people's lips and we recognised that our sister was a fine little actress. La Toya's performer switch also turned on during her tap-dancing routines with Michael, Marlon and Rebbie as they danced up a storm to Peggy Lee's 'Fever'. We'd end the show with a family tap-dance to a big-band number, bowing out to a standing ovation, all smiling, hands linked, united. If I could have taken just one snapshot of a moment in time, it would have been a freeze-frame of me looking down the line and capturing the joy we took from doing what we love: entertainment.

We must have gone down well with the Vegas crowd because we were invited back for a few more stints after that. And then everything slowly started to change.

I knew something was going down when I kept walking into the dressing room and the brothers stopped a hushed conversation and disappeared into their magazines. Michael shifted uncomfortably in the awkwardness that often filled the room. The atmosphere just felt … odd. At the time, I told myself it was nothing; it was just the brothers bemoaning Mr Gordy and they weren't saying stuff in front of me because they didn't want to compromise me.

ONE PHONE CALL SHATTERED THE FAMILY illusion of togetherness. A woman friend of Mother's rang with the news that Joseph had a mistress. What made this betrayal even more hurtful was that the lady was someone Mother had once invited into the house and who had had her eye on Jackie. It seemed that any Jackson would do. Mother was everything a betrayed woman can be: devastated, livid, confused, and torturing herself with the when and where. She had waited in the wings all her life with nothing but 'family' on her mind, so taking that phone call was like being T-boned.

I was in Philadelphia with Hazel, but I know from the others how ugly things turned at Hayvenhurst. Janet and Rebbie pleaded with Mother to 'leave him, divorce him' and couldn't stand the sight of 'the dirty down dog'. Janet yelled and screamed in his face for the hurt he had caused – and Joseph took it. Michael wept with hurt and anger, also advising Mother – quietly – to kick out our father. Joseph had lost the respect he had spent a lifetime building in his children and his actions contradicted every family value of loyalty and decency that he had ever preached. In the heat of the moment, suitcases were packed and Mother needed a few days away, but in the end, she hung on to her old-fashioned and religious beliefs that forgiveness and time can rebuild. 'I had no stomach to fight, no room for ugliness, and a faith in Jehovah,' she said.

OUT OF ALL THE INVITATIONS WE had and the parties we attended, the most-laid back afternoon we ever spent was in 1975 with Bob Marley and his Wailers at his musical haven: 56 Hope

Road, Kingston, Jamaica. It was the year that saw the release of 'No Woman No Cry' – his breakthrough, internationally and in America. We were in town to share the stage at a packed-out concert at the invitation of Jamaica's then opposition leader, the Labour Party's Edward Seaga. We even took along our wives and Mother. As Mother reminded us, it's not every day you get the chance to hang with Bob Marley – and she loved some hip-swaying reggae.

We drove through a rainbow-coloured gateway and pulled up outside a colonial property with a tiled roof, set in a lush landscape of mango trees, drooping palms and the greenest vegetation. Kids seemed to be everywhere, riding bicycles. We 'walked inside' to find a dirt floor; no floorboards or carpet, just soil. It summed up the vibe of our earthy afternoon.

'It's cool to have you guys here … Stick around as long as you like,' said Bob, all sweet-mannered Rastafarian chill, matted dreads, flared jeans and armless vest. So we kicked back that balmy after-noon, and talked about the power of trees, Mother Earth and James Brown. We were too polite to ask about the unidentifiable scent in the air. It smelt like rat's stink, we said. He was too respectful to our innocence so he didn't explain that it was the aroma of recently-smoked ganja.

It was challenging enough experimenting with the drink he had lined up for us: a plastic bottle filled with nasty-looking dirty water. 'We supposed to drink this?' said Michael, and the Wailers laughed.

It's hard to refuse a kind offering from your host so we held it like a specimen bottle in a science class, examining the floating bits in the brown water. Lucky for the rest of us that Michael was the one holding the bottle so all eyes were on him. 'It's herbs and spices,' someone reassured us.

'It's a miracle cleansing cure for all ailments. It's good for you,' another added.

Michael tipped the bottle, dipped a finger inside, licked it hesi-tantly … and pulled the ugliest face. That told us all we needed to know: it was no better than Joseph's castor oil. We skilfully managed to persuade our host that we'd take away this miracle liquid 'to drink later'.

We had so much fun with the Jamaican people who were then experiencing a turbulent, and often violent, political climate. Bob was a forerunner in being a musician and humanitarian, with his lyrical messages of love, peace and harmony. About three years later, he staged a concert in Kingston called 'One Love, One Peace'. There, he famously brokered the moment between warring factions when Michael Manley, the Prime Minister and People's National Party leader, shook hands on stage with Labour's Edward Seaga. That fragile peace wouldn't last, but Michael saw what music – not politics – had achieved. 'That is what I want to do,' he said. 'Make music that makes a difference.'

JAMAICA WAS TYPICAL OF CERTAIN DATES in 1974–5 when the wives – Hazel, Dee Dee and Enid – tagged along to break up the monotony that sometimes came with touring. Michael was welcoming and polite but also quietly irritated by this development. It interfered with our togetherness; it distracted our focus. It meant he and I no longer shared a room. I think it also tempered our wildness on stage, just in case we caused jealousy with the wives. But, as events turned out, that kind of jealousy was the least of our worries.

Disquiet began the day we arrived in Jamaica. A black limo pulled up at the airport and Tito and Dee Dee, walking ahead, jumped in. 'You Mr and Mrs Jackson?' asked the chauffeur.

'Yes.'

'You … Mr and Mrs *Jermaine* Jackson?'

'Oh … no … sorry,' said Tito. He and Dee Dee boarded the tour bus parked behind.

Hazel and I climbed inside the limo and pulled away slowly, separately, awkwardly. This kind of thing had tended to happen since I'd married Hazel because, wherever we went, Mr Gordy wanted his daughter looked after, so he booked her a separate car and her own security detail. What was I supposed to do? Tell the boss to stop acting like a father? Leave my wife to travel alone and go with my brothers and their wives? I went along with it and hoped it wouldn't cause trouble. That was wishful thinking, especially where the other wives were concerned. It was *they* – not the brothers – who resented Hazel receiving preferential treatment. And it was potentially divisive among a unit that had never felt any kind of jealousy before. Ultimately, something had to give, and it blew at airport Departures when we were bound for home.

Jackie's wife Enid was talking real loud as we checked in. She never had seen eye to eye with Hazel and she was going on and on about something, clearly wanting to be heard. Enid moaned once too often and Hazel snapped, 'TOUGH TITTIE, ENID!'

'Jackie!' said Enid. 'You hear what she said?'

'Be quiet, Enid,' said Jackie, as exasperated as the rest of us.

As any man will know, that was the worst thing he could have said – and so it escalated. She turned on Jackie, he pushed her back and she fell over.

Michael was mortified. 'It didn't used to be like this – It used to be fun,' he said. He *hated* discord and this episode only served to prove his point: wives caused drama and proved a distraction. Which was why the myth that Hazel interfered with our choreography sessions was so laughable. No brother would have tolerated it. Especially Michael.

For him, it was enough having to contend with the envies outside the rehearsal room. He even had an expression for wives and their meddling, and he quoted a line from the Ten Commandments, calling them 'sharp-clawed treacherous little peacocks' – based on the woman sent to whisper in Moses' ear. Wives were the reason groups broke up: they had *their own* expectations of what their husbands should be doing. It was this way of thinking that made Michael vow that he was never going to marry until he found his soul and creative match. Besides, he had too many mountains to climb and didn't wish to be held back. But that airport incident was one of many throughout the late seventies. Ultimately, that was what his 1983 hit 'Wanna Be Startin' Something' is about. Hear those lyrics and you're reading Michael's mind about wives always starting some kind of drama.

IN THE MID-SEVENTIES MOTOWN WAS STRUGGLING to keep its family together. There was widespread disillusionment about promotion and record sales. Both the Four Tops and Gladys Knight & the Pips left for new labels (soon to be followed by the Temptations) and Marvin Gaye had taken control of his own singer-songwriting material – following the precedent of Stevie Wonder – to create his unforgettable album, *What's Going On*. When this album was released, Michael considered it 'a true masterpiece' and placed the album sleeve on a shelf at Hayvenhurst: an ornament to be admired; an example to follow. It is still there, propped up where he left it, to this day.

Looking back, everyone seemed to be reinvigorated under new management or granted more freedom. Except the Jackson 5. Michael always said, 'We are each captains of our own ship,' and after the creative freedom of Vegas, the return to Motown was stifling for the brothers. They felt babied and creatively restricted. Michael's song-writing scribbles were growing on paper and in his head, and the brothers worried aloud that 'The Motown ship is sinking.'

There was a difficult meeting with Mr Gordy – to which I wasn't invited – when it was Michael, not Joseph, who asked for more freedom. It was refused. Mr Gordy felt we still needed the Corporation and Michael viewed that as a patronising lack of faith. I stayed out of it because I assumed everything would get resolved. Michael loved Mr Gordy and knew how stubborn he could be – but if you let a matter rest for a few days, he could be persuaded. Just as he was when he first waved away Suzanne de Passe's recommendation to sign us. Just as he had backed down when Marvin Gaye asked for more songwriting freedom and, before him, Stevie Wonder. Mr Gordy was stubborn, but reasonable. All it required was time.

CHAPTER TEN
Separate Ways

'I WANT YOU TO COME OVER *without* Hazel,' said Joseph.

I was driving to my brother-in-law Terry's college graduation ceremony when my car phone – a telecom brick mounted on a plinth between the seats – had started to ring. The wonders of this modern technology meant that I was suddenly reachable anywhere, anytime – ideal for being summoned at a moment's notice to Hayvenhurst.

On command, I turned around and headed for Encino. Joseph might have lost our respect over his affair, but his demands still carried a lifetime's weight. The moment I heard the urgency in the words 'without Hazel' my stomach dropped. I instinctively knew it was Motown decision day. What I didn't guess was that decision had already been made.

Conveniently, no one else was home when I arrived. There wasn't even the sound of a barking dog. 'I'm in my room!' Joseph shouted.

I found him partly reclined on his bed, leaning against the head-board with his feet on the floor. The adamant look on his face said,

'You're going to do as I say, Jermaine.' Before him, fanned out on the floral duvet, were several contracts, flipped open at the signature page.

I walked over, picked up the one with my name on it and saw it was an agreement with CBS Records Group. I started to shake inside.

'We're going to CBS Records. We need you to sign,' said Joseph, straight to the point. It was an incredible opportunity, he said. 'You will write your own material and have the chance to produce,' he added, something he knew each brother wanted to do.

My head was spinning. *You've done a deal behind my back? When? How did the brothers do this?* 'Did Michael sign?' I asked.

'Yes.' He pushed my brother's contract towards me. Nailing me.

I dropped mine on to the bed. 'I'm not signing,' I said.

Joseph stood and walked over to me. It was the first time in my life that I had defied my father and I don't think either of us could believe it. I looked at him, tears welling, and wondered what had happened to the loyalty and integrity we had been taught. But in Joseph's mind, family was the core value to honour.

'Sign it,' he said.

I thought of my wife, Hazel, and my father-in-law, Mr Gordy, and all that he had ever done for us, personally and professionally. The Gordy family. The Motown family. *Damn right this is about family.* 'I'm going to get an attorney,' I said. I hurried out of there. Joseph didn't move.

I headed to the restaurant in Beverly Hills where Hazel was still celebrating her brother's milestone. As I drove, my biggest confusion was Michael. He loved Mr Gordy and remained close with Diana Ross. Why would he leave 'family' and jump ship to a company of strangers? In his heart of hearts, he wouldn't leave Motown under his own steam. I felt convinced about that.

He said differently in his *Moonwalk* autobiography, of course: 'I knew it was time for a change, so we followed our instincts and we won when we decided to try for a fresh start with another label ...'

Financially, they *did* win. When CBS deal-maker Ron Alexenberg offered something like a 20 per cent royalty – compared to

Motown's two per cent – with 'a one million dollar package', Joseph was never going to refuse and it allowed him to reassert his control. But what Michael kept hidden was how his signature was obtained and the truth didn't emerge until the 1984 'Victory Tour'. 'You have no idea how angry I was,' he said. 'I didn't believe another word Joseph said after that.'

Our father had used a lifelong dream of Michael's to tempt him. If he signed on the dotted line, he would have dinner with his idol Fred Astaire, he was told. With that promise, I know Michael would have grabbed that pen and signed eagerly. But the dinner never happened, and he couldn't believe that his own father had made a promise he couldn't deliver. And our father had used that signature to sway me. But Joseph was clearly intent on running to CBS Records, where the new president was Walter Yetnikoff, a man who, by all industry accounts, made our father look like a pussycat. Why? He answers that question in his own autobiography: 'I created a mutual balance of terror between me and my artists,' he wrote in 2004. 'I started seeing myself as a star. Like most stars, my sense of self was dangerously inflated ... I wanted to get high. Drink, drugs, adulation, corporate power, fast women ... made it easy.' I couldn't write a better illustration of the distinction between Mr Gordy and Motown, and Mr Yetnikoff and everything that exemplifies Hollywood. As for Joseph, he failed to see that CBS/Epic – with no emotional attachment to what we had built – wouldn't care about us: they just wanted to own and flog a proven thoroughbred.

When I arrived at the restaurant to see Hazel, Mr Gordy was already there. Apparently my face said it all before I did. He left the dinner table and joined me at the bar. When I told him everything, his hurt was obvious, too. 'What are *you* going to do?' he asked.

'They say the Motown ship is sinking,' I said, unable to look him in the eye.

His reassurances to the contrary were immediate and he was big enough to put to one side the imminent loss to Motown. 'You'll get no pressure from me. I will respect the decision you make,' he said.

If my mind wasn't made up at the bar, I wanted Mr Gordy to know where my heart was: 'If the Motown ship is sinking, then I want to stay and keep it afloat.'

He had believed in us when it mattered, and that debt of gratitude outweighed CBS dollars in my mind. Mr Gordy smiled sympathetically, got up, patted me on the shoulder and told me to go home and think about it.

Another discussion with Joseph and Mother at Hayvenhurst confirmed that nothing was going to change. Not even Mr Gordy's vow – 'We'll do whatever it takes, we just want the boys to stay with Motown' – could sway it. The Jackson 5 was moving to a new label, with or without me, said Joseph.

He reminded me of his mantra through life: that family is the most important thing in the world; that others will come and go, but your brothers, sisters and parents will always be there. Family – the lighthouse, the base camp, the headquarters, the sanctuary, the Kingdom Hall. 'So what are you going to do?' he asked.

'My allegiance is with the Jackson 5 at Motown,' I said.

He exploded. 'IT'S MY BLOOD RUNNING THROUGH YOUR VEINS, NOT BERRY GORDY'S!'

I tried reasoning. 'Mr Gordy brought us to Hollywood,' I said. 'He introduced us to the world. He put steaks on our table and teeth in our mouths!'

Mother quietly interrupted and reminded me that we'd eaten steaks in Gary, and that the cosmetic dental surgery to repair Tito's and Jackie's chipped teeth 'has been recouped by Mr Gordy a hundred times over.'

I desperately wanted to speak with Michael, but what was the point? There was this awkward tension between me and the brothers now, and Joseph had control. It seemed futile. I returned to the comfort of Hazel's company. Without her, I don't know where I would have been and she made her stance clear on day one. 'I'm married to you, not Daddy's business,' she said. 'Whatever you decide, I will back you 100 per cent.' I had some serious thinking to do and took a break from the Jackson 5 in order to reach my decision.

BY NOW, HAZEL AND I HAD moved from Bel Air to a ranch in Thousand Oaks, north-west of LA. It was a Paul Williams-designed home set in 46 acres in Hidden Valley, with 12 horses, 11 dogs, ducks and swans on the pond – and a mountain lion in its pen. We bought Sheba as a cub, and she was evidence of my escalation in exotic pets. It almost rivalled that of our neighbour Dean Martin – he had a bear that was the talk of the valley. We kept a lot hidden in the Hidden Valley.

Our ranch was a sanctuary but there is no better place to meditate than the Pacific Ocean, so we also spent time at our beach-house on the La Costa stretch of Malibu, facing the ocean, backing on to the Pacific Coast Highway. I watched sunrises and sunsets for much of my 'thinking time' deciding my future. In fact, I was sitting on the beach one day when Hazel called me to the phone. It was her father on the line.

'Jermaine,' said Mr Gordy, 'I've just had a call from Michael – he wants you there with him.' The brothers had previously performed in some city on some date without me, but Michael wanted me alongside him for the Westbury Music Fair in Long Island. According to Mr Gordy, he said, 'Please get Jermaine to come out here. I miss him. It's hard being onstage and looking to my left and not seeing him there.'

In his autobiography, Michael explained it this way: 'It was so painful for me … I had depended on being next to Jermaine. When I did that first show without him … I felt totally naked onstage …'

Mr Gordy's advice was unequivocal: 'He's your brother,' he said. 'He needs you. Go support him.'

In the 1992 television mini-series of our story, I was shown wandering the beach on the West Coast as Michael performed on the East. In other written accounts, biographers have turned this entire scene into fiction. What really happened was that I boarded a plane to New York to join the brothers. Hazel stayed at home and

I was accompanied by someone from Motown to 'protect Mr Gordy's artist and interests'. On that flight, all I could think about was Michael reaching out to Mr Gordy. It was a brave call, and it told me two things: (a) Joseph didn't know he was making it; (b) Michael was letting Mr Gordy know there was no ill-will on his part, that he still had Michael's trust and respect.

My anxiety calmed the nearer the flight got to Long Island. I didn't care that Joseph would be on me, thinking I was crawling back. All I cared about was being with my brothers. There were no great hugs when I turned up at the hotel on the afternoon of the show but when Michael saw me, a beaming smile broke out on his face. Some comforts don't need to be expressed, I guess. We talked. He said he couldn't imagine continuing on stage without me. I said I couldn't imagine life at Motown without my brothers. But gradually the reality became clear: in me, there was a determination to stand my ground; in him, there was resignation to a collective decision already made. We slowly arrived at acceptance, not quite understanding how we'd reached this end-game.

That alone was a wrench. I cried. Michael cried.

Joseph interrupted and asked me what I planned on doing. 'I'm not going on stage,' I said.

In that instant, it became clear that my arrival had misled everyone into thinking that I had turned up to perform. It was about one hour before show-time and Joseph was livid. The other brothers accused me of being unfair. I wanted to capitulate, jump into show costume and grab the nearest bass but instinct proved stronger and pulled me back. I remember little else, apart from standing there and watching them all walk off in a bubble that no longer surrounded me. As he headed down the hotel corridor, Michael looked back and the sadness in his face killed me. Joseph's frown said it all: 'You're not with us, your choice.'

I felt guilt; I felt like I had let everyone down but to go onstage would have misled the fans. The brothers ended up borrowing the bass player from the orchestra to make up the five and the Westbury Music Fair went on without me. I stayed at the hotel and slept in a separate room, alone for the first time since I was a poorly three-year-old in hospital. Maybe that was why it hurt so much.

The next morning, I joined the brothers at CBS Records, Manhattan. With the dawn of a new day, I think Joseph had woken hopeful that, when I'd heard the strategy for our greatness, I would see sense. But I was just curious to hear what they had to say. Call it a fishing expedition. The one memory I have is of sitting in an office as a salesman-like A&R man, dressed in all-white to match his teeth, outlined that he was going to do this and do that, and 'We're going to make you as big as the Beatles!'

I looked at Joseph. I looked at my brothers. Nothing. So I said it for them: 'But we're the Jackson 5. We've already knocked the Beatles off No. 1.' All heads turned to me. 'Twice,' I added pointedly.

It failed to divert the A&R man. He cleverly steered his pitch around his self-made obstacle and blew so much smoke up our asses that it was coming out of our mouths. Afterwards, they wanted to take us somewhere to 'meet a few people' but I was wary of photographers hovering around the building. I smelt a contrived photo op, the chance to capture all five brothers together at CBS Records. That was the picture everyone wanted at a time when rumours of a split were rife. I got out of there, said my good-byes and headed back to LA that day.

That is pretty much how we went our separate ways. There was a suggestion for years that I broke up the group by leaving, but I've never viewed it that way. I did not leave them: they left me. They left 'home' – and I will believe that until the day I die. There is no point in revisiting the ugly legalities that followed, between Motown, Joseph and CBS. I've read that Mr Gordy received damages of anywhere between $100,000 and $150,000. I never checked the figures – I just know it proved to be a costly decision and that Motown retained ownership of the 'Jackson 5' name. That meant my brothers became known as 'The Jacksons'. Randy, then 11, stepped into my place.

In six years, according to Joseph, we had recorded more than 400 songs at Motown and we released less than half that number. There is an untapped archive out there somewhere. I hadn't been counting. All I knew was that it felt like thousands and thousands of hours spent in the studio, plus all that time on stage and travelling the world. It had given us the most fun, the most memorable and happiest times of our lives. If I could claim them back at an auction and relive them today, I would.

THE WEEKS OF SEPARATION WERE – until June 2009 – the hardest of my life. The sense of detachment and loneliness was profound. I didn't feel like I had lost my right arm; I felt like I had lost every limb. I had Hazel, of course, but the brotherhood was intrinsic to who I was and everything I knew. When it was ripped away, I felt something tear.

What made it worse was that the brothers didn't speak to me for six months of 1976. Only Mother maintained contact, via phone, reassuring me that I just needed to give everybody time. But it still felt like ex-communication, and I suspected Joseph was behind it because he stopped my weekly allowance and share of royalties – no doubt to teach me a lesson about family.

Occasionally, the house phone rang and it was Joseph. 'How are you doing, Jermaine? How you living? How you eating?'

They were crazy questions, considering how well I was living, but I never took his taunts at face value. Deep down, Joseph was checking that I was okay and hiding it behind his hard front. At least, that was how I read it.

Hazel said she watched me wander lost and aimless for the longest time, but it remains a blur to me. 'Your depression was real bad,' she says, assisting my memory today. 'You just walked up and down the beach by yourself. You walked and cried, and there was nothing anyone could do to get you out of that hole. All I could do was hold your hand and let you cry.'

I wish I could say that a bout of melancholy was the extent of the trauma, but it wasn't. The stress made my hair fall out and I developed a bald spot bigger than a 50-pence piece on the top of my head. I went to see a dermatologist and an 'emotions doctor' and they both asked if there had been a recent trauma in my life. I must have found the only two specialists in Hollywood who didn't read newspapers.

But the fans didn't miss a trick and they were quick to banish me. On several occasions, I had Jackson 5 fans approach me in public and say, 'I don't want your autograph. You left the group – you betrayed your brothers!'

Let me tell you, when you'd known only adulation and praise, and you'd loved those fans back, that was a hard upper cut to the jaw. The upside to a dark period as an artist is that, sometimes, those moods can be translated into song and it was my first experience of loneliness that inspired me to write 'Lonely Won't Leave Me Alone', released on my *Precious Moments* album in 1986. But I think the song that best speaks about this time and the years that followed is 'I'm My Brother's Keeper'. I turned over my hurt to that song, like one of those old diary pages that you wrote as a kid: 'It's been five years or more since we've sung our song / And I wonder why we took so long / Through all the pain and the tears that I cried / Our dream never died inside ...' All I can say is YouTube it. It will always be the song that reminds me of the Jackson 5 split.

ONE AFTERNOON, HAZEL DECIDED TO GET me out of the house and take me shopping down Rodeo Drive, Beverly Hills. While out, we bumped into Barry White's right-hand man Gene Page – the composer and producer whose deft touch and arrangements underpin most of Barry's pillow-talking songs. That evening, Barry was having a party and Gene invited us along. It would be one of the most meaningful introductions of my life.

Barry lived in Sherman Oaks and his vast garden – all dense and tropical with a stunning waterfall – was filled with guests and industry names. Barry, a smile as big as his girth, greeted us at the door and stayed with us the whole evening, sitting in the library. We became friends for life, and I was at his side in his final days.

He was a wonderful man with the biggest heart, and so wise. He knew what it took to reach into the souls of people with his lyrics and in time, we would share a passion for motor homes, horses and sitting up late to watch *The Ten Commandments* over and over. We watched that classic so many times that we knew the script backwards.

Barry's advice about my own minuscule moment in history was invaluable. I lost count of the hours that I bored him with my dilemma, even after the decision was made. 'This is a test of character,' he said, 'standing up for what we believe in. You're good-hearted, J,' he added, 'so follow that heart. You have my support and your brothers will come around. There is family and there is business – don't confuse the two.'

Barry's advice ultimately came good. By the end of 1976, I was invited back into the family fold and the subject was, typically, rarely discussed. I think both sides realised that we could have handled matters better, but we put our artistic politics to one side for the sake of family.

Being a constant visitor to Hayvenhurst again made me realise that although things could change around us, nothing altered between us. We even found room to laugh. Michael would play a demo of the Jacksons and I'd listen intently, looking all serious. 'It's good ... There's just one thing that's missing,' I'd say.

'What? What you think it needs?'

'My voice.' Only part of me was joking. My sense of detachment was vocal, too.

MICHAEL LOVED LIFE AT THE BEACH and at the ranch. He stood in the tranquillity of Hidden Valley and in the ocean breeze of Malibu, and said the same thing in both: 'Never sell this place.' The secluded privacy of those locations appealed to him. That was presumably what appealed to my neighbours, too: actors Ryan O'Neal (four doors down) and Beau Bridges (directly next door). It was during my morning runs on the beach that I used to wave at Ryan's daughter, Tatum, as she stood on the balcony. She was a

13-year-old child star at the time, having won an Oscar at the age of 10 for Best Supporting Actress in *Paper Moon*. I told Michael there was 'this real pretty girl' living nearby and, coincidentally, he started showing up at the beach house more and more at weekends. But here's the ironic thing: they waved at each other but never spoke until they bumped into one another in a club on Sunset Strip.

'It's meant to be,' I joked.

'It's nothing, we're just friends,' he said, playing down its importance. But it was obvious from Tatum's visits to Hayvenhurst that they were boyfriend and girlfriend. She was clearly smitten and he was giddy around her, but Michael was always guarded about when and where he saw her. I don't remember one visit to Malibu when he left my house to see her, or they met on the beach. Which seemed odd, but Michael's sense of privacy and discretion, even among his siblings, was notable.

I am aware that Tatum has publicly distanced herself from being Michael's childhood sweetheart, but I don't think my brother ever suggested that they shared a blazing, passionate love affair. It was nothing but puppy love. But what matters is that, in my brother's heart and mind, Tatum was his first girlfriend.

ON AMERICAN INDEPENDENCE DAY 1977, MICHAEL was with me at the Malibu house to enjoy Hazel's barbecue. As she prepared the sunset feast, he decided to go splash about in the ocean. I watched him from the balcony – he had the beach to himself – sprinting down the slope in his shorts and jumping into the breaking waves. Hazel asked me to help her with something in the kitchen. I ignored her. I was too busy watching Michael as the sun started to drop. Something told me to keep my eyes on him, out there in the fading light, in the surf by himself, about five houses down.

I saw the waves and then his bobbing head … the waves … his bobbing head. He looked like a seal. Fireworks started shooting into the sky from somewhere around Malibu Pier but I kept my eyes on Michael.

Wait. Where is he?

The sunset sky flared with flashes of white, and started popping.

I can't see him. I can't see him.

And then I was running, barefooted, down the steps, towards the ocean, screaming his name. I caught him staggering on rubber legs in knee-deep water. He was gasping for air, shallow, rapid breathing. I got him out of the water and onto the sand.

I helped him up the steps from the beach and got him, dripping wet, into the passenger seat of the Mercedes before breaking the land-speed record on the Pacific Coast Highway, bound for the Malibu Emergency Hospital. I wove in and out of the traffic, foot to the floor. Beside me, Michael said nothing, pinned to the seat, grey-faced.

At the hospital, it turned out that he had pleurisy. After a few hours, he was discharged and I drove him back to my place.

'That was the most frightening journey ever,' said Michael, as we headed home.

'Yeah, you had me worried, too,' I said.

'No, Erms!' he said. 'Your driving! It was scarier than being in the water!'

I TURNED UP AT HAYVENHURST ONE day to find Muhammad Ali in the kitchen, the proudest black man in America sitting with Michael and Mother. The brothers had met him backstage at an all-stars event in his honour in 1975, and so began a happy association with the family, especially Michael. Ali was the sweetest, friendliest of men, like one of those playful uncles you can't wait to visit. Every time he saw us, the first thing he did was skip and bounce around the living room, ducking and diving. Then, he made one of those faces he used to put up against Joe Frazier: all good-looking, eyes big, biting the lip, slight nod. He looked us straight in the eye and jabbed at the space either side of our ears. Before he knew it, one of us was shadow-boxing with him. His aura was shy but magnetic, his presence strong but kind. There was not

190

a hint of 'celebrity'. The Ali you saw jousting and joking on television was the Ali who visited our house.

He spoke so fast and enthusiastically that his passion was contagious. The poetic lines he gave to the media he threw into natural conversation. He spoke in soundbites. His speech had such rhythm that, if you'd put music to it, he could have been America's first rapper. He said life was a mind-game. No one steps into the ring without a strategy, he said, and we each have an equal shot at greatness. Black or white. Rich or poor. 'Tell yourselves every day that you're the best, you're the greatest, no one can beat you. Tell yourselves that you are going to be out of this world,' he said. 'Be the greatest. Become it. Believe it.' This was Ali putting steel girders behind everything our parents had taught us.

Michael loved Ali because of his shared passion for magic. We were outside in the garden once – the photographer Howard Bingham was there – and Ali made us stand back as he stood side on at an angle. Then he was hovering on an inch of air. Floating like a butterfly.

'Do it again! Do it again!' Michael yelled, not taking his eyes off the footwork. Ali did it again. 'How you do that, man?'

'Lots of concentration, lots of magic!' he said.

Soon enough, Ali would pass down the art of levitation when my brother visited his beautiful house in Hancock Park. Michael returned from his first visit raving about the blown-up photos of Ali's bouts, and the belts framed on the walls. Michael went there to learn magic and practise different tricks. Their magic entertained them both for hours, but I know my brother also learned much more about Ali's philosophies on life, religion, his love of music – Jackie Wilson and Little Richard – and what it took to be a showman.

In later life, I would visit his house for a different reason: his third wife, Veronica Porsche, and I started taking acting lessons at the Milton Katselas School of Acting in Beverly Hills, twice a week. It was all part of my long-term wish to be a movie director, and hers to act. She always arrived immaculately dressed for the wonderful monologues she would deliver. And what surprised me most was that she brought her own props. Not in a bag, but a truck. If ever I doubted her zeal to succeed, it ended when a truck pulled up outside the playhouse and a guy started unloading couches, chairs, tables and lamps. It was quite something to see the greatest showman's wife throwing *everything* she had at this opportunity.

Meanwhile, Ali's admiration of Malcolm X intrigued Michael. In fact, it intrigued all of us, especially our school friend John McClain and me, because we were the most militant at that time. Motown had asked us never to speak in public about how Malcolm X went up against prejudice – questions about 'black power' were off limits – but we privately saluted his fight for black justice. I'll never forget a rare television interview Ali did with the brothers in 1977 when he spoke about his recent visit to the White House. 'The pictures I saw on the wall left me with one impression: it's the *White* House. It is the *white* White House,' he said, before he corrected himself and added, 'Oh, I saw a black cook!' One day, Ali added, they might allow a black man to be something more than a servant there.

Ali was a committed and campaigning Muslim, and he introduced the topic of the Nation of Islam into our lives. In the same way that Michael had been interested in Rose Fine's Jewish faith, he was also keen to explore Ali's beliefs, which led him to read about Malcolm X, the National Association for the Advancement of Coloured People (NAACP) and the Nation of Islam (NOI). He shared his mentor's admiration of the NOI's spirit of harmony, love and peace.

Michael looked up to Ali as a personal and professional role model, but I doubt he ever appreciated how much the admiration was mutual. In the year after my brother's death, Ali paid tribute to him. He was asked where he got his strength from to fight Parkinson's syndrome and he said: 'When people ask me, I tell them that I look at the man Michael Jackson looks at when he looks at the man in the mirror.'

I think back to five-year-old Michael shadow-boxing with Marlon in our living room in Gary as Ali floored Sonny Liston and wish I could travel back in time to tell the young Michael that one day he'd be shadow-boxing with Ali in person, learning magic, self-belief and courage – and inspiring him with his music. 'Destiny,' I would say. 'This is your destiny – and it's only the start.'

'*WHAT* IN THE HELL HAPPENED TO you?' I said to Michael, when I walked through the doors of Hayvenhurst one afternoon and saw his nose and cheeks covered with bandages. It looked like he'd gone 10 rounds with Ali: Michael seemed sheepish and the look Mother shot me suggested my question was insensitive.

He had slipped and fallen near the bar in the living room, I was told. Broken his nose. Everything was fine. I don't doubt that he had fallen but the consequent rhinoplasty led to the start of several phases of plastic surgery over the years, which the world seemed to obsess about it. Just as my brother kept his acne trauma to himself, he kept his surgery private, too. It was none of my business, yet people still expect his siblings to point out every stitch and scar with a time, date and place. Maybe some families are that intimate about each other's medical knowledge, but not ours. But even when I found out that he'd had a nose job, it didn't surprise me. It's hard to be surprised by something that is commonplace in Hollywood. The town merely mirrored our upbringing: image is everything. Besides, I understood Michael's need for surgery because the size of his nose had made him miserable for so long. What I never understood were those wild suggestions that he had plastic surgery because he wanted 'to do *anything* not to look like Joseph'. I shared a mirror with Michael for many years and his face adorned countless magazine covers. How *anyone* can think he resembled our father is lost on me.

The main thing was that Michael's surgery made him feel better about himself and, between now and his solo career, he would have surgeries that gave him a slimmer nose and a chiselled chin. Personally, I couldn't see what all the media fuss was about.

OUR SPLIT AS THE JACKSON 5 was a catalyst for change, and I think the Jacksons era was a transition phase for Michael, between him holding on to the security of the group and deciding to let go. Looking back, his immense talent was only ever biding its time, waiting for its perfect moment. When CBS Records placed the brothers with writer-producers Kenny Gamble and Leon Huff, they honed and polished the knowledge Michael had amassed at Motown. Michael said he learned more and more about a song's anatomy.

The Gamble-Huff combo had orchestrated what was known as the Philly International Sound. This soul-funk – heavy on the strings and big on the beats – was, in their words, 'the leaf that blew over from Detroit and landed in Philly'. If you know Harold Melvin and the Blue Notes' 'If You Don't Know Me By Now', Billy Paul's 'Me & Mrs Jones' or MacFadden and Whitehead's 'Ain't No Stopping Us Now', you've listened to their calibre.

So my brothers headed east to make music in Philadelphia, not far from Motown's roots. In this more collaborative environment, Michael and the brothers flourished as songwriters and producers, and they released some great pop music. Their first two albums didn't take off, continuing the struggle we had experienced together. The change in fortunes came with their third album, *Destiny*, which moved away from the Philly sound and was a group collaboration, written by the brothers themselves. It went double-platinum, vindicating their long-time wish for creative autonomy. The album yielded hit singles: 'Enjoy Yourself' which went to No. 6 in the Billboard Hot 100, 'Show You The Way To Go', their first UK No. 1 and 'Shake Your Body', which went to No. 7 in the US and sold over two million copies. 'Blame It On The Boogie' – a cover of a song first released by an Englishman called, ironically, Mick Jackson – also charted, and found its Top 10 audience in the UK.

There was also *'The Jacksons'* TV special with Janet, La Toya and Rebbie on CBS, but Michael privately cringed over its scripted comedy and canned laughter. It was vaudeville all over again, but instead of being restricted to a quiet corner of Vegas, it was broad-cast across America.

Michael worried that over-exposure would jeopardise his musi-cal career. We had always said that too much TV could burn out an artist like a light-bulb left on too long, and this bad experience would turn him off from exposure on television shows.

As for me, life without the brothers was a reality check. Motown put everything into the production of my album, *My Name Is Jermaine*, but it didn't get behind its promotion as much as it could have. It had other priorities, like Stevie Wonder, Marvin Gaye and Diana Ross. So much for everyone's suspicions about me becoming 'the favourite son'.

This reality would hit home hardest in 1982 when the track 'Let Me Tickle Your Fancy' with Devo hit No. 17 in the US and carried Billboard's red dot symbol, signifying it was 'a bullet' set to climb. But Motown didn't harness the momentum. The song lost the bullet and started falling. I remember wandering around London at the time, feeling despondent and marooned. My most notable chart success at Motown was with 'Let's Get Serious', which reached No. 9 in the Billboard Hot 100 and No.1 in the US R&B charts in 1980 before earning a Grammy nomination for Best Male R&B Vocal Performance. People said that a nomination must be nice, but all I heard was Joseph's voice reminding me that it's the winning that counts.

However hard I tried over the years, it was never the same without my brothers. I didn't regret sticking to my principles; I just regretted the new reality. In truth, neither I nor the Jacksons could recapture the magic and heights of the Jackson 5. In that respect, we chased our own shadows for much of the late seventies and early eighties. I continued recording, but also decided to channel my energies into becoming a producer, guided by Mr Gordy. 'Find 'em, sign 'em, mind 'em and re-sign 'em,' he always said. I had my own office and a roving brief to find and produce new talent. With Hazel, we brought in Stephanie Mills, Switch and DeBarge. If I didn't exactly flourish in the charts, I advanced behind the scenes.

MICHAEL COMPARED HIS CAREER TO THE American presidential plane, Air Force One, a 747 like no other, looking to take off and cruise in its own exclusive flying corridor. In his mind, the plane was his 'empire'. It needed to be aerodynamic. He needed to know each and every passenger he was carrying, and every working part. He was 'the pilot, flying solo'. This was an analogy he sketched out on paper as a master plan as early as 1978. He was entertaining the idea of going 100 per cent solo long before he did.

But if the ultimate decision to stand alone was tough for me, it was excruciating for him. He was a people-pleaser who hated the idea of confrontation or causing upset. In the studio, his creative instinct pushed forward a gentle but assertive insistence, but in his personal life, he preferred to stick his head in the sand and hope an issue would work itself out. In his heart, he knew that he carried the Jacksons, which weighed on him heavily.

In my opinion, two key factors brought his solo career to a head. First, the brothers left home one by one. Marlon married his girl Carol, and Randy moved out to find independence, aged 17. Michael – so used to the comfort of brothers around him – was left at Hayvenhurst with Mother, Joseph, Janet and La Toya. Rebbie observed the situation from afar, saying he 'resented the brothers moving out of the house.' She says, 'He didn't see how he could build effectively on the strong musical foundation they had established if the brothers didn't remain 100 per cent focused.'

Michael was married to his work, and it puzzled him that we could allow women to come between us and our music. The echoes of Joseph's conditioning were not lost on me. But Michael's passion and companion was music: he simply had no room in his life for a woman. In the brotherly void, he grew accustomed to being on his own. The more time he spent alone, the more going solo seemed less alien. But the propelling force was Diana Ross. She was in his ear, saying he needed to chase what he wanted, advising him how to use *his* name, not the family name, making him believe in her example of leaving the Supremes. One of the hottest acts around – and a mentor he adored – was telling Michael that if he wanted to be the best, he had to jump ... and fly. At least, that was how the message was relayed back to me.

It was life-changing advice, issued in New York on the set of Universal's movie adaptation of the musical *The Wiz*. Diana played Dorothy, and Michael played the Scarecrow. It was Mr Gordy who handed him this début screen role after Motown acquired the movie rights, proving the lack of acrimony following the split, but my father-in-law was initially unsure how Michael would react to his approach.

I was at the ranch when the phone rang and he sounded me out. 'Are you kidding me?' I said. 'Michael loves *The Wizard of Oz*! It's right up his alley! He's got to play that role!'

It was between him and the Broadway star Ben Vereen (who, ironically, would play the Wizard in the musical *Wicked* in 2005), but Michael landed the part after impressing Universal.

Ultimately, the movie bombed but Michael won plaudits and the highest praise came from the director, Sidney Lumet, who said, 'Michael is the most talented young person to come along since James Dean – a brilliant actor, a phenomenal dancer, one of the rarest talents I've ever worked with. That's no hype.' The whole experience lit another desire within Michael: to get more involved in movies. It also brought him exceptionally close to Diana.

His devotion to our goddess of Motown developed from a teenage crush into a young man's infatuation. I think it's fair to say that, in his mind, Diana was the first woman he fell in love with. I always wondered if she felt for him the way he felt for her, or if she saw him as the little boy she'd first met. Michael felt she no longer viewed him as a boy, but as a man and a respected artist. They had the kind of true friendship that rarely exists in Hollywood and I think that was what he prized most. As for how intimate they truly became, this is where his music – nearly always semi-autobiographical – should speak for itself. Go listen to the wistful lyrics of 'Remember The Time', released in 1992. That song was, as Michael told me, written with Diana Ross in mind; the one great love that, as far as he was concerned, escaped him.

MICHAEL NEVER MENTIONED FEELING lonely at Hayvenhurst without the brothers. He concealed it well, even though he lived under the same roof as my parents and sisters. I don't think any of us knew it was 'one of the most difficult periods of [his] life' or how 'isolated' he felt until we read his autobiography.

Of course, he built a special bond with Janet and she became his virtual shadow. Those two were so alike it was sometimes uncanny. Janet, although a tomboy, was the female version of Michael in many ways: sensitive, gentle, inquisitive, socially brittle but heartily strong, and full of kindness. But she wasn't always around because her acting abilities had landed her a role in the CBS sit-com *Good Times*, playing Penny, which put her on set most days nine-to-five. Michael always had La Toya and they were also close.

He adored his sisters. Without them, he would have been utterly lost. But I think there is something about being brothers that only a brother can know. And I suspect the same detachment that hit me hit him. Maybe it was the shared realisation that we had no *real* friends outside the industry. We never had. Not in Gary. Not in Los Angeles. Our pace of life, the many schedules and our countless dreams had got in the way of forming true bonds. 'Friendship' was a word we heard but never really understood.

So, when he got bored, Michael told Mother he was going for a walk down the street and I guess she assumed he was getting out to clear his head. Ventura Boulevard is the longest east-to-west thoroughfare that links the San Fernando Valley with Hollywood and he had only to turn left out of the gates and walk less than one block to reach the crossroads next to the local supermarket. Michael didn't wander down there to clear his head: he went to find friends – 'to meet people who didn't know who I was … I wanted to meet *anybody* in the neighbourhood.'

It was years later when we briefly spoke about this. 'Why didn't you call me? Or the other brothers?'

'You had Hazel. I didn't want to disturb you.' That was Michael: afraid of coming across as a nuisance or upsetting someone else's plans. Or maybe it was because we had never needed to organise our togetherness before, so the idea of arranging to meet up, unscheduled, was alien among the brothers. Whatever the reason, it was not the first time Michael had been in distress and failed to reach out to his family. He'd rather suffer quietly, walk away and seek his answers in a stranger. It was as if he wished to enter into a bond where the slate was clean. Not that such a hope would be realistic. As he told me, traffic only stopped in Ventura Boulevard when motorists spotted 'Michael Jackson!' hovering on the street. They wound down their windows and asked for his autograph; they took his photo. I can only imagine his sadness when his expectations ran up against that reality.

Michael soon realised that his true self was invisible; all people saw was the image of 'Michael Jackson'. This is what fame does: it eclipses the real you, and someone like my brother had no chance of being 'seen' for who he really was as a private person. From that day on, his friends would have to come from an eclectic group of A-list Hollywood names.

THERE WAS SERENDIPITY IN MICHAEL DOING *The Wiz* because its musical score maestro was Quincy Jones, who became the producer on Michael's first solo album, *Off the Wall*, in 1979. Michael had heard of Quincy before *The Wiz* because Quincy had a high-profile concert group called Wattsline and also ran an LA workshop for unknown artists. When he first agreed to work with my brother, he said: 'If he can make people cry singing about a rat, then he's something special!'

Initially, this album was viewed as another solo project under the group umbrella, just as before, and Michael would ultimately take his material on the *Jacksons' Triumph Tour*, their fourth album. I don't honestly know if he reckoned, based on the performance of his previous albums, it would be a success but the Quincy factor changed everything. He and Michael proved a great team, hand in glove. Quincy helped extract and shape Michael's ideas; the mechanic to his creativity. Together, they carved out Michael's signature sound and *Off the Wall* ultimately sold around eight million copies in the US, achieving two No. 1s in the Billboard Hot 100: 'Rock With You' and 'Don't Stop Till You Get Enough', the latter winning a Grammy for Best R&B Vocal Performance (Male).

But Michael didn't celebrate that first Grammy; he wept. He watched the ceremony at home and felt crushed that he didn't win Record of the Year. For an album that had been embraced by the industry, critics and fans, one Golden Gramophone didn't match his hopes or expectations. He felt snubbed, not honoured; he felt that his great work had been largely overlooked but it didn't defeat him. It made him hungrier and he adopted the 'I'll show 'em' attitude. He decided to 'reach beyond' and set his sights on domination, a clutch of Grammys, and creating 'the biggest-selling record of all time.' This was the ambition he would write on his bathroom mirror at Hayvenhurst: 'THRILLER! 100s MILLIONS OF SALES … SELL-OUT STADIUMS'. It was a desire driven by his conditioning never to be second best and motivated by the same yearning with which he had vowed to have his name in *The Guinness Book of Records*. Michael also knew what it would take to get him there. Focus. Dedication. Determination. Perseverance. He wrote those words everywhere. Aged 21, he decided to take charge of his life.

CHAPTER ELEVEN

Moonwalking

'YOU ARE CONFIDENT ... YOU ARE strong ... You are beautiful ... You are the greatest.'

In my mind, I am relistening to a tape and it is Michael's unmistakable voice. He's talking to himself. 'You are confident ... You are strong ... You are beautiful ... You are the greatest,' he repeats. He is meditative and alone, speaking in a tone as soft as the lightest breath. I hear it today as clearly as I did back then; one of Michael's morning meditations in the eighties, a mantra captured on a voice recorder so that he could play it back as a pep-talk to himself. He was like a sportsman in the dressing room before stepping into the public arena on a must-win day, eradicating any doubt or fear of failure. With Michael setting out to conquer the music world, he needed to be mentally strong. I don't know if it was a technique handed down by Muhammad Ali, but 'the greatest' suggests to me that it was, as an extension of our training: think it, see it, believe it, make it happen.

I first heard this mantra in 1984, in the studio with Michael, when we recorded a song called 'Tell Me I'm Not Dreaming'. We'd

been talking about negativity and he said something about controlling our thoughts, adding, 'Listen to this.' If he were still alive, he
would probably cringe at my sharing this because it was a very
private ritual. But if his legacy is about the empowerment of others
with his music or wisdom, then I think this insight is appropriate
because it shows that Michael Jackson – the King of Pop, the greatest entertainer – was human, too. It says that his self-esteem needed
a kick up the butt just like anyone else's.

Michael used positive self-talk when he needed to feel good or
make something happen: 'When you say it out loud, and you keep
repeating it, the subconscious can make it come true,' he always
said. To him, speaking into a tape recorder – a device never far from
his side to capture an arrangement or lyric that came into his head
– was as natural as making a wish. He wrote about this in his autobiography, explaining how he made wishes while watching
sunsets, casting out those hopes for the sun to take with it. As a boy,
he always made a wish before diving into the pool. These wishes
were focused on creating the best-selling record of all time. We all
believed in positive visualisation, but Michael took it to a whole
new level: messages on his mirror, mantras on his tape recorder,
imagining his name in *The Guinness Book of Records*, and wishes cast
into sunsets and swimming pools.

I have no doubt that he was telling himself that he was the
greatest in the run-up to his 'This Is It' concert in London; a feath-
erweight champion psyching himself up for a comeback. He was
his greatest critic with each new album and tour; he didn't view
himself as the fans did. The adulation may have been Michael's
constant source of love, but it didn't guarantee self-love in a public
environment where the media labelled him 'wacko' and 'weird'.
Mental strength becomes the biggest challenge when the fans don't
expect you to fall but the world's media are waiting for the moment
you do.

Michael believed that if he put something out there – and said
something was so – it would become reality, and everyone in the
family knew that he was promising the kind of solo album that

would astound us all. But that creative process was strictly private. According to Mother, he locked himself away in his quarters and she only knew the song-writing was going well because, occasionally, she'd pass his door and hear a 'Whoo!' and excited clapping.

IF *OFF THE WALL* DIDN'T BRING a clutch of awards, it swelled his 'fan-dom', and the days of Jackson-mania meant he was ready and equipped for it. That was probably a good thing because disturbing incidents started to happen. Once, Mother went into a back room behind the garage and got the fright of her life. There, in a sleeping-bag, lying next to a bunch of discarded food wrappers, was a young girl, looking equally startled. Ever the saint, Mother asked her what she was doing.

'Waiting for Michael,' she said innocently.

'How on earth did you get in? How long have you been here?'

'About two weeks. Will Michael see me?'

We knew how she had gained access but I'm not going to advertise the fact, even if we have blocked it off today. But that's how big the property was: she had been able to go unnoticed for that long.

Yet that was a minor incident compared to the time Mother decided to take a nap in her bedroom. She was probably lying there for about half an hour when she felt a presence. She opened her eyes and, looking down on her, standing beside her bed, were two of the most innocent-looking fans. 'We didn't know what to do ... we didn't want to wake you,' they said, 'but we've come to see if we can ask for Michael's autograph.'

Mother didn't call the police because 'I didn't want them getting into trouble.' But our position would be less forgiving when the 'Billie Jeans' of this world started to show up.

There have been many theories about the song's inspiration, with suggestions that 'Billie Jean' was a specific woman. But, as Michael made clear in his autobiography, she is actually a composition of the most obsessive fans, as witnessed during our Jackson 5 days.

The song tells the story of a woman trying to trap a man with a false pregnancy and its true back-story lies in two incidents. First, one lady mailed me a pair of pink baby shoes to the Bel Air home I'd shared with Hazel. An attached note read: 'These are for the baby we'll be having. I am pregnant with your child.' Then Jackie received a similar fantastical claim in a handwritten letter sent to his home. As the two most prolific boys with the ladies, we were wide open to such claims but they ignored the fact that we practised safe sex. Michael never slept with a fan so no such claim could be made against him.

In later years – after the song became a worldwide hit – the family described a certain kind of fan as a 'Billie Jean'. It wasn't intended to be a compliment – because that song is no love story – but a few people put their hands in the air to claim this notoriety over imagined relationships with Michael.

Billie Jeans were fans Michael was wary of. The interior walls of the guard-house we installed at Hayvenhurst were covered with photos and sketches of what each woman looked like. It resembled a sheriff's office with 'Wanted' photos. The most notorious Billie Jean was a woman we knew as Yvonne, an African-American with three kids. She was always loitering around, convinced Michael loved her. One day, she waited at the front gate until Mother came out to see her. She had shaved the heads of her three children, saying they had lice and she needed Michael's help because 'These are your grandchildren. These are the children I had with Michael.'

Another Billie Jean lived in the UK but the 5,000-mile journey has never deterred her. She actually took out a lawsuit against the family, saying she had married Michael in secret and they'd had a child. She even presented convincing-looking marriage and birth certificates as 'evidence' in a case that obviously went nowhere.

But the most astonishing incident happened later at Neverland when a Billie Jean accessed the grounds. When security found her, she was carrying a bona-fide California driving licence from the

Department of Motor Vehicles with a photo and an address that said 'Neverland Ranch', Figueroa Valley and the zip-code – and the name Billie Jean. It was incredible the lengths these women went to.

I need to stress that the vast majority of Michael's fans were not Billie Jeans; they were the most dedicated, loyal and loving fans an artist could wish for, and he knew this better than anyone. He shared a unique association with the people he called his 'soldiers of love'. Once security had screened groups of fans outside Hayvenhurst, he'd come out to spend a few minutes chatting and signing autographs. He was forever trying to make himself accessible in an increasingly inaccessible reality.

As his brother, it wasn't always easy to keep my patience. One day, I pulled into the driveway to find a man standing alone at the gate, blocking my way in. I asked him politely to move. He refused. I asked him what his problem was. Michael's family, he said. *That* was his problem. 'I'm here to rescue him,' he added.

'Michael doesn't need rescuing. Now get out of my way,' I said.

When he refused, I got out of the car and we started fighting just as the security guards arrived. 'You know nothing about this family! Now leave us alone!' I yelled.

Strangers claiming to know Michael as well as we did were something we would have to get used to. But at least that guy got the message and ran off.

If only it would always have proved that easy to keep divisiveness at bay.

MICHAEL MADE THE DECISION TO REDESIGN Hayvenhurst, gutting its interior, adding a second storey and landscaping the gardens. There had been talk of a move after 11 years in Encino, but he wanted to stick around because he liked it there, so he offered to pay for the remodelling. Everyone moved into a family-owned condo up the road as the house was rebuilt English-style, mock-Tudor. He wanted 'to liven the place up a little' and the new Hayvenhurst – planned in 1981, built in early 1983 – remains infused with my brother's heart and spirit.

After passing by a stone fountain of kneeling horses, the grand entrance is a double-door leading to a lobby with a white marble floor. Library and in-house theatre to the left; living room and kitchen to the right. Ahead the staircase sweeps from right to left, curving up around a central chandelier. At the landing that over-looks the lobby, turn right down the emerald-green carpet to what were Janet and La Toya's rooms. Turn left to Mother's and Joseph's suite in one corner and Michael's in another. Michael's quarters and the sisters' bedrooms were at opposite ends of the house – a point worth noting for later reports that placed La Toya's 'bedroom adjacent to Michael's', suggesting she could easily witness all his comings and goings.

Inside his quarters, there was a brick fireplace, black marble bathroom and a Murphy bed that folded into the wall because Michael often liked to sleep on the floor; a hangover from our Gary days when we'd throw down a mattress or a duvet. There is just *something* about sleeping on the floor that we've always liked. I'm the same to this day. I prefer it, whereas Michael always said it was good for his back.

In his rooms, photos of Ava Gardner were pinned up because he 'loved her grace and beauty'. In later years he had pictures of child star Shirley Temple and then, towards the end of his life, Alicia Keys. His ceiling leaps to a narrow mezzanine-level loft – reached by a white-painted, wooden spiral staircase – which is lined with bookshelves and leads to a door and a set of rooms tucked away in the roof, with a den and a 'hair salon' complete with a barber's swivel chair, sink and mirror. It wasn't the only private place in his quarters – he also ensured he had his own staircase to a back entrance out of the house.

His bedroom opened on to a brick patio with a vast, pergola-like canopy supported by pillars; he placed a giant hot-tub in one corner and a tiled barbecue area in the other. This was where he sat in the mornings, with views of the lawns 90 degrees to his left and the cobblestoned courtyard below, reached by his outside spiral stair-case leading from the patio. In the middle of that yard stands a

Victorian lamp-post with a street sign announcing 'Happiness'. In a corner down to his left, there is a brick building with a mock shop frontage; one display window depicts a 1950s toy store full of porcelain dolls, wooden toy soldiers, teddy bears, a doll's house and a mini rocking chair; the other a flower store, full of artificial arrangements in baskets. This is the façade of Michael's studio. The fun on the outside belied the serious work that went on behind the scenes.

Inside, a painted mural fills one wall. It is a green forest scene, with a cartoon version of Michael perched in a tree reading a green book with a title *The Secret of Life* – required reading for Jehovah's Witnesses. On the studio's exterior wall is an encased image of a Disney-like castle on a hill, lying in the distance at the end of a path leading from a forest. In the foreground, Michael stands with a child leaning into him. 'Of Children, Castles and Kings,' the caption reads, embedded with pin-lights.

But the most striking change was in the gardens: there were flowers everywhere. Michael never used to like flowers 'because they remind me of funerals', but his trips to Disney had changed all that. Now he created blooming flowerbeds, arranged in the colours of the rainbow, five, six rows deep. It is in those gardens that you can't help but notice a wrought-iron web of leaves framing a lantern. It hangs from one corner of the house with a wooden, hand-carved sign that reads, 'Follow Your Dreams Wherever They May Lead.'

There was one surprise renovation we were not allowed to see until Michael was ready. The 'attic' – two narrow rooms above the garage – was out of bounds for weeks. 'No one is allowed up there,' he told Mother. 'It's a gift to you all – I want everybody to see it at the same time.'

He was up in that attic for nights on end, running up and down the short flight of stairs beside the garage, organising his secret project with his assistants and helpers.

Come the day of the grand unveiling, Michael asked every sibling to gather in the dining room with Mother and Joseph. The chef laid on an impressive buffet, so we guessed this was a big deal.

There was a real touch of the ceremonial and then, clapping his hands to seize our attention, he appeared at the door. 'Everyone, my surprise is ready. Follow me!'

In single file, we crossed the courtyard and climbed the stairs to the attic. I was somewhere in the middle of the herd when I heard gasps up ahead. When I reached the top and looked around, I understood why.

Michael had turned the entire space into a memory room.

He had literally smothered the walls *and ceilings* in images, blown up into large prints, running into one another. Every inch of available surface – including the underside of the sloping garage roof and the inside of a closet – is to this day covered with his black-and-white and colour montage. I'm not talking photos neatly arranged in frames like a museum; I'm talking about walls plastered with images that provided a running commentary of our years as a family, our years as a group, and his years as a solo artist; his fondest memories merged together in one place to provide a secret archive of his and our journey.

I was speechless trying to absorb the scale of this monumental project. There were photos of our grandparents, the family, 2300 Jackson Street, our childhood, Jackson 5 days, magazine covers, TV publicity shots, concert stills and crowd shots. You name it, he'd posted it. Even Mother's driver's licence, our parents' marriage certificate and his old school report. The second room, at the far end, would ultimately fill with memorabilia, awards, mementoes and glass cases of his sequined gloves. By the mid-eighties, one wall became his 'celebrity wall' – maybe 50 photos of him with famous people. To name but a few: Julie Andrews, Elton John, Jackie Onassis, Frank Sinatra, Barbra Streisand, Sean Connery, Whoopi Goldberg, Joan Collins, Liza Minnelli, Dustin Hoffman, Meryl Streep, James Brown and E.T., from when Michael narrated *E.T.: The Extra-Terrestial* storybook LP. There was even a blown-up image of our tutor, Rose Fine.

But the walls did not say it all. On the skirting-boards, messages were written in perfect calligraphy, running around the room like one of those news-tickers at the bottom of a television screen: 'Joseph Fulfilled His Dreams Through Us'; 'Thank You, Jehovah, Joseph, Mother, Berry Gordy, Suzanne de Passe, Diana Ross'; 'The Earth Has Music For Those Who Listen'. And in the attic's bathroom, he posted only one telling item: a giant image of the 1981 Diana Ross album *Why Do Fools Fall in Love* – a title which I think points to his own reflections about his relationship with Diana. I found it significant that this was the only image that stood in isolation in all the rooms.

One of the two rooms was dedicated to the Jackson 5 years. He had enlarged one black-and-white publicity photo so that we stood five feet high at the top of the stairs – the first image you see. Above it, he had written his own caption: 'JUST KIDS WITH A DREAM'. Beside it, on a wall-mounted plaque, Michael had inscribed a message, written in gold on black:

> To take a picture
> Is to capture a moment
> To stop time
> To preserve the way we were
> They say a picture speaks a thousand words
> So with these photographs
> I will re-create some wonderful
> Magical moments in our lives
> Hopefully, this journey into the past
> In picturesque form
> will be a stimulant
> To create a brighter, successful tomorrow
>
> – Michael Jackson

This picture gallery was also his office and dancing room. Each Sunday, this was where he locked himself away for two- to three-hour sessions to rehearse a move. I love the thought of him dancing surrounded by memories. When anyone claims that Michael was always running from his past and the Jackson 5 days, I afford myself a wry smile and think about this memory room and the walls that speak to each of us and say: 'Be proud. Never forget.'

SOME FACES ON THAT 'CELEBRITY WALL' Michael classed as dear friends: Jane Fonda, Katharine Hepburn, Marlon Brando, Gregory Peck, Sammy Davis Junior and the inimitable Elizabeth Taylor. He met them while socialising, which he increasingly did once the new Hayvenhurst was completed. He started holding dinner parties, sending out invitations and making an occasion of it, with the chef cooking the finest food and staff on hand to serve. Mother referred to them as his 'star-studded dinners' and still recalls the night when she stayed in her room until there was a knock on her door and it was Michael with Yul Brynner, who had just popped upstairs to say hello. When Yul saw Mother was wearing her sleeping cap, he told her not to be embarrassed.

I never attended one of those occasions, but Mother was almost always there. She said that Michael, who was around 26 at this time, tried to behave in a mature fashion with his notable, older guests. 'He grows up to their age,' was how she put it. Yet the first thing he did was show them his doll collection in the window at the studio and the ice-cream/frozen yoghurt machine he had installed. As much as he tried to be adult beyond his years, his inner child was impossible to contain.

One thing you'll note about this eclectic group of people is that they were all actors in the movie business. He first met Katharine Hepburn when Jane Fonda invited him to the set of *On Golden Pond* in 1981. But whoever he was with, Michael was determined to extract their life wisdom, advice and knowledge, especially about the movie industry and fame; he was eager to tap into their experience as he stepped out as an artist in his own right.

With each friend – at their house or trailer – he took along a tape recorder and discreetly recorded their conversations. This might seem like a strange thing to do and I doubt the other parties knew about it, but it was understandable from his point of view: he captured their sound advice so that he could play it back, like one of his recorded pep-talks. I think he was so enraptured by being with them – especially Jane Fonda, Marlon Brando and Elizabeth Taylor – that he wanted to ensure that he never missed a word they said. At night, back at Hayvenhurst, he played back those conversations, listened and took notes. Michael was a prolific note-taker and note-sender, and he went through cassette after cassette on that tape recorder of his. I suspect there are numerous attorneys, producers, record-label executives and managers who were close to Michael without realising that the record button was pressed to capture a moment or protect his interests.

Over the years, as his fame and success grew, the motivation to record conversations had less to do with capturing advice than what people said about others or harsh words said to him. The fact that Michael was the star and revered by fans was not always respected by some people who came and went. Once Michael was with me when someone he respected started blaring at him down the phone. He held it away from his ear. 'This is how they speak to me. Can you believe it?'

I think many underestimated Michael. They considered him a musical genius yet they also detected his malleable tendency and his difficulty with confrontation. This, I think, was perceived as a weakness rather than kindness. I always liked to see strangers meet him for the first time and walk away impressed, preconceptions shattered. He had the capacity to be one of the silliest, most down-to-earth people you could know, but he was also one of the savviest, with an intellect and a creativity that made him one of the smartest thinkers-outside-the-box at any table.

I laugh now at his use of a tape recorder because it feels almost like he was snooping on his own private conversations, which reminds me of how inquisitive he was. Once, after Hazel and I had moved from Hidden Valley to a new house in the Brentwood area of LA, Michael was over and I was looking for, and failing to find, a flashlight.

'It's in the top drawer next to your bed,' said Michael.

'Oh, you've been rooting around again, huh?' I said.

Going through people's drawers had been a notorious habit of his since way back. He said you could always find out a little something about people by seeing what they kept there and how organised they were. He had started doing it when we'd visited our grandmother, Mama Martha, in East Chicago. He'd go into her drawers and rifle through her keepsakes. 'Michael, stop being nosy! You've no right looking in folks' drawers!' she said, but he didn't listen.

I was terrified he was going to do it at Sammy Davis Junior's magnificent home on Summit Drive, Beverly Hills. 'Michael, don't go looking in his drawers. I'll telling you!' I said. But he just chuckled and kept me guessing.

Sammy was a great guy to hang out with. He, Michael and I shared a love of movies and Sammy turned down the blinds to the California sun, pressed a button and a projector screen slid down the wall. One of the most-watched movies when Michael was over was Shirley Temple's *The Little Colonel*. I think Sammy liked it best, though, when we reminded him about his cowboy movies. Michael once challenged him to a draw and it was game-on with Sammy's fake pistols – old props from Hollywood. They pushed aside the stage-sized coffee-table in the living room and stood back to back. Altovise, Sammy's wife, and I were reduced to spectators. Sammy swaggered dramatically to one end of the room and Michael, all serious-faced, to the other.

Then someone shouted, 'DRAW!'

'BANG! BANG!' declared Sammy, and in one stroke he seemed to have swivelled on his heels, drawn and 'fired', as Michael grappled with his holster.

Michael's pivot as a dancer may have been impressive, but Sammy teased him: 'I'm still the fastest draw in the West!'

A nice footnote to this story is that, some time around the turn of the new millennium, Michael was fortunate enough to meet Shirley Temple at her home in San Francisco. I think he naturally gravitated towards child stars – wanting to meet Sammy, Shirley,

Elizabeth Taylor, Spanky McFarland and, later, Macaulay Culkin – because he felt there would be an instant empathy.

I can only imagine what he and Shirley must have shared, but the only insight I had into their conversation came during Michael's 2001 address at Oxford University when he said: 'I used to think that I was unique in feeling that I was without a childhood. I believed there was only a handful with whom I could share those feelings. When I recently met with Shirley Temple … we said nothing to each other at first, we simply cried together, for she could share a pain with me that only others like my close friends Elizabeth Taylor and Macaulay Culkin know.'

WE HAD GROWN UP LOOKING AT clocks and feeling pressure, from a rehearsal timetable to curfews on tour, from album deadlines to show times in that venue or this city. Time had ruled us, or we had raced against it, but the brother who heard the ticking clock loudest was Michael. If he wasn't doing something constructive – most of the time – he felt guilty. As much as he spoke about time being stolen from his childhood, he never eased up on himself. He thought video games a waste of time, and catching rest idle. He needed to stimulate his mind, not numb it. Even if that only meant reading a book. 'I can't just sit around,' he explained. He always said there were not enough hours in the day to work on all the ideas and thoughts he had.

Michael became a man truly obsessed once he set his soul on creating *Thriller*, the album. This project totally consumed him when he locked himself away with Quincy Jones. He worked between Westlake Studio, Hollywood, and the Hayvenhurst studio (unaffected by the renovation), where he recorded the original ideas. Alone. That way, Michael could capture the feel of the album that was in his mind; the first creative thought that became the foundation to the end product. No matter how many musicians were brought in later, he'd refer back to his original idea for the sound and song as a guideline to keep everybody aligned with his thinking.

We understood his artistic need for space so we hardly saw him for most of 1982 as he pushed himself beyond the point of fatigue to perfect *Thriller*. But when the 'finished' album was played to him, he was 'devastated'. It didn't *feel* right and the final mix was off. 'It's like taking a great movie and ruining it in the editing,' he wrote in his autobiography.

The team who worked with him so intimately will have known his creative ideas better than anyone. In their minds, I am sure *Thriller* sounded ambitiously strong, regardless of Michael's reservations. But Michael could have umpteen tracks laid down and throw them all away – and that was exactly what he did when everyone thought *Thriller* was ready. When he first heard it, he 'cried like a baby', in his words, and said, 'That's it! We're not releasing it.' The story he told is that he stormed out of the studio at Westlake, borrowed some bike from a member of his team and pedalled as fast as he could to get away from the madness he felt. He happened upon a schoolyard packed with kids playing, so he stopped. He said all their laughter and innocence 'put everything into perspective, and I rode back, feeling inspired again'. He then set to work on *Thriller* (take two). About one month later, he had tapped the outer limits of his creative ability and imagination to bring back a classic for the world to enjoy.

Thriller was released in November 1982 and started a blaze. It spent 37 weeks at No. 1 in the album charts, selling anywhere between 50,000 and 100,000 copies a week. But it achieved much more than sales and records: it marked his musical coronation. Not just in America, but worldwide. Joseph had always hoped that one day we would create music for the masses' and I like to think we broke down a lot of racial barriers in the Jackson 5 days. But *Thriller* obliterated all of them and was embraced by young, old, male, female, gay, straight, black, white. It achieved what music's soul was all about: it transcended differences and united people.

IT HAD BEEN ALMOST 18 YEARS since we had first set out as artists in Gary, and 25 since Mr Gordy had launched his label in Detroit. To mark that quarter-century milestone, NBC was taping the telecast *Motown 25: Yesterday, Today, Forever.*

Suzanne de Passe was one of its producers and she called to say that they wanted the Jackson 5 to perform at the reunion concert as part of the salute to Mr Gordy. It sounded amazing on paper. Just the thought of performing again with the brothers elated me. For six years, I'd had a recurring dream that I was on stage with them and I was counting a song off in my head, just about to sing … and then I'd wake. My unconscious had teased me with that promise for too long. Now, it was going to be a reality and I couldn't wait.

I was certain Michael would feel the same, especially since his attic picture gallery celebrated this very era, and considering his love for Mr Gordy. But the reality of the music industry is that advisers have an artist's ear and his camp's brand focus was 'Michael Jackson' not the Jackson 5. It was about the future, not the past. And with everyone caught up in the momentum of *Thriller*, I guess no one wanted to concern him with a night in Memory Lane. As they saw it, Motown 25 would benefit Mr Gordy and the brothers, but what good could it do Michael? My brother also had his own reservations. But although it was reported that he didn't want to perform with his brothers again, it was never about that. His early opposition was about not wanting to perform on TV. Still bruised from his CBS exposure on *The Jacksons*, he was surer than ever that television was a damaging medium to true stardom.

The rest of us felt he was making a mistake. Mother was the first to ask him to rethink his position. 'Motown did give you and the brothers your start,' she reminded him, 'and you'd be performing on the same stage as all the acts you idolised as a boy.'

He said he'd think about it, but that hesitancy didn't sit well with me. I rang him at home. When I heard his voice, I immediately sensed he was exhausted with the subject but I felt strongly that he was approaching this from a negative viewpoint or listening to bad advice, and brothers have the right to challenge another brother's thinking. 'You know, being back together will be spectacular,' I said. 'All our fans will be there and that magic will make good TV, not bad TV.' I reminded him of when he'd done 'The Robot' dance on *Soul Train* and the power of that performance. How it had got half of LA's kids up and dancing; How empowered *he* was by it.

'That was different,' he said. 'That was then. I don't want to do no more TV. I want to be doing music videos and live performances. I don't *want* to do what the Osmonds are doing.' He was calm but resolute. I could do nothing but respect his artistic reasons, and I was resigned to the fact we'd be doing Motown 25 without him. Privately, I was crushed.

The next thing I knew, Mother was on the phone saying Mr Gordy had turned up. I wouldn't have put any money on a positive outcome, because if Mother couldn't persuade Michael, then no one could. But my father-in-law had always said that the defection to CBS Records 'was not only amicable but wrapped in love', as far as the brothers were concerned and he visited Michael to convey how important it was for him to be there on the night.

'Think about it,' he told Michael, 'up there again with Jermaine … together again … back onstage. It will be magic!' Mr Gordy had never forgotten that phone call Michael had made before the Westbury Music Fair, saying he needed me. 'But it's not just Jermaine who needs you now,' he added. 'It's me and the Motown family.' He reminded him that Smokey would be back with the Miracles, and Diana Ross would reunite with the Supremes. No one could imagine the night without Michael reuniting with the Jackson 5.

Michael saw wisdom. 'Okay, I'll do it,' he said. But on one condition: he'd do a Jackson 5 medley but then he wanted a solo spot to showcase 'Billie Jean' – a CBS Records song on a night dedicated to Motown. You have to admire that kind of nerve and maybe that was why Mr Gordy agreed to the compromise. Either way, everyone was in agreement and we all wanted to make this thing feel special.

We got busy and rehearsed our group choreography at both Hayvenhurst and Jackie's house but none of us knew what Michael had up his sleeve for his solo spot. At some point, he had decided he'd use the television platform to try out a move he'd borrowed from street-dancers, one he had been finessing for the past two years. It was a move called 'The Moonwalk'.

The one thing Michael fussed over for this grand performance was his wardrobe. He had the white sequined glove, the Sammy Davis-style half-mast black pants, white socks, the silver sparkly shirt, and he asked his management to order a black fedora, 'something that a secret agent would wear'. But the jacket? However hard he looked, he couldn't find it. He opened the doors of his quarters, looked down the hallway and saw that Mother's bedroom door was open. As a lover of anything shiny, he had once seen her wear a black sequined jacket and he went to her closet to fish it out. He put it on and walked downstairs to find its owner in the kitchen. 'This would be a good jacket for me to do a show in!' he said. 'And it fits good!' He loved it because when he moved it sparkled. 'Imagine it under the lights,' he said. That was how Mother's jacket found its place in history. With a dance borrowed from the streets of LA and a jacket from Mother's closet, Michael was show-ready.

One question fans always ask me about the Moonwalk moment is: 'What was Michael like before and after the performance?' In people's minds, this defining moment of his career has adopted a significance they assume was present in its build-up: that Michael was locked in some kind of trance-like focus, ready to unleash his wonder on the world. The truth was a little less remarkable. He treated the telecast at the Pasadena Civic Auditorium like a piece of cake. It was a big deal for Mr Gordy and Motown, but it was just another performance for Michael. When we asked him what he was planning for his spot, he simply said, 'I'm going to do something that might work.' And then we didn't see him. He just … disappeared. He must have been gone half an hour.

'Where you been?' I asked, when he came back to the dressing room. He started chuckling and that mischievous grin spread across his face. 'Been up in Diana's rooms … She's got some serious suitcases going on!' he said.

Wait. I've just seen Diana Ross – and you weren't with her.

He looked at me. I looked at him, and we died laughing.

'You've been rooting through Diana's stuff!' So that was one part of the question answered. What was Michael like before the show? He was nosing about his mentor's dressing room, wondering what she had in there.

He was also all over the production team during rehearsals, wanting to know every detail of the telecast. Every performer has to run through 'camera blocking' to allow the director to frame his shots, but Michael wanted to know what those shots were, how many cameras he had and at what angles. All this before the editing process! It was part of his methodical approach – and control.

He explained it best in an interview with *Ebony* magazine in 2007 and what he said applied to every live performance and music video he ever did. He said: 'I don't care what kind of performance you are giving – if you don't capture it properly, the people will never see it. You're filming WHAT you want people to see, WHEN you want them to see it, HOW you want them to see it, what JUXTAPOSITION you want them to see. You're creating the totality of the whole feeling of what's being presented … 'cause I know what I want to see. I know what I want to go to the audience. I know what I want to come back.'

For me, the perfect moment came when we walked onstage as the original Jackson 5, and the magic and chemistry returned naturally. All that had altered was that we weren't kids any more and, golly, we had fun that night. I was overcome with this sensation of 'WE'RE BACK!' even if it was for only one night. I didn't care, because this was the moment that, in the back of my mind, I'd known would happen again. I embraced it with a kind of homecoming jubilation. Poetically, when it was my part to sing on 'I'll Be There', during the medley, my mic went out. Michael, alert to every beat, sensed it, saw my lips move with no sound and scooted over to share his mic, putting his arm around me as I sang. There is a wonderful picture of this moment, with both of us smiling. I think many people thought it was staged as we both leaned into his mic, but it was a technical glitch we got away with and that image is one I treasure from a momentous night.

At the end of our medley, Randy walked on and had his moment to recognise his input with the Jacksons, and then we bowed and everyone in the auditorium stood. That ovation meant everything, and we hugged each other before walking off, leaving Michael alone in the spotlight.

Now it was his turn, on his own. 'I have to say,' he told the audience, 'those were the good old days. I love those songs. Those were magic moments with all my brothers, including Jermaine, but ... er ... those were good songs ... I like those songs a lot, but especially ... I like ...'

The crowd started to scream and someone shouted, '"BILLIE JEAN!"'

'... the new songs!' Cue his virtuoso routine, which sent the place crazy with those kicks, toe-stands and spins of his. It was all improvisation, going with the beat. And then, at the bridge of the song, came the rehearsed moment: his first five-second burst of the Moonwalk, followed by another five seconds at the end. Ten seconds that would be talked about forever – and 10 seconds I missed when live.

I was in the wings with a restricted view, standing with the Four Tops and the Temptations, when I heard the audience go nuts and I said, 'He got 'em ... Mike's got 'em!' The other brothers watched it on small monitors and I knew from their reaction that the seventh child had just pulled off something special.

Michael came offstage to a standing ovation but was probably the only doubtful-looking person in the house. 'How was it? Did it work?' he asked.

Marvin Gaye, the Temptations and Smokey Robinson told him they were blown away, and then comedian Richard Pryor idled up. '*What* was that? *That* was incredible – the greatest performance I've ever seen!' We lost Michael in a crowd of praise and superlatives as everyone gathered around him. Mother and Joseph were in the audience somewhere, with our father screaming, 'He stole the show! The boy stole the show!'

That 'Billie Jean' performance was the best performance Michael had ever been talked into. It was also the best I ever saw him do. It poured rocket fuel on the *Thriller* album and sales went even crazier, peaking at a million a week. More importantly, within all the phenomenal success and wealth it generated, Michael finally sealed his name in *The Guinness Book of Records*. *Thriller* became the biggest-selling record of all time, ultimately shifting more than 100 million copies worldwide, and it earned him his desired clutch of Grammys – winning a record number of eight. The kid who used to sing for a plate of cookies had now surpassed even our father's greatest expectations by setting two records, neither of which has been matched or surpassed since.

Unbeknown to Michael, one of his idols was among the millions of viewers watching his Moonwalk from an armchair at home. My brother had no idea how his performance had touched this particular person until the phone rang the next day at Hayvenhurst. And even then, he struggled to believe it when he found Fred Astaire on the other end of the line. 'I watched it and I taped it, and I watched it again this morning,' said Fred, 'You're a helluva mover. Man, you really put them on their asses last night!'

That one call meant more to Michael than any number of Grammys. Fred Astaire admiring him was *the ultimate* as far as he was concerned, and life had finally fulfilled Joseph's CBS signing-on promise in an unexpected way. It might not have been a dinner, it was more important than that: it was praise from his hero, and that carried more meaning.

What's extra-nice about this story is that Michael got to meet this legend some weeks later and Fred Astaire held out the palm of one hand and imitated the Moonwalk with two fingers before Michael gave him a demonstration. Fred apparently told my brother that he was 'the best dancer he had ever seen', but it was the warning he issued that sticks in my mind: he told Michael that his 'Billie Jean' performance would bring social pressure for him to dance at the drop of a hat. 'Remember, you're not a performing monkey – you're an artist. You dance for no one but yourself,' he apparently said. Michael, as ever, made a mental note.

As for Mother's jacket, she never did get it back. Michael needed it for his now-famous routine. Some years later, he presented it to Sammy Davis Junior. In return, Sammy gave him a treasured wrist-watch, which Michael gave as a keepsake to Mother. Seemed like a fair swap to me.

CHAPTER TWELVE

Animal Kingdom

AROUND THE TIME MICHAEL WROTE 'Earth Song' in the mid-nineties, I sat down and wrote an outline for a children's story with him in mind. I called it *The Pied Piper of Hood River* and it was set around the beautiful fields and rivers of Oregon. In this fable, a young musician lives in the wilderness, protects the forest from evil forces and talks with animals. It was partly inspired by Michael: I'd always seen him as something of a Dr Doolittle because he had an uncanny way of communicating with animals. He was not a horse- or dog-whisperer, more an all-round animal-whisperer. 'Give them love, you get love back,' he said.

It didn't matter how wild or exotic, animals seemed to trust him. I once said that if you threw him into a cage of lions, you'd come back an hour later to find him sitting against a wall with two lazing in his lap. Several visits to LA Zoo confirmed his desire to be surrounded by animals and he collected his own menagerie at Hayvenhurst, starting with another snake – Muscles the boa constrictor – three cockatoos and a stunning collection of koi carp in the pond at the far end of the garden. The two of us also kept horses at the ranch of actor Richard Whitmore.

One day, Michael decided he wanted a llama. He asked me to take him to nearby Agora and we ended up at this lot packed with hay and horse trailers. From the car, we eyed four llamas out back. I parked between two trailers, unintentionally shielding my Mercedes from view. It was the only parking spot available. When we walked into the office – two kids dressed casual but smart in T-shirt and jeans – this guy, bent across a counter doing some paperwork, didn't even look up when he said, 'We're not hiring.'

'We ain't looking for no job,' said Michael, wearing his shades. 'We're here to buy a llama.'

The man looked up. Not a flicker of recognition on his face. It took me about two seconds to know that his musical taste ventured nowhere near the *Thriller* album. 'We don't have any llamas,' he said. The look on his face said it all: you can't afford it.

'You have four of them out back,' I said, trying to keep calm.

'You know how much they cost?'

Michael smiled. 'We know how much they cost.'

Then came an incredible bombardment of questions, fired by the man's prejudices and assumptions. 'Can you afford a llama? What do you boys do to afford a llama? Where will you keep it? Have you thought about this?'

Ever patient, Michael explained that we had a house with grounds and were serious customers. 'I know how to look after all kinds of animals,' he added.

The man begrudgingly asked to see some ID. Michael handed over a bank card. I handed over my driving licence. And then night became day.

'You're those Jackson boys?' said the man, his face lighting up. He began to back-pedal about how he had to be careful and he couldn't sell to just anyone; you understand how it is. But we didn't understand: we saw right through him.

'So you're happy to accept me because you now know who I am?' Michael asked. The biggest misconception people had about my brother was that his legendary shyness made him timid, but he was a man of principle, especially where his roots as a proud black man were concerned and he wasn't afraid to speak up on this when riled. Michael took back his ID and came right out with it: 'You are an ass, and we don't want to spend our money in here any more.' Then we walked out to the Mercedes the man had failed to spot when we arrived.

On the drive home, Michael was exasperated. 'Can you believe that? What is this area about? What are they teaching their kids?'

We had always been told by our parents that no one is born with a prejudice. It is something that is taught, ignorance passed down from generation to generation. The more Michael brooded, the more fired up he became. He told me to drive to Tito's.

That afternoon, Tito's acoustic guitar and our free-styling lyrics captured an angry inspiration for a song we called 'What's Your Life?'. That was how Michael liked to work. When a true experience inspired a song, he liked to get it down on his tape recorder or in the nearest studio. We recorded that song within an hour at Tito's studio, also in Encino. It went like this:

FIRST VERSE: All my life I've been asked such questions
As who I am and what I do
When I tell them, they are happy
'Cause I am rich, it gets me through
If I were a poor boy, would they accept me
Am I rich? What's it to you?
And what's your reason for asking?
Is my life one big interview?

THE HOOK: What's your life? What you do?
I do this, how 'bout you?
What's your goal in life 'cause
I want tips, to get through
Are you rich? Are you poor?
Are you bold? Are you sure?
Will you bend, do you break?
Are you strong, to endure?
What's your life? …

Those lyrics sum up the conversation we shared in the car.

Michael eventually bought two llamas from elsewhere. He called them Louis and Lola. Those llamas stood as high as us, and were the most serene and beautiful pets you could imagine. He also bought two deer called Prince and Princess, two peacocks, Winter and Spring, and a giraffe called Jabbar, after the tallest basketball player we knew: LA Lakers star Kareem Abdul-Jabbaar.

And then, there was Bubbles. The lovable chimp was first introduced by a handler called Bob Dunn, who'd raised him for the first six or so months of his life, training him to be domesticated, before his arrival at Hayvenhurst. But Bubbles was more than some novelty pet – he was a constant companion and Michael doted on him. The media would poke fun at this, but millions of dog and cat owners the world over find companionship in their pets, talking to them, treating them as substitute kids. Michael's relationship with Bubbles was no different, yet it was deemed 'weird'.

THE FIRST-TIME WE MET WAS AT Hayvenhurst. I'd heard from Mother about the new addition to the family so I went over to check him out. When I got to the top of the stairs, I heard Michael's voice: 'BUBBLES! No, Bubbles!'

On the way to his quarters, I saw his doors were open. Contrary to what's believed, his rooms were not 'a no-go zone'. The rules were probably no different from many other families: if the door was closed, there was an expectation of privacy. If open, we knocked and walked right on in. We simply respected each other's boundaries. 'I'd heard you had a chimpanzee in the house,' I said, announcing my arrival.

Michael's Murphy bed was down and Bubbles, wearing a diaper, was having a crazy five minutes, leaping and bounding over the bed, then swinging from the spiral staircase that led to the mezzanine balcony. He was throwing stuff around the room. It was like watching a hyperactive kid run riot.

'No, Bubbles. Stop bouncing around!' Michael said – and Bubbles stopped. It was fascinating watching them interact: when Michael spoke like that, Bubbles tilted his head and listened.

My brother's authoritative voice, being all parental, amused me. It was like he had become a father overnight. Chimpanzees are six times stronger than man, so in theory, Bubbles could have yanked Michael's arm right out of its socket, but he was so tame that he responded like a child and did exactly as he was told. It took only one or two 'NOs!' before he realised the command was serious and he then calmed down, skulked over to Michael and jumped into his arms to be petted.

He had his own wooden crib beneath the spiral staircase but he only slept there when his ass got real tired. Most times, Bubbles slept in the bed, under the duvet, and Michael slept on the floor in a sleeping-bag. I think it's fair to say that he was the best-kept ape in the whole of California, if not America. Bubbles wore Poison by Christian Dior because Michael always wanted him to smell and look good. When Mother smells that scent on someone today, she'll whisper, 'Smells like that old monkey!' He even had his own wardrobe, full of the latest designs for a two- or three-year-old boy. One time, in later years, when my son Jeremy was a toddler, I grabbed some clothes from the washroom and dressed him. When Mother saw him, she said, 'You're wearing Bubbles' clothes!' I hated to admit that Bubbles had the better wardrobe.

When Bubbles became hyper, he'd be jumping all over, grabbing candy and tossing it, causing a real mess. You always knew when he was becoming a handful because Mother would shout, 'MICHAEL! Get that monkey out of here!'

The trouble with Bubbles was that he knew his way around the house, and he'd walk into the kitchen, open the fridge door and help himself. And if he wanted you to go somewhere, he'd take your hand and lead you there. Most of the time, he stuck close to Michael. He was so playful and everyone loved him. Michael always liked hooking up his video camera to the television and filming Bubbles with the family, laughing at the images on his 'live cam' screen.

I think the funniest thing was when the two of them played hide and seek. Michael would hide and Bubbles would cackle out loud when he found him. The chimp clearly enjoyed this game because he'd terrorise Janet's poor dog in his own ape-style version of the game. Bubbles would walk up to Puffy, bop him on the head, then sprint off and hide. The dog would sniff him out and start barking. Seconds later, when Puffy returned to the kitchen, Bubbles would scamper back, bop him on the head and run off again.

Michael and his ape were inseparable in the house, in the studio, on tour, and sometimes at functions. Michael didn't care what anyone said. I don't think Bubbles was too fazed, either. Mother says that whenever Michael went to his dancing room on a Sunday, Bubbles went with him. I heard that once when Michael was doing one of his spins Bubbles, unprompted, sat down, closed his eyes and spun on his ass as the music played. Bubbles ultimately went to Neverland, but when the children came along, it was felt there was a potential for aggressive jealousy, a risk no one could take. He had grown into a 170-pound beast, so he was returned to Bob Dunn's ranch in Symlar, California, where Michael visited him from time to time. I know the separation was hard for my brother, but at least he had true fatherhood to look forward to. I suspect that Bubbles was none too happy either at being wrenched from his owner's side after almost a decade together.

Today, as of 2011, Bubbles is still alive and being cared for at the Center for Great Apes in Florida, where they are happy to report that he's definitely turned into his father's son: 'Bubbles can be sensitive and dramatic. If he has any kind of cut or scratch on his body ... no matter how small ... he will show it many times during the day to his caregivers and ask for sympathy. Though he is able to throw sand with amazing accuracy, he is extremely gentle with the youngsters ...'

After Michael's death, La Toya went to visit Bubbles. She found him sitting in a corner 'looking sad'. But the moment she walked in, he recognised her, jumped up and came bounding over. God bless that damn monkey.

IN ANY LARGE FAMILY, THERE'S ALWAYS one dark horse that busts out of nowhere and makes everyone sit up and take note. And I'm not talking about Michael, I'm talking about Janet.

We brothers had nailed our dreams to the mast early on. There were no surprises there. But no one saw the singer-songwriter blossoming in Janet. If anything, we had our youngest sister's career path mapped out as an actress. So had she. After CBS's *Good Times*, she landed television roles in *Fame* (as Cleo Hewitt) and in ABC's *Diff'rent Strokes* (as Willis's girlfriend, Charlene). Janet's acting ability was as crystal clear then as it remains today. But, as she tells it in her 2011 memoir, *True You*, she wandered into the recording studio at Hayvenhurst one day, armed with lyrics 'about my teenage-girl notions of loneliness and love', wrote a melody, worked the mixing board and single-handedly laid down a track she called 'Fantasy'. That was when she was nine. Just like Michael with his Quaker Oats bongos, she had been watching us all the time, especially when Michael and Randy took her along to rehearsals of the Jacksons. We'd watched our idols from a distance in Gary, but Janet had vicariously lived and breathed music with us, and the more Joseph heard her sing, the more he recognised a new talent to harness.

Long story short, my sister was 16 when she landed her first record deal with A&M Records, where our old schoolfriend John McClain had become senior vice-president of the A&R department. Having grown up around us, he was already like a protective big brother to Janet, so he naturally made her one of his top priorities at the label – and she soared on merit.

Unlike us, Janet felt she was pushed into her singing career. She went along with it because Joseph was insistent and she didn't wish to defy him. But when you think of her enduring career, and how many No. 1s she's amassed over the years, that was no bad instinct of my father's. Again.

My abiding memory of Janet in childhood is of this impeccable flower who could do no wrong in any of our eyes. She seemed attached to Mother's lap and couldn't wait for Joseph to fall asleep so she could climb into bed next to Mother, on the other side. And then, before Joseph woke, she'd get up and slip back into her own bed. La Toya was actually the first sister to break into the music industry, releasing her first album *La Toya Jackson* in 1980, again with our father's encouragement. Michael contributed to one of her songs, 'Night Time Lover'.

I remember going to school with my middle sister and being ignored by her in our Jackson 5 days. She was determined to find friends because of who she was, not because of her access to us. For years, she acted like she didn't know any of the brothers. I first realised this when I saw her walking in the opposite direction in the school hallway. 'Hi, La Toya!' I'd say, but she kept her head in the air. We only became her brothers again once we'd crossed the threshold of Hayvenhurst – the one place in the world where all brothers and sisters could be themselves.

WHEN YOU FIRST THINK OF SONGS, like 'Beat It', 'Billie Jean' and 'Thriller', you 'see' the music before you hear it because the visual of Michael's music videos is seared into culture's memory. That is the power and impact he always set out to achieve. Ever since 'Video Killed The Radio Star' by the Buggles became the first video aired on MTV on 1 August 1981, Michael had wanted to stand out within this new medium. He felt the industry approach was lazy, going through the motions of executing just another promotional tool. 'They need to be more entertaining!' he said. 'They need a beginning, a middle and an end – a story!' Echoes of Mr Gordy.

The biggest game-changer of them all was the *Thriller* video, with a theme inspired by *American Werewolf in London*. Michael recruited that movie's director John Landis for his $500,000-budget video. It was an astronomical amount of money for a music video. So much so that CBS Records refused to finance it. They felt the album's sales had peaked and, therefore, it didn't make financial sense. Michael's vision was years ahead of the combined wisdom at CBS Records (which later became Sony) – and *his* balls made

them more money in increased album sales after they had effectively given up the chase.

In the end, MTV and the sale of rights provided the funding
and the 14-minute 'film' that followed was as pioneering as it was
mesmerising. It heralded the start of a story-telling, cinematic
approach to music videos. Michael's thinking-outside-the-box
took everyone else with him. He reset the rules and standard with
everything he did. Before its official première in December 1983,
he had gathered the family in the 32-seat theatre he'd built downstairs at Hayvenhurst with wood-panelled walls and gold-framed
black-and-white photos of Shirley Temple, The Little Rascals and
Charlie Chaplin. We took our places in the red velvet seats and
Michael walked on to the small raised platform in front of the
screen. He was nervous but excited, and explained that his new
video was 'shot like a film' and he wanted our honest opinions at
the end.

I don't think there was one member of the family who wasn't
blown away. It was musical, choreographic, cinematic, makeup
genius. What was funny was the reaction of the youngest kids in
the family. Rebbie's son Austin, then a toddler, freaked out afterwards whenever Michael went to cradle him. He screamed and
bawled, convinced his uncle's face was going to 'change' into that
of a monster any minute. It was hard to explain to a kid that 'I'm
not really a werewolf,' because that was exactly what he'd said in
the video.

Unfortunately, the folk at the Kingdom Hall didn't see the funny
side. That epic video was, in Jehovah's eyes, 'evil and satanic',
because it celebrated the occult and the unseen world; 'the great
princes of darkness and the wicked spirits' that the Bible warned
against. That was why, at the video's opening, there was a last-
minute on-screen disclaimer added that read: 'Due to my strong
personal convictions, I wish to stress that this film in no way
endorses a belief in the occult.' That was not Michael's idea. It was
there at the insistence of the Kingdom Hall after the elders heard
back from two Jehovah's Witnesses who were on set with Michael

and became concerned by the video's theme. He didn't even write the disclaimer – director John Landis did.

This drama caused my brother a lot of unnecessary distress. He felt conflicted between his passion and his faith; he had only ever set out to be creative and entertaining, not offensive. I don't know the full extent of the calls that went back and forth between Hayvenhurst and the Kingdom Hall, but I couldn't believe there was even a fuss in the first place. It made me wonder why the elders hadn't insisted on a disclaimer that said: 'Due to my strong personal convictions, I wish to stress that I am not really a zombie but Michael Jackson.' To me, the whole affair was *that* ridiculous. But Michael was typically compliant and didn't voice any opposition. The whole thing was religion gone mad. I felt for Mother, too, because I know she came under tremendous pressure as the elders lobbied for the video not to be released, collectively failing to understand the distinction between creative brilliance and literal meaning. But contrary to what's been long reported, Michael was not de-fellowshipped by his religion or threatened with it. Far from it. Instead, and from this point on, two slightly serious-looking elders would shadow him on tour just to ensure he didn't stray from God's path. As if Michael's life wasn't restricted enough, these two religious guards were posted as silent witnesses in the background to 'monitor' what he creatively did. When anyone asked who they were, they were just part of the entourage.

For the remainder of 1983 and throughout 1984, Michael still carried out his pioneering work as a dedicated Witness, going door-to-door to spread the word of Jehovah. When he could, he also attended the Kingdom Hall four times a week with Mother. The only difficulty now was that his fame was so great that he couldn't walk up anyone's path without causing a fuss or being praised – which defeated the object of honouring Jehovah. But if the *Thriller* video had taught him anything, it was the art of disguise. Obviously, he had learned not to dress up as a werecat, but he obtained a collection of props that included a fake moustache, spectacles, hats with attached wigs … and a fat suit.

When he experimented with these different disguises, and went from door to door without being mobbed, he realised that his only chance of anonymity lay in becoming somebody else. From inside Hayvenhurst, he had only to look at the CCTV monitors to see the daily crowd of fans waiting at the gate and the numbers swelled after *Thriller*. I suspect it was then that he resolved to become the master of disguise and felt confident that he could fool everyone. Even those closest to him.

OUR FATHER HAD BEEN AN AMAZING coach, but he wasn't really equipped for the Hollywood machine and Michael's world-wide fame had outgrown him. The other brothers also recognised his limitations and had to explain to Joseph – at first in writing – that his managerial services were no longer required. It hurt him, too. 'I can't believe they're doing this. I can't believe they're leaving me,' he told Mother, the one person he allowed to see him vulnerable.

It can't have been easy being dismissed by the kids whose careers he helped make, but as much as he'd lost his power base, it wasn't as if he was shut out completely. All the brothers, including Michael, would continue to seek his advice over the years and we somehow knew he'd never be far away with another world-beating idea.

Ultimately, the managerial change had a knock-on effect to Michael's wider management set-up – the Joseph-appointed team of Ron Weisner and Freddy DeMann who'd arrived in 1978. Michael was encouraged to find new management and his favoured candidate, Frank Dileo, vice-president of promotions at the Epic label, landed the job. With his vast experience and jovial manner, the man from Philly, nicknamed Tookie, was an indispensable asset for a long time. Those two were a double-act that gelled from day one. They reminded me of Abbott and Costello because Frank was the roly-poly guy with a thick cigar in his mouth, while Michael was the one doing all the mad capers. Frank was a deflector and mouthpiece – a front man – but his know-how also brought a new slickness to all that Michael did.

John Branca, a fair-haired New Yorker, had become my brother's new attorney and he, too, would provide expert guidance in the years ahead. The Branca-Dileo combination was the professional operation Michael was happy to have surrounding him. Meanwhile, Weisner and Mann would manage the other brothers as the Jacksons.

By now, all the family knew that Michael's fame was at a level none of us had experienced before, but aside from the sales figures, the non-stop media coverage and the fans outside the gates, it was hard for us to measure. One day, La Toya was out and about in Beverly Hills when she got snarled up in traffic. Every street around her was gridlocked. She waved to a police officer and asked if there'd been an accident.

'There's no accident,' he told her. 'That Michael Jackson fella's just walked into a shop.'

'Oh,' said La Toya. 'Okay.'

When she relayed that story, we started to understand the reality we'd now be dealing with.

THERE HAD BEEN A LOT OF changes in my career, too. Ironically, it was Joseph who suggested that I needed to shake things up a little. 'You've gone as far as you can at Motown – you need a change. You need to go see Clive Davis.'

Joseph had known Clive since he was president of Columbia Records before he had founded and built the growing empire of Arista Records. Everyone in the music industry knew of Clive, a savvy trail-blazer with a nose for hits who had previously signed artists like Janis Joplin, Earth, Wind & Fire, Bruce Springsteen and Aretha Franklin to name a few. Starting Arista from scratch, he'd taken the label from a big fat zero to $70 million in his first four years and his roster of acts was growing all the time. As Joseph told me then, '*That* is a man who knows what he's doing and where he's going.'

Before I went to see Clive, at a meeting that Joseph would arrange, I needed to speak with Mr Gordy. I couldn't line something up and then jump ship without letting him know. When we had the 'big talk', we both knew that my solo career and producer work had exhausted all its options at Motown and our professional relationship had reached a natural end. But that didn't make my heart weigh any lighter. As we talked, he made it easier for me. 'You and Hazel need to see how it is to work with other people,' he told me, 'and get out from beneath my wings. As your father-in-law, I want to see you grow.'

Although several years remained on my contract, he released me and, after 14 years at Motown, I left with immense gratitude, with songs still inside me – and as a ready and able producer. This time, leaving felt right and the circumstances were never in dispute. The difference was that I had no one in my ear telling me what to do.

Clive Davis asked to see me at his bungalow at the Beverly Hills Hotel. When he came out west from New York, that was where he stayed: Bungalow 1B, with poolside cabana number 10. Always. Clive was a creature of habit.

When I parked, I suddenly felt nauseous and uncertain – perhaps because I'd always thought that the day I left Motown would be to reunite with my brothers and this wasn't moving me towards that. So, as I walked up the pathway to the bungalows, I found myself questioning the wisdom of this move.

As I reached Clive's bungalow, a monster bee buzzed around me with the determined assault of an Apache helicopter. I'm petrified of bees, and I took this as a sign that said, 'Stay away,' or 'Danger'. So I headed back down the path.

'JERMAINE! Where you going?'

I turned around and there was Clive – smart, wearing sunglasses – at his door, waving someone off, and waving me in. Ozzy Osbourne said, 'Hi!' as our appointments crossed each other.

'Perfect timing, come on in,' said Clive.

Over the next hour, we had a fine meeting and I liked him enormously. Whatever his mind is spinning with, you always feel like you've got his full-on attention. I told him that I still wanted to make great music and he gave me some pointers as to how he saw things. The upshot was that we shook hands and I signed to Arista.

'Now, before you leave, can you put your producer's cap on for a minute?' he asked. 'I have this new artist ...' He pushed a tape into his VHS recorder and we sat back to watch this tall girl with model looks and an incredible voice singing in a club in somewhere like New Jersey. She must have been about 18. That was my first sight and sound of Whitney Houston. 'She needs material,' he said. 'She's going to be huge. I'm working with other producers. We're not rushing her. What do you think?'

I blurted out what was in my head the moment I heard her voice: Marvin Gaye and Tammi Terrell. That's the gold standard I had in mind. A duet. Me and her. 'I'd be excited to work with her,' I said. 'We'd be perfect together.'

THE FIRST TIME I SAW WHITNEY in the flesh was at a studio in Hollywood. She was even more gorgeous in person. She walked over, we shook hands, and there was one of those recognitions that sends all sorts of wires sparking and fusing on the inside. I caught her during a break in recording, and she was smoking. 'You don't want to smoke those,' I said. 'They'll ruin your voice.'

She smiled. 'You might want to live more dangerously,' she said. *Touché*. This girl was quick-witted with a confidence that trod on your toes. She was that mix of street-smart East-Coast girl with an air of innocence and a vast talent. I found that a hypnotic combination.

Her voice had strength, passion and softness, and she could use every element of her range to tell a song's story. She could sing anything. We would spend a lot of time in the studio together, recording duets and in production, and soon enough, she was calling me Jackson, not Jermaine, setting the easy atmosphere in which we worked. We had an instant mutual respect for each other and a growing attraction. During our increasing time together, it was what we didn't say – yet still conveyed – that sent me into a head-spin. I kept reminding myself about Hazel, the family, and everything I had built and everyone I loved. This was the stuff they didn't warn you about when you got married, aged 19. They didn't tell you that when you grew up there would be super-human forces to drag you towards temptation. No matter your intentions, you shall be tested. And this collaboration, with an as yet unknown artist, was to be mine.

WHEN THEY WORK, COLLABORATIONS ARE LIKE a love affair between sounds and voices. When an artist and a producer, or two artists, find that symbiotic match in the studio, there is no better creative feeling in the world.

Michael was fortunate enough to work with some of the best names in the music industry, but the man he most looked forward to teaming up with was his 'musical prophet', Stevie Wonder. Stevie was, and remains, a big friend of the family after working with us on many unreleased Jackson 5 tracks (and we did the background dooda-waps on his hit 'You Haven't Done Nothing'). We all shared the same precision: building up a song, seeing it as a piece of intricate art that only came together layer by layer, detail by detail, instrument by instrument. It was, Stevie always said, 'about painting a picture using sound'. One sound was one colour. Blended together, music formed – and this was how a blind man approached his craft. He was a regular visitor to Hayvenhurst, as was Michael to Wonderland Studios, Hollywood, where he was allowed to observe Stevie put together his outstanding work on *Songs in the Key of Life*. 'It was like being a fly on the wall of the greatest composer of all time,' said Michael.

During the eighties, we both separately collaborated with this great man and neither of us could get over how many keyboards he had, sent by every supplier in Japan and stacked like folded sun-loungers in one corner.

When the music began, Stevie was like a kid in a candy shop, darting from keyboard to different instrument and back again, 'seeing' its brush strokes, humming its sound with his earphones on, head back, swaying in his seat. When he threw back his head and laughed, you knew he'd nailed a particular sound – and you knew what it meant to him. If my post-Jackson 5 years at Motown were memorable for one thing, it was for the times I got to work with Stevie on 'You Were Supposed To Keep Your Love For Me', 'Where Are You Now' and 'My Cherie Amour'.

I'll never forget the night I went to his Hollywood apartment to start collaborating on 'Let's Get Serious'. We were supposed to leave for a studio in Irvine at 8pm but I arrived to find a lot of Asian folk showing him the latest and greatest keyboards. *Why are you wasting your time on this when we'd arranged to be somewhere?* I thought, irritated. By the time Stevie had stopped messing around, it must have been 10 o'clock and not far from midnight when we arrived in Irvine. I was tired, ready to crank it out, and I couldn't see a mic on a stand. That was when Stevie pointed to the wall and this flat-mounted plate. 'That's the mic? Are you kidding me? I've got to sing with my nose two inches from the wall?' I said. Apparently, this ECM-type mic picked up sound better.

'Before we start, you want a game of air hockey?' he said. Had he been able to see my face, it would have told him everything. 'You've only got a blind man to beat,' he told me. I hesitated. 'Then we'll get to work,' he added.

I took the bait. He was right: it would be no contest. But, of course, I'd walked right into it. He kicked my ass not just in one game but in the second, third and fourth that I insisted we play until I beat him – and never did. Stevie Wonder is not just good at hide and seek, he's a demon at air hockey, too. In victory, he was standing opposite me with both hands on the table and rocking from side to side, head rolling, with that trademark grin on his face.

It was now about 1.30am, and I saw red mist. In a fit of pique, and feeling pissed that I'd been messed about and then beaten at air hockey, I lifted up the table and let it smash back down on its legs. 'Oh, man,' said Stevie, 'you're fired up – you want to sing now?'

And that was how we came to record 'Let's Get Serious' – because the best producers know exactly how to bring out the best in their artists.

MICHAEL'S COLLABORATION WITH HIMSELF WAS POETIC and unique. To imagine his music-making process is to peel back his hit songs to their rawest form: captured on his tape recorder from his mouth. Nearly all the songs you've ever heard that were written and created by my brother were first arranged in full in his head. No sitting at a piano or a keyboard and seeing what came to him; no experiments with technology: his inspiration arrived at any time. If he was in a meeting or a restaurant and you suddenly saw him grabbing a sheet of paper or a napkin to write on, you knew something was forming in his head to be captured on tape at the soonest moment. For example, 'I Just Can't Stop Loving You' came to him one morning when he was in bed. He grabbed his tape recorder and laid it down there and then. These flashes of inspiration were 'God's work,' he said. He would grab his tape recorder and, like the most skilled beat-boxer, he used his mouth as an instrument to create the beat and then imitated each part: the drums, the bass, the horns, the strings and so on. He did this until the structure and feeling of the song were just as he wanted them.

Once in the studio, he'd find the instrument he'd first imagined, then play his recording to get the song from his head into everyone else's heads. As he sang it on tape, they played it – and it had to match *exactly* what he'd first envisaged. In effect, Michael was channelling an orchestra and this sonic blueprint from head to musical imitation was just as impressive to hear as one of his finished songs. He also had the knack of running through a tune once and knowing how to sing it. I don't think he ever struggled for the right sound – or words: when he surrendered to inspiration, everything fell into place. For him, music was an endless source of material from within; a constant stream that he just had to step into and take from.

Then came the writing, and whenever Michael sat down with his pad and pencil, he was always looking at how the video was going to be at the same time. He wrote visually – finding the image or scene in his head, then applying the words. He loved what he did because he felt it was such a magical, spiritual process. As he said, around this time in 1983, 'I just love to create magic. I love to put something together that's so unusual, so unexpected, that it blows people's heads off.'

Which was exactly what I was thinking when I called him in the Fall of that year to invite him to do a duet.

I DON'T KNOW THAT I HAD completely given up on sharing a studio again with Michael, but I'd reached the point of thinking it highly improbable. Especially after his career-defining *Thriller* album. But sometimes it takes just one thought and phone call to change everything. 'Tell Me I'm Not Dreaming' was written for my début album with Arista, *Jermaine Jackson*, and my co-writers Michael Omartian and Bruce Sudan – Donna Summers' husband – helped create a slamming track. The moment I started humming the melody, I knew exactly whose voice was needed for this duet. 'I have a new song … and it's perfect for me and you,' I told Michael on the phone.

He had no problem coming to the studio, even if he hadn't properly understood what was required. 'Am I singing on this? Or doing backgrounds?' he asked. I don't know many 'superstars' who'd ask such a question *after* showing up. I had ensured that no one was there but me, him and an engineer to push the buttons. After *Thriller*, the last thing he needed was a bunch of eyes staring at him, so the fewer people the better.

The moment we got to work and he heard the instrumental, he was dancing. 'I love this … I love the sound of this,' he said, holding the earphones to his head with both hands. What struck me most about that recording session was how well we knew our way around the studio and console. The last time we'd recorded together, in 1975, we were surrounded by a team, being told what to do. Now, there we were, as fully-fledged producers. Just the two of us. We talked about those good old days and how green we were, and we joked and laughed about memories, almost forgetting that we were there to record. But there was that clock again, reminding us that we only had one afternoon to get this done.

I laid down my verse and he produced me, then vice versa. After that we traded ad-libs, singing into our individual mics, across the floor from one another. 'I think this has got No. 1 written all over it,' I said.

'You think it's going to outsell "Thriller"?' he teased. 'What if it does, Jermaine? What if it does?'

'Maybe I should write it on my mirror.' Michael liked that. 'The sales don't matter,' I added. 'I'm just happy that you're singing this with me.'

That's why that record remains special: because it was a personal collaboration between Michael and me. Ultimately, the song was never released as a single in its own deserved right. There was a big conference call between our labels that we both listened in on. Sony didn't want him on a song that would, they said, conflict with his own new releases. I think Michael wanted to help a brother. I think Sony was never going to lift a finger to help Arista with a song featuring its artist. When you're tied up in recording contracts, brothers helping brothers is not an argument. Not that the wily Clive Davis was going to be outdone and I always knew he'd find a way of getting it out there. 'Tell Me I'm Not Dreaming' became the poor-relation B-side to my later hit 'Do What You Do' because, that way, it didn't classify as an official release.

I lived with the setback because the amount of air play that song received confirmed my instinct: it was a deserved No. 1 in everything but name. Anyway, there was increasing talk in the family of doing a reunion tour as brothers. First, the studio. Then, maybe, the stage. It sounded too good to be true.

PAUL MCCARTNEY WAS AN ARTIST WITH whom Michael had always wanted to collaborate and 1983 saw them create 'The Girl Is Mine' for the *Thriller* album and 'Say, Say, Say' for Paul's *Pipes of*

Peace. But two significant things happened behind the music. First, when Michael was in London with Paul and Linda McCartney, one topic of discussion was the lucrative business of music publishing. Paul showed off a booklet from MPL Music Publishing, detailing a catalogue of songs he owned, including Buddy Holly's hit-list. Music publishing is the smart end of the industry: while you can be an artist with a timeless hit it's the person who owns the rights to the song who makes the money each time it's played, covered or performed live. The more prestigious the song catalogue, the more money you make. I can see my brother now, soaking up another lesson from another great artist he admired and quietly telling himself that he, too, must follow suit. One day.

After London, Paul came to California to shoot the 'Say, Say, Say' video in which the storyline was about a pair of vaudeville con-artists rolling through different towns with their horse and cart – Michael built in a cameo role for La Toya. The location was a ranch at Los Olivos in the Santa Ynez Valley, about two hours' north of Los Angeles. It was isolated and idyllic – a world away from Encino, LA's smog and the fame that surrounded him. If he longed for anything, it was for a sense of freedom and the ability to breathe. Ever since he'd spent time at my old ranch in Hidden Valley, he had dreamed of owning one. I don't know if Michael knew it then, but the 'Say, Say, Say' video brought the idea of 'home' to Sycamore Valley Ranch – the very place he would purchase five years later and name 'Neverland'.

CHAPTER THIRTEEN
The Hardest Victory

IF THERE IS ONE YEAR THAT stands out like a trophy across the decades, it is 1984. It was the greatest of years and, looking back, there was a distinct theme of victory, milestone and record-breaking running right through it. Our family friend Jesse Jackson became the first major black presidential candidate in US history. My NFL buddy Walter Payton of the Chicago Bears broke Jim Brown's career record of 12,312 yards gained with a ball (and gave me one of his cracked helmets). And America's newest athletics hero, Carl Lewis, equalled Jesse Owens' four gold medals at the Summer Olympics in LA.

It was also the year in which American Bruce Chandliss became the first astronaut to float free in space with his self-controlled backpack and the Statue of Liberty had her torch removed for the first time in 100 years so the flame could be repaired. *Ghostbusters* set the box office alight, making $212 million in its first six months. It was also fitting that this was the year Michael collected his record haul of Grammys and was awarded the 1,793rd star on the Hollywood Walk of Fame.

And then there was the 'Victory Tour'. This was our monster reunion. Six brothers back together for our most ambitious concert as a group. It would represent the pinnacle of our collective dream because we set a new record for the most consecutive stadiums sold out back-to-back in a summer that saw Bruce Springsteen and Prince also touring. It is a record that still stands today. I'm not embarrassed to boast about it because I have a lot of pride where that tour is concerned and *nothing* about that achievement came easy.

Onstage and in the dressing room, everything clicked as before. Offstage and in the meeting rooms, the whole set-up was fraught with politics and tension, proving that when outside 'advisers' enter a family equation, the whole dynamic changes. Like acid dropped into still water. But no matter how rocky the road, it was like any victory: it doesn't matter how many times you're down in the game, it's the end result that matters. It's about perseverance. And with all the blood, sweat and tears that went into the tour and its accompanying album, *Victory*, it was the hardest-earned triumph I can remember.

THE VICTORY TOUR WAS ANOTHER IDEA that had to be sold to Michael before he agreed. And, as with Motown 25, his change of heart walked him into another page of *The Guinness Book of Records*. It also led to reports that we, as brothers, 'pressured' or 'coaxed' him into taking part. This was the start of a mistaken and enduring belief that we were only interested in coat-tailing Michael's fame for profit, as if he were an overnight sensation and we had just woken up to his talent, as opposed to having grown up alongside it.

I didn't see the barren financial landscape that some have attempted to paint as our motive for touring. My début album with Arista was set to release singles like 'Dynamite' and 'Do What You Do'; I was excited about my collaboration with Whitney Houston, and a duet with Pia Zadora, singing 'When The Rain Begins To Fall' (No. 1 in four European countries). But this would become a

recurring theme for the family: a showdown of fact versus perception – and fact would always be the underdog.

Unlike Epic and then Sony, we never viewed Michael as a
robotic money-making machine. We viewed him as a brother with
whom we wanted to share more glory. Our passion to perform
with him never changed en route from our bunk beds to Hollywood.
That desire between brothers was always consistent, pre-fame,
post-fame. But somewhere in the transition between Jackson-mania
and 'Michael Jackson mania', sacks of fanmail morphed into
printed pages of lies and fiction. We read accounts of constant feud-
ing, rampant jealousy and how the brothers 'refused to talk to each
other on their way to the stadiums'. I guess this was another side
of Michael's new-found fame: that for every public hero, the rules
of myth demand villains, too.

Michael didn't help the confusion over the back-story to
'Victory'. In an interview we did for *Ebony* magazine, he said, 'I
didn't say that I didn't want to tour. I'm doing it for the joy of touring and the family as a whole …' Four years later, in his autobiography, he said, 'I didn't want to go on the Victory tour and I fought
against it …' Both accounts represent the truth at different times
and accurately illustrate his indecision about taking part, but the
expression 'stage addict' best sums up why he finally agreed to
take part. As much as he had vowed to take a break from touring
in 1981, he was like any other performer whose intimate relationship with the stage began as a child: he couldn't resist it.

In fact, in the end, he insisted on the tour. He spent hours
drawing up storyboards for its stage design and concept. He
became *the* self-designated stage designer and, as a result, everything the tour needed it got. Including two giant spiders he
sketched for either side of the stage – costing $250,000 each – plus
stage hydraulics, advanced lighting and full-on pyrotechnics.
Before we knew it, he had presented his vision, complete with
costume designs, to tour co-ordinator Larry Larson. *That*'s the
truth of how hands-on keen he was. He had always been passionate about touring. That is why we never felt awkward about

approaching him with a new idea because creative ideas had filled our childhood, and we knew his heart was tied to that shared past, too, as seen inside his private picture gallery. What he loathed were the politics, the legal posturing and the tension between our individual attorneys and promoters. That was what ground him down, and it was present from the moment Joseph first mentioned the tour.

OUR FATHER WAS NEVER GOING TO accept being sidelined and the thrill of Motown 25, combined with the success of the *Thriller* album, had got him thinking on the same grand scale as his daydreams in Gary had. In partnership with Mother, he was the architect of 'Victory' and, for all the doubts the brothers had shared about his managerial capabilities, it was no small feat to plan a national tour. I think Joseph felt he had a point to prove. His early proposal had La Toya and Janet in the line-up, which was when Michael first balked, no doubt flashing back to Vegas vaudeville and worrying about what our father's vision might be, but Jackie was the most vociferous, insisting it should be brothers only. Then Michael reconsidered his opposition.

I always suspected his camp told him the tour was a bad idea – that it would get in the way of his solo focus; that it was a backward step – just as it had with Motown 25. After *Thriller*, we, Michael's family, saw his people ring-fencing him as an artist and digging a moat around him to keep us out; over time, the moat would grow deeper and wider. Entourages keen on building empires don't necessarily promote family values in Hollywood, as we would learn. As always, when conflicted, Michael turned to Mother, explaining that he'd planned to spend 1984 working on movie ideas. 'I think it's important to grow,' he told her, 'and I've been doing this [touring] for so long I sometimes feel like I should be 70 now.'

If anyone knew that he was wrestling with advice he'd received and his sense of family, it was Mother. 'Just think about it,' she said, giving him space.

Days later, he warmed to the idea on his own. He was aware that CBS Records was not honouring contracted release dates for the other brothers as the Jacksons. I think that made him feel that his success had left his old group hanging. It is a blocking tactic used in the music industry: put the other group members on the shelf and, if they try to leave, wave the contract and say, 'Can't go anywhere – you owe us albums.' Michael knew that a tour would trigger a new album, and help out his brothers, so he agreed to take part. If anything, his decision spoke of his selflessness. But in the back of his mind, he always wanted it to be his last tour with us – even if we didn't. He proposed a tour name: 'The Final Curtain'.

You can imagine how that went down. It sounded so negative, signalling the point of no return. For us, the tour represented the summit of everything we'd built as kids. It was, therefore, a conquering moment. That was why we wanted, and eventually agreed on, 'Victory'. As Michael set to work on the stage design, everyone was committed to making this an event that was 'out of this world'. As he and Marlon both joked later, 'The mothership [the group] was calling.'

THE MOMENT WE ALL SAT AROUND the table at the first meeting to discuss the tour, I noticed one jarring difference between past and present. Instead of being one unit behind Joseph, we now arrived as individual players with different legal representatives. Michael had his attorney and manager, I had mine, and the four other brothers had a manager and attorney they shared. As Mother astutely observed, 'You all brought too many chefs into the kitchen without first agreeing as brothers.' The reality of this set-up was that, in the event of a difference of opinion, Jackie, Tito, Marlon and Randy had the casting vote as a block of four. Their attorney could – and would – say that he spoke for four brothers, not one: the power of veto. In theory, Michael and I were powerless on any issue – and we knew attorneys didn't get rich by brokering peace. With lawyers involved, the odds on harmony didn't look good from the start.

And there was Michael's incredible success. *Time* magazine called him 'the hottest phenomenon since Elvis Presley' and yet there he sat around a table – the now eight-Grammy-award winner – holding a 'vote' that carried least sway. The tone for the way ahead was set when the team behind the four brothers felt it had found the right promoter. A man named Cecil Holmes stepped up and presented a cheque for $250,000 as an upfront fee. It wasn't enough to split individually, and only just covered one of the giant spiders Michael had envisaged.

Joseph ripped up the cheque in front of us all and threw it at the man's feet. 'Are you kidding me? We're not going to be undersold like this!' he said. Michael liked this new attitude. In the old days, Joseph might have taken it.

Soon afterwards, our father announced that he'd found the right man to stage the tour: boxing promoter Don King – a flamboyant man with wild, upstanding hair, white limousines, gold chains and mink coats. But his image preceded him and made everyone doubt him. If he was serious, they said, tell him to put his money where Joseph's mouth was. Within a day or two, Don turned up and wrote each one of us a cheque for $500,000. 'Because you boys need to know I'm serious about making this happen,' he said.

We signed contracts that week. The media had a field day with this appointment, because it wondered what Don – famous as Muhammad Ali and Sugar Ray Leonard's promoter – could possibly know about putting on a Jacksons concert. But a promoter is a promoter: someone who should be able to hype a boxing match or a concert as the biggest and best event of the year – and Don King could. Many in the music industry turned up their noses at his involvement, and that was the grapevine the media tapped into. But the claim that we thought him 'too ostentatious' and not someone we wanted was inaccurate. At the start anyway. If there had been initial doubts, our friendship with Ali convinced us that Don was a good man. Now, what Michael's associates told journalists might have been a different story.

Don didn't win awards for tact and diplomacy, and his giant ego was the reason he was a promoter. He was brash but effective. Had you seen him – the loudest mouth – and Michael – the quietest soul – interacting, you might have thought, There's the kid with the embarrassing uncle he can't help but find funny. I'll never forget being in a meeting when we were discussing something about the show's direction and Michael was talking about how he wanted to pay back the fans and keep pushing higher.

'Michael!' said Don, cutting dead the monologue. 'Remember this. It don't matter whether you're a rich nigger, a poor nigger or just a nigger. No matter how big you get, this industry's still gonna treat you like a nigger.' In other words, and in his opinion, you'll always be a servant to the music industry, so don't ever think of becoming more powerful than that. Everyone in the room froze. If the music industry blew smoke up everyone's ass, Don blew in an icy blast of straight talk.

It was Michael who was the first to laugh, cracking the suspended silence. He found it funny, in a shocking way, and wasn't offended. None of us was. A black man had been addressing black men, and that kind of talk was hardly foreign to someone from Gary, Indiana. Don always came out punching because he had sensed, as had I, a lot of corporate envy about the fact that he'd brought in the big money and was pulling off the biggest-ever tour with Michael Jackson attached to it. If that didn't make the phalanx of record-label executives, entertainment attorneys and cynical journalists look like chumps, I don't know what did. But as Mother observed about the politics and dirty tricks that would soon follow, 'We always knew there was a mood that certain people would do everything they could to stop the tour for as long as Don was involved. That's why I could never be in a business like this – it's dog-eat-dog.'

MICHAEL DIDN'T DRINK PEPSI BECAUSE HE didn't like it. Which was a potential problem when Joseph and Don lined up a $5 million Pepsi sponsorship deal, together with two television commercials that would rewrite 'Billie Jean' and use it as a jingle. When it was explained to Michael that he didn't need to drink Pepsi or be filmed drinking it, he was happier to compromise. During the tour, there was a funny moment which would have given Pepsi executives a heart attack had they witnessed it. Michael was in his dressing room one day when he decided to grind a can into a plate of food, poured Pepsi over all over it like gravy, and then posed for a photo: a close-up of his sequined glove presenting his 'dish'. If ever there was an image that summed up both his devilish humour and the difference between brand Michael and the real Michael, that might have been it.

We got down to the serious business of filming the two Pepsi commercials in January 1984. The first was at a Hollywood lot in a 'New York street', where we free-styled with kids representing 'the new Pepsi generation'. The second was at LA's Shrine Auditorium, where we performed 'a concert' in front of screaming fans holding Pepsi cups. On this second shoot, with our favourite music video director Bob Giraldi, the planned sequence was for the brothers to play Michael in as he made a grand entrance, standing atop a lit stairway as an explosion of magnesium flash bombs showered him with sparks.

We'd already done five takes when Bob wanted Michael to wait a few seconds longer at the top of the stairs so that he could be captured in silhouette. So we did it again. Take six. I was on the bass, right of stage, facing the audience. 'And ... action!' someone shouted. The audience stood and started screaming. Cue the familiar 'Billie Jean' beat. Then the popping sound of flash-bombs. I knew Michael was now skipping down the steps. I turned side-on and that was when all hell broke loose. I glimpsed flames in Michael's hair, but he was oblivious. He kept dancing. Then he spun so fast that he doused the flames, resulting in a halo of smoke, but the damage was already done. Five people raced from the wings and bundled him to the floor. Everything happened so quickly that my brain didn't compute at first what I had just seen. I was convinced my brother had been shot, because the panic reminded me of the President Reagan assassination attempt in 1981, the way everyone pounced on him. I dropped my bass and raced over as Michael was getting to his feet. Dazed. Blowing out his cheeks. I saw him patting the top of his head; I saw a bald patch covering his crown, his hair scorched away. One of the flash bombs had rained sparks that had ignited the flammable hair-spray we all used. Later, when watching the footage back, it was clear that a flame was shooting out of his head as he skipped down the steps. Within five seconds, his entire hair was engulfed. Going up like a haystack.

Backstage, he was lying down, remarkably calm. I think the shock stopped him freaking out. I crouched down and rubbed his arm, and all the brothers huddled around. 'He's going to be okay … You're going to be okay, Michael,' I said, as much for me as for him. Thank God Mother wasn't there. She didn't need to see him like that. Thank God for Bill Bray, too, who carefully broke the news to her over the phone and managed to conceal our panic.

An ambulance rushed him to the Cedars-Sinai Medical Center in West Hollywood and we followed in one car, still wearing our colourful costumes. The whole family headed there, because that's what happens when something bad happens to one of us: everybody drops everything and runs to that person in need. One for all, and all for one. Michael had suffered third-degree burns to his scalp – almost down to the skull – and no one needed telling how lucky he was to be alive. He was later transferred to the Brotman Memorial Hospital in Culver City, where he sat up in bed watching videos, his head swathed in bandages. He actually admitted that he'd got a secret thrill from the ambulance ride. He'd wanted to taste that kind of excitement since he was a kid, he said. Thank God for Michael's spirit.

Michael never intended to sue Pepsi but, after seeing the plight of other burns victims, he developed a plan. Instead of talking damages, he talked charity and renamed the Brotman Burns Unit the 'Michael Jackson Burns Unit' – and got Pepsi to donate $1.5 million. In litigious America, it was humbling to see someone bypass their own suffering to help those worse off. And, trust me, Michael was in pain. Although he'd make a full recovery and be okay to tour, come July, he had to undergo surgery to laser the scar tissue and stretch part of his scalp over the burned area. Michael also had some kind of implant and all of the treatment left him in excruciating pain. Not just for those first few weeks, but for many years afterwards. It was so bad that you'd see him pulling at his head in agony. All he could rely on to alleviate the pain was a prescription drug called Demerol. This was no regular anti-inflammatory. It was a morphine-strength painkiller that brought numbing relief. Imagine the worst pain of your life and wanting to do *anything* to end it – that was what my brother went through. In that state, I doubt he gave a second thought to Demerol's side-effects, one of which was 'can be habit-forming'.

THE NEXT BROTHER TO BE LAID up in a hospital bed before the tour began was Jackie. He was at some movie drive-in when he was hit by a car. It busted his knee. He was in the hospital for days with a cast from thigh to ankle. Like Michael, his injury would heal but, sadly, not in time for him to tour. He was devastated because he knew how special the concerts were going to be. He'd still ride with us, provide input, and come on stage to make appearances, but he couldn't perform. It was a blow for everyone as six performers became five, and I don't think I was the only one wondering if the tour was cursed.

'THEY'RE DIGGING UP DIRT TO DESTROY the man,' Joseph said, as a smear campaign began against Don King. Someone somewhere had put out word that he had a 1966 conviction for manslaughter. Don King had killed a man, and he was promoting a concert with Michael Jackson. This 'revelation' was lapped up by the press – and every enemy Don had on the tour. I felt for him because there was something coincidental and dirty about its timing, and it didn't matter that he could speak from a four-year prison education about the futility of violence. His rehabilitation and plea of self-defence weren't going to get a fair hearing. It was now open season in the badmouthing of Don King.

Long story short, when Michael heard about it, he refused to tour for as long as Don remained in charge. 'He's a crook,' he said, 'and we don't work with crooks.'

Joseph had to intervene to stop him quitting. 'That is what the press does to folk,' he said. 'We've come too far for you to back out now. Don's been working 24/7 to make this a success: don't punish the man.'

Michael went away to think about it and word eventually came back that he'd continue with the tour, but that one revelation changed everything within his team and the other brothers'. Don received a legal letter forbidding him to conduct business or communicate with anyone on the brothers' behalf.

Eventually, one month before the start of the tour, a fourth co-promoter was brought in to balance the picture and take more control. Chuck Sullivan, the owner of the New England Patriots, arrived: he had impressive pull with different stadiums around America. Effectively, his appointment reduced Don, Joseph and Mother to figurehead roles, but Don remained defiant. 'If you want to take this tour away from me, you'll have to pay me,' he said. So they did. He received a diminished role and three per cent of profits.

EVERYTHING HAD CHANGED AND YET NOTHING had changed. The moment we launched into full-on rehearsal, our onstage camaraderie returned like an old friend, with the timely reassurance that everything was going to work out just fine. The difference between brothers performing as One and legal teams looking for conflict was like night and day. We had never toured with the crew around us, yet everything about our strange environment felt familiar. The passage of time hadn't affected the nucleus of our bond. Throw us into a new arena and throw anything at us, we could still bring it.

We set up the full stage at Zoetrope Studios – the Hollywood rehearsal space owned by movie director Francis Ford Coppola, who had directed Michael's Disney movie, *Captain Eo*. Those rehearsals were invigorating because the more we ran through the set, the more excited we became. Michael was like the rest of us: he coasted, running through the motions at 50 per cent. He always saved his 1,000 per cent for the stage.

But what he also did, as he would with every tour, was go home and practise his dancing alone. Each intricate move had to be perfect and he'd push his body until it could take no more. He would run through agreed steps during rehearsals, then work towards perfection at home, repeating a move over and over ... and over. He told me that sometimes he was so tired he could barely lift his legs to climb the outside spiral staircase to his quarters.

At Neverland he had a dancing room, with wooden floors and mirrors all around. You could actually see the swirls ingrained in the floor from where he had been pivoting and spinning. His dance always left its own indelible mark.

AS WE ARRIVED IN KANSAS CITY for the tour's opening in the July, the digging for dirt turned away from Don King to Michael. Journalists were hunting for *anything* and one persistently false rumour wouldn't go away: that our brother was homosexual. This claim first arose in the seventies when some magazine ran a scurrilous story suggesting he was competing with a woman for the love of a male songwriter. It was nonsense then, and remained so throughout Michael's life but by the middle of 1984, he was tired of hearing the same old echo in reporters' questions or reading the sly innuendo in print.

He knew how the media worked it. Ask if Michael's an alien, he'll deny it. Cue the headline: 'MICHAEL DENIES HE'S AN ALIEN!' Ask him if he's gay, he'll deny it. 'MICHAEL DENIES HE'S GAY'. Then everyone would wonder why he was denying whatever it was.

Michael's life would become mapped by headlines. That was why he chose to say nothing in the end and hoped his music would transcend everything and speak for him. But back then, in Kansas, one reporter asked if he had any reaction to reports that he was gay. Michael batted it away, saying he was not a homosexual but wondered why people were so fixed on attaching labels. 'We're all humans. What's the big deal?' he asked.

It wasn't emphatic enough. The press started to read between the lines of what he'd meant by 'What's the big deal?', not understanding that Michael was trying to strike a balance between a denial and supporting the gay community. He couldn't win.

To me, the whole debate about his sexual orientation was preposterous. I think people misinterpreted the fact he was a workaholic. People saw an unmarried man with a penchant for makeup, child-like things, with no facial hair, and an attachment to a chimpanzee, then filled in the blanks. Michael was also unafraid of displaying his creative feminine side and his voice tended to fit society's stereotype of what a gay man sounds like. But none of us in the family have heavy voices and I knew what it felt like to be on the receiving end of such ridicule. When I first started driving in LA, I was pulled over by a police car. When the male officer heard my voice, he laughed, turned to his female colleague and said, 'Who's going to search *her*?'

Michael always said, 'My wife is my music and I'm married to my craft' – and that was why he achieved greatness. But he was also a devout Jehovah's Witness who lived his life in accordance with the Bible. Because of his religion, he was a lot more restrained than his brothers. Michael longed to know what a full and intimate relationship felt like. After *Thriller*, he seemed to be eternally waiting for that elusive lady to walk into his life, someone he could trust, and someone he knew was there to be with him and not 'Michael Jackson'; to be in love with him and not in love with the idea of him.

My brother was a kid at heart and he wanted to find that in a woman, too. Michael's heart wasn't about intensity, passion and drama. It was about playfulness, water-pistol fights, comic books and movie nights. It was about sharing his humanitarian dreams, visiting hospitals and looking at life through a child's eyes. This was his field of diminishing returns when it came to looking for his ideal woman. Until that 'match' came along, he would struggle to let anyone in.

SOON ENOUGH, THE TERM 'WACKO JACKO' would be coined by the *Sun* newspaper in London. It was a nickname Michael found offensive and was the consequence of a public-relations strategy to plant weird and wonderful stories about him. Michael always insisted he knew nothing about this PR sleight-of-hand and I can believe that. His Motown training was the promotion of artist and music, nothing else.

The first story ran in the *National Enquirer* with a photo showing Michael seemingly asleep in a hyperbaric oxygen chamber under the headline 'MICHAEL JACKSON'S SECRET PLAN TO LIVE TO 150'. It was a genuine photo. This chamber was used by burns patients at the Brotman Memorial Hospital and Michael couldn't resist posing inside it during one of his visits. Not because it was part of his treatment but because it looked space-age and he wanted a quick, fun photo. He lay inside for a matter of seconds with his eyes closed and hands across his chest. It ran in the *Enquirer*, which printed quotes from 'close friends', who said he planned to buy one to sleep in to stop the ageing process. Extraordinarily, people believed it. I lost count over the years of how many times I was asked: 'Is it true your brother sleeps in an oxygen tank?' I wanted to say, 'My brother doesn't like sleeping in a bed, let alone a tank!'

The second story was so outlandish that it doesn't deserve an explanation: Michael was intending to buy the Elephant Man's bones, with supporting, on-the-record quotes from manager Frank Dileo. Again, people believed it. Or did they just *choose* to believe it because everyone needs to feel comforted that genius does not come without eccentricity? I never could figure it out. As his family, we read these reports and never gave them a second thought, but when Mother found out that Frank Dileo was behind the silliness, she challenged him. 'You shouldn't be spreading stuff like this,' she told him. 'It makes my son look like an idiot.'

Frank apparently wasn't worried. 'It makes people wonder about him and this is what we want.'

Was this a misguided strategy to build *mystique?* I never did understand the team's thinking. It treated Michael like some kind of wannabe who needed his profile raised when the *Thriller* album had already done all the talking. Such reports led to Michael being ridiculed and that seemed like a travesty when his only intention in life was to be treated as a serious artist. The people around him should have known better, because that kind of transaction with the press is always dangerous.

Michael wasn't prepared for the seemingly daily assault that paraded him not just as 'wacko' but as a 'weirdo' and a 'freak'. And his plastic surgery, together with innocent interactions with animals and children, would add to the twisted portrayal. Eventually he wrote an open letter to the press, expressing how hurt he was by the lies coming from people who didn't even know him. He quoted an old Indian proverb: 'Do not judge a man until you've walked two moons in his moccasins.'

But his best response would come in 1996, via the eloquence of one of his short-film videos for his single 'Ghosts' – a video co-scripted by novelist Stephen King, which broke the record for the longest-running music video ever made at 39 minutes 31 seconds. In it, he played himself as the owner of a haunted house behind Neverland-style gates in 'Normal Valley'. He also wore a fat suit to play his arch nemesis: a white, middle-aged mayor, with grey hair and horn-rimmed spectacles, who was vowing to drive him out of town.

The dialogue in the video's opening sequence mirrors how Michael felt he was viewed and treated. It carried a serious message while poking fun at people's judgements of him. YouTube it and you'll see Michael, in character, acting out what people said about him as he speaks the lines of the middle-aged man who'd led a group of concerned parents, with children in tow, to his house. For

'Normal Valley', read Santa Ynez, California – and Media Land. 'We want you outta this town. We're a nice normal town. Normal people. Normal kids. We don't need freaks like you telling ghost stories … You're weird … you're strange, and I do not like you … The fun's over … go back to the circus you freak … Don't force us to get rough with you, because we will if we have to …' Then watch Michael's reaction as he plays himself, expressing both his calm and his pent-up anger before using his magic to silence every adult who projected their warped thinking on to him.

For me, that opening sequence is Michael venting his feelings through music. I remember his disguise vividly because, during a break in filming, he dropped by Hayvenhurst still in character, still wearing the fat suit, looking like a middle-aged white man with his grey wig and latex face. When he walked in, I instantly knew it was him because he winked at me but, beyond that, he was unrecognisable. Our cousin Tony Whitehead, who was carrying a book under his arm, was with me and he thought this 'stranger' was just another visitor. Michael decided to have some fun: he always liked a good laugh with Tony, who joined his tour crew as a carpenter and familiar face from 1988 onwards. So, Michael walked up to him, in character, as a white man, and said, 'Hey, why do you have a book? Niggers don't read!'

Tony, thick-set and big-necked, not someone you'd choose to confront, couldn't believe what he'd heard. 'What did you just say?' he said, standing over Michael, ready to clock him.

'Tony! TONY!' he screamed. 'It's ME! IT'S ME!'

Our cousin stared into my brother's eyes, trying to find the person he knew. 'IT'S ME – MICHAEL!' And that was when Tony stood down and we all fell about laughing.

IN THAT FINAL MONTH BEFORE THE tour opening, attorneys seemed to argue and vote about every tiny detail, from how many tour dates (40 or 45) to the tour's routing schedule; from this idea to that fee, from 'we want this' to 'we want that', from this cost to that ticket price. It was draining. Watching them feed different advice into different brothers' heads was painful, and I could see it sucking the energy out of Michael. Tour-weary before the tour had even begun. But I'll say this about him: as much as it drove him mad, he never once shirked a meeting or ducked out of a conference call.

At one meeting, where another tiresome debate was going on, everyone was chipping in their two cents' worth when I saw Michael mentally retreat and block out the noise. He leaned back in his chair and began scribbling; he was drawing Charlie Chaplin. Suddenly he looked like a kid killing time while the grown-ups argued around him – and it seemed the smartest escape. We were all brothers thinking the same thing by the end: we just wanted to escape the politics and get out onstage. Become what we knew best. Be all that we loved. As Michael said in his autobiography: 'The tour was like: we're a mountain. We've come to share our music with you. We have something we want to tell you.'

CHAPTER FOURTEEN

The Reunion Party

THE ULTIMATE REWARD COMES ALWAYS AND only via the stage. Politics fade out and pale into insignificance the moment you hear the muffled roar of a capacity crowd from beneath a stadium. For any performance artist, it's this moment that provides the purpose of living: the sweet taste of victory that we relive and chase ever afterwards. As kids, I don't know how much of the Jackson 5 years, when we were packing out stadiums, we'd truly savoured but second time around, we were determined to soak up and capture every second and sensation. Tito said it at the outset: 'It's going to be the tour we never want to end.'

The omens had started to look good when we were kerb-side at Kansas City airport, ahead of our first concert. This happy-looking guy was helping load our bags into one of the vans when he said: 'Remember me?'

I stared at him. 'Wesley?'

It was the catcher I'd collided with that day playing for Katz Kittens in Gary. What a small world we lived in. We compared the scars we still carried above our eyes. 'That collision ended our baseball career,' I said. 'Not sure Jackie's forgiven you!'

'You guys don't seem to have done too badly.' He winked. Everything about 1984 would be tinged with that kind of nostalgia. Memories would be everywhere. Even below the stage: we'd ensured there was a disco club there for crew and friends, and called it Mr Lucky's.

Come opening night, we had massive support from everyone we knew in the industry and Michael boasted about one particular telegram he'd received from Marlon Brando. The line I remember ran, 'MICHAEL – DON'T MAKE AN ASS OF YOURSELF AND FOR GOD'S SAKE, DON'T FALL IN THE ORCHESTRA PIT – MARLON'.

Backstage, as 45,000 people packed into Arrowhead Stadium, we formed a huddle just like we used to, stacked our hands in the middle and then heard that growing sound: 'JACKSONS! JACKSONS! JACKSONS!'

The stage was monster – something like four storeys high, 150 feet wide and weighing 350 tons. But the crowd saw nothing up there at first, except a stone boulder with a protruding sword and two giant images of an oak tree at either side of the stage. There was no set. No instruments. No band. Michael wanted everything hidden at first, and then a city would rise out of nowhere, triggered by Randy, dressed as a knight, pulling the sword from the stone to slay alien-like Cretons. Then the sword glowed and sparkled, the stadium went dark and Randy dashed to join us below as we took our positions and lined up as five, standing on a flight of steps. Facing out, it was me on bass far left, Randy, Michael in the middle, Marlon, and Tito on guitar, all wearing our Aviators and standing slightly stooped to keep our heads below stage level.

'Arise, world, and behold the protection of the kingdom!' declared a booming voice over the speakers.

We heard the screams of old; we sensed a familiar euphoria.

'You all ready?' said Michael, leaning forward.

'Let's tear this place UP!' shouted Marlon, echoed by Randy.

Giant floodlights beamed outwards, bathing the entire stadium in light as we started to rise, five silhouettes, statuesque. Only my eyes moved behind the shades – I couldn't help but suck up the exhilaration at seeing a sea of people, hands in the air, with banners and signs that read: 'We (heart) You Michael!' or 'J5' or 'Jacksons = Victory'. We were standing there for the longest time. Let 'em wait, said Michael. Build the anticipation. Send 'em crazy. On this, his first stepping out since *Thriller*, he knew he held the threads to 45,000 people's emotions.

We took slow, deliberate footsteps down the stairway in sync and each step lit up as we did so. At the bottom we waited, then raised our hands in sync to remove our sunglasses as the lights swivelled and turned on us. Then Michael gave his cue – a jab of his sequin-gloved hand. Cue the beat into 'Wanna Be Startin' Something'. In a 15-song set, we performed a Jackson 5 medley, Michael sent them wild with hits like 'Human Nature' and 'Billie Jean', and we performed our duet 'Tell Me I'm Not Dreaming' at the end of my solo set, which included 'Let's Get Serious', before Michael gave 'Rock With You' and 'Beat It'.

For the first time in years, I was in musical heaven. If Motown 25 had been the reigniting of old magic, this was its explosion. And as much as the press would throw more crap at Michael, he had only to step out on stage to know where the love was. 'MICHAEL! MICHAEL! MICHAEL!' they chanted. I watched him watching them – a crowd aged from five to 70. Saluting them, blowing kisses, disbelieving it. Wearing the biggest smile on his face.

Anyone who says – as many have – that 'Victory' was a miserable experience for him doesn't have a clue what they're talking about. There was always a world of difference between the business and the show for Michael, and it was this kind of love that expunged the frustration that had preceded the tour. It was a buzz that would sustain us across five months, 47 American and eight Canadian cities. You ask any of the brothers today what the best time of their lives was, and I'm pretty sure they'll each say, 'Victory.' Half the time, we just wanted to shut ourselves away as brothers because when it was just the six of us – with no one whispering divisive advice in our ears – we were in sync.

I've read the accounts that would have people believe Michael was 'increasingly difficult' on the road and was suddenly 'unreasonable' in his 'demands'. We apparently feuded so much that we had to have rooms on different floors in hotels; we 'didn't speak *en route* to stadiums'; and we especially 'glared' at Michael's guests. I honestly think some people wanted so badly to believe that the discord in the promoter/attorney meetings extended into the dressing room and hotels which it did not. No one focuses on how we went out there night after night and kicked ass on stage with a chemistry that spoke for itself. I guess success stories fall flat where news coverage is concerned. As Michael always said, 'When they can't pick fault with the performance, they'll pick fault with the person.'

I had a long-time suspicion that it was in the interests of people who worked with Michael to plant subliminal messages of conflict – both with the media and in his ears – because they wanted to be his replacement 'brothers' and it was far more profitable to slice into a financial pie that was for Michael alone, rather than a pie that had to be cut six ways. Many times during 'Victory', I thought back to when Joseph had gathered those twigs in Gary and bunched them together. Inseparable. Unbreakable. Stronger together than apart. Now, in 1984, having endured the wrench of separation once before, I held even tighter to that teaching as the entourage swelled around us.

BAKANA THE BENGAL TIGER JOINED US on the road. Bubbles stayed at home. He would have to wait for Michael's 'Bad' Tour.

Bakana, named after the Fijian island, was my 'plus one', and stayed in my room. After raising a mountain lion, I had bought a cat from a friend and I had been raising her like a child, bottle-feeding her in my arms and taming her for the tour. I appreciate keeping a tiger is not something most ordinary folk would do but in Hollywood as they say, anything goes. Don't forget Dean Martin and his pet bear! Anyway I would sometimes have to give Bakana a little bop on the nose from time to time when she got slightly rowdy, hissed and showed her fangs. As part of this taming process, I posted a photo of myself inside her cage and left one of my old shirts in a corner – I hoped to get her used to my face and smell. But I returned one day to find the photo eaten and the shirt in shreds, so we had to work a bit harder at our relationship. Thankfully, by the time 'Victory' began, she was impeccably behaved and took to touring like a duck to water.

We often had to take different floors at hotels because there were only so many suites per floor. Occasionally, due to a limited number of suites, we stayed in different hotels. The days of sharing rooms were over, but there was still an open-door policy between us and we each had our own assigned security. Michael loved the thrill of us sneaking my tiger through hotel kitchens – entering via back routes as always – after she had travelled to each destination via the crew bus. On arrival in each city, we just threw a blanket over her cage and pretended it was musical equipment. Then, once in the suite, we'd do what we'd always done and blow up the phones of room service, ordering ice-cream, fries, fruit … and lots and lots of raw meat for Bakana. 'What are you doing up there? Barbecuing?' asked the always-agreeable voice in the kitchens.

'Yeah, we're throwing some meat on the grill on the balcony,' I'd say, as Michael muffled his laughter. Room service staff always seemed to accept our story that we took a travelling barbecue wherever we went. 'So much hotel food, we just like cooking it ourselves,' I said.

Bakana loved the five-star cuisine, even if the wardrobe department didn't love Bakana. It was usual for a rolling rack of outfits to be wheeled into our rooms each day, but I'd always find my clothes hanging outside on the door knob and the door frame. As Bill Bray said, 'There ain't nobody going in Jermaine's room when that joker's got a tiger in there!'

Michael helped nurture Bakana on the road and was as unafraid as the other brothers when he fed her meat and gave her a bottle of milk. When we came offstage, all pumped and unable to sleep, there was no better release than wrestling with a growing tiger on the carpet. But, eventually, just as with Bubbles, she became fully grown and the decision was taken to release her into a national park in Oregon. For many years, there was a tiger running wild out there with as many fond memories of the 'Victory' Tour as we had.

MICHAEL DIDN'T NEED PETS AS COMPANIONS because he had his two extra guests in tow: his ever-present shadows from the Kingdom Hall. Following through from the 'Thriller' video, 'Victory' allowed me to see first hand the set-up of having two independent Jehovah's Witnesses travelling with him city to city. This pair – a man and a woman, both nice enough people – were always immaculately turned out and hovered without saying too much. They were just a … presence. I'd like to say that they faded inconspicuously into the background but it's hard to ignore people whose role you know is to 'monitor' everything. I started wondering what their thoughts were about Randy slaying alien-like Cretons at the start of each concert. Nothing was said, so I presumed Jehovah only had a problem with the occult, not encounters of the third kind.

At first, Michael seemed okay with this arrangement because the monitors were presumably as good as having God's eyes watching over him. But if there was one overwhelming characteristic of my brother, it was his need for space – especially creative space. It was as essential to him as food and water. Place him in a straitjacket of discipline in any way and he was always going to rebel. I had never known someone so self-disciplined and yet he struggled to tolerate being disciplined by others. So it was never going to end well when he had to think inside the box when his instinct was to think outside it.

Michael started to make his point at the very start of 'Victory'. We rode together as brothers en route to stadiums, but didn't always share the same vehicle at other times because the elders took up two seats alongside Michael. Often, there was also Frank Dileo and photographer Harrison Funk. Growing entourages meant that it wasn't always possible to travel together. But the following story was a funny memory of Michael's that Harrison – whose friendship and lens was trusted to roam freely with him for many years – has assisted with.

Their van had stopped at a set of traffic lights in Kansas City when Michael spotted three hookers on the street corner, with one wearing sequined hot pants. Michael's eye couldn't help but wander. 'Oh my goodness, hurt me!' he said, playfully – Jackson-speak for 'Oh wow, she's looking hot'. Then, just as the lights were about to change, he stuck his gloved hand out of the window and waved. Three hookers did a double-take, wondering if that was … just maybe … it can't be … Michael Jackson. Just to make sure that they were certain, Michael opened the van door a little and, looking back as the van began to move away, he showed his face, chuckled, and then slammed the door tight. He twisted around in his seat to watch three hookers jumping up and down with excitement. I don't know what the two Jehovah's Witnesses made of this interaction but it made Michael's day and made one thing clear: he wasn't *always* going to be squeaky-clean.

The 'monitors' would stay in place for three more years. But then, in 1987, each side's tolerance of the situation mutually expired when he shot the video for 'Smooth Criminal'. Ironically, the inspiration behind this hit would have been enough for the Kingdom Hall to get stirred up again, but they never found out because Michael kept that inspiration hidden, for understandable reasons. The video had an Al Capone-style feel, but 'Smooth Criminal' was actually inspired by a serial killer who spread fear throughout Los Angeles and San Francisco between 1984 and 1985. Richard Ramirez, a self-confessed devil worshipper, was the 'Night Stalker' who took 14 lives. In most cases, he forced his way into people's homes before brutally murdering them with a knife (hence the appearance of a flashing blade in the video). As Michael's first verse described:

As he came into the window
It was the sound of a crescendo

He came into her apartment
He left the bloodstains on the carpet
She ran underneath the table
He could see she was unable
So she ran into the bedroom
She was struck down, it was her doom ...

There were two reasons not to reveal this inspiration at the time: first, so that the media didn't accuse him of glorifying such a heinous crime; and second, he didn't want the elders to know that a worshipper of the occult partly 'inspired' this song. But if he thought he had been clever in swerving trouble, he was mistaken because, in the end, the elders found something else to be upset about. During the music video, there was a scene where Michael sprayed an underground bar with bullets, using a machine-gun. It was a real firearm, and one that he'd been trained to use by ammunition experts on set. It was fun, harmless and necessary for the story-line. But no Jehovah's Witness is allowed to hold or possess a firearm, let alone use one. The official rebuke from the Kingdom Hall was harsh. It asked Michael to consider where his priorities lay: as a Jehovah's Witness or as an artist. As distraught as my brother was by this implied choice, it was the final straw: what church asks you to reconsider the very gift that God gave you? Michael had been the perfect 'disciple', going door to door in Encino, but that seemed to count for nothing when his creativity was up against the rule book.

That same week, before the 'Smooth Criminal' video was even wrapped, Michael wrote to the Kingdom Hall disassociating himself from the Jehovah's Witnesses and specifically asking not to be recognised as a baptised Witness. I know it broke his heart because he was severing such a long-standing tie, but he felt he had been placed in an impossible position. It devastated Mother, too, but she made it clear that he was her son and she supported his decision because she understood his need for artistic freedom. The matter was never discussed again. Jehovah's Witnesses don't discuss with the disassociated or the de-fellowshipped their reasons for leaving and that seemed to suit everyone.

MICHAEL'S SENSE OF HUMOUR NEVER MATURED and I suspect that anyone who ever spent time with him will confirm that he was still playing hide and seek, and still acting chief prankster beyond the age of 40. Bill Bray remained a merciless target for his jokes and his new manager Frank Dileo wasn't spared either. Michael would toss a bunch of his 100-dollar bills out of the hotel window for fans or dump a bundle of cash in the bath and turn on the taps. Only one thing could have been worse to Frank and that was wetting one of his big fat cigars.

Being back on the road meant we could revert to being ourselves and the fun we had was silly, infantile but *fun*. Michael, Marlon and I dropped water bombs from hotel windows high above a table of suited businessmen having an al fresco lunch, knowing the water would turn into a mist of 'rain' halfway down. We then drenched each other in water-pistol fights. Placed eggs in people's shoes. And Michael held a toilet roll and let it unravel from the balcony. Tour boredom didn't get any easier as we got older so we spent a lot of time goofing off, making our own entertainment and no doubt retaining the title of Best Behaved Group in the History of Music. I think we made the Osmonds look devilish by comparison.

The post-concert food fights were always the best. Michael would be standing and talking, looking all serious with Frank Dileo and someone else from the tour, and I'd be watching. With Michael's back to me, I'd hurl a handful of peanuts or almonds, peppering them. You could always tell when innocent bystanders on the crew weren't used to our historic bombardments because they'd hold their arms and hands to their faces, asking us to stop. Responsible adults being bombed by the 'kids'. Michael would crack up laughing. 'ERMS! You're going to get it now!' he'd shout. Before you knew it, all the brothers were at it, unleashing tracer fire of a thousand M&Ms. When they ran out, we'd throw pieces of banana, shrimp, berries and cake, re-enacting our favourite scenes from *The Three Stooges*.

Harrison Funk captured most of this fun on camera and we had to get used to him walking into our dressing room without knocking as he started blasting away with his flashgun. As a trusted member of the team, he had *carte blanche* to take photos whenever he liked. Unguarded. In private. Then, one day, Michael asked him to put his cameras down and take a break. Harrison thought this a very nice gesture – an artist recognising the hard-working photographer. Then, as he stood there picking at the fruit plate, Michael came up from behind him and poured an ice bucket full of shrimp cocktail over his head. Welcome to the family.

AS VICTORY PASSED THROUGH JACKSONVILLE, FLORIDA, Bill Bray had taken a decision not to tell us about the numerous death threats the team had been receiving. Especially the one from a worrying individual named James Huberty. Every tour and group gets its share of crazies and we knew that; we just didn't need the distraction of a reminder.

But two weeks into the tour all that changed. We knew nothing of what was going down until we were resting up in our individual suites. I was alone in my room, kicking back on the bed, when there was a fierce knocking on the door. I sprang up and Bill rushed in with a fire marshal, uniformed officers and sniffer dogs. Lucky for them that Bakana was in her cage. These guys were 'clearing' each room, said Bill, as he tried to explain what was going on. Just a precaution, he said. But it was the most frantic precaution I'd ever seen. Once the all-clear had been given, it was explained that there had been a shooting at a McDonald's restaurant in San Diego. A man had walked in and gone mad with an Uzi, shooting dead 22 people and injuring 19. 'What's a shooting in San Diego got us panicking for in Florida?' I asked.

'Because the shooter was James Huberty – the same guy who's been threatening you jokers,' said Bill. Even though he had been killed in the shootout, no one was taking any chances after he had hinted at a little surprise for the Jacksons while on the road. At least, it was something sinister like that. Understandably, everyone was freaking out as the San Diego incident played itself out on television.

If the room search seemed a little over the top, it was nothing compared to the increased security. The atmosphere of the next few days was one of lockdown just in case the shooter hadn't acted alone. We transferred out of the tour vans and into one of those armoured bank vans, steel-encased with no windows and certainly no leather. So the seats normally reserved for bags of money now had our costumed asses parked on them. Once we were clear of Jacksonville, we thought the red alert was behind us, but then we moved on to Knoxville, Tennessee, where the local newspaper had received a threat, predicting that one of us would be shot during the concert. We were again spared the details, but we found ourselves back inside the armoured van. There was talk of cancelling the Knoxville dates – but there was no way we were letting down the fans. We took advice from the head of the police unit, Lieutenant Vitatoa, and we had outriders wherever we went.

With increased security, both around us and at the stadium gates, we couldn't have felt more over-protected – especially when we were bumping around in the back of the windowless bank van on the way to Neyland Stadium. As we rumbled along, we got talking about how serious this all was and then one of us – can't remember who – said, 'What are we going to do if he [a shooter] is out there?' Before we even arrived at the venue, we had convinced ourselves that one person out of the 48,000 fans was out to get us. We started laughing. Nervously.

'Hey, Michael, you're up front! You're the biggest target!' said Randy.

'Yeah, Mike,' said Marlon, 'what are you going to do?'

Michael looked at us like we were dummies. 'I'm going to keep moving! I'm going to move so much and so fast that he'll have a hard time getting *me* …'

That was true. It would be hard to train crosshairs on a bolt of lightning.

'Why should I be worried?' he continued. 'I'm not the one tied to the spot with my guitar.'

I looked at Tito, and Tito looked at me. Michael suddenly seemed to have the safest position on stage. That's what I've always said about the bass and guitar players – we're the unsung heroes.

THANKFULLY, IT WASN'T ALWAYS ARMOURED CARS and ass-bruising seats. We had some cool experiences. It was a lavish, no-expense-spared tour, from the lasers and special effects onstage to the spoiling treatment off it. The size of the operation meant that Michael always flew in his own private plane with his team and we flew in a separate one with some of the band. Sometimes, I commandeered the fleet of seven private jets that belonged to my friend Meshulam Riklis because I was collaborating with his wife Pia Zadora – he was the most generous man on earth. All in all, 'Victory' was what a tour should be: rewarding, crazy, exhilarating, spectacular and full of memorable performances.

In New York, the scenes were incredible. We were told the city had 1,000 police set aside for crowd control, which best illustrates the scale of what we found ourselves in the middle of. Tour co-ordinators told us that they sealed off Midtown on the west side when we played Madison Square Garden, which is one to tell the kids and the grandkids. A few days earlier, we had played the Giants Stadium in New Jersey and had decided to arrive in style, by Chinook helicopter. Michael and I were not the most relaxed air passengers at the best of times and there was limited seating capacity, but everyone ignored that and piled in. We had the managers, security, makeup, and Michael's guest Julian Lennon who, contrary to what's been reported, was accepted warmly into the camp without a fuss. An extra kid aboard was the least of my concerns. All I was thinking as we stood on the helipad was, We don't have to cram in like sardines. The pilot can come back in 20 minutes for a second group – otherwise we're going to be swallowing the Hudson River. But, no, everyone wanted to travel together.

Remarkably, Michael was the calmest, but as that helicopter started to take off and swing, I was convinced its alarm would sound with an electronic voice that would echo what was running through my mind: 'Too much weight! Too much weight! Abort! Abort!' It dipped and swayed, and I wasn't happy. 'There's too many of us in this thing,' I said.

'Calm down, Erms, we're flying in style,' said Michael, laughing at me.

How things had changed since Mobile, Alabama. It was evening, heading into dusk, and I painted headlines in the pink sky: 'JACKSONS WIPED OUT IN HELICOPTER TRAGEDY'. And then we flew over the Giants stadium, skimming its noise. We looked down into this bowl crammed with people waiting to see us and saw every one of those minnows looking skyward and cheering. They knew it was our helicopter, presumably because it had been announced. We landed about two blocks away before jumping into limos. I think that that night we gave one of our best performances, which goes to show that there's nothing like a bit of fear to get you pumped up before a show!

I was always happiest riding to a venue when the tyres remained in contact with the ground. The pre-concert atmosphere in the van was always the same: going over last-minute reminders about this turn and that cue. But all Michael could talk about was the segment where he got to show off his love of magic. In a scene he'd dreamed up under the guidance of tour illusions master Franz Harary, one of my brother's two giant spiders crawled electronically onstage to eat him, trapping him under its legs. Michael played dead. He was lifted on to a table covered with a bed-sheet. When Randy pulled that sheet away, he had vanished into thin air. If there was one element of the show Michael wanted to get *just right*, it was this moment. *En route* to the stadiums, he'd be running it through with Randy, who was struggling in his role as magician's assistant. 'Give it a beat ... wait a little more until you pull the sheet away,' said Michael. 'You're doing it too soon, and the audience is figuring out the trick!' Randy kept pulling the sheet too hard, too soon.

Sometimes, you could still see Michael rising into the air, attached to wires and cables. We'd be back there, laughing, and Michael would be getting so frustrated. I'm pleased to report that Randy eventually nailed it, proving that magic is just as much about timing as music is.

Those rides to the stadium reminded me of the times we'd squeezed into Joseph's VW van back in the day. Our routine and mind-set had not altered over the years. We still plotted and planned and laughed. There was only one thing missing from the flashback: our old driver Jack Richardson. Those cigarettes had taken their toll and he had died of lung cancer. We missed him badly, from the van and from our lives. 1984 was a tough year in that respect because we also lost an idol in Jackie Wilson and a dear friend in Marvin Gaye, shot by his father during a drunken dispute. We wept for all three of them and dedicated the tour to their memories, because each had been an important influence on our lives. 'Victory' was a reunion in which we toasted absent friends.

A NEW FRIEND WHO STARTED HANGING out with us in New York was Madonna, whose star was rising somewhere between her first single 'Holiday' and her movie, *Desperately Seeking Susan*. Dressed in all black with a proud cleavage, navel-baring cropped top and wild, scrunchy hair, she seemed to be a constant presence backstage at Madison Square Garden and the Helmsley Palace – Michael's favourite hotel in New York. At first, she actually came across as shy. She seemed like more of a VIP fan than a fellow artist as she moved between rooms at the hotel, being social, spending most of her time with Michael and Randy. It was certainly a productive networking time for her. Not only did she end up being managed by the Jacksons' management, Weisner and De Mann, she would recruit our keyboard player, Pat Leonard, as her musical director, and our drummer Jonathan Moffett for her 'Virgin' Tour.

In later years, it would also become obvious how much Michael inspired her artistically: his signature crotch-grabbing dance was all over her 'Express Yourself' video, and take a listen to 'Material

World'. That beat, that bass line? In my opinion, that's 'Can You Feel It' right there. I always sensed that Madonna was hovering with intent, looking to get some action from somebody, but Michael was indifferent to her back in 1984, which was probably why she turned first to Randy. The obstacle with him was overcoming the girlfriend who was not only with him but on his arm. Short of walking around with a sign saying, 'I'm taken', the situation couldn't have been clearer. But we soon learned that very little deterred Madonna. Ignoring his girlfriend, she walked up to Randy, grabbed his face and stuck her tongue down his throat.

You would have thought that kind of directness would be enough to put off someone as delicate as Michael when it came to future dating prospects but, come 1991, he and Madonna 'dated' for the shortest time. Out of all the combinations Hollywood could throw together, this was probably its most ill-matched. As Michael soon found out.

Here was a gentle man in touch with his feminine side, and here was a wild woman with a tight grip on her masculine side. She was everything his ideal woman wasn't: brazen, outspoken, opinionated and with an unashamed shock value. I think Madonna sincerely adored Michael but the feeling wasn't mutual and she committed two cardinal sins. The first was that she played on the fears he had about relationships: that every woman tries to change a man. It seemed she was hell-bent on loosening him up, bringing him out of his shell, getting him to see life through *her* eyes. The second big mistake was when they were at dinner one night and she had the temerity to criticise Janet. Michael was furious and, not surprisingly, they never went on another date.

Shortly afterwards, he started a more suitable courtship with an old friend, actress Brooke Shields. She was demure, elegant and the epitome of beauty and grace. Brooke had been in his life since the mid-eighties and Michael was extremely fond of her. I know she spent time with him in the studio as he worked in 1991–2, and this was a time they were seriously dating. Even though it ultimately didn't go anywhere, they remained lifelong friends and Michael always felt able to reach out to her. That line of communication never closed until the day he died.

VICTORY'S SCHEDULING MEANT WE WEREN'T SOLIDLY on the road for five months. We had periods back home and we had off-days built in, which gave me time to continue my collaboration with Whitney Houston on her début album. Clive Davis was still building the hype about his *protégée*, throwing parties on both coasts and clearly wanting to ride this collaboration on the crest of the brothers' tour. There was always some club to attend, like the Limelight in New York, or a promotional party in LA, where Whitney and I made our well-choreographed entrances. I didn't know at the time, but someone from Arista was always nudging the writing elbows of gossip columnists in the hope of building an are-they-or-aren't-they mystery. But it seemed the press was more interested in the fact that Whitney spent a lot of time with a woman named Robyn Crawford. Whitney once described their friendship as being 'closer than sisters' – and that was all journalists needed to read between the lines. They were curious about her sexual orientation before her album was even released.

Having witnessed this kind of false diversion play itself out in Michael's life, I had every sympathy, but we also laughed about it in the studio because, trust me, if you had spent more than two minutes in the charged energy of the 'Whitney whirlpool', you didn't need to ask how that fire smouldered.

I knew I was in trouble in the face of that fire when Clive booked us on to the CBS soap opera *As The World Turns* to test our duet 'Nobody Loves Me Like You Do' for the wedding scene of Betsy (Meg Ryan) and Steve (Frank Runyeon). I remember when she held my hand mid-song as the cameras rolled – an unrehearsed moment – and something hit me. The frisson just kept developing the more we worked together.

Back in the studio, we recorded and produced songs like 'Take Good Care Of My Heart', 'If You Say My Eyes Are Beautiful', 'Sweetest Sweetest' and two unreleased ones called 'Don't Look

Any Further' and 'Someone For Me'. With each session, we were in each other's eyes, almost cheek to cheek around the mic, selling the lyric, feeling the song – and that intense professional chemistry crossed over. Come the end of a powerful rendition, Whitney would just stay close to the mic, close to me, and say, 'What are you going to do with me, Jackson?' She held the seductive gaze. I lost my words. Then she walked away.

These were turning into duets between temptation and forbidden love, and the studio sessions gave us what felt like stolen time together. I arrived on those days with butterflies, because the whole experience of being around Whitney was intoxicating. I admitted silently to myself that I had the strongest feelings for a remarkable woman, whose heart was as beautiful as her face, and it became increasingly hard to sing love songs with all that emotion and unspoken passion between us. I spoke to no one about this until the day Michael raised an innocent enough question: 'So how's it going with Whitney?' He'd heard me predict that 'She is going to be the biggest thing when people hear her voice.'

'We're getting along very well,' I told him, smiling.

'You like her?' he asked.

'Yeah, I like her.' Still smiling.

'Oh, you *really* like her!' He started chuckling.

'I really like her,' I said. Smile now gone.

Michael got excitable. 'You in love with her?'

'I can't be in love,' I said. 'I'm married.' That was a deliberate lie. I was caught between the guilt of saying it out loud and the respect for his position because he was, at this time, still a devout Jehovah's Witness. I guess I didn't want to be a disappointment to him having for so long been an example. I can't remember what his exact words were in the back and forth that we had, but for a man with limited experience of this kind of thing, he had the wisdom of a sage. He didn't fuel the temptation as some guys would. He reminded me about Hazel. About family. About not getting wrapped up in the moment. He gave the soundest advice, and I knew that doing 'the right thing' was ultimately what I had to do.

Clive Davis was a true friend, too. 'How are you and Whitney going? Things good, Jermaine?' he'd ask. He always knew more than he let on and always said his door was open, before giving me a big hug followed by a pinch of the cheek. Whitney and I spoke endlessly about our shared predicament and as much as I wanted to lose myself in all these feelings, I told her to wait. I spoke of 'one day' and 'maybe'. Ultimately, we had to go our separate ways and it killed us both even if it was the right and sensible option.

I don't think anyone punched the air harder than I when the album *Whitney* became the biggest début album ever, selling 16 million copies worldwide after its release in 1985. Two years later, her follow-up album turned her into the first female artist to have an album début at No. 1. We didn't see each other for years after we finished recording. In fact, she saw more of Michael than of me: backstage at one of his concerts in New York, and then again in 1988 when she was onstage with Quincy Jones to help present Michael with an honorary doctorate in humanities from Fisk University. I saw newspaper photographs of them together in this moment and I observed the irony of them side by side.

In 1985, I received a phone call from someone close to Whitney, telling me that she was releasing her new single 'Saving All My Love For You'. Like Michael, she expressed herself through song. And when I watched the official music video, I soon realised that it was also autobiographical with its parallels – and coded message – to what we had recently shared in the studio together. I guess we had both left a deep and abiding impression on one another and her positive impact has never left me.

WE ENDED THE TOUR VICTORIOUS AT the Dodgers Stadium, LA. Seven nights of back-to-back sell-outs. We had played to a total of two million fans across America – a long way from 30 or 40 people at Mr Lucky's. I remember those final dates for the rain that lashed down, soaking the fans. And yet they still had a good time and danced, like most Californians tend to do when the heavens rarely open. If there was one thing the brothers were certain of, it was that we had made an impact with our reunion, and Europe would have heard about the excitement we had caused. We couldn't wait to take Victory across the Atlantic and retrace our steps from the good old days.

Our American ride finished on the evening of 9 December 1984 and we went through a range of emotions. Tito's prediction was right: it was the tour we never wanted to end. But I looked forward to the as yet unplanned European leg. As we reached the show's climax and the crowds cheered, Michael took the mic. We thought he was going to speak for us all. He didn't. He spoke for himself. 'This is our last and final show. It's been a long 20 years and we love you all ...' He hadn't prepared us for that one. I initially thought he was referring to the last and final show on American soil. I'm pretty sure this was how the other brothers felt, too. Maybe it was our continued wishful thinking, but there it was: finality.

What's absolutely not true is that we said to each other things like 'the little prick' or 'what a creep', as was reported because (a) that's not how we speak at all and (b) that's not how we viewed it, even when we realised Michael had announced his detachment from the Jacksons. It was actually not something we addressed or confronted with him. As was typical between us. Anyway, Michael had explained to Mother that, 'This is something that I just need to do alone,' so we had to accept it – and who were we to hold him back? I'm not going to pretend it didn't hurt because it did: it hurt deeply. But not once did we ever criticise or blame Michael because we knew he loved us and this was an artistic decision. If there is one thing to understand about our family, it is the pride we have in one another. However hard someone's decision might be, family trumps everything. Brothers first. Artists second. But I believe the outside world has struggled to understand that thinking because it has only known us as artists, *and we just happened to be brothers.*

On reflection, Michael wasn't just detaching from the Jacksons as a group, he was also disentangling himself from the messy politics. I knew he couldn't tolerate another round of all that. When you are a giant talent, why put up with it? We had wanted to ride with him, but what we carried with us was too much of a weight, I think.

So, with that one decision, a single branch was removed from our tightly-bound bundle. Separated. Weaker. Breakable. Not as an artist – because his career would go from strength to strength – but as a brother, as a person. Michael was riding high within a never-ending glory and, for as long as the good times rolled and the success brought in untold wealth, everyone wanted to hang on to his magic carpet ride, now that the excess baggage had been removed.

IF THERE WAS ONE THING I always prided myself on, it was the ability to spot my brother from 1,000 yards. Even when in disguise, like that day when he was taking a break from the 'Ghosts' video. His eyes and aura were unmistakable. He could never fool me. I knew it. Michael knew it.

For most of 1985, we had only seen one another intermittently because we both returned to the studio to concentrate on solo projects. He started his pursuit of topping *Thriller* by working on his follow-up album, *Bad*, and I began work on my second Arista album, *Precious Moments*. By the time the spring of 1986 rolled along, Michael was still cutting tracks but my album was out and included my duet with Whitney 'If You Say My Eyes Are Beautiful' and a song that would become a Top 20 hit in the US, 'I Think It's Love'.

I then kicked off the 'Precious Moments' Tour with dates around America, which eventually brought me home to the Universal amphitheatre in LA some time that May. In the back of my mind, I'd always hoped Michael would come to see me, just like the rest of the family, but I had accepted that he was consumed with *Bad*. At least, that was the impression he gave. What I didn't know was how much he wanted to attend the gig as a surprise, but hadn't wanted to cause a fuss in the crowd. 'It's Jermaine's night, not mine,' he told Harrison Funk. Michael couldn't so much as step outside without causing a mob scene, let alone attend a concert with a few thousand people.

I was in my dressing room backstage, in costume, with my daughter Autumn and son Jermaine Junior, hovering near the door where my Israeli security guy stood guard. And then I saw Harrison in the frame, with a battery of cameras slung around his neck, accompanied by Kevin Wilson, the son of comedian Flip Wilson, whose shows we had always done as the Jackson 5. I allowed Kevin and his buddy Marcus to open the show with a comedy act and they had people with them backstage.

'And this is Uncle Willy,' said Harrison, introducing a fan, a pasty-looking white man, aged in his forties, wearing a hat and looking a bit long in the face. I wasn't really paying attention because show time was approaching, but I shook this guy's hand and thanked him for coming.

'I'm a huge fan of your music,' he said.

'Thank you,' I said – and everyone burst out laughing. So hysterically that I looked behind me to see if anyone was pulling a prank. But there was nothing.

'Jermaine,' said Harrison, 'it's Michael … Uncle Willy is Michael!'

I looked hard at 'Uncle Willy' and even though his face was dead-pan, his eyes were laughing. 'Oh, no, no, no, no, NO!' I screamed. The disguise was so incredible that I'm pretty sure Michael looked at himself in the mirror that night and wondered who the hell was staring back. I've included a photo in this book to show you just how unbelievably unrecognisable he was. During the 'Bad' Tour, it was this disguise, along with others, that allowed him to mingle and sight-see among the crowds in places like Vienna and Barcelona.

Not only had he succeeded in fooling me, he'd made my night by turning up to watch the concert. As I took to the stage, now feeling on top of the world, I knew that out there in the crowd somewhere, together with Janet and La Toya, 'Uncle Willy' was blending in, unnoticed. He was sitting among people who, for one night only, shared a row with Michael Jackson and didn't even realise it.

MICHAEL'S DISGUISES WERE HIS ONLY CHANCE to become fleetingly anonymous. He worried now that his fame might lead to him being assassinated, like John Lennon.

The fan and press attention outside the gates was relentless and he became more and more anxious each time his car pulled into the driveway. Fans surrounded him on both sides and from his seat, all he could see were bodies. He started to freak out any time he saw someone approaching the window with their hands in their pockets. 'What happens if one of these days someone has a gun in their pocket when I think they're reaching for a pen?' he asked.

Michael knew all about John Lennon's death at the hands of a disturbed fan, David Chapman.

It reached a point where he became paranoid about a similar outcome. It was impossible for him to feel calm as he arrived or left home, and this was the prime reason why he sought solitude elsewhere, hunting for a secluded property within acres of land away from the city. He knew exactly what he had in mind, and he knew exactly the right place.

THE END
THE NEVERLAND YEARS

CHAPTER FIFTEEN
Once Said …

BETWEEN OUR LAST TOUR ENDING IN December 1984 and 1992, the family saw Michael sporadically, say three or four times a year in those eight years. When those occasions came around, at Hayvenhurst or Neverland, I found myself snatching time with him before he'd disappear again for the longest periods without a phone call. It actually *felt* like eight years without contact because the contact was so fleeting. His move to the solitude of the Santa Ynez Valley only made matters worse: we grew used to this foreigner called Distance moving between us and making itself at home. I don't really know how that came about. Maybe I had first invited it when I'd stayed at Motown and broken the team pact. Maybe we had each become too preoccupied with trying to reach beyond our reach. But regardless of decisions taken as artists, had you said to me during the Jackson 5 years – and even during 'Victory' – that career and stardom would turn us into distant brothers, I would never have believed you. 'We had each other *before* success and our love will outlast it,' I would have said. 'The synergy and team spirit that formed our backbone were built not in Hollywood but forged in the steel furnaces of Gary.'

I understood where Michael was at this time of his life. He was consumed with the *Bad* World Tour for most of 1987 and into 1989, and returned home to move into Neverland. We also knew that dropping off the radar was his creative habit. But before we knew it, the gap had widened and we had drifted towards an uncomfortable reality. Michael didn't carry a cell-phone so it wasn't as if we could call him. Communications technology was never his forte and the system dictated now that we call his offices at Neverland or in LA and leave a message. And another. And then another. They all went unreturned and I didn't know what to think. *Are our messages even being passed on? Is he ignoring them? Are we being blocked from talking with our own brother? If our messages aren't being passed on, does he think we're being distant?*

Publications like *People* magazine ran reports about the Jackson siblings being 'at odds – and out of touch'. It was only half-true: we were never at odds.

Of course we heard the snipes of strangers who claimed to understand our brother, suggesting he had chosen a place like Neverland because it 'guaranteed space between Michael and his pesky family'. There was talk that 'the brothers only want Michael for his fame to make a name for themselves'. Even though we had already made a name for ourselves: the Jacksons.

And then came the best claim: 'Michael doesn't need his brothers – he's a success on his own.' Hear that again: *Michael doesn't need his brothers*. As if his success was all that mattered to him and us. That is the biggest misunderstanding about our family: few grasp that our love for each other was always the most important thing, regardless of perceptions built by headlines. 'Family' was all we knew, our platform to success, and it came before everything else.

It was only when this splintering happened that we realised that, away from the stage and outside of entertainment, there was no actual coming together because we didn't celebrate holidays or birthdays due to the rule of Jehovah. We never sat down together at the dinner table or spent Sundays visiting one another. That was why, around 1988, I inaugurated 'Family Day': it would be a chance for us all to get together at Hayvenhurst, catch up, have a barbecue, watch a movie, or see our kids dress up and put on a show on the stage in the movie theatre. A couple of times Michael made these occasions, but not every time. What I liked about these days was the fact there was no business talk – we had 'Family Meetings' for that. 'Family Day is a chance for us to be family again,' said Mother. Meanwhile, Joseph observed that he felt like he was fighting to keep us all together.

It was because of our parents that we recorded the song '2300 Jackson Street' in 1989, featuring Michael. He also wanted to film Mother and Joseph talking about the family and themselves – how they met, their first date – and he started the 'interviews', but they were never finished. He kept the material in his own archive, under lock and key, with his deeply personal diaries. Michael recorded everything on paper: his first song lyrics, his memories, feelings and notes about the different people he met and what they meant to him. It is a memory collection that should remain as he intended: private and sacrosanct. (He also saved trinkets, keepsakes, family videos and memories from his past, like Rebbie's first pair of baby shoes, his nieces' and nephews' first pacifiers – dummies – or first dolls.) During 'Victory', it was his idea that we all join Mother on a trip down Memory Lane to visit her roots in Alabama and he wanted to capture us on camera as we visited distant relatives. This meticulous collection of everything 'family' made his distance seem at odds with who he was and what mattered to him in life. I guess every family has a distant member – I just never imagined that ours would be Michael, or that he'd become so absent from our daily lives. We went from 'always together' to the point at which we couldn't get to him at all.

We knew Michael thrived in seclusion – I think artists need to retreat from life to some extent if they are to observe, sing and write about it. We understood that need in Michael – and I never forgot that he gave his first public performance, singing 'Climb Ev'ry Mountain' on the school stage on his own. But he would learn that there is a fine line between creative solitude and personal loneliness. He found himself caught between what he chose and what his fame imposed on him; he would discover that solitude was not always his friend, and that the life of a genius can be the loneliest in the world. But there is one guarantee about family: you know where its members are, and that the day will come when you'll be there for one another, come what may.

I needed solitude for very different reasons.

My marriage to Hazel had ended in 1987, mainly because I wasn't, in the end, strong enough to resist temptation. I let her down and shattered something special. I met a woman named Margaret Maldonado and we ended up moving into Hayvenhurst after Michael moved out. But I needed to get away and find balance, so in 1989, I headed to the Middle East – a concert by Rebbie was my excuse. She remained the incredible dancer of old and her voice had blossomed, too. Michael had written her début album's title track, 'Centipede', in 1985 and she had lined up shows in Dubai, Oman and Bahrain, which offered me my chance to show support and see her live for the first time. I didn't know exactly what I was searching for on this trip because I couldn't put my finger on what was missing. I just packed my bags and followed my instincts.

THERE'S NOTHING LIKE A DRIVE THROUGH the Arabian desert to clear the mind. I had the windows up in the Range Rover and the air-conditioning turned high during the four-hour journey between Bahrain and Riyadh. It was the most serene, scenic – and dusty – drive of my life. A ribbon of road unfurled across powder sand, with giant dunes on either side. I saw camels running loose, children stopping to pray, and we passed tented communities of Bedouins as Middle Eastern music played on the radio. *Everything* about the place was hypnotic. Ali Qamber, a friend from Washington DC who'd met me backstage during 'Victory', was driving. He was

BROTHERS UNITED: (Clockwise from top left) Michael comes to my rescue with the mic during Motown 25 – the spark for the 'Victory' tour; Michael with his record-breaking clutch of 8 Grammys; Indulging in some magic backstage during 'Victory'; Show time!; A food fight is about to begin backstage, with Michael at its centre.

JUST KIDS WITH A DREAM.

TO TAKE A PICTURE
IS TO CAPTURE A MOMENT.
TO STOP TIME.
TO PRESERVE THE WAY WE WERE.
THE WAY WE ARE.
THEY SAY A PICTURE SPEAKS A THOUSAND WORDS.
SO WITH THESE PHOTOGRAPHS.
I WILL RECREATE SOME WONDERFUL.
MAGICAL MOMENTS IN OUR LIVES.
HOPEFULLY THIS JOURNEY INTO THE PAST.
IN PICTURESQUE FORM. WILL BE A STIMULANT.
TO CREATE A BRIGHTER SUCCESSFUL TOMORROW.
MICHAEL JACKSON

PICTURE GALLERY: Going up the stairs into Michael's 'memory room' – the first image you see is 'Just Kids With A Dream' with my brother's poem on a plaque alongside it.

HAYVENHURST: Inside one of the 'memory rooms' with Michael's 'celebrity wall' to the left of the door; Hayvenhurst from the rear garden, showing the studio on the left, the picture gallery across the courtyard in the middle, and Michael's quarters and balcony on the right. In the foreground hangs one of his signs: 'Follow Your Dreams Wherever They May Lead'.

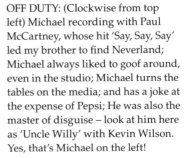

OFF DUTY: (Clockwise from top left) Michael recording with Paul McCartney, whose hit 'Say, Say, Say' led my brother to find Neverland; Michael always liked to goof around, even in the studio; Michael turns the tables on the media; and has a joke at the expense of Pepsi; He was also the master of disguise – look at him here as 'Uncle Willy' with Kevin Wilson. Yes, that's Michael on the left!

GOOD COMPANY: (Clockwise from top left) Michael with Berry Gordy and Bill Bray; Randy and me with Madonna during 'Victory'; Michael spent a lot of time with Elizabeth Taylor; Whitney Houston and me walk towards the set to perform our duet 'Nobody Loves Me Like You Do'; A precious memory for both of us was being guests of Nelson Mandela; Michael and Bubbles, seen here on stage in Tokyo, were constant companions; Michael meets Muhammad Ali; and his idol Fred Astaire.

HAPPY AND SAD: (From top to bottom) In love, and in the truest relationship he'd known, Michael with Lisa Marie Presley; Performing at the 30th Anniversary special in New York on the eve of 9/11; With Michael at the 2005 court case when Michael cried that he was 'the most misunderstood person in the world' before his infamous 'pyjama day'; 66 days after the trial started, I hold up news of the verdict: Not Guilty.

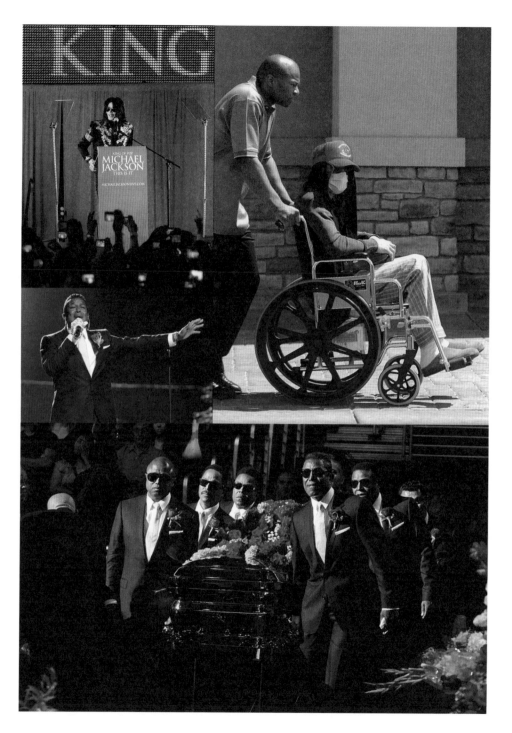

THE GREATEST ENTERTAINER: (Clockwise from top left) 'The Comeback King' announces his 'This Is It' concerts in London; Months earlier, he had the world fooled with a deliberate act of frailty, being pushed in a wheelchair … but it was all part of his clever plan!; The brothers wheeling in Michael's coffin at the memorial service – there's Randy and me (right) up front, then Jackie behind me, Marlon opposite him and Tito at the rear; Singing 'Smile' at the memorial service, the toughest performance of my life.

A HAPPY, FINAL MEMORY: Our last 'Family Day' with Michael as we all came together on 14 May to celebrate 60 years of marriage between Joseph and Mother. It was the last time we'd see our brother alive – but I'll always remember his good spirits and laughter from that day.

my guide and translator; he would help to change my life and become my closest friend.

As we drove, he pointed out a palm tree in the desert. 'Remind you of Hollywood?' he said.

This is nothing like Hollywood, I thought, but I smiled and nodded.

He talked about the Bedouins. Nomads. Big, strong families. Can weather anything. Family, family, family – that was what those people were about. I smiled and nodded again.

I had teamed up with him at one of Rebbie's shows in Bahrain. The following day he had taken me to a reception at his house to meet his family. Despite the fuss that having 'a Jackson' in the house caused, the kids were well-mannered and respectful. Even in their excitement, they waited for each other to finish a sentence before another spoke. In this Muslim household, every negative perception I'd heard in America about the faith fell away. Everything that Muhammad Ali had said came flooding back. I remembered the day when he'd taken me into Mother's office at Hayvenhurst, closed the doors and pulled up a chair opposite mine. 'Listen up. I've got something important to say. Look at me. Believe what I am about to tell you.' He started thumbing through the pages of the Bible, jabbing his finger at what he believed to be contradictions. Right under Mother's roof. Taking the fight to Jehovah's door. His guidance had led me to meetings of the Nation of Islam, when Minister Farakhan spoke to something inside me that wasn't quite ready to listen.

Now, in the bosom of the Qamber family, I felt something so profoundly that I can only describe it as a calling. I told Ali then and there that I wanted to drive to Riyadh, fly to Jeddah, then drive to Mecca.

In my eager conversion to Islam, I found myself walking a well-worn track inside the holiest of outdoor arenas, the Al-Masjid al-Haram, in Mecca; seven circuits of the Ka'ba – this big, black-clothed square block. It is the sacred centrepiece around which Muslims walk in silent prayer. As I prayed – for my family, for the brothers to be watched over – I started to feel as if I was gliding, not walking. From nowhere, I felt that rush of being onstage and hearing a crowd's roar. I felt euphoric without anything tangible before me.

'You're used to "seeing is believing",' Ali Qamber would say later. 'Now you see that feeling is believing.'

I became aware of the dozens and dozens of people around me, walking the same circle, in the same direction, united in worship. Connected. It's the same with Ramadan. No matter where people are in the world, they fast from sunrise to sundown, together. I observed more synchronicity and harmony, and everything resonated with me. I saw how, at the Call to Prayer, everyone prayed side by side in neat rows. They washed themselves before prayer because hygiene is imperative. They never placed the Qur'an on the floor at their feet because that's disrespectful. Order, cleanliness and respect. Just as I was raised.

I returned to California reinvigorated. I moved out of Hayvenhurst and into a duplex in Beverly Hills with Margaret and our two children, Jeremy and Jourdyn. I was also keen to record my next album with Arista. The nineties would represent a fresh start. I vowed to live my life according to God's will and become a better human being.

However, I would discover that seven laps around the Ka'ba is no guarantee for achieving that goal because life continues to test you – and sometimes you fail. Sometimes becoming 'better' is about making the worst decisions and learning from them.

I HEARD VIA THE TELEVISION NEWS that Michael had been taken to hospital with 'chest pains'. It was June 1990, and he must have been staying at his new condo in Century City because he was in the emergency room at St John's Hospital, Santa Monica. I remember thinking, I need to be there or he'll have no one with him – the rest of the family must have been out of town.

It was easy to locate the hospital because of the television satellite trucks parked outside and the news helicopters hovering above. Michael was forever besieged now.

When I got to his room, he was resting in bed, wearing a hospital gown, propped up by a stack of pillows. He told me he hadn't got 'chest pains' but severe headaches – a throbbing pain that I assumed was related to the old burn injury on his scalp. He was receiving his painkiller – Demerol – intravenously, but he was complaining more about a burning sensation in his arm. I called in a nurse, who adjusted the needle. I noticed two books on his bedside table: one about marriage and divorce, the other about taxes. For a man not contemplating marriage and who had his own accountant, it might seem odd but it was typical of Michael, who always wanted to be learning something new, however random.

I made a joke about his light reading material. 'Maybe that's why you have the headaches,' I said – which raised a smile. If he wanted to tackle something new, I suggested, he should start on my ton of books about Islam. This hospital visit was my first real chance to share my experience in Mecca, and he was as intrigued as I'd known he would be. We spoke about spiritual matters generally, which was nothing new between us because we had often imagined standing outside our bodies to observe ourselves so that we could improve as performers and people. 'Imagine what another person sees,' Michael used to say, 'and that will make us better in every way.'

'That is what Islam is all about,' I said, 'to make us better humans.'

He asked me to bring him all the books I had, once I had finished with them. 'But there's something else I really need now,' he said, all serious.

'I'll get the nurse. What do you need?'

Michael smiled. 'Chocolate cake … They have this great chocolate cake here … Do you want to split a piece?'

Over the cake, we caught up on everything and then I told him my big news: I was moving to Atlanta to start work on a new album in the studio of two of the hottest producers around, L.A. Reid and Babyface, who had founded LaFace Records in a venture with Clive Davis and Arista. Nowadays, people in America will recognise L.A. Reid as a judge on the US version of *The X Factor*, but back then he and Babyface were starting to carve out their names as the biggest hit-makers in the industry. 'These guys are going to be my Quincy Jones,' I told Michael – an indication of how excited I was about the opportunity.

He wished me luck. 'Just make sure you do your own melodies,' he said, throwing in some late advice.

By the time we had finished talking, day was turning to dusk and he was feeling tired. He said I should go home. I said I wanted to stay to make sure he was okay. 'You don't have to,' he said.

'But I want to. Don't worry about me, just go to sleep.'

On that first night, I didn't want him to be alone in a hospital room. I drew the curtains and turned out the lights. There was a big armchair in the corner. It seemed comfortable enough. As Michael closed his eyes, that was where I curled up and fell asleep till daybreak.

MY MOVE WAS A BIG DEAL. I took everything but the kitchen sink and enrolled the kids in a new school as Margaret and I set up home in Buckhead, Atlanta, in a nice colonial-style property in West Paces Ferry Road. I signed a year-long lease and spent the initial weeks ensuring the family was happy and settled into the community. We even took in a baseball game or two and adopted the Braves as our team.

Meanwhile, I placed calls with L.A. Reid and Babyface's people to chase the album start date, but was told there had been a delay. Never one to sit around doing nothing, I made the most of the lull and started talking business with Stan Margulies, the producer of the TV mini-series *Roots* and *The Thorn Birds* (and later *The American Dream*, our family's life story up to 1992). Stan told me that he had 17 hours' footage from research he'd done on Tutankhamun and wanted Michael to play the pharaoh in a movie. He asked if it was something my brother would be interested in. 'He'd jump at the chance,' I told him. 'Just give me a few days, let me put it to him and I'll come back to you.'

I left a message for Michael with his office. I waited up in Atlanta until 3am for his call back. Nothing happened. I did this – leaving a message and waiting up – for the following few days, but there was still no response. I couldn't understand why there was silence when the Michael I knew didn't like wasting time when such an opportunity arose. But this was becoming the norm.

Before I knew it, three months had passed in Atlanta and nothing had happened on any front. Ninety days of nothing going on is a long time when you're raring to go, revving on the spot. It was the slowest, most wasteful, most frustrating of times. Eventually someone at the record label called to give me the heads-up. They told me I wasn't going to be happy about it, but they thought there was something I should know: L.A. Reid and Babyface were working in California with another artist. I was furious. No wonder they didn't have the guts to pick up the phone and tell me themselves, I thought. 'Who's this other artist?' I asked.

'That's the bit you're not going to like,' I was told.

'Why? Who the **** is it?'

'It's your brother, Michael.'

I put the phone down and Margaret asked me what was wrong. I couldn't tell her, because I couldn't find the words. I was too busy fighting the forces of gravity as my head spun with questions. *Michael had shared my excitement about my project: why would he retain the very same producers? Why, when I was committed to LaFace Records, wouldn't they have the courtesy to tell me? Why would everyone go behind my back, leaving me hanging in Atlanta?* Over the coming weeks, those questions festered unanswered. I heard nothing from the producers or my brother. Instead I embraced the teachings of the Qur'an, as I tried to become a better human being. I hung on to one particular *hadith* – a piece of wisdom from the Prophet Muhammad – and recited it in my head over and over: 'The strong is not the one who overcomes the people by his strength, but the strong is the one who controls himself while in anger.' As with all wisdom, though, it's not about reciting it, it's about living it.

I WAS CONTRACTED TO LAFACE RECORDS and obligated to Arista for one more album, so I had no option but to wait for my producers and get used to the sour taste in my mouth. But when they were finally ready to start work, it turned out that they, too, were upset with Michael. I don't know what studio set-up L.A. Reid and Babyface had expected with my brother, but I don't think it included the prominence of his preferred audio engineer/producer Bruce Swedien. He was integral to capturing and finessing Michael's unique sound over the years and was viewed as indispensable to his production team. At Michael's insistence he *always* sat behind the boards in the control room. Something about Michael's reliance on Bruce didn't go down well with L.A. Reid and Babyface. Nor did they appreciate the fact that Michael wasn't going to continue with any of their songs. That, I think, was the real slap in the face. That much was obvious when, during a phone call, they shared a hook from a song they had already written for me called 'Word To The Badd'. The hook that resonated – because of its implied selfishness – went like this:

> It ain't about your world
> It ain't about the things you do
> If you don't care, I don't care
> You keep thinking about you
> You been taking all of my pie
> You been taking for a long time …

The lyrics they had written in anger met with my still-brewing anger towards Michael. Not only that: all my pent-up energy to get into the studio combined internally with a deepening sense of injustice. It was a perfect emotional storm in which no one was thinking, just letting fly. If a studio session is an outlet for anything, it is for releasing unexpressed emotion. Music can be cathartic that way and I won't have been the first artist to arrive at the mic with an intention to get it all out. In fact, it was typical of me to vent on my own instead of saying anything direct to Michael.

It's one thing to write vocals, quite another to release them as a single. I guess it's like keeping a diary: you let the emotion pour on to the page. You write it and in the moment, you believe it. But you'd never think of publishing those words. When I arrived at the studio to start work, I was presented with the finished song and L.A. Reid and Babyface had come up with one particular verse that went like this:

Reconstructed
Been abducted
Don't know who you are
Once you were made
You changed your shade
Was your colour wrong?

It was a clear dig at Michael, and I knew it. Those lyrics were consistent with a mistaken perception about him and I didn't agree with them – but I did agree with the angry tone. I was mad. I embraced this secret retaliation. The moment that song sheet was in my hand, I was singing with an anger that therapists would have applauded, even if Michael's fans would not. In my naïvety, I didn't expect for a single second that those words would be heard outside the audience of two producers and one engineer because, in my mind, they were lyrics never intended for release. After I'd laid down my angry vocals – and felt much, much better for getting it off my chest – we recorded another version: the *intended* version of 'Word To The Badd', featuring T-Boz from TLC. It kept the same hook but ditched all of the innuendo towards Michael. I didn't think about it again as we went on to cut the rest of the album – due for release in 1992 – which included my biggest hope: a high-energy song with an explosive beat that never lets up. It was called 'You Said, You Said'.

I CAN'T REMEMBER WHERE I WAS when the bomb dropped. I just remember a phone call asking if I'd heard the radio, and that was how I found out that the angry, boot-legged version of 'Word To The Badd' had been leaked.

Someone had found it irresistible, and it was receiving blanket air-play on a radio station in Los Angeles and its affiliate in New York. Some smart-ass DJ had a field-day swapping between the lyrics 'you changed your shade / Was your colour wrong?' and Michael's soon-to-be-released single 'Black Or White'. I was mortified: I was the man caught on some surveillance videotape holding the gun in a crime I hadn't committed, yet the evidence was damning. Now my image was being flashed everywhere with the headline: 'HAVE YOU SEEN THIS ASSASSIN?' Guilty as sin. With a sense of shame to match.

My stupidity in trusting the catharsis of the studio, and leaving that version floating around, came back to haunt me and I was damned by the face-value evidence: Jermaine Jackson singing lyrics that attacked and ridiculed Michael Jackson. Crimes against loyalty apparently didn't get any worse.

I got on the phone straightaway to Mr Gordy, the one person I knew who would be calm in a crisis.

His advice was as straightforward as I needed it to be. 'Did you write it?'

'No.'

'But you sang it?'

'Yes.'

'Were you upset when you sang it?'

'Yes.'

'Well, you have to take full responsibility, Jermaine. There's nothing more I can say.'

I must have sat in my car for an hour after that call, berating myself, wanting to slam my head first against the dashboard and then through the windshield. I wanted to ring Michael instantly, but what was the point? I'd only leave a message that would go unreturned. Especially now. I wanted to tell the world that I hadn't done this and hope they believed my lie. Because the real me hadn't done it, and that was the truth. But I had to own up and step up.

I owned up on CNN with Larry King. I tried to explain, find context and plead mitigating circumstances. I tried to explain it was a song I should never have sang, let alone recorded. But none of that public stuff mattered in the scheme of things. What mattered now was repairing the damage with Michael. Inevitably, he called Mother, wanting to know what the hell was going on, and he wanted to double-check that it was *really* me singing those lyrics. He couldn't believe it. No one could. Everyone I cared about looked at me and asked, '*What* were you thinking?' and I had no answer. Anger never has made sense after the fact.

But Mother has always been one for brokering peace in the family and it was she who called a meeting at Hayvenhurst so that we could speak one-on-one. 'Don't listen to the media,' she told Michael. 'Don't listen to your advisers. Listen to what Jermaine has to say and sort this out like brothers, like men.'

For the first time that I could remember we were going to confront an issue face to face. We were going to point to the biggest, fattest elephant that had ever taken refuge in one of our rooms and we were going to call it what it was.

I WAS UPSTAIRS AT HAYVENHURST WHEN I heard Michael in the lobby and formal, ominously hushed voices – a sound you'd normally associate with a grim summit. I came down to find him, Mother and Joseph waiting for me in the library. He looked solemn as he took the sofa seat 90 degrees to my right, our knees almost touching. He had Mother at his side, and Joseph took the sofa directly opposite me, at the far end of the coffee-table. I cannot remember a time when we'd previously had a bust-up of any kind, not even as children. So the awkwardness between the two of us was alien. First, the distance. Now the discord.

At first, we avoided eye-contact. Michael looked down. I stared at Mother. Joseph looked like he wanted to bang our heads together, but said nothing: a father intently watching his sons work something out on their own.

It was Mother who got things going, reminding us about love and how close we were; that it should never have come to this. I went first. Not with an apology, but with the undercurrents. It is a conversation that remains vivid. 'We used to be close,' I said, 'but it's been eight years … eight years, Michael. Eight years that we haven't spent proper time together. I'm speaking for all of us, not just me.' He looked at me. Now we had eye-contact. I continued: 'In those eight years, everyone has said everything they can about this family as if they know us and know you, and we should have stuck together but you went off and –'

'And for those eight years you thought I deserved that song?' he interrupted. '*That* is hurtful, and I didn't expect that … not from you, Jermaine.'

'I didn't write it.'

'You sang it.'

'I sang it when I was upset, but those lyrics don't reflect how I feel about you and you know it,' I said.

'You put *your voice* to those lyrics,' he said, forcing his point home.

I could see in his eyes how hurt he was, and it killed me, knowing that I was responsible. 'I'm sorry I hurt you,' I said. My betrayal acknowledged, I tried to explain how I had reached out to him numerous times, leaving messages, and how frustrating that felt. 'Like the King Tut movie idea you ignored …'

'I don't know anything about a King Tut movie,' he said, looking genuinely surprised. 'I didn't get any of those messages.'

'Doesn't that tell you *something*? That the people around you are not passing on messages from us!' I said, feeling agitated all over again, renewing my suspicion that our messages were being filtered by his gatekeepers.

Michael promised to look into it.

'But that still doesn't excuse how much time you let pass during those eight years,' I reminded him. *If we're going to do this, let's bring it all out*, I thought.

Michael went into a long-winded justification, saying it wasn't deliberate, he was just busy. There had been a lot of travelling and touring, and recording and shooting videos. He went on and on with what I considered to be rationalising.

Eventually I had heard enough. 'BUT, MICHAEL, WE'RE YOUR FAMILY! You've GOT to make time for family!' I yelled, and in a fit of frustration, I slammed my fist on the coffee-table. The cups and saucers jumped on the silver tray and Michael almost leapt out of his skin. There was something so timid and fragile about him, so easily startled, that I felt bad for raising my voice. 'I'm sorry,' I said. 'I didn't mean to make you jump …'

Then he smiled. 'Look at your face,' he said, and then he started to laugh. 'You're so uptight!' As kids, we'd laughed nervously in the most serious of situations and Michael's chuckling, made me laugh now. With that, everyone relaxed. Everything that had seemed so serious now seemed silly and pointless, and we wrapped up the big talk by mutually accepting fault. We both stood, gave each other the biggest hug and said, 'I love you,' almost in unison.

From that day on, Michael turned up to more Family Days, even if he never again became regularly available to us, as he had been in the old days. The main thing was that we had cleared the air.

To this day, some of Michael's fans hold 'Word To The Badd' against me in a way that he did not, but ultimately what mattered was forgiveness between brothers. As family, you don't look at a dispute in the same way the public does – the issue was blown out of proportion on the outside, increasing the perception of us as a dysfunctional family. Sometimes it seemed that we weren't allowed to argue, lest someone suggest we were a family 'at war'. The truth was that our difficulties were no bigger or smaller than any other family's, but they became magnified by my actions and Michael's fame. Thankfully, we've always been able to put matters into perspective and move on. It takes a lot more than a few ill-considered lyrics to break the ties of kinship between us.

CHAPTER SIXTEEN

Forever Neverland

NEVERLAND WAS INTENDED TO BE MICHAEL'S happy-ever-after. It wasn't quite his romantic castle on a hill, but it was still perfectly removed from the outside world, and it had a breathtaking charm. I doubt there was a more magical place on earth away from Disney. I may have fewer memories of it than I do of 2300 Jackson Street and Hayvenhurst, but they are just as rich.

To this day when a warm breeze blows across my face and I hear water trickling from a fountain to merge with a child's laugh, I'm back in my brother's happy valley and I see him surrounded by children playing. I see him wearing one of his hats, sprinting across the freshly-mown grass beyond the swimming pool, armed with a water balloon or a pump-action water pistol, chasing and soaking the opposite 'team'. I see him on the back row of the giant Pirate Ship at the theme park, waiting until it is suspended in its up-swing … and then he pelts everyone sitting below with candy.

I see him in the bumper cars driving better than he ever did on LA's freeways, doubled up with laughter as we smash into him from all sides. I see him in the movie theatre, slouched back in his chair, tossing popcorn in the dark at anyone on the first few rows – the last person they suspect is Michael. I see him walking around the grounds near the lake, holding an umbrella to shield himself from the sun, heading to the cluster of Indian tepees. I see him in a golf cart, customised to look like a mini Rolls-Royce or a Batmobile – complete with stereo sound-system.

I see him lazing at home with the 'Michael Jackson image' hung up in the wardrobe as he shuffles about the kitchen – morning or night – not so pristine in a white V-neck T-shirt, pyjama bottoms or sweat pants, and black velvet house slippers with a gold crest and the letter 'J' on the toe. I see him as clear as if it was yesterday. I see him as I never want to forget him.

And if, as you just read that, *you* see a grown man acting like a child – not conforming to how things should be and feeling free to let his inner-child run wild – then you, too, see the unashamed truth of who Michael really was, being himself in the one place where he was *allowed* to be himself.

How people judge this truth, and project *their* views of 'normal' behaviour, will always say more about them than it ever did about Michael. Take Martin Bashir, the British documentary-maker who brought his lack of understanding of anything child-like into Michael's world in 2003. On camera, Michael told him how he loved to climb his favourite oak tree and sit in its branches and write songs, at one not just with nature but with his past: the tree outside our bedroom in Gary; the tree trunk he touched for good luck at the Apollo; Joseph's twigs that taught us togetherness; and then my image that a tree is like our family – the parents are the trunk, the children its branches. 'I love climbing trees,' Michael told Bashir. 'I think it's my favourite thing. Having water-balloon fights and climbing trees.'

Bashir didn't get it, so he projected his idea of normal: 'Don't you prefer making love or going to a concert? You really mean that? You *prefer* climbing trees and having a balloon fight?' He would later remind Michael that he was, at the time, a 44-year-old man. And that was where this journalist's 'examination' instantly failed:

regardless of whether or not others can identify with how Michael was, it doesn't change *who* he was. The core fact is that my brother looked at life through a child's eyes. Age, status, persona and other people's expectations of him had nothing to do with it. He had a child's heart and he never outgrew a child-like enthusiasm for fun – and *this* was why he had a natural affinity with children.

People with suspicious minds would turn this characteristic into something it wasn't, but if you accept his child-like spirit, you are at the starting point to understanding him and his joy in 'elementary things'. Is this 'normal'? Probably not. But I'll never forget a quote that someone once read to me: 'Normal is just some-one you don't know very well.' A privileged few knew Michael very well, and he was as 'normal' as can be when holding the cards that life had dealt him within an extraordinary life. Running back-wards to chase after his childhood was the most normal thing in the world for him to do. Michael might not have fitted many people's idea of 'normal', and that's because his sense of compas-sion was rare. But to *truly* know him was to love him, and to see him was to appreciate what Neverland was, too: a toy town filled with innocence and fun. I always said that my brother might as well have been the offspring of Walt Disney or William Hamley or Frederick Schwarz. At face value, it really was as beautifully simple as that.

HOWEVER VISITORS APPROACHED NEVERLAND – by air or road – one landmark guided them there. A mountain peak, with one side shaved clean and the other still thick with brush and trees, was the first thing we looked for in the distance either from the helicopter or from Highway 54 heading inland from the coast at Santa Barbara. If you kept your eyes on that highest point, which ducked in and out of view on the winding road, it was impossible to get lost. Michael named it Mount Katherine in honour of Mother because mountains represent something solid and serene and spiritually strong. Katherine Street ran in front of the train station, which he called Katherine Station. Mother was celebrated in the detail and in the distance, always part of Michael's landscape.

She was the first of the family to lay eyes on his new home, joining him after his European tour with *Bad*. As mother and son arrived at the property, they were greeted by two magnificent Clydesdale horses that pulled a Cinderella carriage driven by men wearing top hats. At the end of a winding road through open fields, she arrived outside the main house on the right. Huge oak trees cast shadows on the brick-paved forecourt and a statue of Mercury stood inside a decorative mini-roundabout. On her left, across the courtyard, were the guest-houses that overlooked a four-acre lake. Mother wasn't surprised to find that Michael had chosen another Tudor-style property and the previous owner had done it up inside: oak walls and beamed ceilings with varnished wooden floorboards. Think dark oak tones, exposed brickwork, brass features and mullioned windows, and you have the feel of this dreamy home – a 13,000-square-foot residence, surrounded by canyon stone paths, shingle and manicured lawns as lush green as the finest golf courses in the world.

Michael also had rainbow flowerbeds again, the most spectacular being the Geneva-inspired giant flower clock on the grass slope beneath the train station – you reached it by following the driveway from the house up and around a slight incline. Inside the house, standing in the widest foyer, the life-size model butler stood to attention, holding his tray of cookies. To the left, there was a den-like room, with a grand piano that bore framed photos of the family and a five-feet-high miniature model of a medieval castle on the floor as its centrepiece – a château that Michael had his eyes on in France. To the right, there was a library, filled with the smell of old books and velvet photo albums. Finally he had the grand library that would make Rose Fine proud.

But what visitors probably missed as they first stepped inside that foyer was the big wooden door immediately to the right. It could almost have been dismissed as a tiny restroom, but this was the entrance to a long narrow hallway running along the front of the property before it turned left and led to Michael's quarters. Inside, there was a living room, bathroom, pinball machines and stairs to a bedroom. He also had a second bedroom – a master suite – upstairs in the main house, reached by the varnished staircase that climbed out of the foyer. Everything about the house was grand.

I stood on the stairs, on my first visit, taking it all in, and remembered the boy who had wandered around awestruck inside Mr Gordy's Boston House. *Did you dream this back then? Is this what you were always shooting for?* I found one element of the answer downstairs in the country-style living room. There were huge self-portraits of Michael. One was of him being crowned, looking regal, another of him in military dress, decorated with medals and epaulettes, looking commanding. I had a flashback to Mr Gordy's Napoleonic self-portrait and smiled.

Neverland was regal in its slick operation. It had its own small army of about 60 staff with seven or eight chefs in the kitchens, a housekeeping department, a team of attendants at the theme park, a crew of animal handlers for the zoo, and a host of gardeners and security. Michael even had his own health and safety officer, a fire department and fire truck, manned by two full-time fire-fighters.

I knew instantly why the house and its solitude appealed to Michael: it was the size of a planet compared to Hayvenhurst. Instead of having a limited suburban garden and being fenced in by a main road, he had acres to roam and the horizon was his boundary. He could leave his front door, go on a long walk and then take a morning drive in a golf cart. Neverland was as much about freedom as it was escapism. To place its vastness in context, the developed part of the ranch – including zoo, theme park and all buildings – probably covered something like 50 acres but that still left another 2,650. Michael would climb into his 4x4 truck and get lost in its beauty. When he drove away from the developed land, he could take numerous dirt roads, arrive in other valleys and still be on his land. It was almost cowboy country in those parts – all oak trees, twigs, tumbleweed and brush – and you half-expected a convoy of wagon trains to appear, with land-grabbers on horseback to hammer their flags into the ground, vowing no one would take away their dream to own a corner of the world.

FROM THE OUTSIDE, NEVERLAND DIDN'T LOOK much. Even when the brown gates slowly opened, you felt as though you were driving into a rambling game park, not a home. There was a private road with nothing but trees and fields for about half a mile. Then the first thing that came into view was Michael's double-decker Neoplan motor-home, a jumbo bus parked and covered in its own court-yard on the left, waiting to be taken out on tour or to a video shoot. It was fitted out like the finest condo, with flat-screen TVs, sumptuous bed and sofas, and a big bathroom. On the upper deck, it had cream aircraft seats with burgundy piping – the windows were so high that when the vehicle was on the road, Michael said it felt 'like you were flying.' Even his tour bus was an experience.

Then the visitor arrived at the main grand entrance to the house, which was familiar to me because the black-and-gold wrought-iron gates were from my old house in Brentwood. They were put in storage after my neighbours had complained, 'Living next to you is like living next to a Saudi prince.' When Michael was looking for an impressive set of gates, he knew exactly where to come. He added the golden replica of the United Kingdom's coat of arms: the lion and the unicorn and the motto *'Honi Soit Qui Mal Y Pense'* which, when translated, apparently means 'Shame be to him who thinks evil of it'. He posted that motto long before the police and Martin Bashir passed beneath the black archway announcing 'Neverland' in gold, with Michael's name set within a crown motif. Michael had a fascination with royalty, and he absolutely *loved* the pomp and ceremony of the British monarchy. The entrance summed up Neverland for me: very Hollywood in its extravagance yet very English in its inspiration.

Just inside the gates, on the left, a little shop-front displayed candy and several mannequins in costume depicting old Hollywood and the 1950s period, an ornamental museum-like welcome. A few feet further on, you came to the track for the small train that toured the estate's circumference, taking passengers to the theme park and the zoo. Bubbles and the Hayvenhurst menagerie had been joined by giraffes, elephants, lions, tigers, alligators, wolves, an orang-utan, a camel and every kind of reptile and South American bird you can think of, each housed in its own pen or cage. Not forgetting the Clydesdale horses. In the distance, you could see the main house but, before arriving there, you crossed a double-arched stone bridge, two lanes wide and spanning the narrowest stretch of the lake, where there was a mini waterfall near the flamingos – they roamed the banks as underwater jets spouted huge towers of water.

It was instantly obvious that you were entering a child-centric haven. Signposts warned 'Be Careful, Children Playing' and there were bronze statues of happy children: a child with a flute, a group of children dancing as a circle linked by hand, a girl pulling a boy's arm, a kid hanging upside down from a rail, and a child kneeling down, playing with a dog. Inside the house, Michael had paintings of children from all over the world, black and white, from east to west. And all around the property, all the time, there was piped music: soothing instrumental pieces, strong with flutes and harp, and children singing, from the speakers that Michael had camouflaged as rocks and boulders.

Visitors could never tire of the amenities because, away from the zoo, theme park and quad bikes, there was also a two-storey arcade with every conceivable game and simulated ride, plus a tennis court, basketball court and a full-sized movie theatre that would put most local cinemas to shame. You name the movie, Michael had it, from modern-day smashes to Hollywood classics. If Blockbuster didn't have a movie in stock, my brother would. You stepped inside the theatre foyer, and the ceilings vaulted about 30 feet. On one side of the entrance there was a glass case housing a miniature animatronic version of Michael dancing to 'Smooth Criminal' and different buttons triggered different dance moves. There was also, of course, the biggest candy store, with yoghurt, ice-cream and popcorn on tap.

But the most incredible feature of the 50-seat theatre were the two rooms at the back of the screening room: one to the far left, one to the far right. Each had a window and a bed, oxygen tank and medical monitors. These were mini-hospital suites designed and installed with young cancer patients and terminally ill kids in mind. Unable to attend the theatre in the outside world, and too sick to sit in a chair, Michael wanted them to be able to lie in bed and enjoy the cinematic experience. Each child in each room had a bedside intercom that allowed them to speak with Michael, sitting just outside the window in one of the upper rows. Wheelchair ramps were built into every ride and facility because Neverland was designed not just with his own childhood in mind, but the childhood of others less fortunate. This was a side of Neverland that you never heard the media shout about, and whenever I heard the lie – from people whose knowledge was media-educated – that Neverland was some kind of predator's lair to lure young children, I wanted to drag them here, into this theatre, into the inside of my brother's heart, and make them see this truth about Michael's humanitarian spirit.

THERE WERE MANY DOWNSIDES TO MICHAEL'S fame, but he recognised early on that it gave him a platform and the power to make a difference with his music, and messages of hope, love, basic humanity and Mother Earth. He recognised the unity in music and felt its galvanising force as the only universal medium that made everyone listen, speak the same language, and brought communion between every race, creed and culture. Michael was one of those rare artists whose music shook hands with the world and brought people together. He had the biggest heart and he truly wanted to help children, nurse, nurture and make them happy, especially the unloved, the less fortunate, the sick, the infirm and the dying. This was not some trite, trendy mission statement on behalf of a pop star, it was a purpose that he lived and breathed, dedicating vast amounts of time to many causes and donating hundreds of millions of dollars to numerous charities.

Neverland's privacy meant that no one witnessed the busloads of charity groups and terminally ill children who, month after month, visited Neverland as invited guests. Like the 200 deprived children from the St Vincent Institute for the Handicapped, or those kids from the Big Brother, Big Sister organisation. Michael never publicised these visits because he'd only have been accused of a publicity stunt. So let me remind everyone that in the millennium issue of *The Guinness Book of Records*, Michael was named as the pop star who gave to and supported the most charity organisations. It was the one record he never boasted about. Not that he needed a public pat on the back because the gratitude came via the thousands of letters from charity leaders and parents, who wrote to explain how a visit to or a weekend at Neverland had provided either a long-needed therapeutic day out for a sick son or daughter, or a dying child with happiness. The busloads of children and the army of grateful parents – who trusted what they saw and not what they read – are worth bearing in mind in the context of what came later.

I witnessed my brother's sincere connection with kids when we visited hospitals in almost every city during the 'Victory' Tour. Throughout his career, he would build time into every schedule to visit children's hospitals, cancer wards and orphanages around the world. In those privileged moments that I shared on such visits, I saw him using the craft God had given him to give something back. His interaction with a child was the most unquestionably pure thing to witness.

I guess you had to be there to see a dozen bald kids running around Neverland, temporarily forgetting their chemotherapy. But I saw what happened when he walked into a room at a hospital: a child's sickness seemed to vanish for a moment as his or her face lit up and their eyes widened. I often saw parents and nurses crying at this breakthrough. I used to compare Michael's impact to the joy that Santa Claus or Mickey Mouse caused when they walk into a room.

No one in our family was surprised by any of this because his empathy with children had always been an intrinsic part of him and Mother remembers him watching television and crying over some terrible event on the news. Central to this hyper-sensitivity was his religious upbringing and, as he always reminded us, 'Jesus said to be like children, to love children, to be as pure as children, and ... see the world through eyes of wonderment.' He always believed that we 'should give our hearts and minds to the little people we call son and daughter because the time we spend with them is the Sabbath. It is Paradise.' This thinking – this mind-set – is essential to understanding how my brother approached and viewed his relationship with children.

When fans listen to his song 'Speechless' from his *Invincible* album, they are listening to that kind of wonder because he wrote it seated high in the branches of that oak tree at Neverland, while watching a boy and girl at play. That was because both girls and boys visited the ranch: I stress that because of the loaded myth that only 'young boys' were guests and that was never the case.

He couldn't bear to witness suffering in children. Mother always tells the story of how she and Michael were at home watching the news in 1984 when the cameras focused on the famine in Ethiopia. Michael saw images of skeletal starving children, with flies clustered around their mouths, and just wept. That was the spark for his 'We Are The World' collaboration with Lionel Richie and a life-long dedication to charity.

The story that best sums up my brother's humanitarianism was when he heard about a gunman opening fire in a school playground in Stockton, Northern California, killing five children and wounding another 39. It was February 1989 when such incidents were not as common as they seem today and his devastation was overwhelming. His instinctive response was to rush to Cleveland Elementary School, but then he checked himself. 'Will my presence help or hinder? I can't sit here, but I don't want to cause more problems.' He was torn between the mayhem his fame could cause and his sincere wish to help.

In the end, after allowing three weeks to pass, he followed his instinct and flew up. As photographer Harrison Funk tells it, he wanted to make his visit as low-profile as possible and was sneaked into the school in a detective's car. When he arrived, he walked into an assembly of children in a large classroom and gave a passionate talk about hope, comfort and God. Then he handed out toys and recordings of his song 'Man In The Mirror', which contains that lyric about making the world a better place. Afterwards, he visited a local church to spend time with parents of the victims. Remember, this was at a time when Michael was at the pinnacle of his career and yet – without having to and without prompting – he took time to reach out to a community recovering from a terrible tragedy. For me, the biggest cheer for that compassion came from eight-year-old Thahn Tran, who had lost his younger brother in the shooting. He spoke to a reporter of the strength my brother had given him: 'I didn't want to go back to school, but Michael made it all right again. If he goes there, it must be safe.' Michael found this kind of response 'more rewarding than anything I can get from a sold-out stadium or a No.1 hit' because he knew he was doing good and not just entertaining. There are many similar stories about him the world over.

And this was the man whom the authorities would later want the world to believe had a perverted mind and was capable of harming children.

PRINCESS DIANA WAS A FELLOW HUMANITARIAN Michael had always admired and they finally got the chance to meet backstage at Michael's *Bad* concert at London's Wembley stadium in 1988. In my mind, they were fame's kindred spirits: both hugely misunderstood, both ridiculed for heartfelt missions, both hounded by the paparazzi, and both reduced to wearing disguises to gain a little privacy.

From what I understood, Michael and Diana spoke on the phone irregularly between 1991 and 1994, and I know that more calls were placed from Kensington Palace to Neverland than vice versa. And they apparently shared one other trait: the ability to spend literally hours on the phone. It seemed that Princess Diana didn't care for time differences and when she wanted to speak, she called, and Michael – who had never been the best of sleepers – was often wide awake. Once they got going, they could talk for hours. When I asked him what she was like, he said she was 'a wise, sweet, sweet woman', and she had told him that Prince William and Prince Harry loved playing his music loudly in her apartment. Given my brother's admiration for anything royal, I'm sure he liked hearing that!

In 1995, Diana gave a BBC Television interview to Martin Bashir and it was seen as a PR coup, helping the world better understand her. Michael made a note of it: if she trusted Bashir, that was good enough for him.

ALMOST THREE YEARS BEFORE DIANA'S TELEVISION confessional, Michael gave his own broadcast interview to set the record straight via an up-and-coming host who, because of her unfamiliar face, had to introduce herself to the viewers: 'Hello, I am Oprah Winfrey.'

Michael, who had since parted company with his manager Frank Dileo due to differences of opinion, wanted to speak out for the first time in 14 years because newspaper headlines were increasingly poisonous. 'Wacko Jacko' journalists were now making up headlines everywhere, but Oprah confirmed one lie when she searched Neverland high and low for a sleep-in oxygen chamber and admitted: 'I could not find one anywhere ...'

The bully mentality of the British tabloids – picking on his appearance, making fun of him – was particularly upsetting because it had the effect of denying Miachel's humanity, making him a simple caricature to poke fun at. He decided on an at-home interview with Oprah that would go out live to remove any chance of clever editing. That willingness to leave himself wide open before a global audience indicated how sincere he was: there were no prima donna rules, question approval or conditions. Just give it your best shot. What you see is what you get. Watched by one hundred million viewers.

For me, the 'world exclusive interview with the most elusive superstar in the history of music' turned out to be more of a career-changing triumph for Oprah than it was for Michael: it seemed to kick up more dust than it brought clarity. Although Michael never used the word 'abuse', this was the interview that would cast Joseph as abusive. It was also the occasion on which Michael publicly revealed that he suffered from vitiligo, which destroyed his dark skin pigmentation, answering speculation that he was bleaching his skin because 'you don't like being black'. I always felt that his honest answer was greeted with cynicism and led to more, not less, speculation about his skin. The truth is that Michael noticed a small white patch on his stomach around 1982, just as I had found a spot on one thigh. Where mine didn't worsen, his spread. I had suspected something was going on as early as 1984 and 'Victory', because he started to cover up all the time.

It is *not* true that his vitiligo was the reason behind him wearing his sequined glove: that was an idea first suggested to him by Jackie. In fact, Michael only wore a glove or wore a white forearm cast to draw attention to his hand movements; his trousers stopped short to show the white socks that drew attention to his feet. He even wrapped his fingers with white tape so that when he performed, 'the white follows the light'. Little details like this had artistic reasons in my brother's mind and that was his genius.

But his daywear and show costumes on 'Victory' revealed as little skin as possible: round-neck vests, high-buttoned shirts, and sleeves that showed only a hint of wrist. I suspected something but really had no idea how serious his vitiligo was getting.

By 1990, the family was aware of Michael's condition and how distressing it was for him. You only have to imagine waking day by day to find increasing patches of blotchy pale skin to understand how traumatic that was for anyone, let alone someone so image-conscious. This was a time when he relied heavily on his ever-present makeup lady, Karen Faye, to cover the vitiligo that had spread to his face and neck. A spiritual soul with blonde hair and animated by a bubbly energy, Karen had first been assigned to Michael's team some time around *Thriller* and she quickly evolved from a trusted professional to a true friend he affectionately nick-named 'Turkle'. Soon Karen's wise words and comforting friend-ship proved as indispensible as her brushes and makeup.

I know from Karen that she had first noticed pale patches on Michaels' skin when she was with him on the 'Say, Say, Say' video in 1983. Back then, it was a simple case of colouring them in to match his dark skin tone but it reached the point where his condi-tion left him with tufty patches of his natural colour. This meant that his skin *without* pigment predominated so Karen had to camou-flage the dark areas by matching them to the lightest skin. Trying to keep a darker tone over his body when it had lost the majority of its dark pigment was impossible, especially when he sweated.

These necessary cosmetics had everything to do with the *appearance* that he was lighter, and his heavier use of makeup was also, I suspect, the reason behind the cruel jibes that Michael was 'a drag queen'. That saddened me because, for him, it was a neces-sary mask. When you understand how sensitive he was about his condition, you also understand how much he trusted Karen. It was invasive work but every professional choice she made was designed to give him freedom and confidence, and make him look like the star he was. And he equally relied on her keeping all her work confidential. Some members of his entourage, video direc-tors and photographers, didn't understand that Karen's challenge was to keep Michael looking perfect and she couldn't explain her actions because she was sworn to secrecy. So observers only saw an overly fussy makeup lady – one who sometimes inexplicably disappeared with her client. This was misconstrued: people decided she was competing as a woman for his attention. The truth was that she was working her butt off to keep him feeling safe and secure, ensuring none of his vitiligo was visible to anyone crowding near him.

To make medical matters worse, Michael was also diagnosed with a mild form of the auto-immune disease lupus, which, when it flared, caused reddening blotches across his nose and cheeks. The vitiligo and the lupus together led doctors to advise him to stay out of the sun, which was why he started walking around with an umbrella on balmy California days. The saddest thing is that it took Michael's death, via autopsy reports and doctors speaking out, to confirm everything he had said about his skin. He told the truth in 1993. It was finally believed in 2009.

Thankfully, Oprah brought other truths to the world, too – from her own mouth, back at the time of that blockbuster interview. For me, what she observed about Neverland *before* any of the nonsense started to poison the true picture is significant. Just before the interview ended, she noted the movie theatre's two hospital beds for sick children and said: 'What I realised when I saw this is that you have to be a person who really cares about children to build it into your architecture.'

And her overall experience of Neverland? 'I loved being here because it made me feel like a child again,' she said.

AS MOST PEOPLE ARE AWARE, MY brother was as keen on preserving his privacy as he was his memories and it is widely assumed that, once away from Neverland, there was no escape from scrutiny. But he kept his small victories equally private and there was one other place on earth that the world never did find about.

From the early nineties onwards, and when in L.A., Michael headed to Santa Monica Airport – but he didn't go there to catch a plane: he went there to find refuge. As flight instructors took up student pilots in their Bonanzas, and different limos dropped off VIP clients at waiting Gulfstreams, one man in a baseball cap slipped between them and walked to an anonymous-looking hangar not far from the runway. Once Michael pulled down its giant shutter of a door, he was able to relax. This was his secret windowless bunker where no one could find him. And he didn't come to this place to sing or dance, or rehearse: he went there to paint. It was an 'art space' found for him by Australian artist Brett Livingston-Strong – whom he'd commissioned to do some portraits. The two of them could disappear there for hours. Michael said this bolt-hole and 'the therapy of art' allowed him to 'escape the craziness and take my mind off everything'.

In 2011, the world finally found out about this secret refuge when Michael's art work was first revealed. I don't think anyone had, until then, appreciated what a superb artist he was, but he derived endless pleasure from experimenting with watercolours and pencil sketches. He even designed his own furniture – with the number '7' detail. It is a priceless collection which Michael requested be kept at the hangar because of its anonymity and because most of that work was done under the tutelage of, or in collaboration with, Brett.

I visited the hangar after Michael's death. His art from across the years was still on display, unframed, surrounding the large worktops in the middle of the floor and the clutter of art materials in the corners. There must be upwards of 50 pieces. As I stood there and imagined him locking himself away, immersed in his work, all I could do was smile and think, Golly, you've come a long way from splashing paint on Diana Ross's carpet.

AS A FAMILY, WE KNEW MICHAEL reached out to befriend children and if you knew his heart like we did, the idea that we should have been concerned by this trait is ridiculous.

I knew of two children Michael had invited into his life. Dave Rothenburg adopted the name 'Dave Dave' to sever all connection with his own father's surname because, when he was six, his father had set ablaze his hotel room and the bed he was sleeping in, causing him 80-degree burns and leaving him scarred all over his face and body. As Dave Dave so eloquently said at my brother's funeral: 'Michael reached out to me, befriended me, and the first time we met, he hugged me – and he never stopped hugging me through-out my life as he continued to provide emotional support.'

Then there was Ryan White, the boy from our home state of Indiana, who contracted AIDs from a blood transfusion and was first invited to Neverland in 1989. His mother Jeanne spent time at the estate before allowing her son to stay on his own for long week-ends. Michael liked Ryan because he didn't treat him like a pop star. Ryan liked Michael because he didn't treat him like an AIDs victim. When Ryan got sick, my brother tended to him the way a true care-giver would. He was devastated when Ryan passed away in 1990. The song 'Gone Too Soon' was written in Ryan's memory.

But it wasn't just sick children who stayed at Neverland. Michael liked being surrounded by his nieces and nephews; he kept gravitating towards child stars and that was how child actors Jimmy Safechuck, Emmanuel Lewis and Macaulay 'Mac' Culkin became friends; and then there was an Australian boy, Brett Barnes, and brothers Frank, Eddie and Angel Cascio, whom Michael bent over backwards to help financially in life. Michael just wanted to help any sick child and any child star struggling with the less happy sides of celebrity.

He became particularly close to an Australian kid called Wade Robson. Michael went so far as to describe Wade, his sister Chantal and mother Joy as 'my second family' and he expressed this to them in writing. Over the years, there would be other surrogate families but I can only speak of his fondness for the Robsons. First, it was mother, daughter and son who visited and stayed at Neverland. Then, as Joy trusted what we all trusted, Wade was allowed to stay at the house on his own. This fact was always conveniently overlooked by the media: no child ever stayed at Neverland without their parents also being present, or without their parents first getting to know and trust my brother as the child's guardian. Newspaper coverage always erased the parents, preferring to build the image of Michael having an isolated rela-tionship with the boys, as opposed to his all-embracing relation-ship with the families. Nobody ever mentioned that the families of

Marlon Brando, Tommy Hilfiger, Chris Tucker, Kirk Douglas and the master of positive-thinking, Wayne Dyer, were also regular visitors but I guess it seemed more titillating to think of unchaperoned children as the only guests.

The Robsons had met Michael in 1987 as his *Bad* Tour passed through Brisbane. Five-year-old Wade had won a contest to dance with him on stage – and he wowed the stadium. Michael was blown away and later said that watching Wade was 'like looking in the mirror at myself all over again.' All he wanted to do was harness this kid's talent and make his dream come true, so to cut a long story short, he ended up moving the family to LA when Wade was seven. In that two-year gap, Michael had built a solid phone friendship with Joy, spending hours on long-distance calls. By the time they pitched up in California, they were not strangers. Michael then took Wade under his professional wing, putting him to work with his choreographers, Bruno 'Poppin' Taco' Falcon and Michael 'Boogaloo Shrimp' Chambers, two guys whose invisible input was all over Michael's routines, and especially the Moonwalk. Then, in an echo of our childhood in Gary, Michael sat with Wade for hours in front of the television watching dance videos, mentoring him and pointing out which moves to watch and what detail to note. The upshot was that Wade became a dance teacher *aged 12* at Millennium Dance Complex, North Hollywood, where Michael held many of his by-invitation-only dance auditions. Four years later, he became choreographer to Britney Spears and then, later, to Justin Timberlake. A talent – spotted, harnessed and nurtured by Michael – passing down his teachings to Britney and Justin.

Many parents saw Michael making a difference to their kids' lives in so many positive ways, and not once did anyone see or sense anything untoward about leaving them in his company. There was a consensus in parental instinct. Every time. It wasn't 'allowing a young boy to sleep over at a house with a grown man', it was entrusting a child to the responsible and tender care of Michael – the difference between an impersonal connotation and personal, cast-iron knowledge.

In hindsight, there was always going to be a problem in an untrusting world that, by now, was becoming celebrity-obsessed. The more strangers you befriend with good faith, the more the odds shorten that, one day, someone will walk in, smell wealth and opportunity, and decide to take advantage. My brother's trusting nature and, perhaps, naïvety wouldn't discern that day coming.

MICHAEL DESPERATELY WANTED TO BE A father and have children of his own, but he never stopped being consumed by work and the perfect woman hadn't come along. But that didn't stop him *talking* about wanting kids and he made no secret of his desire to have nine. That was the number he quoted, just as we had been nine.

Both of us had mentioned having 'lots and lots of children' when we grew up. Maybe when you come from a large family, you want to repeat it. I don't know. I just know that we love kids. Michael had an upstairs room at Neverland filled with a collection of porcelain dolls, dressed in velvet and lace dresses. I could never go in there because I didn't want a million non-blinking doll faces in my dreams. As Mother said, 'That's one scary room with all those faces staring at you.'

I think this room was more than just a collector's prized possession. In my mind, it was a positive visualisation of what he wanted: a house full of children. His bedroom and games room were also busy with mannequins dressed in all sorts of fashions he admired and then there were his life-size superheroes like Superman, Darth Vader, Batman, R2-D2 and Roadrunner. I think at Neverland he missed being surrounded by people – having grown up in a full house – which was also why he invited relative strangers into his world, constantly building surrogate families for himself. I am also certain that he found echoes of his boyhood in the child friends who became his new 'brothers'. Through them, he relived his own childhood after he had rebuilt his playground.

People failed to understand that what Michael created for himself was a comfort blanket – it had no ulterior motive.

Everything he surrounded himself with substituted something in his past. He wanted to be solitary yet struggled to sit with it and he was to struggle with it until the void was filled with a family of his own.

CHAPTER SEVENTEEN
Body of Lies

I REMEMBER 1993 MOSTLY FOR WHAT happened behind Michael's back. It was the year when the dream lost control and everyone seemed powerless to stop it – or content to let it happen. From now on, there seemed to be schemers, plotters and planners everywhere, triggering a destructive chain of events that would affect my brother for the rest of his life. Outside his fan community, it was no longer about loving and appreciating Michael Jackson the entertainer; it seemed to be about the authorities and media ghoulishly anticipating his downfall.

Not for a second did the family think that success could betray him in such a way. It wasn't the kind of lesson we had been taught at Motown University and Michael wouldn't understand the forces he was up against until he was staring the living nightmare in the face. We had spent our lives as the Jacksons trying to control our goals, strategy, image and music: we woke up one day to find all hell had broken loose. It's at such moments you realise that, in life, you're never in control. Only God is – and Michael's unshakeable belief in Him would pull him through the biggest injustice I've ever seen.

VENICE BEACH IS ONE OF THOSE laid-back towns I've always avoided because of its crowds. It's a log-jammed tourist trap at weekends with its mime artists, psychics, performing dogs, rappers, musicians and dancers all taking their chance on the ocean-front boardwalk. One weekend, Wade Robson was one of those street performers, trying out his moves. He was about 10 and he, his sister and mother Joy were still regular guests at Neverland and had set up home in a condo in west LA. Michael had used Wade, with Macaulay Culkin, on his 'Black and White' video, but he was still an anonymous face in the crowd, especially in Venice Beach. There was no way anyone should have known who he was, let alone linked him with his mentor.

Until, that is, some 'freelance writer' named Victor Gutierrez sidled up to his mother and explained that he was investigating Michael Jackson for 'being a paedophile'. How did he know who she was? Joy took his business card and immediately phoned Michael's office. It was early summer 1992 – a year before any formal allegation or police investigation – and a butterfly started to beat its wings near the beach.

IF HE WERE STILL AROUND TODAY, Michael would tell you that he was wary about the people he engaged with. He only mentored, nursed or nurtured maybe 10 or 15 children over the years. And that, to him, was doing good deeds in the eyes of God. The more he reached out to help, the more he was practising what he'd been taught all his life. Michael was his mother's son. We all are: each of us has been taught to see the good in everyone. Ever since Mother had invited fans to sit at her kitchen table while we were on tour as the Jackson 5, our artist-fan relationship has been finely balanced. Even at Hayvenhurst, we'd be seated at the dinner table when the bell would ring at the gate – 'Hi, we're visiting from Australia and we're just here to see the family.' Joseph would invite them to join us.

We were probably the only family in Hollywood with an open-door policy and the irony was not lost on me: don't let the outside world in when you're working towards the dream, but let anyone in once the dream has been achieved. In our minds, we were still folk from Gary, with temporary citizenship of California. We never wanted to lose the common touch. As Mother always reminded us: 'There would be no Jackson 5 and no Michael Jackson without the fans.' With that in mind, maybe it's easier to see why Michael wasn't street-smart when it came to letting random people into his life.

One day in May 1992, he was driving along Wilshire Boulevard, Beverly Hills, and broke down. Fortunately, there was a Rent-A-Wreck nearby so he could hire a replacement car. The owner of the business was an elderly man named Dave Schwartz. He had a younger, attractive wife named June, and she had a son from a previous marriage: 13-year-old Jordie Chandler. At first, everything seemed okay. It turned out that the kid was a huge fan of Michael's – the boy was rushed to his step-father's offices, with his sister Lily, before his idol left. Michael apparently spent no more than five minutes with them, but was told he wouldn't have to pay for a car if he took Jordie's telephone number. It would make the boy's day if he called him sometime. Please. It would be a dream come true.

The pressure on my brother was, apparently, polite but forceful, and he would have been sympathetic because at 13 he'd have done anything to meet Fred Astaire. So, he took the kid's number, promised he'd call and was a man of his word.

Somewhere along the line, he clearly felt comfortable enough to stay in contact. He called the mother and the boy over the next several months as he travelled. Before anyone knew it, they were part of his entourage and snatched press photos referred to them as 'Jackson's adopted family'. Such reports went over our heads, but one person was apparently really happy about it: the boy's father, Dr Evan Chandler. He was a dentist who didn't have custody of his son, and who harboured a dream to become a screenwriter. He'd already had one story idea picked up, which would evolve into the Mel Brooks' movie *Robin Hood: Men In Tights*, but he wanted more. Only one thing stood between him and his Oscar: the money to fund that dream. But his son now appeared to be Michael Jackson's new best friend and, as the dentist told his ex-wife – as we heard in court, many years later – the relationship was 'a wonderful means for Jordie not having to worry for the rest of his life'.

MICHAEL HAD INCREASINGLY SHUNNED contact with the outside world. Sadly, in consequence, he drifted away from the brothers again. We knew that he called Mother and asked about us, checking that we were okay, but I was unhappy that we had slipped back into lazy-communication mode.

This time, instead of leaving futile phone messages, I sent numerous letters, reminding him of what we had agreed about family and how important it was that we stick together. A lot of those letters were sent in the blind hope they'd get passed on and, in April 1993, I made that point to him by writing: 'I've sent a lot of letters to you. I hope you get them all.'

When I didn't get a response, I wrote again: 'I really need to talk to you about our relationship. I'm your brother and I miss you a lot.' The following month, I wrote again: 'Dear Michael, it would be great if you and I *only* could spend some time together and just talk about things … What's important to me is our friendship now. Please respond asap – Jermaine.'

Again, there was no response. I just kept praying he was okay.

BY FEBRUARY 1993 – AROUND THE time of the big Oprah interview – Jordie Chandler, his sister and mother were guests at Neverland. Sometimes a whole bunch of families were staying there together. As with every other parent, Jordie's mother June 'never' had a problem with her son spending time in Michael's bedroom because, as she put it, 'it was a boy's room … a big boy's room, lots of toys and things', and everyone seemed to be crashing there. She then invited Michael to stay at their house in Santa Monica, which he did for a total of 30 nights, we found out. Even

Dr Chandler played host and was happy for Michael to stay twice at his house with his son; all three of them ended up having a water-pistol fight. I know this from the court hearing.

In time, Dr Chandler was clearly getting on so well with Michael that he asked my brother to pay for 'a new wing' to his property. Thankfully, Michael had the good sense to dodge that one. But maybe it sparked Dr Chandler's resentment – a resentment which, however it started, would deepen as Jordie missed his weekend visits to his father so that he could stay instead at Neverland, where Michael treated him to expensive gifts, trips on Sony's private jets with his mother and stays in five-star hotels. This would later be misrepresented as a seduction technique 'to force a minor to comply with his sexual demands'. But Jordie Chandler wasn't alone in receiving such treatment. My brother had always been generous to a fault with his nieces and nephews. He'd allow them to have whatever toys they liked from his games room or he'd take them on a Toys R Us hunt, where they would close the store and he'd say 'Go on! Buy whatever you want!' For me, his generosity was his over-compensation for those years as a child when he'd only ever known what it was like to shop at the Salvation Army; his way of giving back something he'd never known.

He didn't just treat the boy Jordie, though. He bought the mother, June, Cartier jewellery, a $7,000 Fred Segal boutique gift certificate and even allowed her to use his credit card to buy two designer handbags – and no one one ever accused him of trying to seduce her.

Meanwhile, as more time passed, Dr Chandler became inreasingly angry because Michael had stopped calling him; he felt left out. Suddenly he said something 'was not right' about Michael's relationship with his son. None of us could have known what his remedy would be and if Jordie's step-father, Dave Schwartz, hadn't secretly taped a telephone conversation to protect his wife's interests, we would never have found out the truth behind what happened next.

Dr Chandler – presumably using his 'set routine of words that have been rehearsed', as he put it – would demand $20 million from Michael to fund his screenplays ($5 million for each of four scripts). If Michael refused to pay, he'd go public with allegations that his son had been molested. A month earlier, he had said as much to Dave Schwartz in the call that was recorded. It was an extortion that was presented in person to my brother at a hotel on 4 August 1993. Michael ultimately refused to pay.

For a lone man who was, it turned out, $68,000 in debt, Dr Chandler had supreme confidence in taking on the most powerful and wealthiest artist in the industry. Maybe he felt like he had nothing to lose, but it didn't sound like he was acting alone. As he said, 'Everything is going according to a certain plan that isn't just mine … There's other people involved that are waiting for my phone call that are intentionally … in certain positions.' I presume he was referring to his legal team, even if he was only advised by one attorney. Either way, he would stick to his 'plan'.

From now on, the focus would be on the spectacle of this episode, not on the absence of fact. No one would listen when my brother's team held a press conference playing back some of Dr Chandler's taped conversation. No one would listen even when his malicious motivation came across loud and clear: '… that's all I regard him [Michael] as … an attention-getting mechanism. It'll take on so much momentum of its own that it's going to be out of all our control. It's going to be monumentally huge …

'I mean, it could be a massacre if I don't get what I want …

'… Michael has to be there. He's the main one. He's the one I want. Nobody in this world was allowed to come between this family. If I go through with this, I win big-time … I will get everything I want, and they will be destroyed forever.'

'Michael Jackson … is gonna be humiliated beyond belief. You'll not believe it. He will not believe what's going to happen to him … beyond his worst nightmares … he will not sell one more record.'

A father was using his own son to extort money. And people wondered why Michael was so keen to give love to children.

MICHAEL WAS IN THAILAND ON THE Asian leg of his *Dangerous* World Tour when police raided Neverland with search warrants and a locksmith. We wouldn't find out until two days later when it broke on the television news. We had no means of contacting him immediately, but we thanked God that Bill Bray was with him because he was as good as family being there. All we could do was sit on the sidelines and watch the nightmare unfold.

When Michael had refused to pay, the dentist had taken his son to a psychiatrist to discuss child molestation. Standard procedure led to a call to the Department of Children and Family Services (DCFS), who brought in the Sexually Exploited Child Unit of Los Angeles Police Department (LAPD). Glory-hunters smelt blood. Then two things happened. Dr Chandler started a $30 million civil lawsuit, citing child battery, seduction and negligence. At the same time a criminal investigation was launched, overseen by two District Attorneys: Tom Sneddon for Santa Barbara County and Gil Garcetti for LA County. That was when an LAPD convoy arrived at Neverland, looking for evidence. They left with nothing more than memorabilia. There was nothing subtle about the raid: the police got as carried away as anyone else who came into contact with Michael's world. One of America's greatest entertainers was being treated like one of America's most wanted.

Days later, they also searched the condo in Century City, but Michael was truly devastated when they searched Hayvenhurst because he didn't want to bring trouble to Mother's door. Thankfully, she and Joseph were away so were spared the ordeal as police went through medicine cabinets, asking what this and that was used for. They hammered open a safe in Michael's old quarters and found it empty, but seized private notes and writings, which turned out to be his scribbled lyrics – the seeds of his ideas. Those notes were never returned and yet, over the years, they appeared in magazines. In all three properties, the police found nothing but word reached us via attorneys that officers believed Michael to 'fit the profile of the characteristics of a paedophile' because he used words like 'pure' and 'innocent' and he preferred child-like activities and bought gifts for boys. Gone were the days of true detective work, replaced by the psycho-bullshit of a one-size-fits-all template. No one looked at my brother's unique background, his character or what he'd done for people.

In the meantime, Jordie Chandler – now under the control of his father – had sworn an affidavit that built a false picture of intimate allegations and descriptions of my brother's body. Armed with that testimony, two detectives turned up with a camera and video-camera to subject Michael to what he rightly described as 'a dehumanising and humiliating' body search. He was compelled to undergo it because refusal 'would indicate guilt', they told him. Once they had stripped him of his dignity, Michael was made to stand naked in a room and lift his penis so that it and his scrotum could be photographed from front, right and left. As he turned to have his buttocks, chest and back photographed, a detective stood with a notepad, taking down every last detail. None of the markings on Michael's body matched the boy's description. In fact, the imagination bore no resemblance to the actuality.

When we were kids growing up in Gary, we had believed in the American Dream – that each citizen, black or white, has the freedom to chase opportunity and deserve success; that self-motivation would be rewarded. We had believed in the 'Land of the free, Home of the brave' – that if you earned your prosperity, you would be acclaimed as an example of what makes America great. It was a lifelong belief unravelling by the minute.

THE QUESTION NEVER CHANGED, AND HOSTS put it to Michael in every television interview he did: 'What is a grown man doing *sleeping* in a bed with children?'

I can still see ABC's Diane Sawyer and the BBC's Martin Bashir straining to comprehend the logic of the sleepovers; this habit that Michael willingly offered up and never once tried to hide. It was interesting to me that the question was never why Michael *shared* his bed with children: it was always posed with the sexual connotation of 'sleeping with'. Especially when it was about getting into bed with hot milk and cookies and putting on a movie.

Unless you knew Michael, it is hard to convey to you the trust and understanding innate to the sleepovers, because the simple answer to the question – that it was about giving love and providing hugs – immediately runs into a wall of suspicion that has nothing to do with Michael and everything to do with the modern concern about child abuse. Nowadays, a panic-stricken parent sees danger at every turn.

I would simply ask: who is the one man in your family, or in your circle, who you would trust implicitly with your child? That man who you would say 'I'd trust him with my life'. Because that man was Michael to us, and to every parent who entrusted their child to his care; parents who didn't appreciate strangers on television or in newspapers telling them what was appropriate for their kid. It worries me that our minds have taken over our hearts, and fears and stigmas and blanket judgements now stand in the way of basic love being expressed to children. If we know that a man shares a bed with a child, and we ignore the merits of that individual and immediately leap to suspicious thought, what is this world coming to? But beyond that, it was also misleading to focus on Michael sharing a bed with only boys. Young girls played in his bedroom and jumped into those same beds – like Chantal Robson or Marie-Nicole Cascio or the sisters of Macaulay Culkin and Brett Barnes. I also know that some of the parents would join their sons and daughters and Michael in bed and snuggle up to watch a movie with popcorn. It was, at times, like that lullaby 'There were ten in the bed, and the little one said, roll over, roll over ...'

It was about being with children who had the innocence to accept him for who he was; with kids whose presence brought him comfort and probably took him back to the days of sharing with Marlon, and cramming brothers into one bunk bed. I wondered how many people have considered that Michael had an anxiety about being alone in his bedroom and that was why he filled it with mannequins, and with children that asked nothing of him. The real clues about the real reasons he opened his bedroom to children were always there, but others would choose to see what they wanted to see.

I also wish people could have seen how children were naturally magnetised to him. Tito's three children, together with my kids, would trail Michael around both Neverland and Hayvenhurst, following him like ducks, upstairs, downstairs, to the kitchen, and even to the toilet, and it would have Michael in fits of laughter. Ironically, the person who best summed up this human 'magnet' was June Chandler when, in 2005, she told the courts that she had once told Michael: 'You're like Peter Pan. Everybody wants to be around you and spend 24 hours'.

AS A FAMILY, WE WENT BEFORE the cameras at a press conference in North Hollywood. It was a deliberate show of strength at a pre-booked event to announce a television special on NBC, *The Jackson Family Honours* – a celebration to honour the humanitarian work of Mr Gordy and Elizabeth Taylor, who was, by now, a constant presence and source of comfort in our brother's life. Mother had spoken with Michael on the phone and everyone had agreed that 'the show must go on', with our television special and his Far East tour, even though we knew he was struggling. Bill had told us he was 'sick to the stomach but keeping strong.' We suspected that his reassurance was to stop us worrying.

Our show's humanitarian theme provided an apt platform for us to demonstrate solidarity. Every one of my unanswered letters seemed irrelevant now; it was about shouting for the truth as the media invited ex-employees to run with their wildest allegations, induced by large six-figure payments and the racier the allegation, the bigger the cheque. I've since learned that Wade's mother Joy Robson was approached by the *National Enquirer* and offered a six-figure sum if she changed her story 'to say that Michael had molested your son'. Thankfully, people like Joy had scruples and she, like every other parent and child who'd spent time at

Neverland, would not corroborate Dr Chandler's claims or anyone else's, even when the police turned the screw.

One investigating sheriff was caught on tape – as we would hear in 2005 – saying to a child witness about Michael: 'He's a molester … great guy, makes great music, bullshit …'

As the US and UK media wrote out life-changing cheques, there was a 'while stocks last' stampede to this open season on my brother's reputation. With everything that we have learned over the years, it is hard for us not to view this police-media pursuit of Michael as the starting line for a hostile campaign designed to bring about his downfall.

Back then, my eyes were less wide-open as Mother, Joseph, Rebbie, Tito and I took our seats in leather armchairs on that stage in North Hollywood. I thought the transparency of the case would become obvious when television pundits had caught their breath. I took that optimism into the press conference as we faced a jostling stack of lenses and television cameras. Not too dissimilar to Jackson-mania, only without the love. As the room echoed to the sound of a hundred shutter speeds, I could only think, If it's this intense for us, what the hell is poor Michael going through in Singapore?

When everything quietened, I spoke for us all: 'Michael has been made a victim in a cruel, obvious attempt to take advantage of his fame and success. We know, as does the whole world, that he has dedicated his life to providing happiness to young people everywhere. His compassion is legendary and we are confident that his dignity and humanity will prevail in this difficult time.'

After that, there was only one place to be: Joseph, Rebbie and the brothers started making plans to join Michael in Taiwan.

OUTSIDE THE RAFFLES HOTEL WHERE HE was staying in Taipei, the first people to greet us were a bunch of kids, excitedly telling us how they had followed Michael around Asia every step of the way. Michael's 'soldiers of love' were all over the world; an army standing shoulder to shoulder, never once doubting him. As isolated as he may have felt at times, Michael was never alone when it came to love, support and millions believing in him.

Elizabeth Taylor had joined him before he left Singapore. Out of all his friends, she and Marlon Brando had remained constant. Elizabeth had a unique bond with my brother and he found her 'playful and witty'. Their common ground was child stardom. Their connection was built on respect, loyalty and love, and she was always there for him.

At the hotel, we didn't immediately see Elizabeth because the first person we met was Michael's publicist Bob Jones, whom we'd known since our Motown days and that first trip to Australia. He had joined Michael when he went solo. My problem with Bob was that, rightly or wrongly, I felt he formed part of the barrier to our direct communication with Michael. Hollywood entourages spend their days standing in front of the artist – often without the artist knowing – but I was damned if that shield would be used against us after we'd travelled halfway round the world to support our brother, who knew we were arriving that day. When Bob explained that 'Now is not a good time … Michael is sleeping', I lost patience and the conversation turned into a dispute.

Eventually I'd had enough. 'Bob, get out of my way … you don't tell us when we do or do not see our own brother,' I said.

'I'm just doing my job, Jermaine.' He stepped to one side.

Sure enough, Bob's blocking tactic was false. We knocked at Michael's door and walked in. He was happy to see us, even if we were a little surprised by what confronted us: he was sitting with an intravenous drip leading from a bag above his head into his wrist.

'What's going on?' said Jackie, forever protective. He wandered over to the bag, no doubt to confirm that it was saline.

Michael explained that he'd collapsed before his concert had begun in Singapore; the show had been cancelled. The doctor, who was also in the hotel room, told us he was suffering from 'dehydration'; Michael was still struggling and they were worried about his blood circulation and …

He kept talking and I stopped listening, because I was watching Michael, who looked the saddest I had ever seen him before going on stage. Normally, he'd be focused and energised. Now, he seemed drained, sitting down like one of those exhausted marathon runners at the finish line, desperate for fluids – and yet he had a 90-minute set ahead of him. 'I'm stressed, that's all,' he said, 'I just need liquids.' His eyes, which were usually smiling, were clouded; he had lost a lot of weight. Michael wasn't into his food at the best of times, but when stressed, he just stopped eating. My guess was that he hadn't eaten or slept for about a week, based on how emotionally shattered he looked.

Attorneys and media commentators would wonder if Michael was 'playing the victim' on the public stage yet the man I saw in private looked like he was using every sinew to keep standing and performing. I didn't see a man folding or pleading for understanding, not until that degrading body search which would come two months later. Physically, it was clear that the ordeal was taking its toll, but his spirit was indomitable.

Before we left, we reminded him that we were there to support him, and said we'd return tomorrow. Which we did. We told him he was going to get through this. We said the tough-talking things that brothers say, but the outcome of the investigation didn't seem to worry him too much. Instead, the next day when we met, he seemed preoccupied with another puzzle. 'What are they trying to do to me? Why do you think this is happening?' he wondered aloud.

AS A FAMILY, WE FELT OUR solidarity was unbreakable. As long as we stood as one, we felt sure that justice would prevail. So when La Toya popped up on television from Tel Aviv to denounce Michael, it felt like being T-boned at a crossroads. 'Michael is my brother,' she said, 'and I love him a great deal, but I cannot and will not be a silent collaborator of his crimes against small children.'

I watched that press conference and her follow-up interview with NBC the next morning, and couldn't believe how freely she was talking on camera, seemingly ad-libbing. To the watching public, La Toya's interviews looked like a damning and convincing condemnation but we knew our sister and the kind of language she'd normally use. The moment she said Mother had referred to Michael as 'a damn faggot', we knew the truth: they were the planted words of her manager-boyfriend Jack Gordon who, according to La Toya, would have knocked her black and blue, had she not said what he wanted. This is not my story to tell. It is La Toya's, and she's shared her version of events in her own book, *Starting Over*. The main thing to know is that Michael, and the rest of the family, forgave her.

ABOUT TWO MONTHS LATER, IN NOVEMBER, just when we thought that life couldn't get much worse, we heard Michael had suffered some kind of meltdown and been taken into rehab in England. It seemed to take us an age to get a handle on what was happening, but we knew Elizabeth Taylor, Bill Bray and Karen Faye were with him and he was cancelling the rest of his *Dangerous* World Tour. He had left Mexico City and flown to London. It was obvious that, in the time since we had left him, his physical and mental state had deteriorated.

Michael had developed a dependency on his prescribed painkiller, Demerol. With all the suffering he was going through over the false allegations, it had hit him hard. A doctor had recognised what was going on and now Michael had to face up to a six-week rehabilitation programme under the professional care of Dr Beechy Colelough. Inevitably the timing led to accusations that this was a cynical ploy to delay the legal process. It has always struck me that when Michael was alive, everyone was keen to say that he was feigning this condition, yet when he was dead, they were happy to call him 'an addict'. We had known Michael was taking Demerol ever since he was burned in 1984. I know little about his time in rehab so I can't talk about it here but it's not right for certain impressions to persist, especially when people label him 'an addict' or 'a junkie'.

There is a world of difference between someone becoming an addict due to bad choices and someone accidentally becoming dependent on a prescribed medicine. Michael was vehemently anti-drugs and was devastated to find himself trapped in a dependency primarily caused by the medication's side-effects. I've read accounts that hype up how, on occasion, his speech was slurred and he appeared glassy-eyed and 'high'. But what few have perhaps considered is that Demerol, to the best of my limited knowledge, affects the nervous system, blocks pain and creates a sensation not dissimilar to a high.

In 1997, Michael wrote a song called 'Morphine', which ridiculed the hysteria that surrounded this issue. The lyrics – 'Demerol/Demerol/Oh God he's taking Demerol' – say it all. That song was his response to the critics 12 years before he died. Sadly, it was never going to be the final word, but he was a man in pain from 1984, as caused by a terrible accident. Then, he was diagnosed with lupus, which itself can cause untold pain. I can't talk about that because I don't know how chronic it can be, but there are, apparently, another two million Americans who can. And all Michael ever wanted was for the pain – internal and external – to leave him alone.

WHEN MICHAEL FINALLY RETURNED TO AMERICA, stable after his stint in rehab, his health and well-being were paramount to everyone, but things didn't look promising. First, he was in the intensity of the media spotlight. Then both District Attorneys decided to convene Grand Juries in seeking an indictment. Michael was adamant that he wanted to clear his name but it didn't seem that he would be walking into the great Courts of Justice of California; more as if he would be sitting at the tables in Las Vegas and gambling his liberty and career. At least, that was how his camp viewed it. But here's what most people don't know: Michael's *personal* choice was to take the risk and go to trial – a criminal trial with the penalty of prison, not a civil trial with the possibility of financial damages. That was how confident he was of his own innocence. He even instructed his attorneys to file a motion to delay the civil case so the criminal trial could go ahead, putting the 'beyond all reasonable doubt' test before 'the balance of probability'. That way, an acquittal would seriously have weakened Dr Chandler's lawsuit.

But, in November 1993, a judge denied that motion because no charges had been brought. Instead he allowed a speedy trial for the civil case because no one wanted the boy's memory to fade and a trial date was set for the following March. That decision changed everything: if the civil lawsuit went against him, how could he possibly expect a fair criminal trial? In those circumstances, it was no surprise when a decision was taken to settle the case out of court. This payment – said to have been in the region of $15 million – was not hush money and it was not about cheating justice because justice was cheating Michael. It was, if anything, about saving him from a travesty of justice. People forget that the insurers governing his personal liability were also involved in this decision. Remember, Michael's intention was to fight this case. In the ever-changing circumstances, and amid all sorts of other legal motions, a team decision was taken to settle but that settlement stated in writing that payment was not an admission of guilt.

Another myth that needs debunking is that Michael bought the Chandlers' silence with this money: the settlement only prohibited the Chandlers from talking to the media; it did not prevent them testifying in any future criminal proceedings, as time would prove. This settlement was the only way to end the nightmare quickly. At the time, it seemed the best choice among bad options – and Dr Chandler really wasn't the winner because it was said that he and his wife only received about $1.5 million each from the settlement, with the rest going to the boy, Jordie – who grew up to become estranged from his parents.

In November 2009, four months after Michael's death, Dr Chandler, then 65, was found dead in his apartment in New Jersey. He had suffered a gun-shot wound to the head and was found lying with the gun in his hand.

BY EARLY 1994, AND AFTER SPENDING millions of dollars, convening two Grand Juries and talking to more than 150 witnesses, including all of the kids who'd spent time at Neverland, the LAPD and District Attorney Tom Sneddon conceded there was no case to answer.

Unfortunately Sneddon refused to close the case. It was, he said, 'suspended', leaving the door open for anyone who came forward in the future. The media wouldn't stop its pursuit, either.

Two years later, in 1995, my partner, Margaret, received a phone call from a friendly journalist warning us that a rumour was circulating about a 'secret' videotape. 'And what was this tape supposed to show?' I asked.

'Michael in the shower ... with Jeremy,' she said. Our son. Michael's nephew. 'They're printing a story saying Michael has paid us off to keep silent.' We could only despair, not knowing whether to weep for the truth or scream at the madness of it all.

Our attorneys immediately made the *National Enquirer* understand that if it so much as published the first sentence of that lie it would be closed down within a week. For once, it listened. Sadly, the producers of a 'hard news' television show called *Hard Copy* – a.k.a. Hard Copy, Soft Facts – ran a story about a videotape being found and its correspondent Diane Dimond breathlessly reported to viewers, and later to radio station KABC-AM, that the police would be re-examining the case against Michael. That same week, LAPD confirmed no such videotape existed.

It transpired that the source of this lie was none other than Victor Gutierrez, the freelance writer from Venice Beach. Michael's legal team launched a lawsuit for defamation. A judge and jury found that the story was false and malicious, and awarded my brother $2.7 million in damages. Gutierrez filed for bankruptcy and fled to Mexico. But despite that small victory, I think I knew then, in the back of my mind, that this whole saga would never go away.

WITH THE HORROR OF 1993 BEHIND him, a vindicated Michael moved on. He had resolved not to change his philosophy of life or his attitudes towards children based on one experience with one family. In his mind, love never surrendered to hate. He trusted what was in his heart, and that God knew the truth. He did not allow those events to taint his love for children and he would not permit outside influences to reshape who he was. That is strength, not weakness. He would install certain safeguards: he'd never again share a bed with a child, and he wouldn't be alone in a bedroom with one. Otherwise, Neverland would continue to operate on its foundations of trust, love and charity.

THE JACKSON FAMILY HONOURS WENT AHEAD in February 1994 at the MGM Grand in Las Vegas. We had specifically wanted Oprah Winfrey to host the evening. As the one person who had given Michael a sympathetic television platform almost a year earlier, it seemed fitting that she should welcome him on an evening that was all about humanity. In December 1993, she joined President Bill Clinton at the White House to support a new law against child abusers, the National Child Protection Act. Now, we thought, she could line up alongside Michael, the biggest champion of children, and declare her support.

We were surprised to hear her decline, saying she didn't think she would be a good host, but she wished us the best of luck. It was a shame – we knew how much she loved Michael – but it didn't detract from the occasion. When he walked out on stage, the entire auditorium gave him a standing ovation that must have lasted beyond 10 minutes. It was wonderful to see him onstage looking so revitalised and healthy after all the bullshit. He was radiant and happy.

Moving into 1994, there was good reason for him to feel on top of the world because he had *finally* found his true counterpart in a woman: someone who had had a restrictive childhood, wasn't impressed by his fame, had experienced living under a spotlight and didn't need him for his money. Someone who absolutely understood his world and needed nothing from him but love. Lisa Marie Presley ticked all the boxes.

CHAPTER EIGHTEEN
Love, Chess and Destiny

LOOKING BACK, LISA MARIE PRESLEY WAS always popping up on the periphery of Michael's life, sporadically flashing by unnoticed until their paths converged. Retracing destiny's map today, it seems clear it was always God's plan that they unite.

I'm not one for coincidences; I don't think there is such a thing. And I know that Michael felt there was a strong element of 'meant to be' when they first met as adults in late 1992. He viewed destiny as a game of chess: we, the people, are the pieces and God was the player, moving us around the board until King takes Queen.

By the time of the big Oprah interview, Michael had already started a phone relationship with Lisa Marie, building up towards their ultimate romance – which ends the lie about a 'publicity marriage to restore his reputation' after the events of 1993. As a couple, they were flirting and talking, and starting to feel something long before the extortion nightmare began.

In fact, destiny's journey began in 1974 when we were in Vegas doing the family variety show. Somewhere between those bookings, we went to nearby Tahoe for a performance at the

Sahara-Tahoe casino lounge. That sort of intimate venue seated about 1,000 people and pulled in the likes of Frank Sinatra and Charlie Rich. At some point during our down-time, Jackie must have wandered off with Michael because they found themselves in one of those wide, service-type elevators. Apparently, they were standing around, watching their feet, when the elevator stopped. The doors opened and Elvis stepped in, slicked hair and sparkling white jumpsuit with high collar, a thick towel around his neck. He looked at Jackie and Michael. 'You're those Jackson boys?' he asked.

They nodded, dumbstruck. You'd think that once you'd met the likes of Smokey Robinson, Sammy Davis Junior and Jackie Wilson, nothing could faze you, but the randomness of that shared elevator ride was the biggest unexpected thrill. Not that it lasted long. Seconds later, the doors opened again and Elvis was on his way. 'Good luck, fellas!' he said. That was the day Michael met the future father-in-law he would never know.

I was mad to have missed out, but some years later, back in Nevada, I found myself in a hotel – I can't remember which one – and spotted Elvis's right-hand man, Colonel Tom Parker, amid a cloud of cigar smoke. He was a legend: the manager of all managers. Bespectacled and rotund, with his trademark red scarf around his double-chin, he was sitting at a restaurant table near the casino. I dared to venture over and say hi. Before I knew it, we were sitting down, talking all matters Elvis and the Jackson 5, as 20-year-old me pretended to puff on one of his big-ass cigars. He was fascinated by Mother and Joseph. 'Tell me, how did they produce all that talent in just one family? That's what I wanna know,' he said, probably working out the commission percentages in his head and multiplying it by nine.

When he asked me to fire at him any question about Elvis – and after I had found out that 'The King' loved doughnuts and the blues group Muddy Waters (not to be confused with the artist) – I couldn't resist asking the one thing that had always intrigued me: 'Is it true that you split everything 50:50 with Mr Elvis?'

He laughed at my audacity. 'Yeah.' He let out another thick swirl of smoke.

I was still pretty green about all matters business but even I was thinking Elvis must be mad to give away *half* his earnings, but Colonel Parker was shrewd. He sat there all relaxed but commanding – like he owned the very spot where we were seated – and we spoke about how much of a partnership he'd shared with Elvis, how trust was everything in this business, and how Elvis set the bar as the hardest-working man he knew. Later, when I told the brothers about this inspirational meeting, Michael only wanted to know one thing: 'Did you ask him if Jackie Wilson was one of his favourites?' Now there was a question I should have asked. 'Because it sure looks like he stole his moves!' he joked.

We did find out one thing from Colonel Parker: Elvis's six-year-old daughter Lisa Marie was a 'big Jackson 5' fan, who had already seen us perform – she'd attended a show with one of her father's backing singers. Years later, someone said that she was brought backstage to meet us.

The next time I saw Lisa Marie was maybe 17 years later around 1990–1 in a pharmacy in the Brentwood district of LA. I wondered about going over to say hello but she looked frazzled and I hesitated. Soon afterwards, in 1992, she and Michael discovered that they had a mutual friend in the Australian artist Brett Livingstone Strong, and the man who had found my brother his secret hideaway in an airport hangar now played unintentional match-maker. He brought them together at a dinner and from that day – when she was still married to Danny Keough – an innocent friendship began, the slow-forming foundation to a very real romance.

Throughout Michael's ordeal in 1993, Lisa Marie was one of those friends he called on for advice by phone wherever he was in the world. There were others: hotel owner Steve Wynn, talent manager Sandy Gallin and MCA Records' David Geffen but she impressed him with her no-nonsense, straightforward, hard advice. With so many voices around him, she was a refreshing sounding-board. She took no bullshit, and when she saw it around him, she made her feelings about certain people very clear. That kind of frankness always made my brother chuckle. There were no show-business airs and graces, and she was feminine, fine-looking and strong. I'd say the attraction was obvious.

The world didn't see them step out together until 1994 – which is presumably why there was talk about a marriage of convenience – but she had actually joined Michael in public in May 1993 at some charity kids' event out east as a guest of ex-American President Jimmy Carter.

Michael never missed an opportunity to meet a president! Not only had he read up on nearly every one of them, but his coffee-table in the living room at Neverland was decorated with framed photographs of him meeting Presidents Carter, Clinton and Reagan. Michael was very proud of that presidential showcase and he became particularly friendly with the Clintons. Soon the house would be filled with photographs of Lisa Marie, her two children, and Michael. It had taken 20 years since they first flashed by one another in 1974 and now Jackson was in love with Presley. The King's daughter and the King of Pop – God doesn't write better movie scripts than that.

IT WAS A QUIET WEDDING. SO QUIET that we didn't even know it was happening. The ceremony took place in the Dominican Republic in August 1994 and a decision was clearly taken not to inform either family: a 'we-want-no-fuss' affair. The fewer people who knew about it, the less chance there was of the press finding out. Had Mother been there, she might have reminded the officiating minister that her son's name was not 'Michael Joseph Jackson', as was said in the vows, much to Michael's amusement. Once they were declared man and wife, the over-excited groom phoned Mother from their hotel suite with his 'big news', but she thought it was one of his pranks. 'You're telling me you married Lisa Marie Presley? No, you did not,' she said.

'I did! I *did!*' he said, starting to laugh.

'I don't believe you!'

'You want to speak with her? She's here with me now ...' he said, and there was, apparently, a lot of laughter in the background before Lisa Marie said hello and eventually put Michael back on.

Mother still didn't believe it. 'That's not her – you've just got some black girl pretending to be her,' she insisted.

By now, Michael was laughing so hard that he could hardly speak. Bless Mother, her Alabama ears had expected Elvis's daughter to speak with her father's drawl. As she recalls it today: 'She sounded so unlike what I had imagined. Goes to show ...'

There was probably another reason why Mother was sceptical: Michael was always ringing either her, Rebbie or Janet, disguising his voice and pretending to be someone else. His English-gent impression was apparently very convincing, and always had them fooled.

In that phone call from the Dominican Republic Mother loved hearing how excited he was to have a wife. I only witnessed rare glimpses of this marriage because they were so wrapped up in each other. My previous concerns about him being alone – surrounded by professional advisers or filling the void with random people – evaporated. Now he had someone very real, firm and big-hearted, who wasn't afraid of the vultures around him.

I laughed at media suggestions that they were 'faking it' because we all knew in the family the intensity of their relationship and how they always wanted to be together. Michael's joy couldn't have been faked. The intimacy you see in the video for 'You Are Not Alone' was art imitating life; a sweet glimpse as to how easy they were with one another and how they liked to laugh. Reports that we 'loathed' our brother's new wife could not have been further from the truth: she was only ever embraced and there was never one iota of doubt that she had Michael's best interests at heart. She grew particularly close to Janet and Rebbie. When my sisters spent time with Lisa Marie and heard her speak about Michael, they always came away saying the same thing: 'That girl is crazy about him!'

Now that Lisa Marie had arrived in Michael's life, I stopped throwing out my lines of communication. For me, it was only ever about 'Is Michael okay?'

Once I knew he was okay, I was, too.

IF MICHAEL WAS INTENT ON ONE thing, it was securing his future. From very early on in his career, he vowed not to become 'just another black artist who ended up with nothing.' Of course, he first said that at a time when he had no idea how phenomenally successful he was going to become, but he had told Mother he wanted to make business decisions that meant 'our family will never have to worry about money any more.'

With him now married and looking to start his own family, financial security was paramount. No matter how many miles he put between himself and Gary, Indiana, and no matter how enormous his success, nothing removed the memory of our parents' struggle. It never leaves you; it never stops pushing you.

Perhaps now, people will better understand why Michael landed, and so ruthlessly pursued, what everyone referred to 'as the biggest deal in music publishing history'. He had followed Paul McCartney's advice, given in 1983, that the real security was in the ownership of copyright to songs. One year later, in 1984, Michael spent $47.5 million on the richly historic ATV Music Publishing catalogue comprising about 4,000 songs, including 'Tutti Frutti' by Little Richard (which, I'm sure, made Joseph happy). But the big fish was the Beatles' hits, and every song they had written between 1964 and 1971. What made this deal ironically controversial was that Paul McCartney had tried to buy back the copyright he'd sold in the 1960s. He reportedly wanted to go halves in a $20 million bid with John Lennon's widow, Yoko Ono. Nothing came of it and his interest fell away, so he didn't take it very well when he learned about Michael's deal. A lot of injured pride found its public voice, but Yoko Ono said it was 'a blessing' that such a prestigious catalogue was in the hands of someone like Michael. As ever, I guess it depends on which side of the fence you sit. Michael followed the rules of the game, came in with the highest bid, and if Paul McCartney had wanted full ownership that badly, he'd have put his money where his mouth was. But he didn't: he lost. That's business. Like so many people, I think he underestimated who Michael was. If there was any advice I could have given to anyone who thought they had my brother's measure it would have been this: don't be fooled by the big-kid act, the gentle voice or the headlines. He was a shrewd businessman with a futuristic vision. Now when you placed his ATV library alongside his own MIJAC catalogue (which includes all his music as well as some Ray Charles and Sly and the Family Stone), he was suddenly sitting on the biggest-paying prize in the music industry. With the help of attorney John Branca, he had out-manoeuvred Hollywood to guarantee his future.

Nine years later John Branca would take this coup to the next level. Michael's own label, Sony, had said it wanted to buy half of the ATV catalogue, but it was not for sale. Sony wanted to do business, Michael wouldn't budge. The record label presumably had to think again. The deal that was eventually struck appeared to give Michael an even firmer grip on the music industry, because Sony agreed a partnership in which each side would share half their catalogues, creating a merger of interests within Sony-ATV Music Publishing valued at around $1 billion. Michael, with 50 per cent of Sony's publishing, as well as 50 per cent of ATV, had now become a significant stake-holder in his own label.

Even more impressive was the clause that stipulated Michael could not be subject to an aggressive buy-out. As he himself explained it, his part ownership was cemented forever and 'there was no way Sony or anyone else could do anything corporate to take it away from me.'

On paper, it looked like a marriage made in heaven.

I DIDN'T KNOW THERE WAS FRICTION in Michael's marriage until crisis phone-calls were going back and forth between Lisa Marie and Mother, Janet and Rebbie. I wasn't privy to those heart-to-hearts but it was obvious that the intensity of the romance at the start was mirrored in its falling apart.

The compromise needed in a marriage was, I think, a more difficult shift for Michael to make than he'd imagined. I'd honestly thought this one was going to last because they seemed suited, but when there was a problem, one of them needed to bend first and neither partner knew how to do that. Michael struggled with the demands of married life, and I think Lisa Marie struggled with his isolating creative process. I'm guessing now, but when you think how she had grown up, with a father who was always away, always performing, always in the studio, the last thing she needed was an absent husband. She couldn't understand why he had to be gone all the time, and he couldn't understand why she had a problem with him being in the studio, sometimes sleeping there. So, when Lisa Marie questioned his decisions, he thought, wrongly, that she wanted to tie him down.

They spent most of their time living at Lisa Marie's house in Hidden Hills, north of Los Angeles, but there was added pressure because Michael had taken under his wing the grandkids of our uncle Lawrence, Joseph's brother. There were problems in that family and my brother had stepped in, feeling that the kids needed real love at a difficult time. I'm sure Lisa Marie had every sympathy but she understandably wanted her husband to be emotionally there for her, too.

As the weeks went by, she realised she was not spending enough family time with her own kids, even though they spent some weekends at Neverland, which still remained a place where visiting families came together. At times, and no doubt in response, Lisa Marie disappeared for a few days and when she wasn't around, Michael became insecure. A vicious circle developed: she wondered where he was and he wondered where she was – jealousy and distance never were a good combination in Hollywood. Now, instead of coming together, they were pulling apart.

On one occasion, Michael spent the day in the studio with his protégé Wade Robson, working late into the night. He decided to stay at Wade's family home at the invitation of his mother instead of returning to his wife – it was easier that way. Michael hated arguments or raised voices and preferred to avoid a problem rather than confront it. But Lisa Marie wasn't putting up with it: she stood up to Michael and challenged him. That was what he needed, even if he didn't appreciate it. Also, he was still contending with the remnants of his Demerol dependency. I don't know how much of it Lisa Marie saw, but I do know that Michael wasn't finding his recovery easy and he was still suffering pain that agitated him and kept him awake at night.

Another uncomfortable factor for Michael was Lisa Marie's beliefs as a Scientologist. She gave him lots of reading material about her religion and he devoured it all. At some point he discovered that Scientologists don't necessarily rely on medication to treat a child's sickness. Michael's first port of call would be a paediatrician and he worried about what that might mean when they had children. As it was, he didn't have to concern himself for long. The one big factor that tipped things over the edge came when Lisa Marie – in Michael's eyes – reneged on her promise to give him kids. As soon as they got married, he started his countdown to having his nine little Moonwalkers. When he became convinced she had broken a pact he felt they had made, it would have taken him back to that time when Joseph promised him dinner with Fred Astaire and never delivered. I'm pretty sure Lisa Marie would have felt, from that moment on, as if she was living in Siberia because he would have shut down and gone into retreat.

Soon enough, Lisa Marie ran out of patience. Eighteen months after their wedding, she filed for divorce.

The saddest thing about this whole breakdown is that there was genuine love and friendship between them, but all that got eclipsed and scarred within some power-struggle. At the end of the day, it came down to two people with different temperaments and different outlooks, but I had always wished for a compromise that never happened.

In the months that followed, I know that she reached out to Janet, Rebbie and Mother for their advice on how best to get through to Michael, to see if there was any way back. For me, that illustrated the love she had for him. But when my brother built those walls, he built them high. What I am thankful for is that Michael only ever wanted to know what a real relationship felt like, and he wanted to be loved, and find true love. As much as the reality didn't work out in the end, his heart finally got to know true love and I think a part of it stayed with Lisa Marie right until the very end.

WHENEVER VISITORS ARRIVED AT NEVERLAND, THEY were handed a colour map of the grounds, just as you receive at any theme park, and it was then that you first saw Michael's logo for the ranch, which he designed in 1988: a boy wearing a blue pyjama jumpsuit sitting inside a blue moon with his legs dangling over the front as he looked down on the world. When I went to the movies and saw the logo for the DreamWorks studio, it was like looking at my brother's logo: the DreamWorks logo is silhouetted in blue, with a boy sitting back in the curve of a half-crescent moon with a fishing rod dropping its line.

An amazing coincidence, I thought.

But, like I said, I don't believe in such a thing. So maybe it was telepathy between Michael and Steven Spielberg. Proof that great minds think alike.

The shrewd businessman in Michael had actually believed he was going to be part of DreamWorks when it was set up by director Steven Spielberg, ex-Disney studio chairman Jeffrey Katzenberg and record producer David Geffen in 1994. He had worked with, and known each of them well, and he told me he had been 'instrumental' in bringing them together. Whether the trio would agree with that, I don't know, but that was Michael's belief.

As he explained it, he believed that all four of them would approach Michael's friend Prince Al-Waleed, of the Saudi Arabian royal family, to fund the venture. The Prince was keen to partner Michael in business and make all sorts of creative visions come true. (They would later set up Kingdom Entertainment in 1996, with an eye on movies, theme parks, hotels and children's books.)

I don't know why Michael ultimately didn't feature in the DreamWorks equation, but the moment he was out of the picture, Prince Al-Waleed wasn't interested either. What then happened was that Spielberg, Katzenberg and Geffen went to Microsoft's Paul Allen, who injected the necessary $500 million to get the studio launched and operating.

For a time, Michael licked his wounds and felt he had missed out, especially when the studio won the Oscar for Best Picture for three consecutive years with *American Beauty*, *Gladiator* and *Beautiful Mind*. But its creative successes with high-grossing movies didn't necessarily translate financially and, soon enough, there was talk of a hundred-million-dollar debt, bankruptcy, and some crash and burns at the box office, come the start of the new millennium. And that was when a certain rumour spread that Michael was behind this run of bad luck.

'Can you believe this?' he said. 'I'm now being accused of putting a voodoo spell on the studio and apparently that's the reason they're not doing so well. I didn't know I had that much power!'

There was some crazy story – later perpetuated by people like Bob Jones – that he had consulted a witch doctor in Switzerland. This wasn't a report in the *National Enquirer*: this was gossip published in *Vanity Fair* in 2003. It said Michael had put a curse on Spielberg and had paid $150,000 for a ritual that included the slaying of 42 cows! I would say you couldn't make it up, but someone did. Out of all the excuses I've heard for financial troubles in Hollywood, the sacrifice of a herd of cows 6,000 miles away in Europe is probably the best one yet. Ultimately, DreamWorks' founders would sell the studio to Viacom in 2005. My Indian friends, the Ambani family, at the Reliance Group took over in 2008. Interestingly, the studio's music-publishing rights were later licensed to Sony-ATV Publishing. I guess what goes around, comes around.

VANITY FAIR RAN ANOTHER ARTICLE IN September 1995, quoting Santa Barbara District Attorney Tom Sneddon, who didn't appreciate my brother's statements on television that there 'was not one iota of information' linking him to those old allegations. Tom Sneddon decided to comment on this publicly, pointing out that my brother had not been 'cleared' of sexual involvement with boys and his comments 'were not consistent with the evidence in this case', leading to a rash of headlines that immediately screamed, 'JACKSON LIED IN TV INTERVIEW'.

Two years on, Mr Sneddon was making Michael aware that he was still watching.

WHEN YOU TAKE INTO ACCOUNT MICHAEL'S yearning to be a father, the snap decision he took next was hardly surprising. As ever, he kept his lips sealed about his plans to have children, with or without Lisa Marie, but when a motherly blonde admirer offered to bear him children, it was 'an offer from God' that he wasn't going to ignore.

Debbie Rowe was not a stranger to Michael. She was the nurse at the Beverly Hills clinic of his dermatologist, Dr Arnold Klein, who treated his vitiligo. Because of the intimacy of his treatment, Michael knew her to be trustworthy and discreet. When I heard Debbie was a nurse, I knew she would be soft, gentle and spoiling; someone who knew how to catch flies with sugar, not vinegar. Someone who was happy to roll along with Michael's wishes. This was a chance for him to have children entirely on his terms: with 100 per cent custody and a mother prepared to waive her parental rights. Looking back, and understanding how important fatherhood was to him, I don't see what other choice he had when there was a volunteer willing to make his dream come true at a time when he was standing in the rubble of his marriage in an already-isolated world, not knowing when – or if – his next ideal 'mate' would come along. Besides, it was a practical procedure rooted in love – Michael's love for children. I viewed this arrangement as a blessing because of the devotion these young souls would be born into. I've read all sorts of accounts and imagined dialogue that claimed Michael was somehow pressured into marrying Debbie, and that Mother played some kind of role in this decision because of her beliefs as a Jehovah's Witness. That's not true, and it ignores the fact that my brother had his own values and relationship with God. If he felt the pressure to marry, it was from Him and no one else; 'to do the right thing' and deliver his kids into a holy union.

Michael married Debbie in November 1996 in a ceremony at his hotel in Sydney during the Australian leg of the 'HIStory' World Tour. His first son, Prince Michael, was born on 10 February 1997, followed by a daughter, Paris Michael Katherine, on 3 April 1998. The moment Prince arrived, Michael ensured he had the support of a full-time nanny. The ideal candidate was under his nose: Grace Rwaramba was already working as his trusted secretary. He bounced the idea off Mother and me: 'What do you think?' he asked. 'I need someone I can trust, who understands what I want for my children.' It was at times like this that Michael returned to family as his sounding board, and both Mother and I gave Grace our full support. Originally from Uganda, Michael felt she was not only solid but would bring to his children her African values of absolute dedication to family and community. 'I also want them to grow up knowing where our journey began,' he said.

From the very beginning, Grace was brilliant with the kids and was an integral part of Michael's mission as a parent to keep his children respectful, polite, grounded and loved. During their infancy, as the media began to focus on these additions to the family, Michael became distressed – more so for his children – by speculation that questioned his paternity. At first, this seemed to be aroused by headlines about the children's faces being covered by veils or party masks – suggesting they were used to obscure their lack of similarity to their father. But those veils were not, at first, Michael's idea. It was actually a privacy measure, first instituted at Debbie's insistence because there was anxiety about the threat of a kidnap. Newspaper talk about the finances behind the arrangement between Michael and Debbie had apparently led to the typical crazy correspondence from sick minds threatening abduction, the idea being that Michael would pay anything for his children. Crazy threats were par for the course, but it was new to Debbie and she was understandably freaked out. Later, Michael maintained the veils for privacy reasons.

Then people were wondering whether Michael had used an anonymous sperm donor. Why anyone thought my brother was incapable of fathering his own children was beyond me, as was the idea he'd use a donor when it was *his* personal legacy that mattered to him. I think it's fair to say that Debbie had a dominant gene (Prince had white-blond hair when he was born) but when I look into that kid's eyes or catch his profile side-on, his similarity to Michael as a boy is obvious. But, to nail the myth once and for all, Michael has passed on his vitiligo to Prince. My brother's paternity is irrefutable when Prince removes his shirt. What really matters, though, is that my niece and nephews know without a shadow of a doubt that Michael was their biological father and they were born out of love.

WHEN I LOOK AT PHOTOS OF Michael from this period – post-marriage and pre-children – it is difficult to ignore the facial changes that he underwent through further plastic surgery. In fact, over the following decade, I would say that he reached the point of over-correction because he got so caught up in a negative self-image that he tried to find in the mirror what he had set in his mind: unattainable perfection.

I don't know the exact extent of the work he had done but there were several more surgeries to his nose. He was someone whose wealth allowed him to do something about his insecurities, but he hadn't changed to us because we looked in his eyes and they were the same, and his heart was still the same: he was still Michael.

Personally, I think his preoccupation with plastic surgery was some form of body dysmorphia, a condition often rooted in child-hood or puberty, where the sufferer finds exaggerated flaws that do not exist. This is my opinion, not a diagnosis. Over the years, I wanted to shake him and say, 'Michael, can you not *see* how damn handsome you are?' But it was such a sensitive issue that I felt I could not, and he failed to realise that his self-esteem was not something a knife could correct.

That is why I get angry with the doctors who enabled him to go too far. I always thought if you went to see a doctor and nothing was wrong, they had a duty to tell you so. The saddest thing was that Michael was never happy with his final look. Ultimately, I think he learned a painful lesson that the face is not a piece of music; it cannot be endlessly tinkered with and made perfect. The mirror lied to my brother more than anyone in his life, and it saddened me to know that he never saw how beautiful he was. As I wrote for the memorial programme in 2009, Michael, this world was never meant for someone as beautiful as you – and with that, I referred to not only how he looked, but how he thought and viewed the world.

THE MOMENT THEY MARKED MICHAEL'S FOREHEAD – and especially his 'third eye' – with the mixture of sandalwood paste, turmeric, clay and ash, he felt something resonate: 'I instantly felt like I had come home,' he said.

He had just landed on India's soil and the country was, he said, his 'spiritual home'; the one place he'd always wanted to visit since we started travelling the world as brothers. When they greeted him at the airport with dancers and the thumbed touch of *tilak* – the sacred blessing for good health and auspiciousness – it confirmed to him, as he had once said, that in another lifetime he was Indian. He'd always known there was a reason why he had an Indian chef and a friendship with Deepak Chopra, he joked. Native-American Indian by ancestry, Far East Indian in soul.

When he was drawing up the schedule for the 'HIStory' World Tour, he booked one performance in India and arrived there two weeks before he took his vows with Debbie. The scale of his visit was illustrated when they *closed* Mumbai International Airport for his arrival: 10,000 people had turned out to welcome him. Three Russian cargo planes touched down with the stage. Then his own 747 jumbo followed, the words 'The King of Entertainment' emblazoned across the sides of its fuselage. On his return, Michael showed off his Indian outfits and the mini-Ganesh statue he'd been given.

I heard about his time there, and the way he raved about it afterwards, from the promoter Viraf Sarkari who, with Andre Timmins, brought Michael to the Andheri Sports Complex and 25,000 fans. But it is the story of what happened outside the arena on day one that has stayed with me.

As he drove away from the airport in a Toyota people-carrier, he was standing through the sun-roof, wearing one of his scarlet military jackets, with gold buttons and a white arm-band. His vehicle was somewhere in the middle of a 20-car cavalcade as Mumbai came to a standstill. The orders to the drivers beforehand were not to stop: they should sweep through to the hotel as quickly as possible.

'Wait! Stop!' said Michael, when he came to the first junction. He had seen a small group of urchins – street children, wearing nothing but rags for clothes, who probably had no idea who this visitor was. They had been playing by the roadside, only to stop and gawp at the spectacle passing them. Michael ducked down into the vehicle, then stepped into the street to greet them. He approached them with a smile and communicated in a universal language: he took one child by both hands and started dancing. Then, as all the officials and politicians watched from the cars, the other children started laughing and dancing, too. He was there for two or three minutes, whipping them into giddiness before he hugged each one, kissed them on the cheek and handed out candies before he jumped back into his vehicle. The cavalcade set off again, with Michael waving.

At the very next junction just down the road, it happened again. 'Stop! *Stop!*'

He'd spotted more street children, and got out and danced and handed out more candies. He repeated the stop-start dance routine at every junction he came to on the way to the hotel. As Viraf remembers: 'It was the most incredible sight of humanity I have ever seen.'

Once those three days in Mumbai were over, and before he checked out of his suite at the Oberoi Hotel, Michael politely vandalised the entire room. He took his pen and signed the mirror, the bed-sheets, the room-service brochure, the pillows, the towels and every piece of furniture in there. Then, he left his instructions: 'Sell all of this and give the proceeds to charity, please.' It made a small fortune. Viraf remembers the message on the pillow that today someone, somewhere is treasuring: 'India, all my life I have longed to see your face ... I have to leave but I promise I shall return. Your kindness has overwhelmed me, your spiritual aware-ness has moved me, and your children have touched my heart. They are the face of God ... I adore you, India.'

SPIRITUALLY, WE HAVE ALWAYS BEEN CONNECTED as broth-ers, as family, even when there was physical distance. You don't grow up as tight as we were and lose that sense of connection. There have been countless moments of serendipity to remind me of how interconnected we will always be, but the two most memorable came courtesy of Nelson Mandela and Charlie Chaplin.

It was March 1999, I think, when I travelled to Johannesburg for a function to honour the most incredible man of our times. I was almost making a habit of booking meetings with Nelson Mandela: we had appeared on a South African talk show together and then I was invited to perform for him twice, first, at his eightieth birthday celebration in 1998, and then at the inauguration ceremony the following June, when he handed presidential power to Thabo Mbeki. I performed in front of 90,000 people and it was a momen-tous occasion, which I shared with comedian Chris Tucker, who was wearing an attention-grabbing red tie.

Three months prior to that historic day I had walked into a big reception room at another presidential function buzzing with people from all over the world. Someone tapped me on the shoulder. 'Jermaine? Your brother's here.'

'Which brother?'

'Michael – he's over there,' he said, pointing to the black military jacket and mirrored sunglasses on the other side of the room.

I walked over and decided to stand in a position that meant he came across me unexpectedly. 'Erms! WHAT are you doing here?' he shrieked, looking as surprised as hell.

'What are YOU doing here?' I said, laughing.

'I'm here as a guest of Madeba,' he said, using our host's clan name.

'Me too!'

Mandela had been a big fan of Michael's since seeing him perform during his 1997 tour of South Africa, but I don't think either of us could believe the odds of turning up at the same function 16 hours away from home without anyone mentioning it. We agreed to grab some time afterwards before I left for Swaziland and then we drifted into separate pockets of people to continue rubbing shoulders.

Then it was time for the ceremony and we went to take our seats. I saw Michael cutting across the room, heading in the same direction as me. Our parallel paths came together at the same point: standing directly in front of the 'throne' where Mandela would be sitting. That was when we realised the organisers had seated us either side of him: Michael to his right, me to his left. We laughed again. Brothers in arms. Side by side with Mandela. It was a beautiful honour for both of us, flanking the most dignified crusader of our age. It was almost as special as walking in the footsteps of one of the best entertainers there has ever been.

It was when I was walking around the basement of Charlie Chaplin's home in Vevey, Switzerland that all I could think about were the umpteen sketches of his hero that Michael had drawn over the years. He might have borrowed from Fred Astaire and James Brown for his craft, but there was something about Chaplin's silent mystique as an entertainer that had fascinated Michael. So, it was a privilege for me to be invited by Chaplin's sons to the family home on the shores of Lake Geneva, with the Alps in the background. Eugene and Michael Chaplin were holding an annual film festival and I was to help judge certain independent films.

When I arrived at the house in its postcard setting, I found it easy to understand why Chaplin had left America, besieged by the media because of his political views and love-life. He found solace and a sense of 'normality' in this retreat. Nothing much had changed between the days of Charlie Chaplin's greatest fame and Michael's.

In my school days, when the teachers passed around the geography books, I always turned to the pages that showed Europe and found Switzerland. I would stare at the map, then find pictures and day-dream about being there. One day I told the teacher I would end up living in Switzerland and she humoured the delusion of the steelworker's son. And now I stood in my day-dream, simultaneously entering Michael's. Just as his fans would imagine walking around Neverland, he imagined retracing Chaplin's footsteps.

That thought stayed with me as I was shown the Chaplin family archive in the basement. It was more vault than museum, with tiny slits for windows near the ceilings. Everything was there: photos of Chaplin out of costume as a father, minus the moustache, looking distinguished in a suit with brushed-back wispy white hair. There were movie posters and old films spooled in silver tins. I was thousands of miles away from the madness of Los Angeles yet was now in the seat of Hollywood's founding father, picking up his Oscars from the shelf – and suddenly realising that once the Academy had expected its award-winners to be weight-lifters. Those things were *heavy*!

I remember returning to America and calling Michael to tell him about what I had seen. 'You should have been there!' I said. 'You would have found out everything and –'

'Jermaine,' he interrupted, 'I was just there a few weeks ago! – I didn't know you knew the Chaplins!'

That was when we swapped our stories and talked about the small world again.

Mandela in South Africa. Chaplin's ghost in Switzerland. It didn't seem to matter where we roamed, we were always walking to the same beat. There were actually several occasions where he would show up and then be told I'd been there before, or vice versa; it never stopped amusing us. Wherever I went in the future after all these episodes, I always had my eye out for Michael, half-expecting him to come walking around the corner or tap me on the shoulder. In fact, I still do.

FOLLOWING MICHAEL'S DEATH IN 2009, THIS kind of serendip-ity – these signs from God I take comfort in – didn't stop. Strangely, it was in Mumbai that I felt a tap on the shoulder. I was in India doing a music video for a song I'd done, 'Let's Go To Mumbai City', in memory of the victims of a series of terrorist attacks in November 2008, and we were filming at the railway terminus where 58 people had been shot dead. At the end of the day, I decided not to return to the hotel. Instead I started walking and found myself near this souk-like marketplace filled with tailor's shops and shoe shops, and teeming with people. Wherever I looked there were shops filled with fabric and suits. I followed the street aimlessly until I saw an incredible outfit, which looked out of place in the window of an appliance store: it was one of those long shirwani jackets, fine-looking and embroidered. It drew me inside to where a line of people had formed at the counter. 'Where is the store that has that outfit?' I shouted.

'Roopam … you are looking for Roopam store, sir. Three floors up,' said a man.

I took the elevator and found myself walking into a corridor that had women's clothes to the right, and men's to the left. I stepped into a room with fabric and suits hanging in rows on each wall, surrounding a tailor's workbench in the middle. The owner – his name was Viran Shah – came out of a back office to greet his customer. 'Oh … my … God!' he said.

'What?' I said, looking around to see if he was talking to some-one else.

'Ooooh ... my ... God!' He scurried back into his office, did some noisy fishing around and came back out with a folder, which he laid on the wide desk. 'Your brother Michael – he was here! He bought clothes from here!'

There, in the folder, were photos of Mr Shah and my brother from 1996. Out of all the stores and streets in Mumbai, I had walked into the very one where my brother had been almost 14 years earlier. I had the best kind of tears in my eyes, as the tailor kept patting his cheeks, still disbelieving the coincidence. I wanted to tell him that there was no such thing as a coincidence, but instead I told him to get his tape measure. 'I've obviously been guided here, so I would like to buy some of your suits, sir,' I said.

CHAPTER NINETEEN
Unbreakable

AS WE MOVED INTO THE NEW millennium, Michael's fans looked forward to the next decade of his music. A new album, *Invincible*, was to be released, and a follow-up tour across America and overseas had been planned. First, though, on 10 September 2001 a televised concert would commemorate the thirtieth anniversary of his solo career, from his first solo single 'Got To Be There' with Motown. A host of artists were booked to perform at New York's Madison Square Garden. For us, it promised to be a truly special night because CBS executives had insisted on a Jackson brothers' reunion as part of the deal: we would be on stage together for the first time in 17 years.

It was hard to believe it had been so long, but it was even harder to accept that we had three decades behind us as performers. The show's promoter was David Gest, a man probably best known to the world as Liza Minnelli's ex-husband, but we had known him from our schooldays through one of our classmates at Walton School.

As with everything that involved a brothers' reunion, things didn't go too smoothly at first, though. Four months before the show, I discovered that David was charging $2,500 for a top-tier ticket. I immediately saw profit margins wider than the stadium itself, loyal fans being out-priced and not a hint of Motown in the show. We hadn't forgotten the bad press we'd received during 'Victory' when fans had criticised us for the promoter-set prices of 30 dollars, to be bought in multiples of four. I thought we'd learned a lesson. But David was adamant, saying his focus was to create a spectacular salute for Michael. That was everyone's focus, but the important details – like the fans and Motown's role in our lives – seemed, in my opinion, lost on him. Randy and I found his attitude impossible, so we issued a public statement condemning the 'exorbitant' ticket prices and suggesting that we wouldn't perform. He issued a counter-statement, pointing out that Jackie, Tito and Marlon would be taking part even if we weren't.

I backed down because 'Victory' had taught us some sore lessons about politics so we signed the contracts, put it behind us and focused on what was important: creating a special night for Michael.

Many came in artistic homage, including Slash, Britney Spears, Usher and Gloria Estefan, while Elizabeth Taylor and Marlon Brando took the opportunity to say a few words.

That night Madison Square Garden was one big musical party and the 'reunion' segment a virtual flashback to 'Victory'. We appeared first as silhouettes, backs turned, Michael centre-stage, the crowd going crazy. We delivered an in-sync performance that hadn't faded with time. Sean Coombs, a.k.a. Puffy, had been watching us earlier: 'It's amazing the way you guys just line up, fall in and are on point after all these years.'

The dynamics hadn't changed and when we got together, Jackie was always the eldest brother, fussing about detail, getting everyone organised. I think Michael was as amused as I was during rehearsals when Jackie started marshalling Tito who, because of recent surgery, missed the odd step. 'Tito, you got to keep up, man!'

'Hey!' Tito shot back, 'All you got to do is sing and dance. I gotta sing, dance and play the guitar, and guess what? I've been doing this for 30 years …' Always brothers, never changing.

Come show time, we never skipped a beat and we knew it felt and looked special. Mother and Joseph said it was just like old times, and Michael was appreciative, too: 'It wouldn't have been the same without you up there with me, thank you … thank you,' he said, as we went backstage and gave quick hugs to Prince and Paris.

Other than that we didn't see much of Michael. He was the star of the show, producer, director, lights consultant and father, making sure everything was right and everyone was happy. He had a different dressing room from us and stayed in a different hotel – his usual haunt, the Helmsley Palace.

Back at the Plaza Hotel where the rest of us were staying, I told myself we needed to keep doing this, maybe every two, three or five years. Every time I was back in that performance zone with the brothers, the click of pieces fitting together was loud and proud. It was that buzz and those possibilities that kept me awake that night.

As my family slept, I stood at the hotel window looking out into the city that couldn't sleep either. Madison Square Garden had felt so alive, New York City felt so alive, I felt so alive … There seemed so much euphoria in the air that night.

THE NEXT MORNING I WAS LYING on my hotel bed when one of the brothers rang and told me to turn on the television. Like everyone else, I watched the events of 9/11 play out their horrible sequence. Being in Manhattan, cocooned in one of the city's hotel rooms and feeling that flying bombs were everywhere, it didn't feel so much like a terrorist attack, more an alien invasion. There was a sense of not knowing what was out there, how many there were in number, and when they'd strike next. And these were 'beings' that attacked us, not Muslims. True Muslims don't abuse Islam like that, and they certainly don't take down towers containing fellow Muslims. It was surreal watching the city being attacked and I never again want to feel such helplessness for myself, my family and the country. Also, we knew that Marlon was in the air. He'd left early that morning to head home to Atlanta. Later, we found out that his plane had been turned around and landed safely. Thankfully, none of us had had a clue that Michael was due at a meeting that morning at the top of one of the Twin Towers. We only discovered this when Mother phoned his hotel to check he was okay. She, Rebbie and a few others had left him there around 3am. 'Mother, I'm okay, thanks to you,' he told her. 'You all kept me up talking so late that I overslept and missed my appointment.'

We agreed to get ourselves back to California. But how? No flights were taking off, and although Janet was in LA and had booked two tour buses, she was told that they wouldn't be allowed on to Manhattan., We were feeling marooned when Randy had a brainwave. He decided we should 'hijack' a bus. Seconds later, we were standing in the middle of the street and flagging down the first one that came along. It just so happened that the driver was also the owner of the bus company. We told him we needed two buses for the Jacksons. 'Where you headed?' he asked.

'California,' we said.

'How much you paying?'

I can't remember the cash amount, but he and a second driver were hurridly loading our luggage before we changed our minds. Michael was making his own getaway plans, so with everyone else aboard, we crawled towards George Washington Bridge. I remember looking back at the island as we pulled away and seeing all that evil smoke hanging in the air. It was an impossible reality to comprehend, but all I needed to understand was that everyone was safe as we headed home, leg by leg, state by state.

MICHAEL WAS DESPERATE TO DO SOMETHING for those who had suffered on 9/11 and he dug out an old song from his unreleased archive, 'What More Can I Give?', first written after the LA riots of 1992, as inspired by Rodney King, the black guy whose police beating triggered the unrest. For years, this song was called 'Heal L.A.' It was one of those songs with a universal message, which is why Michael resurrected it in the hope of raising millions of dollars for the victims' families and survivors in New York. This was a mission that brought together the likes of Céline Dion, Gloria Estefan, Beyoncé, Mariah Carey and Usher. They, too, felt that the song's message was powerful and timely, and Michael wanted to share it with the world. But Sony didn't agree and the song wasn't released: it received airplay, but it didn't do what it should have. Creatively speaking, it was a crazy decision. Crazy to everyone but Michael, because he felt that tactical decisions were now being taken to hamper him commercially.

Slowly but surely, as his working relationship with Sony's new head Tommy Mottola unravelled, he started to open up about what was going on inside the empire where he was a partner. It would turn out the politics that snared his 9/11 song were just the start.

Meanwhile, a family meeting was called at Hayvenhurst. An issue of family politics first needed to be dealt with.

EVER SINCE THE THIRTIETH ANNIVERSARY SPECIAL, there had been whispered concerns about Michael's welfare. Some in the family had intuitively picked up on certain things in New York and suspected he was struggling with his prescription-drug dependency again. I hadn't noticed anything that worried me, but looking back, I saw how he'd kept his distance – a different hotel, different dressing room, spending little time with us, post-show or -rehearsal. Initially I had put that down to Michael being Michael, wanting his space. Then someone explained to me that Michael hadn't wanted to be near us, and had made certain people around him promise not to tell his brothers or sisters how he was; from nanny to members of his entourage to management to guards. Suddenly, everything fell into place. I have learned that when someone is aware of their struggle, yet cannot get on top of it, the last people they need close to them are those who see through the social mask. Family is not an employed 'yes-man', or an adoring fan-base.

When those kind of realisations started to dawn, the family decided to act on its suspicions and Michael's siblings descended on Neverland in early 2002. I was out of town but Mother, Jackie, Tito, Randy, Janet, Rebbie and La Toya all headed north, with a doctor, ready to carry out an intervention. When they arrived, unexpected, the guards wouldn't let them in so one of the brothers scaled the wall, jumped over and pressed the button to open the gates for the cars.

As they reached the main house, they found nothing untoward. Michael was apparently heading for the pool with Prince and Paris, walking hand in hand – Nanny Grace took them away so everyone could talk with their father.

The confrontation was emotional. Tito suspected something wasn't right and pleaded with Michael for the truth – if anything was wrong, he stressed, Michael must reach out: the family was always there for him. Michael was reassuring and relaxed. He said everyone had got it wrong. He was fine; there was nothing wrong with him, he insisted. Even the doctor had to agree. So *there was actually no intervention* and everyone departed happier, if not 100 per cent reassured.

We know that Michael would admit, in later lawsuits, that his judgement could have been impaired by the painkillers he'd been taking, so there was no doubt some concealment was going on, but it's hard to get to the truth when someone hides behind distance and those serving them.

We would also find out that the chief reason why Michael had once again fallen foul of a reliance on pain medication was because of an incident in 1999 that had left him in more pain than ever before. He was doing a half-hour set during some charity show in Munich, Germany, and was standing on a bridge that rose up on hydraulics as he performed 'Earth Song', taking him higher and higher above the stage as the song reached its crescendo. The bridge was supposed to lower slowly, returning him to the stage.

Instead, the mechanics failed and the bridge just fell from its four-storey height with Michael gripping the rails, but still singing. In that instant, an engineeer hit the emergency stop button and that one action probably saved my brother's life – it didn't stop the fall, but it slowed the collapse to what one band member described as 'fast slow motion'. Michael landed hard, hitting the concrete floor at parachute-landing speed.

Everyone backstage and in the band feared the worst, thinking he was sure to have broken a few bones in such a crashing fall. Meanwhile, the audience cheered, thinking this was all part of the show. Amazingly, Michael got to his feet, clambered back on stage and finished the song. Those in the wings knew he was struggling but he refused to come off. In fact, after 'Earth Song', he performed 'You Are Not Alone'. Adrenalin was, it seemed, carrying him through. But as soon as he got offstage, he passed out and was rushed to hospital. When one of the band members later asked him why the hell he didn't just come offstage, Michael told him: 'Joseph always taught us that no matter what, the show must go on' – a mind-set that would also become telling in June 2009.

Miraculously, Michael had not broken any bones but he had seriously put his back out and this would cause him constant pain and suffering for the rest of his life, which was why Demerol brought him relief. I'm not sure my family knew of this backstory when it descended on Neverland, but what has frustrated me is that news of their non-intervention only broke after Michael's death but was reported as 'an intervention'. There is a big difference between an intended intervention and one that actually happens. More importantly, an event in 2002 – and the circumstances behind it – can have nothing to do with a sudden death in 2009, and I am confident this truth will be proved by justice and time.

MICHAEL'S RELATIONSHIP WITH SONY HAD TURNED sour after he realised a few things about the contract he had signed, and it turned a harmonious relationship with Walter Yetnikoff into an acrimonious divorce from Tommy Mottola.

First, after reading the small print, he found out that Sony retained the rights to his masters until 2009/2010 when he'd understood they reverted to him in 2000. Second, he discovered that the attorney who'd advised him had also advised Sony, leaving him to wonder if his interests had ever been best represented. He felt there was a clear conflict of interest that freed him to negotiate an early exit from the label, on one condition: he'd deliver one more album (*Invincible*), a greatest-hits compilation (later titled *Michael Jackson Number Ones*) and a box set. Michael resented these terms but he had to deliver if he was to be free, taking with him his 50 per cent stake in Sony-ATV Music Publishing – a move Sony hadn't seen coming when it had merged interests back in the nineties.

Sony's new reality was that Michael was now the artist/partner in the uniquely powerful position of leaving the label as a free agent yet retaining influence in all matters Sony-ATV, rights, licences and profits. Michael's confidence in his strategy showed when he took to the stage of a London club to bemoan the fact that companies take advantage of artists. He told fans pretty much what he had told the family: 'I have generated several billion dollars for Sony ... several billion ... and they really thought that my mind is always on music and dancing, and it usually is, but they never thought that this performer would ... out-think them. I'm leaving Sony a free agent, owning HALF of Sony ... and they are very angry at me,' he said, then added a gentle taunt to those listening in Hollywood: 'I just did good business, you know.'

Michael was setting out to show that the power rests with the artist who has the fan-base, not the label with the smart attorneys. He said to me later, 'From that very moment, they needed me to fail and they wanted control of the catalogue.'

INVINCIBLE WAS RELEASED IN OCTOBER 2001 and Michael felt Sony executives were only doing what they were contractually obliged to do. They didn't go mad on music video budgets and didn't release the album's strongest songs, like 'Speechless' and his favourite album track, 'Unbreakable' – a song about his spirit and defiance: 'It's saying nothing and no one will stop me,' he declared.

Instead, Michael disagreed with Sony and felt they were putting out its weakest numbers. This doesn't surprise me because there is a saying in the music industry, 'Why fatten the frog for the snake?', usually heard when a recording artist's contract is about to expire, or he/she wants to leave. No label throws its promotional weight behind a want-away artist to big them up in the marketplace.

But Michael felt it went deeper than that with Sony, especially after he'd heard from fans who couldn't find the album in certain stores.' He based that on information received in a phone call from someone he trusted. He felt strongly that everything was designed to back him into a financial corner: the less successful his albums, the less royalty income. The less he earned, the more reliant he'd be on his share of the Sony-ATV catalogue, which he'd already borrowed against to the tune of $200 million from Bank of America … guaranteed by Sony. And the more debt he had, the stronger the chance he'd be forced to sell his interest in the catalogue. At least, that was Michael's thinking. But he also felt a subtle pressure because I know that someone had suggested to him – before 2003 – that he could solve all his money worries by selling his 50 per cent share. But to me that missed the math of his inbuilt equity: he had borrowed $200 million against a stake-holding worth $500 million. Plus at the start of the new millennium, he could still command $80–100 million per tour. In fact, this was the mathematical argument Michael used all the time to friends. He was confident that once he was released from Sony, he would be America's greatest artist roaming free – and there was only one bottom line: he wasn't letting go of his greatest asset.

He wasn't going to stay quiet either. Driven by his feeling of injustice, he took open double-deckers around London asking his fans to boycott Sony, holding up signs that said, 'SONY KILLS MUSIC'. That demonstration told me how upset he was; that a man of such controlled emotion and discretion could take to a battle bus waving placards like a protestor proved to me how angry and cheated he felt. I wanted to punch the air and cheer because *finally* he'd found his voice and was stepping into confrontation; I admired him for not being brow-beaten by corporate muscle.

Despite the weak promotion, *Invincible* still went to No. 1 in both the US and UK, but Michael was furious about its sales performance, believing that 13 million albums sold worldwide was not a reflection of the blood, sweat and tears he'd poured into its creation.

IT WAS REPORTED SOMEWHERE THAT *INVINCIBLE* didn't max out on sales because Michael didn't want to take it on tour, but that was never true. An album tour was planned, designed, and he was ready and willing to go on the road in spring 2002, nationally and overseas. But then 9/11 happened, and it was cancelled at Michael's request. I know this led to a bust-up over the phone with Tommy Mottola. Michael blamed him for not promoting his album, and Tommy blamed him for not doing the tour that would have promoted the album. I didn't understand Sony's argument because my brother was one of countless artists who cancelled tours that year, including our sister Janet; the mood at that time was not to travel within the heightened sense of alert. If American targets were at risk and those terrorists audacious enough to take down the Twin Towers, then a stadium filled with fans for America's greatest entertainer could be hit, too. Michael took the decision not to put his fans or his tour staff in that position: it was common sense.

Personally, I think that when Michael backed out of that tour in the September, Sony put the brakes on a full-on promotion in the October. It kept telling Michael that it had spent $24m on the album and needed an artist who was prepared to promote it. At one point, Michael attempted to win over the situation by playing politics with Tommy, seeking to appease him by inviting his wife, Thalia, to sing on the Spanish version of 'What More Can I Give?' I don't know if that version was ever released in Latin-American territories, but if Michael had hoped it would increase the level of promotion for *Invincible*, he would have been disappointed. The big sadness was that if 9/11 hadn't happened, the tour would have gone ahead, keeping him performing into the year 2004.

Since 2009, there has been a lot of debate and misunderstanding about my brother's appetite for the road because he made no secret of the fact that he didn't like touring. It induced anxiety, insomnia and dehydration, and left him feeling miserable. His insomnia was the curse of live shows that left him filled with adrenalin. Other artists may empathise with this, but Michael suffered chronically. That was why, on most tours, he took a qualified anaesthetist with him. This choice had *nothing* to do with a prescription-drug dependency, and everything to do with the desperate need to sleep when on the road: he needed to be knocked out in order to rest. But with a specialist alongside him – *and his intake closely monitored*. Michael also trusted that his physicians would monitor him at all times while he was under. While this may seem unorthodox, it was his coping mechanism when touring – a quick fix to a long-term problem that illustrated the downside to touring.

On the other hand, a strong force willed him on to that stage. Getting out there, performing for his fans, immersed in his music, brought a euphoria that he struggled to resist. He'd talked about 'no more touring' since as far back as 1981 – and look how much he toured after that. Michael could turn to the person on his left and say, 'I'm never going to tour again,' then swivel around and say to the person on his right, 'I'm going to tour again.' He was born to entertain and was forever torn between what his head and soul said. Touring drained him but it exhilarated him, too. Once *Invincible* had been cancelled, it was inevitable that Michael would tour again but he would do it when the time was right, and on his terms.

WHENEVER MICHAEL CHECKED INTO HIS HOTEL suite in any city, in any country around the world, hordes of fans waited in the street in all weathers to see which balcony he'd appear on, because they knew his routine: he'd always step out to wave and acknowledge them, and toss out a pillow with his autograph. Balconies were his stage, too.

In 1988, he was staying at the beachfront Negresco Hotel in Nice, France, during the *Bad* tour and some sweltering August days; it was so hot that firefighters had to spray the fans with hoses at the concerts. On one 'off night', and with Michael restricted to his suite as usual, he threw 'souvenirs' out of the window – fruit, pens, mini-bar snacks, grooming kits – to the fans below. At first, all anyone outside could see were these hotel missiles. But then Michael, the clown, put out his gloved hand. Everyone cheered. Then he extended his arm. Everyone cheered some more. Then he leaned out to wave and say hello. Everyone went crazy. When photographer Harrison Funk, who was in the room with him, relays that story to this day, it still makes me smile. Once Michael had run out of objects to throw, and seeing that the crowd had now multiplied tenfold, he decided he wanted a photograph to capture the moment, but with just his sequined gloved hand in the foreground and the mass of fans in the background, probably a hundred feet below.

'How can we get *that* shot?' he asked excitedly.

It was an impossible shot, even if Harrison stood on top of wardrobes or hung from the curtain rail. 'I can't get it,' he said. 'We'd need a crane or a helicopter.'

'Okay, let's do it!'

Harrison knew he wasn't joking. Michael was one of those pull-out-all-the-stops artists and when he had an idea, however outlandish, he wanted to execute it. Ultimately, after logistical calls with hotel management, he accepted that (a) a helicopter couldn't get close enough and (b) health and safety wouldn't allow it – but he'd had to face up to the impossibility before he'd give up on his idea. That was Michael: not really thinking, just acting on the spur of the moment.

MICHAEL'S THIRD CHILD, PRINCE MICHAEL II, a.k.a 'Blanket', was born on 21 February 2002. Debbie was not his mother: she had asked for a divorce three years earlier. I know little about that separation, except that I don't think heartbreak was involved because they had never lived together, never been a conventional couple, and their arrangement had run its course. But Michael wanted more children so 'Blanket' came along as a result of artificial insemination with an anonymous surrogate mother. Nobody knows who she is, not even the family. I think it's wonderful because that woman kept her privacy – and Michael achieved something that rarely happened: nobody got to the bottom of something personal to him. Such were the small victories he earned in his private life.

'Blanket' became unintentionally famous at the age of nine months old when Michael stood at his hotel balcony in Berlin, Germany, with a sheet over the baby's head, holding him momentarily over the balcony's top rail. He was in and out of those double doors in less than five seconds flat, and it was *supposed* to be a moment of playfulness, but then came the condemnation. Suddenly, back home in LA, we were reading reports about how he was 'a reckless father' who had 'risked his son's life' by 'dangling' him over the balcony. Dangling – 'to hang loosely so as to be able to swing freely' according to the dictionary – was the word everyone used, making it sound like the poor kid was hanging on for dear life from a fraying rope, when the truth is that Michael always had the firmest grip on the baby, with one arm tight to his chest under his chin, and the other holding the sheet to his head. I'm not saying what he did with 'Blanket' wasn't foolish because it was – he knew it was – but the whole episode was blown out of proportion, with talk of child protection services and Berlin police interviewing him for child neglect.

Michael issued an apologetic statement, admitting his 'terrible mistake', but privately he was furious. 'I was proud [as a father]. I wasn't thinking,' he told me, 'but I knew the grip I had – yet they came after me like I'd held a gun to Blanket's head!'

Eventually, the media interest faded and I told him, 'Just be happy the press don't know how forgetful you are!' He laughed, because we both remembered *that* memory.

Michael was probably the most forgetful person I knew – because, as an artist, he was preoccupied with creativity. One Family Day at Hayvenhurst, Prince and Paris were there with 'Blanket', who was still in diapers, tucked up in a carrier-cradle. At the end of a happy afternoon, Michael's chauffeur loaded every-thing into the trunk and the children got in the car. We were all on the steps and Michael was all smiles, with his arm waving out the window as they drove away. We knew what he had forgotten, even if he didn't. How long would it be before he realised?

We waited and waited. About five minutes later, we saw the nose of the car turn back into the driveway. The car door flew open and Michael jumped out, looking all sheepish and with his hand to his mouth, dashed out, rushed by us and hurried back inside. 'Oh, I forgot Blanket!'

MICHAEL BECOMING A FATHER WAS THE completion of every-thing. No matter what he faced on the outside, his happiness – his reminder of what was important in life – now centred on Prince, Paris and 'Blanket'. They made him happy: they took away his loneliness and provided him with a greater purpose than music.

His performance as a father was an example of what fatherhood should be. He instilled in them the love Mother gave us, and he provided the kind of emotional fathering that our father, through no fault of his own, could not. Michael was father and mother rolled into one and he took that dual role very seriously. That didn't mean he was a pushover, though: his discipline was authoritative without being physical. I remember once when both Prince and Paris were acting up and I was visiting with my children, Michael's voice was no whisper in the wind that day: 'I'm so ashamed of you acting like this!' he told them. 'Now go to your rooms!'

He was huge on teaching them manners, respect and kindness, and he would insist that they spoke when someone walked into the room. He would tell them: 'Introduce yourself ... Say hello ... Say your name.' When an adult walked in, it was no excuse to be distracted by toys. His directness was part of the honest communication that he felt was paramount in raising a child: always tell them, every single day, that you love them; hold them and be with them when they fall asleep so that they trust you will be there for them – as he always was.

WE ALWAYS KNEW WHEN TROUBLE WAS going down. Our early warning system – which paradoxically always came too late – were 'the eyes in the sky', the news helicopters hovering over Hayvenhurst. The moment we heard those rotor blades, we'd turn on the television and, nine times out of ten, the breaking news involved Michael. We'd start ringing round and regroup, reaching out to Michael and ensuring Mother had support. It took place so many times that we might as well have instituted a practice drill. Sometimes we'd wonder where the next big one would come from. It was like living with California's earthquakes – you just learn to live with the daily risk that the very city you call home could implode at any minute. It's the 'Big One' that is always in the back of the mind, locked away with the survival kits. Michael always said that he'd climb a tree and take cover in its branches. I don't know if he did that when the 1994 Northridge earthquake struck, though. But when that terrible event happened, it made up Joseph's mind: he was moving to Vegas and safer ground. God had found the one thing to terrify our father, but Mother refused to move out to Nevada. So, after 35 years of marriage, they decided to live apart and split their time between two homes, finding a late independence they were both happy with in what is not an uncommon arrangement with people of their generation. Their marriage had survived much worse than distance, and our family had survived more earthquakes than most. Ones that shake you to the core and shatter everything you've built. Ones that make you come together and fight harder than you've ever fought in your life. No matter how big the earthquake, we survive. And they always start with a tremor that seems like nothing at first.

EAST LA IS ONE OF THOSE low-income districts of social challenges, housing projects and gangland turf. In many ways, its spirit and work ethic remind me of Gary. Good people. Tough lives. Michael's heart went out to one of its number, 10-year-old Gavin Arvizo. This kid was stricken with cancer and had 'a bucket list' of celebrities he wanted to meet, 'the King of Pop' among them. Anyone who'd heard of his plight – stage-four cancer, losing a kidney and spleen, vomiting blood and seemingly at death's door – couldn't help but do their part. It was our mutual friend Chris Tucker who brought him to Michael's attention after Gavin's mother had contacted him, fellow comedian George Lopez and basketball star Kobe Bryant. Michael responded typically, keen to help. Wherever he was in the world, he took time out to call Gavin in his hospital bed or at his grandmother's house, promising him a visit to Neverland. Gavin was in and out of hospital for an entire year: he had never met my brother but he came to know his voice in many hour-long phone-calls. When Michael said he'd call, he called, and they would talk 'forever – literally for hours,' said the boy's mother. And, as Gavin said later, the thought of going to Neverland 'would always make me happy because Michael would always put a smile on my face.' The imagined visit, with the aggressive chemo, pulled him back from the brink and defied some doctors' prognosis. The power of thought: survive to see Neverland.

In August 2000, when Gavin was well enough, Michael's personal assistant Evvy sent a limo to pick him and his family up from their cramped studio in East LA and transport them to Santa Ynez. It is sad that a one-time friend of Michael's, Rabbi Shmuley Boteach, has said that 'Michael's characterisation of the boy as having arrived at Neverland unable to walk, and Michael having to carry him, is entirely fictitious.' The rabbi clearly had no idea how it had been at the very beginning. The truth, as seen on film in a courtroom in 2005, was that this boy arrived without hair, without eyebrows, and so weak he couldn't stand. His brother, Star, pushed him around the grounds to all the places he had imagined in his hospital bed, and Michael walked with them and *did* carry him. As the mother Janet would say later: 'Michael took us from way behind in the line and pulled us up to the front and said, "You matter to me. You may not matter to many people, but you matter to me."'

Gavin put it differently, in the Neverland guestbook: 'Thank you for giving me the courage to take my hat off in front of people. I love you, Michael,' he wrote.

I doubt this back-story is one you will have seen in the newspapers because this wasn't the humanitarian starting point that the authorities or the Arvizo family wanted to highlight once Gavin had recovered and then alleged, with the support of his mother, that Michael had molested him and tried to hold him against his will. Not just an alleged child molester but now a kidnapper. Santa Barbara DA Tom Sneddon was, predictably, all over it. He would later say that my brother had used his celebrity to invite this boy to the ranch as part of a paedophile's grooming process.

But Sneddon didn't come across Gavin because he had gone to the police or child protection services with a complaint: they were only alerted to him *after* Michael had, in 2002, invited his once-sick friend to sit with him on camera during taping for a television documentary. He had wanted to show how he'd helped this kid. After the loss of Ryan White, this was the story of a survivor; an example of what love could do. The documentary was called *Living with Michael Jackson* and the journalist Martin Bashir was granted access to shadow my brother for eight months. Michael trusted his gentle approach and Princess Diana credentials. Bashir had done his job: he had won my brother's trust.

I HAD NO IDEA WHAT WAS going on until the evening of 6 February 2003, when the documentary aired in America – and I watched it with my head in my hands. All I seemed to say throughout the entire programme was 'No ... no ... no ... Michael,' and the more I heard Bashir say, 'Really?' to things my brother said, I wanted to put my foot through the screen.

Michael's true character was torn up by a warped edit – but this edit was the one that brought the authorities rushing in again as it played to every twisted, wacko, weird, eccentric cliché that had dogged my brother's life. This wasn't a world exclusive: it was a hatchet piece that could boast about its access, not its truth.

It was heart-breaking to see Bashir take Michael's sincere love for children and use it against him. The saddest scene was when Michael was sitting on the sofa, with Gavin Arvizo next to him, affectionately leaning his head into my brother. As bare footage without commentary, it was nothing but a tender, innocent moment with the man who was apparently central to his recovery. But in the editing suite, Bashir applied his most grave, worrisome voiceover: 'And so it was that we came back to our meeting at Neverland with 12-year-old Gavin …' Cue a close-up shot of Gavin holding Michael's hand. '… I'd found this easily the most disturbing moment of the past eight months.'

Then Bashir was back in interview mode, referring to how Gavin had spoken about sharing Michael's bedroom. Gavin was in the bed *on one occasion* and Michael and his producer friend Frank Cascio *slept on the floor*. Bashir suggested people would be worried by that.

'Why should it be worrying?' asked my brother. 'Who's the criminal? Who's Jack the Ripper in the room? This is a guy trying to heal a child. I'm sleeping in a sleeping-bag on the floor … I gave him the bed and he has a brother named Star, so him and Star took the bed.' He explained that he'd never shared the bed with Gavin, but openly volunteered he had 'slept in bed with many children.' Smiling at the memory, he added: 'When Macaulay Culkin was little, Kieran Culkin would sleep this side, Macaulay Culkin on this side … his sister's in there, we're all just jammin' the bed. Then we'd wake up like dawn and go in the hot-air balloon! We have the footage. I have all that footage …'

'But is that *right*, Michael?' asked Bashir.

'It's *very* right ... it's very loving ... that's what the world needs now ... more love ...'

'The world needs a man who is 44, sleeping in a bed with children?'

'No, no,' said Michael, 'you're making this all wrong ...'

IF THERE WAS ONE SAVING GRACE in the fallout that followed, it was that Michael was smart enough to have the 'insurance' of his own camera crew filming the journalist's unit. This would become the basis of his own documentary aired on Fox: *The Michael Jackson Interview: The Footage You Were Not Meant To See*. It wouldn't immediately save my brother's reputation, but it would show Bashir's two faces and how his ego-stroking statements made my brother feel falsely safe to open up.

For example, in the documentary, Bashir said, 'One of the most disturbing things is the fact that a lot of disadvantaged children go to Neverland. It's a dangerous place for a vulnerable child to be ...' But privately, he told Michael, 'I was here yesterday and I saw it, and it's nothing short of a spiritually kind thing.'

Or when Bashir told the world about Michael as a father, raising Prince, Paris and 'Blanket': 'They are restricted ... they are overly protected. I was angry at the way his children were made to suffer.' Privately, he told Michael, 'Your relationship with your children is spectacular. And, in fact, it ... it almost makes me weep when I see you with them.'

There were so many sly things about that documentary, but the most priceless moment came when Bashir, in his unused footage, asked my brother, 'Do you sometimes despair at human nature? Can you ever do anything right?'

And Michael replied, 'No, no, no ... No matter what you do, no matter how good your intentions, there is always some mean-spirited person who wants to bring you down.'

In 2009, after Michael's death, Bashir had the gall to pay tribute to my brother. He had since joined ABC's *Nightline* show and asked viewers to remember 'the greatest dancer and musician the world has ever seen.' He then talked about his documentary: 'There was a small part … which contained a controversy, but the truth is that he was never convicted of any crime, I never saw any wrong-doing myself and whilst his lifestyle may have been a little unorthodox, I don't believe it was criminal.' Nice words that were too little, too late. His truth and fairness mattered to Michael in 2003, not 2009. Besides, the damage was done, and nothing could undo the events that his documentary set in motion. With the hullabaloo that followed, the authorities felt compelled to act again, and the Department of Child and Family Services and the Santa Barbara Sheriff's Department launched investigations.

CHAPTER TWENTY

14 White Doves

I HAD ALWAYS WONDERED WHERE MICHAEL'S breaking point was hiding, because I knew that the kid from Gary who lashed out in his tantrums against Joseph was in there somewhere. In the back of my mind, I had always been waiting for him to smash out and scream.

That inevitable day came six months into the police investigation as Santa Barbara DA Tom Sneddon sent his cavalry into Neverland with a search warrant, moving towards an arrest. It was 8.30am on 18 November 2003 – the same day that Michael's penultimate album, *Michael Jackson Number Ones*, was launched. There was a horrible synchronicity to everything, and one inevitability: there was no way his album would be a success now.

When Michael heard that around 70 officers were at the ranch, he exploded. In his hotel suite, he picked up plates of food from the room service trolley and hurled them at the walls, swiped two lamps, pushed over a sculpture, turned over a coffee table and sent all sorts of objects flying from table tops.

Meanwhile, in Santa Ynez Valley, the police were searching high and low, using knives to slit the backs of valuable paintings and his mattress during a *14-hour* raid that turned up nothing. I know the damage they caused because Michael later showed the brothers, and he vowed never to sleep in the main house again (and he didn't – he always stayed in the 'Elizabeth Taylor' guest quarters). They had seemingly waited for him and the children to leave for Vegas for a video shoot before carrying out the raid while he stayed at the Mirage hotel, taking over an entire floor.

I was heading for Las Vegas too – the MGM hotel – with family friend Steve Manning to discuss a deal with the CMX entertainment group for a Jacksons' album featuring Michael. He'd said he was willing to 'record two or three songs' with us 'as long as the brothers get in the studio and do what they need to do without no messing around.' That meant no politics, no attorneys bickering, no voting systems.

I was at Burbank airport, soon to depart, when Mother called about the raid. She was understandably frantic. All I could think about was the state Michael would be in and how quickly I could get to Nevada. When I finally got to Michael's hotel and walked through the door into the hallway of his suite, the remnants of his rare fury were littered all over the floor. 'What the …??! Michael? … MICHAEL?'

His room looked like a typhoon had hit it and my immediate thought was that the cops had been there, too. I don't remember seeing the kids, so I guess Nanny Grace had them out of there by the time I arrived. Randy and Rebbie were also on their way. As I trod among the debris, I walked into a back room, where I found Michael sitting in a chair, calmer but still simmering, trying to distract his agitation with an animation project he'd been working on.

'You okay?' I asked.

Head down, he didn't say anything.

'We're going to get you through this,' I said.

His eyes looked up at me and all I saw was my kid brother again, hiding in a hotel room, not wanting to fly through turbulence. Scared and lost, and as Rebbie said later, looking 'deranged' by the insanity of the situation now encircling him. He looked up at me. 'I haven't done anything – I haven't done *anything!*'

'We know,' I said, 'We know.'

'So why? Are they going to arrest me? For what? They can't do this to me! I haven't done ANYTHING ...' He was pacing now.

Rebbie and Randy had arrived, with Mother not far behind. Rebbie was bent down, clearing up the mess, saying nothing in the awkward silence. The phone was ringing off the hook. Outside, the paparazzi had descended. In the air, the 'eyes in the sky' were hovering. Then, hotel management told us the activity was invasive for other guests and asked if we 'would consider vacating the hotel.' We decamped to the Green Valley Ranch, but everything was happening so fast and the pressure felt overwhelming.

After blowing up and venting, it was amazing how Michael restored his composure for the sake of the kids. Children are intuitive and they kept asking questions but their father reassured them that everything was going to be okay, even if he couldn't tell himself that. I saw him hold and hug Paris; she squeezed him tight. He closed his eyes and gulped it down.

Time to be courageous now, little brother. Your reason to fight is here and all around you.

THE DAY AFTER THE RAID, DA Tom Sneddon held a press conference, announcing that he had issued a warrant for Michael's arrest on 'multiple counts of child molestation.' He called on my brother to turn himself in and surrender his passport. Giving it the whole, unnecessary fugitive vibe.

He didn't reveal the accuser's name but everyone knew it was Gavin Arvizo and his allegation would be that he was abused and held against his will to make him co-operate with the damage limitation PR *after* the Bashir documentary. Sneddon would ask a jury to believe that Michael and his associates had done this when his friendship with Gavin was under the media's scrutiny, rather than before the documentary when no one had known the boy. Standing before a cluster of microphones, he said bail was set at $3 million and the maximum prison sentence per count was eight years. His presidential-length speech went on and on to justify why this case was very different to the 1993 allegations, and then he fielded questions.

'Could Michael Jackson's children be taken away from him?' shouted one reporter.

'That's a decision that would be made by a juvenile court,' he said.

You mother-f*****. Go on, add to Michael's torment. Make him think about the loss of all that is precious to him, I thought.

'Is there a possibility of any more victims?'

'Yes,' he answered. 'We would encourage the public to come forward if they have any information about other victims in the community.'

You've got nothing. That's why you're inviting more onto the bandwagon.

'If Michael Jackson's watching this right now, or his people, what's your message?'

'Get over here and get checked in!' said Sneddon. The press conference burst out laughing, but the humour wasn't over as another reporter waded in with another vital point: 'Excuse me, I haven't asked a question yet. Sheriff, are you going to be serving us members of the media lunch after this press conference?'

'You obviously don't know we have a budget problem!' said Sneddon. More laughter.

'What do you say to parents who let their children go to Neverland?'

'My advice is don't do it,' said Sheriff Jim Anderson. More laughter. It was a double-act now.

They say fame dehumanises people, but I think authority does a much worse job.

As everyone laughed, all I could think about was Michael wrecking his suite, curled up in his chair, pacing the rooms, going out of his mind. Holding Paris. I thought about Mother crying and praying. I saw Rebbie picking up the pieces of Sneddon's work.

And I felt this anger bubbling. Then, to drive it home, the DA reminded reporters that he hoped, 'you all stay long and spend lots of money because we need your sales to support our offices'. Presumably, that was a joke, too.

But he underestimated Michael. By now, my brother had gone through 24 hours of every possible emotion and, as hesitant as he was about co-operating with authorities he didn't trust, he started talking about wanting his day in court. He knew he'd left the door ajar for trouble with that civil settlement in 1994. 'It was bad advice,' he said, 'and I knew it then. Now I'll show them what I wanted to show them before – that I am innocent.'

Sneddon had presumably forgotten that Michael had requested a criminal trial in 1993, but a judge hadn't permitted it. But, as Michael would say: 'Lies run sprints, but the truth runs marathons. The truth will run this marathon in court.' And that truth had been running now, gathering pace for 10 years.

MICHAEL FLEW BY PRIVATE JET INTO Santa Barbara, where the police were waiting by arrangement in an airport hangar. Every move was played out on television: his take-off, his landing, his transfer to the police station, and his arrival there in handcuffs. As he got out of the police car, he bounced his bound arms behind his back – a gesture to the news helicopters, as if to say, 'See! See what they're doing to me?!' He wanted the world to know.

Afterwards, I wanted to know what that world was being told. Some in the family couldn't bear to watch the television coverage, but I couldn't stop myself from tuning in to CNN. Its anchor, Kyra Phillips, was with a blonde girl from *Entertainment Tonight* and a court expert, both of whom were making disparaging comments about Michael and condemning him. First, the Sneddon side-show. Then, the handcuffing, and now two rent-a-quotes pretending to sound informed. I might have been extra-sensitive at this time, but this kind of speculative opinion is a media game that the public takes seriously and it left me fuming.

The final straw was when the blonde said something derogatory about the family and I flipped, smashing my fist into the television screen, shattering it. I then dialled CNN and demanded to be put on air, because it's very simple in our family: if you hurt one of us, you hurt all of us.

I don't think Kyra Phillips believed it could be me with everything going on, but I wasn't there for a friendly one-on-one and my voice was shaking with anger. I've never gone on radio, television or stage so spontaneously or furious but I'd heard enough. 'Michael is a thousand per cent innocent,' I said, building up to my rant, 'and we're tired of people – I'M SICK AND F****** TIRED of people – speaking on my brother's behalf and my family's behalf, who do not know us. You put these people on national TV, international TV, and they say these things and the public is saying, "Oh, wow, is he really like this?" My brother is NOT an eccentric. My brother is about peace. At the end of the day, this is nothing but A MODERN-DAY LYNCHING. THIS IS WHAT THEY WANT TO SEE – HIM IN HANDCUFFS. YOU GOT IT! BUT IT WON'T BE FOR LONG, I PROMISE YOU!'

She said she had no idea what we were going through.

'NO, YOU DON'T! You don't walk in my shoes or my family's shoes, but you put these people on television to say things. We are family, and we will continue to be family. That's my love right there. And we support him one thousand per cent. I have nothing else to say. Goodbye.'

When I slammed down the receiver, my hand was shaking. I sat down, looked at the shattered TV screen, put my head in my hands and just wept.

ONCE THE FIRST PHASE OF INDIGNITY was out of the way and we had all released our pressure valves, Michael returned to Vegas and started to talk. It was less an opening up and more of an unloading of concern about a group which I'll call 'The Men's Club of Beverly Hills' – a group of well-connected power brokers from the music industry who, he said, were behind everything and 'trying to bring me down' and he added: 'They don't want me around … They want me in jail … They want to finish me.'

When he said this – to Mother, to me, and several others, inside and outside the family – his fears were calmly expressed, like someone who could see clearly once the dust had settled. He would also hint about his suspicions later during a radio show hosted by Jesse Jackson, saying there was 'a big fight going on … and there's a lot of conspiracy.' That fight he referred to centred on his music catalogue.

When he spoke about this, it was the sincerity of his tone that got me thinking because – whether true or not – we as a family could see the financial rationale in where he was pointing us: that if he went to prison, what control would he have over the catalogue as a convicted criminal? And with countless lawsuits against him lining up like planes from certain business dealings, he'd likely lose them all from prison. This outcome would have ultimately led to big losses and him defaulting on his bank loan – and his share of the catalogue would revert to Sony. That wasn't some theory; that was a distinct probability in the event of a conviction.

In my opinion, his fears were legitimate: he held the music industry equivalent of the Koh-i-Noor diamond. But it was more than that: he had been talking about a 'conspiracy' long before events turned against him and his suspicions now seemed to be increasingly valid.

THE POLICE INVESTIGATION STARTED TO STINK when we learned of an official letter from the Department of Child and Family Services and discovered that its social workers had been *the first* to speak with Gavin Arvizo and they closed their file within *13 days because there was no case to answer.*

The letter, 'a brief summary of a child abuse investigation completed by the Sensitive Case Unit', explained that 'the child was interviewed … and denied any form of sexual abuse.' The mother, Janet Arvizo, had said Michael was 'a father figure' and had never shared a bed with her son. The Department had 'concluded the allegations of sexual abuse to be unfounded' – a view shared by the LAPD, it added.

That letter vindicated Michael, and was dated 26 November 2003 – five days *after* his arrest. But, of course, Sneddon would dismiss its significance, saying that to call the DCFS case 'an investigation is a misnomer – it was an interview.' I don't what know he thought there was left to investigate when the boy, backed by his mother, had categorically said Michael hadn't touched him, let alone sexually abused him. He had said the same to the Dean at his school, but none of this would matter. All we knew was that in February 2003, the Arvizo family was adamant about my brother's innocence, as were the authorities, but by the June, Gavin was saying he had been molested and he said it took place *after* that interview with social workers. What he did not say was that his family had also consulted an attorney about a civil lawsuit – an attorney who had advised on the 1993 Jordie Chandler case. And with that about-turn accepted in law, Sneddon convened a Grand Jury and decided the case should go to trial.

AFTER HIS ARREST, AND BEFORE WE left Vegas, Michael wanted to discuss his security arrangements and he said, 'I don't feel as secure as I should, and that feeling imprisons me.'

Nanny Grace had already explained to me that the current security set-up wasn't working for him and I suggested to him that he needed people who were not afraid of anyone and shared his trust in God. I knew the sons of Louis Farrakhan, leader of the Nation of Islam, and he had a team of bodyguards ideally suited for the job. Sure of what he had read about Islam, and everything Muhammad Ali had told him, Michael liked this idea but 9/11 was still America's open wound. He knew the distinction between true Muslims and the extremists who abuse Islam, but the matter had to be handled discreetly.

'You're going to have a set of new suits and ties with black faces around you – no one will notice,' I reassured him.

Of course, people did notice, which led to suggestions that 'fundamentalists' surrounded him and would brainwash him. People forgot that Michael's faith in God was too strong to be swayed by any movement and the Nation was there for its effective security, not any kind of ideology. But the fuss amused us both and we wondered what Ali would make of it all. Anyhow, after a meeting in Vegas with the Nation of Islam, Michael was happy with the people who called him 'Sir' and gave him respect. He felt comfortable that everything was locked down again.

Meanwhile, our brother Randy had started working for Michael as his right-hand man and once more they shared the closeness they had enjoyed at Hayvenhurst before Randy left. Randy's contacts led Michael to defence attorney Tom Mesereau, a man unfazed by the celebrity culture and uninterested in grandstanding. His only concern was 'the integrity, decency, honour, charity, innocence and vindication' of Michael. There was no doubt we had the right man for the job.

The moment I met this unflappable character and heard his optimism on how each witness would fold under cross-examination, I felt a sliver of hope that had been impossible to find in Sneddon's injustice. That hope would grow during the trial as Tom exposed a prosecution case built on sand. He'd also found out that the 1993 accuser Jordie Chandler had refused to testify and 'even if he had, we had witnesses who were going to say he told them it never happened and he would never talk to his parents again for what they made him say.' (The boy hadn't spoken to his parents for 11 years.) No wonder Michael felt emboldened by Tom's presence as the case went to trial.

It was the end of February 2005.

COME DAY ONE OF THE TRIAL, the family were at Neverland. Michael rose early to make sure he was mentally prepared, his hair done, his costume pristine, and his makeup perfect, as applied by Karen Faye. Everyone was pensive; everyone ate lightly. It was hard not to view the whole scene as some backstage venue, waiting to walk on for a show we never wanted to do. And this was our time to find out what we were made of as a family, as brothers and sisters. Everything we had ever avoided or not confronted came down to the following weeks because this was about looking an ugly reality in the face; it wasn't about superficial fame or success, or being the best or Michael being the King of Pop – we had to leave all those cloaks at the door. Inside that courtroom it was about raw human truth – the good, the bad and the ugly – and being out of control.

On that first day, as we sat inside Sneddon's house of cards, I looked at Michael, dressed in a military jacket with red arm-band, and was amazed by how crystal-sharp he seemed; arriving with an attitude that said: 'Bring it on. Give it your best shot'. He walked in there head held high … and smelling good. That was because he wore a Dolce & Gabbana cologne with a red top that was my favourite, too. If I wear it today around Prince and Paris, they say, 'You smell just like Daddy!'

There was one day when we were driving into court and Michael was spraying it all over his clothes in a swirl of mist. Mother – who complained that she was allergic to perfumes – started coughing. 'You all putting on too much! I cannot breathe! Stop it now …'

Michael started laughing and sprayed some more. 'It smells good, Mother … you want some, Jermaine?!'

So I added a quick squirt to my neck. Mother tutted, tried to keep a serious face and then couldn't help but smile at the wind up. Moments like that always did help break the tension that preceded a day in court.

On the days when I travelled with Michael in the black SUV, security sat up front and Joseph was seated behind. Mother, Michael and I shared the same row. Leaving Neverland, there were always lots of fans at the gate, holding up their banners of love and innocence, cheering us off. I'll never forget the moment when Michael made the driver stop because he'd spotted an image a woman was holding out. He lowered the window, shook her hand

and took from her a photo of a baby that caught his eye. 'It's beautiful … what a beautiful child,' he said.

'I love you Michael!' she said.

'WE LOVE YOU MICHAEL!' the entire crowd cheered, and we pulled away. He often took the seat on the right against the blackened window, ear-phones plugged in, listening to music. One time, during that first week, I passed him my CD player and ear-phones. 'Listen to this … it's a strong song,' I said.

'Run Johnny Run' was a song I'd written for Tito before any of this police stuff happened, but its theme seemed kind of apt because this secret soundtrack to our ride into court was about a black man falsely accused of raping a white woman in an old southern town and 'Johnny' needs to run because the whole town's convinced he did it. As those first lyrics say: *'You telling me and I know you didn't touch her/But the white man don't trust ya/He'll bring you in and handcuff ya/Tie you up on a tree and then cut ya/All the things said is what they say/It goes around and become heresay …'*

Michael was listening as he looked out the window, foot tapping to the chorus. By the time we took the off-ramp to the court house, he was playing it for a second time (not that anyone would have told Tom Mesereau because he didn't want no race talk in the public arena). As the SUV pulled up and security jumped out, Michael handed me back the ear-phones. 'Great story. Would make a great video!' he said, mischievously.

'Are you ready, Michael?' asked his security, interrupting the spark of an idea.

One. Two. Three. Open the doors. And the silence of a Santa Maria morning was broken by 100 fluttering cameras, the cheers of fans and yelled-out questions from the media as Michael took his composed walk into court.

THE COURT HAD ALLOCATED SIX SEATS for the family so we supported Michael in shifts.

When I was there, I sat on the front row behind him, maybe seven feet away, my eyes boring into the back of his head, wondering what he was thinking. I did that with everyone as I scanned the room. I guessed at expressions on different jurors' faces, and watched when they did or did not make notes. I stared at Judge Melville and wondered if he realised how he wasn't really presiding over this débâcle: God was. I looked at Mother, who attended every day without fail, poised and beautiful in her vigil to the truth. I don't think I truly understood her strength until now: she was crushed inside but never showed it. Her pride and belief in her son were evident to all and I have this indelible image of Michael in the corridors, holding out his arm for Mother to link so that she could be steadier as she walked, and yet her very presence every day was his stability. Joseph was also there. Rock-solid in support. His stern, daily frown never gave away his innermost feelings and he was a man of few words privately, too, never voicing anything but his belief that Michael would be freed. It was that kind of certain belief that gave all of us strength, I think.

I also watched the media who packed into that room as Sneddon's witnesses provided their lewd testimony – and journalists rushed out of the door to spread the prosecution allegations that Michael plied his 'victims' with alcohol, had read porn with them, had touched the boy and kept his family 'captive'.

The media rushed to be first to break the latest evidence – and somewhere in the stampede, trampled into the ground, was the truth that Tom Mesereau extracted during the cross-examination. Like when it was revealed that Michael hadn't plied anyone with alcohol but the boys had known where the wine-cellar key was kept. Or when Gavin Arvizo said, yes, that was the porn magazine Michael had used with him – only for Tom to point out its issue date was August 2003. Or when Janet Arvizo confirmed they were held 'captive' at Neverland – only for Tom to prove that they had left and returned on three separate occasions of their own free will. Or when Gavin told the pre-trial Grand Jury that he was molested on 7 February – but the charges at trial related to 'some time between 20 February and 12 March 2003'.

But Tom's greatest coup was to reveal that the Arvizo family had once sued the department store chain J. C. Penney for millions and settled for $150,000 when the mother said she was inappropriately touched by security guards after they had stopped her son for taking an item of clothing. Janet Arvizo was also charged with (and later convicted of) welfare fraud against the Government. I think the jury had this family's measure after that.

It was actually on day one when it was obvious Sneddon had no case because his first key witness was Martin Bashir. I couldn't believe that his warped documentary, which was shown to the jury, was the foundation to the case but, apparently, it demonstrated 'motive'.

And people wondered why we called it 'trial by media'.

THE COURT CASE DIDN'T JUST IMPACT on Michael's reputation: it hurt his finances, too. His focus had to be on clearing his name for 18 months, not making music, and that pushed him further into debt, especially after the cancellation of the *Invincible* tour had cost him at least $100 million. Meanwhile, his bank loan had risen, with interest, to $272 million and Neverland cost $1 million a month to run, which *didn't* include payments on a $23 million line of credit taken out against the ranch. It was clear to me that since the *Invincible* album, Michael had started to feel the squeeze even if matters were not yet at crisis point, because the music catalogue was providing him with a yearly income of $25 million. The problem was that his spending matched what was coming in.

During the trial, I had to go to Bahrain for a few days. I stayed in touch with Mother and Tom by phone, but didn't tell anyone I was there to do a deal that would ease Michael's financial worries. Once he was free of court, I wanted him to be free of debt's burden, too. That was what I was aiming for as I spent time with Prince Abdullah, the King's second son. My good friend Ali Qamber had introduced us. He had explained that the Prince was producing a local artist but was keen to expand not only a record label but a leisure entertainment arm, too. Michael had tried to do this with Kingdom Entertainment years earlier and his vision for hotels, theme parks and movies never tired – it represented 'the next level' in a direction away from music. Also, after his experience of American justice, he had been talking about finding sanctuary in the East with the children once the trial was over.

The timing of everything presented an opportunity to bring together the Prince and his wealth and Michael and I as collaborators in not only music but movies. This was a win-win, but more importantly, a chance for him to get back on track.

When I arrived in the Bahraini capital of Manama, Ali drove me to a little recording studio. He told me that the Prince was 'excited to meet a member of the Jackson family.'

'That's a good starting point!' I joked, thinking he was humouring me. But when I arrived, the Prince rolled out a Jackson 5 poster and asked me to sign it, then started to talk about his musical ambitions and bank-rolling a whole new venture under a new label and company called Two Seas. Next thing I knew, we were sitting in the desert in one of those red royal tents, signing contracts to share the company between him, Michael and me with a 33.3 per cent share each.

When I returned to California, I put Michael on the phone to Prince Abdullah one morning on the ride to court. They spoke excitedly about plans for the future, exchanged numbers and, from then on, remained in regular contact.

DURING MY TIME AWAY, IT WAS obvious from looking at Michael that sitting in court listening to lie after lie was a withering experience. It was, for him, the legal equivalent of putting a man in the stocks to have everyone and anyone throw lies at him.

Often, he returned to the ranch in the evening and locked himself away in his room until the next morning. On security advice he had also started to wear a bulletproof vest – the crowds outside the court were growing, and who knew what kind of nut was out there? The mere fact he was *having* to wear one did nothing for his spirits.

His case was the biggest news story in the world. We were told there were 1,800 accredited reporters and producers outside, and the media tents looked like the command centre for a military operation. On another corner of the court premises stood a mass of Michael's fans, with their banners and flags. And in the middle stood Michael, whose tolerance for the whole circus had long expired. His exasperation had first blown that day in hospital in his pyjamas, but I also remember the day when he was fed up of all the rules and formalities that had dominated his life for almost five months.

I was sitting behind him when he tentatively raised a hand to the judge, like the kid in class interrupting a lesson to ask a question, only Michael wanted to be excused to go to the restroom. It was more of a raised index finger, held at eye-level, but he seemed unsure whether he could interrupt proceedings or not. When he went unseen, he lowered his hand and waited for another minute or so. Then, he tried again, but Judge Melville never acknowledged his gesture and this must have been a time during Tom's cross-examination because he wasn't next to him to ask.

Fed up at going unnoticed, Michael's bladder reached the point of not caring, and he quietly got up, turned, and tapped me on the shoulder. I followed him out of the door and, surrounded by his security, we walked down the hallway and up the steps to the restroom. We left the guard at the door and Michael rushed into a stall and peed like a racehorse.

'Can you believe that?!' he shouted out, 'I try to get his attention and he just ignores me! What did he want me to do – pee in the courtroom?' As he washed his hands at the sink, he kept venting to my reflection in the mirror.

'You did the right thing – don't let it get to you,' I said.

'*Everything* is getting to me! I don't understand how people can twist things so horribly,' he said. I could tell this toilet break was as much about respite as anything else and he just stood there, appreciating those briefest moments of being in a room with no eyes on him and no lies being heard; able to speak, able to be heard.

'It takes many people to lie, it takes only one person to tell the truth. Remember that,' I said. And with that, he straightened himself up in the mirror, took a deep breath, turned on his heels and we headed back for the court room.

SIXTY-SIX DAYS IS HOW LONG THE justice process took before Michael's freedom was placed in the hands of the eight women and four men on the jury.

And God.

We were all allowed to decamp to Neverland, where we waited in limbo for the next six days as the jury considered the 14 counts: the felonies that would carry a prison term and the misdemeanours that would see him walk free but with an indelible stain.

As each day came and went, our minds spun: *If they're taking this long, it must be a good sign, right? Or are they taking so long because some are convinced and some are not? What if they can't decide – will it be a retrial?* Waiting for a jury and watching your brother wonder whether he'll be free to make music again is torturous.

The authorities had surrounded Neverland with sheriff patrol cars and men in beige police uniforms stood guard at every conceivable entry and exit point. It seemed excessive, but everything about the case had appeared so.

As I waited, and as a glutton for punishment, I turned on the television news channels in my room. Nancy Grace on CNN was characteristically breathless in her prediction of guilty verdicts. I hopped around different channels but that seemed to be the consensus. So, Sneddon had the media with its shallow examination. All we could hope for was that Tom Mesereau had the jury.

I was sitting with Tito on the edge of the fountain near the theme park. Every ride, and every memory of fun we'd ever shared, stood still as we shelled peanuts and made them our lunch. We talked, speculated, worried. Above us, two news helicopters kept hovering. For once, I was able to ignore them. Then, from behind us, we heard a speeding car. 'They have verdicts!' the driver shouted.

In the car, we learned that Judge Melville had given the family 45 minutes to get to court. It was now about one o'clock on the afternoon of 13 June 2005.

We ran to the main house and grabbed our jackets. Everyone was climbing into the convoy of vehicles. Michael, wearing his sunglasses, was already in the car. He was sitting next to Rebbie, who had the Bible in her hand: she was reading from the scriptures. As he listened, he rocked in his seat. 'Why? Why? *Why?*' he kept repeating, beating a fist into his right knee, 'Why does it have to come to this?' Rebbie went on reading as Randy climbed in beside her – and she continued to read all the way to court. During the previous weeks, Michael had privately attended two meetings at the local Kingdom Hall, returning to his Jehovah's Witness roots in his darkest hour. We laughed because both services were in Spanish but I don't think he had to hear the content, he just needed to feel close to all that he knew, forgiving all that had gone before.

I was in the car behind them as we set off for court. Around my neck was a gift from the new woman in my life, my future wife: Halima Rashid. We had recently met in line at Starbucks. Destiny's chess board. King takes Queen.

Come verdict week, she had given me a gold chain with a Muslim prayer in Arabic inscribed on the medallion: 'He knows what is before them and what is behind them, they do not comprehend any of his knowledge except what He wills …' I clutched it in my palm and held it to my lips all the way there. 'My brother is coming back home to this ranch … my brother is coming back home to this ranch,' I kept whispering, as we pulled away from Neverland, passing the fans who had remained there the whole time. '1000% Innocent!' said a banner.

Please, God, let it be a sign.

THE COURT REFUSED TO ALLOCATE US four extra seats on verdict day. Six seats only for the family. Rules were rules. Janet and I decided to let the others go ahead. Part of me didn't know if

I was capable of watching my brother stand, surrounded by marshals, as the jury foreman read out 14 verdicts.

My sister and I went to an upstairs room. Just me, her and security in this windowless box, deaf and blind to whatever was playing out in the court room beneath us. We prayed. We hugged. We paced. We waited.

And then I heard a cheer from outside. Followed by another.

I rushed out the door, chasing this cheer like it was a missing child that I was desperate to find. Then came another, louder this time.

Down the hallway, I found a small window all taped up. I ripped it off and pulled the window ajar just enough to see outside. That was when I saw a woman releasing white doves with each cheer. 'JANET! JANET!' I screamed and started running back to my sister, who rushed out the doorway. 'THEY'RE RELEASING DOVES!'

At that very moment, a lady came bounding up the stairs. 'He's freed on all counts! They've freed him on all counts!'

I wish I could convey the elation that I felt in that moment but put me in front of 200,000 people in the biggest venue in the world and it wouldn't match it.

We raced downstairs and waited outside the doors until they opened, and out walked Michael, surrounded by the rest of the family and Tom Mesereau. Michael wasn't smiling, like everyone else: he looked stunned, and we just kept walking. There was no time for hugs. We could do all that back at Neverland. I didn't even have a chance to enjoy Sneddon's humiliation. He, with his crack detectives, will go down in history as the team who took on my brother and lost. Twice.

We walked outside as a family, and were greeted by the biggest cheer. I wanted to find the lady who had released the 14 white doves at each 'not guilty' verdict – she had done the greatest thing and we all, even Michael, commented on it. On that walk to freedom beneath his umbrella, he ignored the media and saluted his fans. Just before he got into the SUV, he turned to shake Tom

Mesereau's hand. And then the convoy took us back to Neverland, where Prince, Paris and 'Blanket' were waiting with Nanny Grace. Life could finally return to normal, and we honestly thought that the worst was behind us.

CHAPTER TWENTY-ONE
The Comeback King

I SAW THE PERFORMER'S GLINT RETURN to Michael's eyes around the Fall of 2008 – the period when his life was back on track, his health was nearing peak fitness and he was physically preparing for the greatest comeback ever seen. He was, for the first time in a long time, *just happy*. I wasn't the only one who observed this rebirth: people who had worked with him for years saw it and they, like me, could detect when the creative flame had started to burn again inside him, lighting him up. The world has read that Michael was reduced to a frail old man in faltering health, forever broken by the trial, a performer physically unable to tour again, whose voice would never be the same, and the tabloid myth that he was slowly being killed by a drug dependency. None of this was true, as borne out by the sweat stains on the walls of his dance studio and the vocals he'd been laying down on sublime, but unfinished tracks.

The guesswork about his health, especially after his death, summed up the theme of Michael's life: gossip and wild interpretation warped the true picture. People point to a particular photograph, taken in July 2008, of my brother being pushed in a wheelchair, with captions like 'too weak to stand, looking frail and in no condition to perform …' That was exactly what Michael wanted the media and his biographers to write because the man who was forever underestimated was fooling everyone. It was an act. He was in one of his disguises, making everyone *think* he wasn't ready or capable. He of all people knew the power of an image, and he was aware that everyone doubted he still had 'it'. So imagine – just imagine – if he bounced back and surprised the world, going from *that* state to *this*; from that 'before' shot to this 'after'. Michael was doing a Willy Wonka, walking out of the chocolate factory to greet the crowds with a crippling limp as everyone gasps with shock – and then he stumbles … tosses away the cane, does a somersault and everyone cheers. Gotcha. Because no comeback is truly a comeback until the odds *seem* impossible.

Michael's life had long been defined by indelible images that captured a myth: from oxygen chambers to surgical masks, from hotel balconies to 'whiter' skin. This was him having the last laugh. I knew it. The people around him – the ones he trusted – knew it. The rest of the world would find out in London. But the clues were always there because he was such a fiercely private man, knowing when to turn on and turn off the PR tap. He never, ever turned out in public unless pristine and immaculately dressed, and he did everything possible to cover his vitiligo, illnesses and self-perceived flaws because he didn't want the mask to slip; he wanted no one to see any imperfection or doubt his greatness. Yet in Las Vegas that private man chose to go *shopping in public*, with his children, in a *wheelchair*, wearing a red baseball cap, slippers and sky-blue pyjama pants? (Remember how mortified he was when forced to show up in court wearing pyjamas?)

Think about it. Michael was a master manipulator of image, knowing that the media and paparazzi would like to think they'd 'caught' him off guard, looking frail, showing no sign of motivation. He wanted the ultimate vindication in the court of the world. The King of Pop turned Comeback King. Restored to the best and the greatest. Silencing every doubter and hater. And here's a fact to place alongside that wheelchair image: about two months later, he was engaged in a brutal choreography regime for a comeback tour that had not yet been revealed. He was dancing *hard* in four-hour sessions every day, even tiring out his choreographer LaVelle Smith Junior, whom he'd hired to get him back in shape. LaVelle was a dancer in the video for 'Smooth Criminal', who then became my brother's trusted choreographer, which was why he was booked for private one-on-one sessions in Vegas.

Michael got stronger and stronger, week by week, and he shed weight when I didn't think he had any more to lose. Again, some people point to this 'thinness' as if it were a disturbing sign, but he had shrunk ever since the trial and his fitness regime made him skinnier. It was also normal – during each tour he ever did, he'd lose three inches off his waist. Michael was simply shedding weight *because of those daily four hours of dance*. Not bad for a man who, according to one biographer, 'needed a lung transplant'. In late 2008, he was so fit that, further down the line – *eight weeks before he died* – when he bumped into a friend in a doctor's office, he lifted his shirt and said, 'Have you seen my six-pack?' The private truth versus the public image.

Those around Michael sensed he was warming up again when he started requesting CDs, just like old times. He was so obsessed about staying up-to-date with musical trends that *every week* he was sent the Top 10 from the *Billboard* Hot 100 burned onto one disc, plus four other discs with songs from the R&B, electro, dance and Euro scenes. He would listen to every track to determine what was hot and what was selling because he wanted to stay ahead of the curve. He hadn't done that for a while. As one of his inner circle put it, 'He was getting ready for his close-up again. He was writing songs, looking better, looking sharp, getting his act back together. He was at peace with himself.' To me, this is both the beauty and the travesty: Michael was so excited about what the future held, and he had so many plans. He was buying a new property in Vegas and was determined to build a new Neverland, unstained by a police raid; he looked forward to a short residency tour so that Prince, Paris and 'Blanket' could see their daddy on the road properly for the first time; he also knew that touring offered him the chance to regain control and make enough money so that he could, finally, clear his crippling debts. His outlook was positive again. His body was back in shape. His focus was the future.

After his 'This Is It' concerts were done, and he'd had a few weeks off, he looked forward to performing spot dates in China. In 2011, he was eyeing up the half-time slot at the Superbowl (the one that the Black Eyed Peas would end up doing) to repeat his legendary show of 1993. And then, some time before 2014, he had two more tours up his sleeve: the 'back by popular demand' dates that no one knew about. Despite what everyone thinks, the comeback concerts in London were the beginning, not the end. I know what Michael said in March 2009: 'When I say this is it, it really means "this is it" … This is the final curtain-call.' That was his great tease: he was a master salesman, too, and if the world thought that London would be their last opportunity to see him perform, then they would rush to buy tickets. The rules of limited supply and big demand. Many misunderstood his commercial astuteness because he excelled at smoke-and-mirrors, mystery and big surprises.

Admittedly, it wasn't all hype. He worried that the tickets might not sell, so the tour announcement was also a toe in the water, to test the temperature of the public mood – his confidence had been shattered by everything he had been through. Could he sell out five concerts, let alone 10? That was why he chose London, not America: he was concerned that America wouldn't accept him the way Europe would. That's not a reflection on his fans: it's an indication of how scarred he was by those years of child-molester headlines and the treatment he had received in his own country. It had made him doubt that his popularity had survived the allegations. Remember, it had been a long time since the 'HIStory' tour, and he was 50 years old now. It was also why the O2 arena, with 20,000 seating capacity, was chosen by a man who had once played to 180,000 people on Aintree racecourse in northern England. Start small with the rebuild. Ease yourself in. I think he needed to see the scale of the love before he believed that his fans hadn't turned against him.

Come 2008, Michael was not only hungry again, he had a five-year plan sketched out. But to make sense of all this, and to understand how this secret future started to form, I first need to take you back to 2005 when he walked out of court, vowed never to live again at Neverland, and went to make music in Bahrain with Prince Abdullah.

THE MOMENT THE AUTHORITIES RETURNED HIS passport, Michael headed east with the kids and Nanny Grace, and explored the option of permanent residence. He viewed America as a great friend who had betrayed him and he wanted nothing to do with her for a while. But as some friends who didn't step up in his hour of need will know, Michael always came around. He needed time to decompress because he suffered bouts of depression after the trial, which I believe was a natural reaction to the stress. When he boarded that plane, he was a shadow of his former self and he was immensely grateful to the Bahraini Royal Family for providing him with sanctuary.

I had initially worried about the outcome of everything out there: having been instrumental in setting up the framework for Two Seas Records, I found myself cut out of the equation. Suddenly it became a partnership between my brother and the Prince. In theory, I could have waved my signed contract but that was never an option because the last thing Michael needed was a lawsuit with himself stuck in the middle. Some grievances are not that important when measured against other priorities. What mattered was that Michael was having fun and everything seemed to be going well: the Prince paid for much of his lifestyle while he was in Bahrain. This kind of 'hospitality' is often customary with some of the Middle East's ruling families. 'Gifts' are the norm, and that was why Michael, in good faith, considered the hospitality he enjoyed to be a gift; he didn't realise this was all part of his contract. He just felt he was there to create one album only – and that was when the project hit a giant misunderstanding. The signed contract had Michael tied up in some general management lock-down on music, musicals, movies and books. When Michael realised that, he walked away: he wasn't being 'owned' by anyone. He diverted to London before switching to Dublin, Ireland, where he collaborated with will.i.am of the Black Eyed Peas, first staying at the dancer Michael Flatley's house before renting another place. Then he flew over producer Ron Feemster: Ron had worked with the likes of Ne-Yo and 50 Cent.

Collaborating with these music-makers dovetailed with Michael's need to stay current. But back in Bahrain, the Prince was not happy and, long story short, he filed a lawsuit in London, which cost Michael $5 million. It was disappointing to see a king's son scrambling around like that, especially after my brother had done more to put Bahrain on the map in many minds than Formula 1 ever could. But it was also frustratingly characteristic of Michael to sign a contract without reading the small print – just as, in 2000, he had discovered his masters weren't being returned by Sony. His blind faith in his advisers and the face-value honesty of others was his own Achilles' heel and had been since Joseph handled our contracts as boys. The power he'd vested in others dawned on him one day when he overheard an attorney's arrogant remark: 'Michael can't sign off on his own stuff! He *can't approve anything* … We approve it.' It was a stinging reminder that he was viewed as a business first and foremost, a person second.

It was that kind of comment, I think, which spurred him to try to assert his authority with certain agreements, but the reality was that his quest for autonomy left him vulnerable to lawsuits or being controlled. It always amazed me how, over the years, many professionals came and went through his revolving door and tried to control, manage or interfere in his world, always ring-fencing him. It was the strangest phenomenon to see professionals change when they were with him, adopting delusions of grandeur at having his ear, access to him or otherwise holding the reins. It was also hard to hear my brother complain about different people being 'controlling', especially when he felt unable to speak up or take responsibility because of his dislike of confrontation. He terminated many associations by letter. As he always said, 'I'm like my mother – I can't fire anyone!'

But I don't think we understood how much people took advantage of him – and how much he allowed it – until the 2005 court case, when we heard he had given June Chandler free rein with a credit card, and that almost $1 million was unaccounted for under one person's watch because he'd signed over Power of Attorney. It was this kind of incident that prompted me to find the right kind of people to put around him. To be fair, Prince Abdullah appeared to be a fan, a good man and earnest. Unfortunately Michael misunderstood the contract; he often didn't read contracts and so ended up walking into a $5 million debt that he simply couldn't afford.

IT IS NO EXAGGERATION TO SAY that Michael was under siege from lawsuits: they were flying at him from all directions – and from people who must have known he was in difficulty. He was the man everyone decided to kick while he was down: he was facing litigation totalling in excess of $100 million, with the added burden of his $300 million-plus borrowings. Had those lawsuits cashed in simultaneously, he would have been wiped out financially. Michael had tried to stop the buckling by restructuring his loans. The New York-based Fortress Investment Group bought his $272 million Bank of America debt, releasing him a new loan in excess of $300 million to free up more cash. I had thought that by paying off his first loan, as guaranteed by Sony, the record label would be out of the picture. I was wrong. It would become clear that Sony had helped facilitate the restructuring and in return, it secured *the option* to purchase 25 per cent of Michael's half of the music catalogue. If his finances worsened, it held the right to match any future offer on his remaining 25 per cent to ensure it didn't end up with an undesirable partner. But these were rights on paper: Michael still held his 50 per cent, even if the arrangement strategically weakened his position.

In a crumb of good news, he bought back a 5 per cent share of the catalogue that his now ex-attorney John Branca had held. Michael was happy that John no longer had any financial interest in, or influence over, the catalogue. In my mind, this once great business relationship had floundered because John hadn't nailed his colours exclusively to Michael's mast when it mattered.

Meanwhile, Neverland was in trouble because Michael had struggled to meet the staff payroll and veterinary bills. As a result, he was forced to pay employees $300,000 in back pay. Not only that: composers and musicians had been unpaid for months. But those who loved Michael didn't complain or pressure him because they trusted that he'd look after them once he'd turned his life around. That is the response of true friends.

Michael was furious, of course, over his financial situation. In his mind, he had paid accountants to settle his bills and distribute his money. Like any artist, he entrusted a team to keep his house in order. By March 2006, his circumstances forced him to shut down the ranch and all the animals were sent to sanctuaries or specialist centres. It saddened me to see Neverland's demise – I knew how much of his heart and soul was invested there – but it was a time for salvage, not for sentiment. He had to trim the fat and keep the rump of his assets: the ranch and the catalogue.

THAT SAME SUMMER, MICHAEL RECEIVED A set of documents that made sense of everything, he said. I never saw them so I don't know their content, but he shared his discovery with Randy, who was bringing in a host of advisers to get to the bottom of everything. Those documents were sufficient to convince Michael that there had been a deliberate plan by named individuals to 'solicit other attorneys, vendors and creditors' to file lawsuits that would have forced him into involuntary bankruptcy. He immediately instructed his new legal team to investigate and explore his rights. He also wanted the documents forwarded to the US Attorney

General. In a statement, his team said, 'Based on the timing of events that have impacted his personal and professional life in recent years, Michael has long been suspicious of some of those that he entrusted to act on his behalf.' I don't know what happened to those documents – after his death, a lot of things simply disappeared.

MICHAEL TRUSTED FEWER AND FEWER PEOPLE, but there was one individual he trusted as he would a friend; this person had advised him discreetly behind the scenes in a non-professional capacity ever since 2000/2001. Over time, though, and because of two incidents, Michael grew ever more concerned about this person's loyalties. The first came when, at a private social gathering, his friend suddenly asked Michael to dance. He chuckled, thinking it was a joke. 'No, Michael, I would like you *to dance for my friends*,' said this man. Michael remembered the advice Fred Astaire had once given him: 'Remember, you're not a performing monkey. You're an artist. You dance for no one but yourself.'

'I'm not in the mood to dance,' said Michael, 'but thank you for asking.' Point made. Character flaw noted.

Ever trusting, he stayed in touch with his friend to the extent that he was often a guest at his house. But, of course, Michael was never a good sleeper … and he still liked to snoop. One night when he couldn't sleep, he went for a wander and overheard his host talking about him on the phone. As he listened, it became clear the person at the other end of the line was a high-powered Sony executive. This was around 2002/2003 – during Michael's self-declared war on people like Tommy Mottola. Michael had shared all his feelings with his host about different people, what he was thinking and what he should do. He felt that person was loyal. But when he heard that furtive late-night conversation, he realised that his 'ally' was friendly with the higher echelons at Sony. Michael was freaked out because he heard things that were not favourable towards him, but he said nothing. The next morning, he packed his bags and was out of there, leaving his guest to wonder why he was departing early.

Once again, the brothers felt the need to protect Michael. He struggled to trust his own shadow now, but all we could do was bring in new people to come up with a different strategy and turn his life around. By 2007, he was seriously in danger of falling into a financial black hole that would have cost him everything. The clock on his assets was ticking loudly.

He probably couldn't hear it because his head was full of too much noise concerning his safety. Around this time, whenever Michael visited New York, and sometimes in other cities, he discreetly wore a bullet-proof vest but made no big deal about it. It probably gave him peace of mind. *That* is how worried he was.

THE WIZARD OF OZ AND *WILLY Wonka & the Chocolate Factory* were two of Michael's favourite movies. Through his network of producer friends, he had heard that Warner Bros. was in development to re-adapt Roald Dahl's book and he was desperate to play Willy Wonka in what would become the modern version of the movie, *Charlie and the Chocolate Factory*. However, events in 2003 soon made everything impossible, and what he called 'my dream role' fell to Johnny Depp. But, in 2007, he got excited by a chance to re-create a *Wizard of Oz*-style Emerald City in the shape of a leisure and entertainment vision.

'Crystal City' was devised so that Michael and I could create our own leisure kingdom, which, on paper, would have incorporated a Neverland theme park and a Jackson Academy of Performing Arts. We had four meetings in which we let our imaginations run riot. The plan was to build an entire city in the Middle East, on reclaimed land rising out of the ocean. It would have included a replica Rodeo Drive built on a Venetian-style canal with gondolas, Bel Air-type estates and neighbourhoods, a shopping mall shaped like an octopus, a technology corridor, an 18-hole golf course, an amphitheatre for concerts, a marina, and a monorail system connecting every facility. 'And we could do what Disney does,' said Michael. 'We could do a Crystal City parade and have the most spectacular light show at night ... every night!' He wanted to place giant crystals on the top of each of the 14 hotels and then, in the light show, each crystal would refract a beam to the next, connecting the hotels with a web of light that would radiate across the city. But we didn't have the money to fund the dream.

So, when I found myself sitting in Gabon, in Africa, among a delegation of businessmen in December 2007, I put out feelers and came across a potential introduction: an architect friend mentioned that he knew of a 'doctor', who 'knew a lot of people' and lived in the Brentwood area of LA. I'd gone to Gabon and been recommended someone in my old neighbourhood, but I guess that's how life works. 'His name is Dr Tohme-Tohme,' said the architect. 'I'll hook you up.'

DIRECT, TOUGH, PULLING NO PUNCHES, THE Lebanese Dr Tohme-Tohme was no smooth-talking businessman and he certainly hadn't earned his doctorate at Charm School. But when my wife Halima and I visited him at his home in March 2008, he was gracious and everything about him supported the glowing testimonial I'd received. At first he seemed out to impress, showing us old military photographs and albums he had sung on in his younger days, but we were soon talking business and Crystal City. I deliberately didn't mention Michael because I wanted someone to see the value of the project first.

Over the next four meetings and two weeks, Tohme-Tohme seemed genuinely interested to explore the project with his contacts in the Middle East, looking for a consortium of oil-rich investors to raise $6 billion. He said he would report back.

OUT OF NOWHERE, NEWS BROKE THAT the lender was to foreclose the $23 million debt on Neverland because my brother was way behind on his payments. The idea that the ranch was under threat made me feel sick. I watched reports on television, and read newspapers over the following days, then said to Halima, 'Over my dead body are any of those bankers going to sell Neverland!'

It seemed that the only way out for Michael was to sell his $500 million share in the music catalogue. My mind went into over-drive, worrying about something I couldn't control, until a thought flashed into my head: *Dr Tohme-Tohme*. Halima was hesitant. 'But you hardly know the man,' she said.

'And our other options are where right now?' I said. If he could lead me to people of wealth to create something as vast as Crystal City, then saving Neverland would cost the equivalent of small change. I called our new friend and we met at his house on 13 April 2008. I hadn't told Michael what was going on because I needed to get my ducks in a row first. Once there, I outlined my brother's difficulty and explained his suspicions surrounding his debt. 'Is there *anyone* you know who'd be willing to help?' I asked.

Tohme-Tohme picked up a business magazine. The cover photo was of a suave, bald-headed gentleman in his sixties with a deeply furrowed brow. 'This guy.'

'He will?'

'I'll make sure of it,' he added, with a certainty I didn't need to understand. All I needed to know was that Tom Barrack, the Lebanese chairman of a real-estate investment firm called Colony Capital – controlling an estimated $40 billion in private equity – was on his speed dial (as well as the board of Miramax, Hilton, Fairmont and Raffles hotel chains). As a serious player, he seemed tailor-made for this SOS.

When word came back some days later that, yes, he was inter-ested in having a meeting, I was straight in the car and heading to Vegas, where Michael now rented a temporary home. Sadly, when I arrived – as was tediously routine with whoever was around my brother – the security detail from Nation of Islam wouldn't let me in. 'Wait,' I said, through the gate intercom. 'I'm the one who put your asses in this job and now you're telling *me* when I can and cannot see him?'

'He's not here, Jermaine,' said a voice. Click.

Undeterred, I checked into the MGM hotel. I went to the house three more times that day and was turned away each time. I felt like a stalker. Eventually I ran out of patience and rang Mother, who rang Nanny Grace … and the electric gates opened. Some suit with an ear-piece told me I had '20 minutes, and 20 minutes only' because Michael was going to the mall. As I waited downstairs in the lobby, I looked in the living room. It was filled with stacked storage crates and boxes. Everything about the new place felt unlived in.

Michael came down the stairs with a smile and we hugged. As usual when I – or any of the family – breached his team's artificial firewall, it was as easy between us as it had been in the good old days. I told him how his people had spoken to me and he leaned forward to whisper, 'Everyone *thinks* they're in control around here – there'll be changes made soon.' I didn't believe him – he'd been talking about changing his current personnel since the World Music Awards in London, in 2007. I moved on to the reason why I was there – and that was when my security-allocated 20-minute slot turned into hours. When I outlined the financial possibilities that came with Tom Barrack, it blew Michael's mind. I know that my sister La Toya has said she wished she could have 'protected' him from the likes of Tohme-Tohme, but had she known the history and the dire reality of the situation, I doubt she'd have held such an opinion. Everyone's intentions were nothing but good but all that mattered was that Michael understood this because maybe, just maybe, the two businessmen had the key to unlock the ball and chain that were dragging him under.

I WAS DRIVING ACROSS THE NEVADA desert with Dr Tohme-Tohme on 23 April 2008 for his first meeting with Michael and he obviously felt he had a good voice because he insisted on singing 'Lonely Teardrops' by Jackie Wilson all the way through California and across the state line. It's hard to tell someone they suck when they're about to throw your brother a financial lifeline. Diplomatically, I pushed in a CD and 'Earth Song' came on. *Nice timing, Michael.* For the rest of that journey, all I could think was that I was about to introduce chalk to cheese. Tohme-Tohme was blunt, opinionated and had a trip-wired temperament but I knew he wouldn't blow smoke up my brother's ass: he was not an enabler-type, and he took no bullshit. Just what Michael needed for the interim. Anyhow, this 'fixer' was brought in to facilitate the rescue of Neverland; that was his sole purpose as far as I was concerned.

As things turned out, that first meeting went well and Michael also spoke with Tom Barrack on the phone. He was reassured that all the 'talk' seemed likely to be followed up. Tohme-Tohme was decisive. He took the situation by the scruff of its neck and made clear that it was time to get this Jackson house in order. 'We'll fly in next week with Tom,' he said, 'and we'll start getting you back in control of your life.'

THE SPEED OF EVENTS WAS DIZZYING, and I could only thank the spiritual connection between Michael and me for what happened next. A particular email dropped into my lap and, if Neverland was to be saved, it had to be acted on. For reasons of discretion, I'll keep hidden its origins but it was sent to my management's email from the lending house that was attempting to talk with Michael about his pending foreclosure. It was seeking to co-operate with him to find a solution. A bank that cared. Go figure. If only it had been that easy in Michael's world.

That email to me was someone's last-ditch effort to help. Dated 29 April 2008, it read: *'Dear Jermaine, A team has been working on this file for two months but has been running into numerous road blocks through attorneys. It was very upsetting to see how something so beneficial to Michael was being turned down. It compelled me to get in contact with you and Michael.'*

I immediately alerted Tohme-Tohme. He – on behalf of Michael and without anyone else knowing – held a meeting a few days later with the lender in one of its boardrooms. It was there that the full scale of the emergency was revealed: Michael had until 10am the following day to pay off his $23 million ranch loan or they'd foreclose. He was under the impression that he had until 3pm. Had I not received that email, he would have waited until 3pm – and lost the ranch with a market value of $66.8 million. Then all the other dominoes would have started to fall. In that meeting, as witnessed by the lenders, Tohme-Tohme rang Tom Barrack via speakerphone and 'made him' wire the $23 million, apparently saying, 'You have to do this. I'm asking you to do this.' By 9.54am the next day – six minutes before the egg-timer ran empty – the $23 million was wired in exchange for Tom receiving 50 per cent ownership of Neverland. The ranch was saved and if I was overjoyed, I can only imagine what Michael must have felt.

When people ask why Tohme-Tohme was appointed his manager in June 2008, that was the chief reason because, regardless of what happened down the line, he and Tom Barrack were heroes. Not just in my eyes, but in Michael's too.

WHAT UNFOLDED OVER THE NEXT FEW weeks, as Tohme-Tohme got to grips with the true state of my brother's affairs, was eye-opening. It made me realise just how close Michael had come to financial Armageddon. 'Jermaine, the expenses are outrageous. We've not won the war yet,' said Tohme-Tohme, as he pored over every last detail. It was then that he told me Sony was docking exorbitant amounts for such things as stationery; $150,000 a month was being spent on security and another $150,000 a month on flowers – and Michael had only $600,000 in accessible cash in the bank. Michael was the classic example of cash-poor asset-rich: his Sony-ATV catalogue share was worth $500 million, his own MIJAC music $85 million, the now-saved ranch $66.8 million, and personal possessions, art and antiques were estimated at $20 million.

Thankfully, Tom Barrack's financial rescue changed everything. He didn't just save the ranch, he saved my brother's ass, because he also took on the operational costs. It gave Michael the breathing space he'd desperately needed.

Michael had come out the other side with all his assets intact. He might have suffered some scrapes, bruises and scares from all the debt and lawsuits, but he'd survived everything thrown at him.

He still had huge debts – borrowings tied to both of his music catalogues – but, with prudent planning and more cost-cutting, he could begin to concentrate on building a new future. Michael had turned the corner. He was going to be okay now – especially with the deal that lay around the corner. It was May 2008.

'TELL ME WHAT YOU THINK OF this,' he said that summer, on what would be my last visit to see him in Vegas. He pulled out some exterior and interior photographs of a mansion set in 16 acres in the middle of the city, with palm trees all around the pool. 'I really, really want it,' he said.

'You want to live full time in Vegas? How can you stand it out here?'

'I love it here ... look at the woodwork and the grounds,' he said enthusiastically, guiding me through the photos.

That was when I discovered the property belonged to Prince Jefri of Brunei.

'The woodwork alone is worth millions,' Michael added. The house did not match his previous taste – there was no hint of Tudor. It was palatial, with terracotta-tiled roofs. Everything in his life seemed to be about change and turning over a new leaf. If there was one similarity to Neverland, it was the lake, the fountains and waterfalls: he always needed to hear the sound of trickling water. Michael first spotted the house in 2007 and now, in 2008, he had set his heart on it. One year later, negotiations for its sale (however much it was later publicly denied) were ongoing and Michael was about to make a $15 million down-payment on what he called 'my dream home', funded by his 'This Is It' contract. America had been forgiven and he was putting down roots in Vegas for himself and the children.

THE MOMENT MICHAEL MET TOM BARRACK, they hit it off. I was amused when Tom said afterwards that he had been pleasantly surprised by him: he had half-expected some dizzy pop star, 'and I was impressed by how intelligent your brother is.'

'That's what everyone says,' I told him. Blame the headlines.

I'd joined Tom and Tohme-Tohme on the Colony Capital private jet from Santa Monica airport to Vegas. When we arrived you could tell from Michael's smile how grateful he was to these people, who had turned up in his life with such perfect timing. 'The first thing I see, Michael,' said Tom, 'is that you've had a lot of people around you who've taken advantage and I look forward to being a partner you can work with and trust.' They would speak that day, and many other days, about different ideas. Michael always became animated in the company of men who could make those ideas reality. Tom wanted to build a 'Thriller Tower' in the grounds of his Flamingo Hilton Hotel, complete with a 3-D experience. Apparently, it was to be part-funded by Sheikh Tarek of Dubai. 'It will be in your name, and you perform as and when you like,' said Tom.

At that, Michael reached behind him and brought out his Koh-i-Noor diamond: the Sony-ATV music catalogue. That slab of paper, about a foot thick, landed with a thud on the table; the sound of 400,000 songs making their weight felt. 'Are you interested in partnering with me in this?' asked Michael. A discussion ensued about the difficulties he'd experienced with Sony and how much money he'd borrowed against the catalogue. Tom said he was 'very interested to hear more', but I don't think it went any further than that. I wouldn't know for sure because, after that meeting, my services were no longer required, save for a few phone calls.

Tohme-Tohme seemed to turn against me the moment I installed an attorney in the mix. The past is our teacher and I wasn't going to allow my brother to be surrounded by two strangers without independent advice, however trustworthy they might be. Attorney Joel Katz had been a friend of mine since our Motown days and my counsel during the 'Victory' tour. He was the most honest attorney in town and I knew he'd watch over Michael. But Tohme-Tohme didn't appreciate it, saying he didn't 'want to meet with the son-of-a-bitch attorney'. That was his fiery side, which Michael would

412

come to know and dislike. Our new friend's temperament was never going to work long with any Jackson. In fact, Michael at first joked about how 'scary' and 'intimidating' he was, but I do know that Tohme-Tohme's heart was in the right place, however abrasive his manner might have been. I kept fighting for Joel's place at the table and finally got my way. Michael liked him, too, and nicknamed him 'Roosevelt': when Joel wore his spectacles, he reminded him of Franklin D. Roosevelt. If Michael gave you a nickname, you were sticking around.

But Tohme-Tohme's days were numbered from when he orchestrated an auction of Neverland's possessions in the hope of raising more money to cancel more debt. Michael approved it but understood that only furniture *in storage* would be sold. The next thing he knew was that a wholesale dismantling of Neverland was taking place. He was horrified and furious to learn that personal possessions of sentimental value, even his Lladró collection, were due to go under the hammer at Julien's auction house. He had to take legal action to halt the sale.

One month later, Tohme-Tohme would be fired by letter. Before that day arrived, though, I tried arranging to see Michael only to find that Tohme-Tohme had, like everyone else before him, turned gate-keeper. As he reminded me, 'I don't understand why you keep coming around. Your brother does not want to see you. If someone does not want to see you, I wouldn't keep humiliating myself and showing up …' I'll be honest, that one stung, but when I talked it through with Mother, she had wise advice, as always: 'Jermaine, look at it like this. You've helped your brother at a time when he really needed it and he knows that. Now walk away …' I was down but philosophical: I'd done my best and, regardless of the likes of Tohme-Tohme, who didn't understand the revolving door they were caught in, I was a constant in my brother's life and would remain so.

IT WAS AT A DINNER MICHAEL shared with Tom Barrack that the seed for 'This Is It' was planted, some time around March/April

2008, when all the refinancing talk was going on. It became clear to everyone, including my brother, that there was only one way to earn the big money that would secure his future: to go back on tour. Michael knew the realities. As he would later tell his makeup artist Karen Faye, he'd have ended up working at McDonald's otherwise. But he had long envisaged a residency tour. Before his court case, he had often said, 'Why can't I stay and perform in Paris? Then the fans from all over Europe can come see me.'

It was Tohme-Tohme who had got the ball rolling by reaching out to promoters AEG and Live Nation to determine what interest there would be. AEG had first flashed up on the family radar in 2004 after I met with them about a Broadway musical centred on the Jacksons' life story. As interested as they were, they wanted to await a verdict in the court case and that lack of belief just turned me off.

But, come 2008, Tom Barrack ultimately sealed the deal for Michael's tour by getting fellow billionaire Phil Anschutz on the phone during that dinner. Phil is the owner of Anschutz Entertainment Group (AEG) and Tom said, 'I've got Michael Jackson with me. What can you do for him?' That introduction kick-started an entire comeback strategy. On paper, it was a good union because Phil was a fellow humanitarian – he'd donated something like $100 million to charity – and he had a controlling interest in some of the world's largest sports and entertainment venues, including the Staples Center in LA, and the O2 arena in London. As one of America's wealthiest people, he also had a chequebook to match Michael's vision. That was probably why my brother received almost everything he asked for in a long-term deal worth a guaranteed minimum payment of $36.5 million 'with an upside potential of $300 million' based on ticket sales and other attached projects, which included a three-movie deal. From what I understood, he also ensured that a $15 million fee was built in as a down-payment on his new Vegas home. In other words, Michael didn't just negotiate a single residency tour, he ensured that his future was secured. It included an agreement to do other spot dates and two other tours with AEG. Some time after 2011, one of those extra tours was to be a final reunion with the Jackson 5, and that was for one reason only: Mother had said to him that she was nearing the age of 80 and before she left this earth, she wanted to see her sons tour together one last time. 'I promise we'll do that for you, Mother,' said Michael, and he was always a man of his word. He then planned on doing one more solo tour – his true final curtain. 'After that, I will be done – done!' he said, looking towards an official musical retirement age of 55. Then he'd crack Hollywood with his movie ideas.

So, when people claim my brother was suicidal with no plans to look forward to, they cannot be more wrong. On the back of 'This Is It' in London, the money would come in, a new house was being bought, and there were exciting plans to keep him busy until 2014. He had everything to live for, and most especially the wonderful life he was building for Prince, Paris and 'Blanket'.

WHEN MY BROTHER TOOK TO THE 'This Is It' podium to make his comeback announcement in London, I knew, watching in LA, that he was teasing 'the final curtain', but also that something wasn't quite right with him. His demeanour, and lateness, that afternoon also caused comment in the press. There was speculation, too, as to why he had appeared for only five minutes, with some claiming he was having second thoughts. That was simply not true.

Earlier the same day, Michael had learned that his dearest friend and guitar player David Williams had died. He was shattered. David was an integral part of his signature sound, especially that guitar lick on 'Billie Jean'; he was one of those rare guitarists who can just lock into a groove. If Michael could hum it, David could play it. Perfectly. He was like keyboardist and musical director Brad Buxer, drummer Jonathan Moffett and audio engineer Michael Prince: my brother simply could not imagine doing a tour without him. Yet now he had to walk out onstage and announce his comeback, knowing David was gone. As ever, he was the consummate professional. He pulled himself together and put on his show face for five brave minutes: he walked out as the overexcited performer, said his piece, saluted the fans and left with a wave. However, he broke down in tears when he returned to his suite.

But at least the world knew: Michael Jackson was back. Toss aside the wheelchair. Stand by, London. Stand by, world!

FAMILY DAY ON 14 MAY 2009 was a special occasion to celebrate 60 years of marriage between Mother and Joseph. We had told our parents that we were treating them to a quiet dinner with their children at an Indian restaurant called Chakra in Beverly Hills, but Janet had prepared a surprise. What they didn't know was that the whole family, first and second generations, were waiting in one room in silence. Michael was with his children towards the back of the crowd, loving the suspense as the door opened, Mother walked in and everyone cheered. The room was set up like a mini wedding reception, with a top table running across one end, facing three vertical rows of long tables. It was a fun, relaxed, family occasion.

Michael was by now four weeks into tour rehearsals at Center Staging in Burbank, LA. All of the dancers had been auditioned and chosen, signing a two-year contract in line with the plans for what would take place after London. The first thing he had worked on, with LaVelle Smith Junior, was a routine for 'Dangerous' – he wanted to devise a new adaptation. He was apparently doing 'amazing work' and 'kicking ass' – working on twirls and other moves – showing tour choreographer Travis Payne how hard he had been rehearsing in preparation. When I spoke with my brother at the Indian restaurant, there was no question that he was fit, healthy and focused. He was skinny, but only in an athletic sense, and the photos that still stand on an end table in my living room confirm it. More importantly, he was *genuinely excited* about 'doing something special for the fans' and there was talk of special guest appearances by the likes of Slash and Alicia Keys. At least, that was an idea he had been toying with.

The only thing he complained about was that he'd signed up to do '10 shows only' as advertised but somewhere along the line, due to the demand for tickets, AEG had added an extra 40 dates. Even they sold out within five hours on-line. Michael said no one had checked with him first, but at no point did he give me the impression that the schedule was too punishing or beyond him, because it wasn't. Not for a man in his condition. Two shows a week, which was what it was at the start, was a country-club schedule for my brother and it was exactly what he'd done on 'HIStory', but now he didn't have to travel because he was rooted in one city. He was 50, but he was dancing in rehearsals like it was 1996 all over again.

'This Is It' should have been a walk in the park for an entertainer like Michael. He had found a mansion in Kent, which was a 30-minute drive from the arena, and I know he was looking forward to exploring the south of England with the kids. That was what really mattered to him. He couldn't wait for Prince, Paris and 'Blanket' to see him perform, but he'd ensured that he'd have plenty of quality time with them. At this time in his life, he'd found a rare work–life balance. Gone were the days of staying up and writing songs until 3am. He always had breakfast and dinner with his kids, and while they went to bed at around 8pm, he soon followed around nine. He had been sleeping soundly (his insomnia was only ever tour induced) and he seemed the most centred and content I had seen him in years.

I had got talking with him at the bar before we all started eating, and I was raving to him about his song 'Fly Away'. I started singing its harmony – *Baby don't make me, Baby don't make me, Baby don't make me flyyyyyy awayy*. He started to join in, and we were going back and forth, just like old times, and laughing. 'I love the way you do backgrounds, Michael,' I told him.

'That means a lot coming from you,' he said. 'I love the way you do backgrounds, too.'

During dinner, he was seated with the children at Jackie's table and Janet was on the far side of the room when, out of nowhere, she started making this weird Jim Carrey-type sound that was half-scream, half-cackle … and Michael put his hand to his mouth, chuckling. It was clearly an in-joke they shared from way back and the more Janet did it, the more he laughed. Like brother and sister of old. Eventually Michael was laughing so hard – throwing his head back, unable to contain himself – that his hoots were all you could hear. Freeze-frame that moment, and hold it in time. I love that this is the abiding memory that has stayed with me.

When it was time for him to leave, everyone hugged and said their goodbyes. 'You're all coming to London, right?' Michael asked us.

'Yeah! We'll be there!' I said, as we all did.

'Okay, everyone. See you in London!'

CHAPTER TWENTY-TWO

Gone Too Soon

I WAS OUT NEAR PASADENA, THE city at the foot of the San Bernardino Mountains, at a business meeting with people from China when a good friend – CNN host Larry King – called my wife's cell-phone to ask if we knew anything 'about a TMZ report saying Michael has been being rushed to UCLA hospital'.

I wasn't immediately alarmed because it was hardly the first time the media had got excited about my brother being 'rushed' to hospital. But then I called Mother and caught her hurrying out of the door at Hayvenhurst. As soon as I heard her voice, I knew something was very wrong: she sounded fraught with anxiety.

'Jermaine! I'm rushing down now. I'll call you when I get there! Leave now,' she said.

Halima and I jumped in the car, not knowing what to think for the next hour or so as I sat in the passenger seat and she fought traffic, waiting for Mother or someone to call back.

En route, attorney Joel Katz called. 'Jermaine, I hear it's really, really bad,' but he knew little else. Details were scant, it seemed, and I couldn't bring myself to turn on the radio and listen to the media grapevine.

Halima was driving like she owned the highway, and I'm glad she was because I would have been incapable behind the wheel. I felt physically sick and I was trembling – which, looking back, was probably my body's way of bracing me.

Janet called from New York and she was losing it, too. I don't even remember what was said but we seemed to be talking only to hold on to one another. No sooner had I ended that call than the phone rang again. Mother's number flashed up – the only time in my life that I didn't want to take a call when her name illuminated the screen.

'Mother?'

'HE'S DEEAAAD!'

I don't know what has haunted me most about that moment: hearing the hardest news or the sound of Mother's pain, a guttural wail that I can't describe.

I started yelling. 'HE'S DEAD? MICHAEL IS DEAD?'

'He's dead.' Softer now.

Halima was crying. I was crying, and the rest of the journey to the hospital was a blur. I remember seeing about 12 news helicopters in the sky, circling the same spot. The surrounding streets in Westwood were taped off and the crowds were growing, all walking in the same direction. When a policeman spotted us, he waved us through and Halima dropped me by an alleyway that led to the hospital's side door as she went to park. Half running, half walking, I hurried inside, down corridors and through double doors.

'Where is she? Where's my mother?' I called to a nurse.

She showed me into a conference room. Inside, Mother was alone, just sitting there in the silence, at the far end of the table, wearing her dark glasses: not crying, just staring into space. There was no possibility of denial now.

I walked over, knelt beside her and hugged her as tight as I could. She was rigid. I kept holding her – we both needed comforting – until my cousin Trent walked in, allowing me to leave her in his strong company. All I could think about now was getting to Michael.

Outside in the corridor, La Toya rushed past and then Randy, looking shell-shocked. 'Somebody did this,' he kept saying. 'Somebody did this.'

That comment didn't really register. I wasn't capable of listening. Randy showed me the way to the room where our brother lay, pointing to a door that he clearly didn't want to walk through a second time.

It was like a sitting room, with a lamp and a sofa, but a window looked into a room within the room. La Toya was already there, standing alone, leaning down into Michael's face, like she was talking to him. He was lying on a trolley in a hospital gown. Momentarily I felt like an observer, looking through that window, as if being on the outside somehow didn't make it real. But then La Toya looked up, tears streaming down her face.

I steadied myself, took a breath, and entered the side door to the right. I went over to the other side of Michael, reaching down to take his hand, rubbing his still-soft skin, like you do when you comfort someone. I couldn't believe how skeletal he was. He seemed half the size he had been a month earlier. If a stranger had walked into the room, they would have assumed he had been ravaged by cancer or anorexia. Or, as one of the paramedics would later say, that he had been 'a hospice patient'.

What's happened to you? I knew no amount of rigorous dancing could have left him in this state. Grief didn't allow me to process the impossibility of how he looked. I was still coming to terms with seeing him lifeless. I leaned down and kissed him on the forehead, telling him I loved him. I found I couldn't pull away. I lifted one of his eyelids because I wanted to look into his eyes, 'see' him one last time.

Look at me, Michael. Look at me.

I rested my forehead against his and wept.

I did this despite the Islamic teachings that told me I was looking into a shell whose spirit had already flown; a spirit that was

421

probably looking down on me, telling me not to cry, telling me he was okay. I remembered how we both said we liked stepping out of our bodies to observe and critique ourselves. That was what I thought he was doing now, watching over us.

Prince, Paris and 'Blanket' walked in with a nurse. What they said and did deserves to remain private, between them and their father. But the moment I saw those kids crumple, I had to get out of there and leave them with their auntie. I wasn't strong enough for them and I could feel my legs giving way.

People describe grief as a physical pain, but I didn't know how wrong they were until that day. It's not a wound that can be stitched and there is no surgeon who can heal it; it's an emotional pain. It's a resident pain that just moves in and you have to look at and sit with it every day for the rest of your life. And, for us, we'd have Michael's fans look at us and measure our grief, to see if we were grieving enough for the grief they felt. Because, beyond those hospital walls, an entire world of fans – the millions of strangers he referred to as his second family – were inconsolable, too.

Outside in the corridor, I saw a cast of suits standing around: AEG's CEO Randy Phillips, Frank Dileo, the manager fired long ago by Michael but rehired by AEG, and Tohme-Tohme, also recently fired by my brother, but I didn't have a chance to focus on them. Someone walked over to me and said they wanted me to read a press statement that confirmed Michael's death. 'Of course,' I said. 'His fans need to know.'

'We just have to find a room without a window, because there's so many fans out there that if you go out front, there'd be a crush against the glass,' I was told.

Some fans have wondered why I made the announcement and not a doctor. All I can say is that it was the idea of the attorneys and the medical staff, and it felt right to me that someone with a personal connection to Michael should do it. Let the fan community hear it from family first.

I stood in a back room, waiting to walk on, going over lines written for me. Just reading them once to myself left me short of breath. I couldn't process this script. *He was ready to make his comeback and prove everyone wrong. He can't be dead. This can't have happened. How can …?*

'They're ready for you now, Jermaine,' someone shouted.

I walked in, greeted by the flutter of cameras. As I stood before a cluster of microphones and spotlights, I took a deep breath and started: 'My brother, the legendary King of Pop, Michael Jackson, passed away on Thursday 25 June 2009, at 2.26pm. It is believed he suffered a cardiac arrest in his home. However, the cause of his death is unknown until the results of the autopsy are known. His personal physician, who was with him at the time, attempted to resuscitate my brother, as did the paramedics who transported him to hospital. Upon arrival, a team of doctors attempted to resuscitate him for a period of more than one hour. They were unsuccessful …'

We would later come to understand the futility of these attempts, because Michael had been dead before anyone dialled 911. It was around 12.05pm when he had apparently stopped breathing in his bedroom and, it seems, 12.21pm before an emergency call was placed.

After the press conference, I walked back to the room where Mother was. Joseph was on his way from Vegas. She hadn't moved from her seat, but she responded as I walked in this time. 'Hi, baby, you okay?' she asked, reverting to the mother's role, making sure everyone else was all right. We were sitting there, holding hands, and she told me how she had prayed all the way to the hospital for Michael to be alive. Tears rolled down her face as she re-lived that hope with me.

Our conversation was interrupted when a tall black guy walked into the room, wearing a heavy face. Security, I told myself. He sat down, looking uncomfortable. Everything about him was awkward. He was across the table from me and sitting side on to Mother. It dawned on me that this was Dr Conrad Murray, my brother's personal physician. He said he wanted to express his condolences. He had travelled in the back of the ambulance and had broken the news to Mother when she arrived: 'I'm sorry, Mrs Jackson, but he's gone.'

I would later learn that he had been in my brother's life long before 'This Is It' was ever planned. Apparently he had been called out for the first time in Vegas to treat Paris for something and Michael had retained him soon afterwards. At Michael's request, he was hired by AEG for the tour. I don't know what, if any, checks they made in regards to his suitability but, by having him on their payroll, they were, in my opinion, responsible for his duty of care to their artists.

The house where Michael died was in Carolwood Drive, Holmby Hills, a neighbourhood next to Beverly Hills. It was a mansion that AEG had rented for him and his children while he was in rehearsal – the previous month he had stayed at the Bel Air Hotel. I couldn't face going there after his death; none of the brothers could. In our numbed state, we came together at my house and comforted one another.

Meanwhile, Mother, Janet and La Toya felt the need to be there. In fact, La Toya's boyfriend Jeffre Phillips stayed there overnight by himself for two weeks, presumably to guard against vultures.

Around July, it would become clear that the house was a no-go zone for anyone because it had become 'a crime scene': the LAPD elevated its accidental-death enquiries into a homicide investigation.

The autopsy report ruled that Michael had had a healthy heart and had died from 'acute propofol intoxication', with no other factor related to the immediate cause of death. The media would go on to portray him falsely as a 'junkie', trying to make the link with prescription-drug usage but that, and drugs like Demerol, were not the reason why his heart stopped: what was clear is that the anaesthetic propofol was everywhere in his system.

I didn't even know what propofol was, but I've since learned that it is not a recreational drug and it was not prescription medicine. propofol is what people are given intravenously as an anaesthetic before major surgery, or doctors use it for sedation. This, I would find out, is what Michael relied on to be knocked out when desperate for sleep. According to the instructions it should be given only by a trained anaesthetist and the patient's intake must be carefully monitored with the appropriate medical equipment in place.

Michael was usually beset by sleeping problems only on tour so it was, to the best of my knowledge, a departure for him to be using this kind of sleep-inducer during rehearsals. It's also worth noting that the last time Michael would have needed something like propofol would have been during his last tour, 'HIStory', in 1996. It didn't surprise me that his insomnia was returning in the run-up to his London dates because of the unimaginable pressure to which he was subjected, most of it self-imposed. He was his own biggest rival in the relentless drive to be perfect within the great comeback he'd envisaged.

Pressure. It would become a theme in everything I went on to discover about the final days of his life.

We, as a family, would face a struggle in our pursuit of the facts. Understandably, the LAPD had its investigation to conduct and Dr Conrad Murray's actions would be central to its enquiries. But I didn't expect to run into a wall when I wanted to know what really happened during rehearsals for 'This Is It'. We needed to understand how, from 14 May when we had last seen him, Michael could lose his life – and all that weight – so rapidly. He had gone from 150–155 pounds to what his autopsy report said was 136 pounds: that is not only abnormal, it's frightening. For a man of his height (5ft 9in), it was thinner than anorexic-thin.

Many fans, understandably passionate to know the truth, have criticised us for not banging the drum loud enough for justice, but it has taken two years of quiet work to establish a mere outline of events. What I shall share with you next is what I have discovered. It has made me understand that the movie *This Is It*, showing Michael in rehearsals, was not the whole picture. Like everything else in his life, it was just another clever edit. That footage might have provided a glimpse of what could have exploded onstage in London, and I know it can be argued it's a great film that portrayed who Michael was as an artist. But that well-chosen footage didn't show the truth of what went on at rehearsals: that was a whole other disturbing story.

BY THE START OF JUNE, REHEARSALS were taking place at the Forum in Inglewood and Michael was apparently still focused and business-like. Everything was going wonderfully well. Some people who saw him dance said he wasn't on fire, but he had always held back, reserving his 100 per cent for the concerts. That was why no one saw any electric moves or signature magic. Anyone who truly knew his method would have known this was his normal half-speed.

By now four opening tour dates had been pushed back and there was speculation that the reason was health-related, but the truth, which didn't please my brother, was that pre-show rehearsals in London had been booked in error at Wembley Arena. No artist was going to perform without rehearsals at the actual venue, so the dates had to be moved to build in essential rehearsal time at the O2.

Outwardly, and apart from the insomnia that was creeping in and getting him down as usual, there was no alarm about his health at this stage, even if some people around him were worrying about how loaded the schedule was getting. In fact, Michael had told his friends that he 'was going to have a word and change things', so those concerns had been heard.

One potential problem with Michael was that only a handful of people were recently used to working with him and I suspect there was little familiarity with his character and particular ways. This probably had something to do with the fact that AEG seemed intent on bringing in some of its own people. Director Kenny Ortega hadn't worked with my brother in a long time. Musical director Michael Bearden was chosen over Michael's preferred Greg Phillingains, and choreographer Travis Payne, who last worked with Michael during 'Dangerous', was left in charge when my brother's preferred choice of LaVelle Smith Junior was dismissed. Meanwhile, I don't think AEG CEO Randy Phillips could have had any idea who or what he was dealing with, except 'Michael Jackson'. Outside of the dressing room personnel, there was a sense of 'starting from scratch' instead of trusting proven practices from the 'HIStory' tour. This was important: to get the most from Michael and to alleviate some of the pressure he put on himself, he had always needed to feel comfortable with the set-up around him. He needed people who understood him and how he worked. On 'This Is It', I'm not sure he felt that on every level, especially with some of the art direction, costume choices and the musical mixes coming back in his ears. As he confided in someone close to him after rehearsals: 'Wait until I get to London. I'm changing everything! We're going to do things my way.'

Michael's strategy was to honour the 10 dates he'd agreed to and then he was 'going to renegotiate the contract' based on the 40 dates he hadn't approved, knowing that public demand and the headlines would be behind him. That was what he told people he trusted, and that was why he seemed strangely indifferent at meetings to discuss the concerts. He was biding his time.

I also know Michael was not happy when AEG brought in his old manager Frank Dileo and then, a week before his death, when his ex-attorney John Branca arrived on the scene (and would later become an executor of Michael's estate together with our old school friend, John McClain). Michael had dismissed them yet I think AEG clearly felt that it needed familiar faces whose experience could 'build a wall around him to protect him', as one person involved with AEG put it. I think there was a sense that Michael needed handling so AEG turned to those with historic, if not recent, knowledge of him. The move seemed more about bringing peace of mind to the promoter than to Michael. John Branca would later say that Michael asked him to come up with an 'agenda' of ideas for the future, which seemed odd when a five-year plan was already sketched out. Maybe that was my brother's way of testing his ex-attorney. Either way, Michael had had a game-plan since 2008, regardless of what he did or didn't tell John in their seven days of reacquaintance.

When Frank Dileo showed up, the people Michael had trusted at rehearsals were nudged out and 'blind' to his schedule because Frank treated everyone on a need-to-know basis. This was no doubt a protective measure in Frank's mind, but it bred a feeling of unease in others that Michael seemed to be under the command of someone who couldn't read him, his habits or his nuances. To illustrate how little Frank knew about the modern-day Michael, he suggested my brother's moans about the tour going from 10 to 50 dates weren't relevant because 'he'd had the contract read to him and knew what was in it.' But by mid-June there seemed to be bigger concerns than clauses in contracts because Michael's health inexplicably started to deteriorate. It all seems to have begun when Michael missed rehearsals on 13, 14 and 15 June. Even on the days when he did show, there were occasions when he'd turn up at 8pm for a 2pm start, as if just getting out of the house was a struggle. This coincided with the time when, instead of there being two guards around Michael, his security became 10-strong – and no one seems to know why. I don't know if it was at Michael's request or his security, but someone was clearly worried about something to bump up the numbers in this way.

It was when Michael was at the Forum on 17 June that someone mentioned the noticeable deterioration in his appearance when he took to the stage. 'That's not Michael up there – he's like a ghost. You seen how skinny he's getting?'

During the week that followed, further worrying signs stacked up for those who knew how on-point and articulate he normally was. In the routine for 'Thriller', he turned left when he knew he had to turn right. That was odd in itself, but then he did it a second time. He also started repeating himself – a sentence or a phrase – like someone with Obsessive Compulsive Disorder … but he didn't have OCD. He struggled to finish one song and he sometimes needed a teleprompter for lyrics. Plus, he had to be helped up and down ramps and flights of stairs. This weakness was also apparent in the 'Thriller' routine when he was supposed to come out from beneath a giant bug which was made feather-light for him to lift – but he couldn't push it up without assistance.

His inner circle started to worry that something was wrong because his behaviour was so disturbingly out of character. In fairness to AEG, maybe its people didn't observe the same signs as those with a closer proximity? But, even if that was the case, people would still sound the alarm bells to those in authority to actually do something to help.

Meanwhile, at home, different observations were made. Paris remembers, 'Daddy was always cold,' and always slept in front of the fireplace. I know that makeup artist Karen Faye, who knew my brother better than anyone, noticed how cold he was at rehearsals. Even Michael must have been worried because he called a nurse from home, complaining one half of his body was hot, the other cold. It is interesting that he sought the advice of a nurse, not Dr Murray. Why would he reach out to a nurse instead of his personal physician? It doesn't make sense to me.

The nurse told Michael to go to a hospital. For whatever reason, he chose not to.

Meanwhile, back at rehearsals, it was clear that somewhere along the line, patience was running thin with Michael's absences and lateness. This is where I suspect – based on what I've heard from people who were there – that AEG's people believed Michael's condition was related to the drug dependency they had presumably read about and believed. I can think of no other reason for the collective blindness that followed.

Certainly, no one was giving Michael the kid-glove treatment. Instead, I know that he felt belittled on several occasions and he was also yelled at, as witnessed by people who were there. On one occasion, he deliberately spoke into his mic as he walked offstage: 'I just want someone to be nice to me today ...'

A voice from the floor yelled back: 'If we could just have a coherent person here today!'

'They wouldn't speak to me like that if Joseph was here,' Michael muttered, off mic.

At times Michael hated the way he was spoken to.

Whatever assumptions people made about the reasons for his condition, how could anyone have missed his plummeting weight? I know the people around him voiced real concern about his weight, vocally and in writing. On one occasion when someone expressed worry that he wasn't eating enough, they were told – out of Michael's earshot – 'Just get him a bucket of chicken!'

The thinner Michael became, the colder he got. He began shivering onstage; he was given a thick coat to wear. In fact, he ended up wearing three layers of clothing to keep warm while rehearsing in a place where everyone else was baking. Presumably this was why Kenny Ortega noticed he was 'chilled' on 19 June. 'Chilled' was his choice of word, but I've been given an alternative description by someone else who was there: 'Michael wasn't chilled – he was like a block of ice to touch.'

That was when someone, without any AEG authorisation, placed a discreet call to a doctor whom Michael had consulted in the past. After the symptoms had been explained to him, the doctor said it sounded as if Michael was suffering from 'toxic poisoning of the brain' and should get to a hospital. AEG could never have known about this call, but for reasons that remain maddening to me, he didn't go.

It is clear to me that something was very wrong. Even taking into account the belief of some people at rehearsals that Michael had a prescription-drug dependency, the suspected neurological symptoms, the frighteningly low body temperature and drastic loss of weight – which he had never before displayed – don't line up with the theory of a prescription-drug dependency.

Not that Dr Murray was giving AEG any sense that there was an emergency. Instead, after Michael was sent home on 19 June, he sent them a fax saying that Michael needed to rest for two days and would return once rehearsals had moved from the Forum to the Staples Center. Some around my brother also said he tried to put on a brave front for AEG and 'could appear as sharp as a tack' on occasions in that final week. As one person put it, 'Michael didn't want anyone to think anything was wrong.'

But it's still hard for me not to worry and wonder in light of his suspicious death. I have lain awake at night wondering what was making him so ill. Was his doctor giving him so much anaesthetic that it was slowly poisoning his system? Could my brother have known how much propofol was being injected into him?

Whatever was happening to him, those closest to Michael at rehearsals – Karen Faye in Makeup and Michael Bush and Dennis Thompson in Wardrobe – were seen to be frantic with worry, pleading for someone in authority to intervene. It was obvious that something was seriously wrong when in that final week while still at the Forum, Michael was seen being taken out of the building, his arms draped around the shoulders of two bodyguards, looking like someone who had either collapsed or was too weak to stand.

That was on an afternoon when Travis Payne stepped into Michael's shoes to do the run-through. But still, to the best of my knowledge, no one thought to get my brother urgent medical attention – presumably they were relying on Dr Murray.

Had anyone reached out to us – Michael's family – we would have got him to hospital. It is hard for me to accept that no one called us. But for me the responsibility to act was AEG's because I cannot escape the strongest sense that it owed him a duty of care and that his welfare lay squarely with AEG.

I know that most people – and the LAPD investigation – have so far focused on the fatal events of 25 June, but the disturbing incidents and symptoms in the days prior suggest that something was seriously wrong long before that. And yet rehearsals would carry on regardless and switch to the Staples Center in downtown LA.

If anything, instead of easing up on Michael, the pressure would now increase. As someone involved with AEG told me after witnessing everything backstage: 'Michael was this great bird with two broken wings standing near the edge of a cliff. And they kept pushing him, and pushing him and pushing him, expecting him to fly and soar … but he would fall.'

THE MORE I HEAR ABOUT THOSE final rehearsals, the clearer it seems there was a focus on getting to London and hitting that target of 50 concert dates. Somewhere in the pressure that everyone felt, AEG viewed the King of Pop as a performing robot and lost sight of the human being.

Out of anybody, the director Kenny Ortega was seen at rehearsals doing what he could to help: once sending Michael home to rest, asking on-camera if there was anything anyone could do for him. He also ensured Michael ate something by cutting up his chicken and feeding him and he even gave him a foot massage. It was clear that Kenny felt Michael needed to eat. But I believe AEG should have gone further because it seemed blindingly obvious to anyone that this tour had to be – needed to be, should have been – cancelled, because my brother was in no fit state to continue.

Instead there seemed to be an attitude of 'the show must go on' as different AEG delegations were sent to Michael's home on 18 and 20 June to discuss his no-shows for rehearsals. The purpose of these summits was not to offer tea and sympathy but to 'have strong words with Michael' and remind him of his contractual obligations. It was in one of those meetings that he was 'read the riot act' – Michael's words – and, based on conversations he shared afterwards, he was left in no doubt that if he didn't step up and start delivering, they would not only pull the plug but he was in danger of 'losing everything'.

This was, apparently, the 'tough love' my brother needed if the concert was to meet its obligations. 'Tough love' was the expression some people used when referring to how Michael should be handled.

I guess the definition of 'losing everything' included his prized music catalogue. His contract with AEG stated that if he failed to perform, he would be liable for all production costs and lost revenue, meaning his assets – and most notably his Sony/ATV catalogue – were collateral up for the taking. In this scenario, with Michael's 50 per cent share going to AEG by default, Sony would have found itself with an 'undesirable partner' and would no doubt have tried to exercise the option rights it had taken out. If Michael failed or was 'finished', he would have lost his precious catalogue.

Whatever he was told during his meeting of 18 June, it was enough to make him show up for rehearsal at 9.30pm. I doubt he was well enough to rehearse but he wanted to show willingness. He did nothing but watch a pyrotechnic show and discuss certain concepts, staying until 2am. That was typical of Michael: not wanting to let anyone down, not wanting to be perceived as a failure, not speaking up for himself when he had clearly felt cajoled into attending. As one person there told me: 'He tried his best to fulfil his obligations, especially when he felt there would now be consequences if he didn't step up.'

Meanwhile, loyal fans who followed him everywhere had started to notice his deterioration, based on the briefest of meetings outside the rehearsal space. As one fan said in an email to Karen Faye: 'I think there is something wrong with Michael's health ... I think he is at the point where something bad and regrettable could happen to him. Please help him.'

What the fans couldn't know was that people like Karen did not just speak up; they were heard forcibly pleading for something to be done. I know that someone went to Kenny Ortega and Frank Dileo, and asked for a doctor and a psychologist to be brought in. This person was assured everything was under control.

On the final rehearsal day at the Forum, on Saturday 20 June, Kenny Ortega clearly did see something that concerned him when he visited Michael at home because one hour after he left, choreographer Travis Payne received a phone call from Kenny telling him to urgently get to the house, leaving his assistant in charge to do the run-through that day. Whatever happened and whatever was witnessed are known only to those who were present, but that same afternoon the musical director Michael Bearden made a bizarre announcement to dancers and crew on stage, telling them: 'Everyone needs to pray for Michael and send him good wishes.' This was four days before Michael died.

Why would he say such a thing? And why – if we're at the point of prayers and good wishes – would the tour continue? Yet the show apparently had to go on.

And then, again bizarrely, everything changed on the final two days of rehearsals, the 23rd and 24th. Michael suddenly showed up at the Staples Center looking upbeat, sharp and reinvigorated. It was this version of my brother that the world saw during the *This Is It* movie because it was those last two days that were filmed and captured as the best rehearsal footage; the temporary two-day truth for the box office, not the horrible truth of the preceding weeks.

Not that this sudden transformation was good enough for AEG. Instead, it kept up its pressure, posting a man in a suit inside Michael's dressing room on 24 June. I cannot imagine how invasive this must have been on what would be the last full day of his life. Presumably, Randy Phillips wanted someone to keep an eye on Michael and maybe this was in the interests of his welfare, but Michael clearly detested this measure: he resorted to holding discussions in the bathroom, away from the stranger posted to monitor him.

That last night of his life, rehearsals ran late because Michael was preoccupied in the 'video world' section, where he signed off on the visuals and computer images that would come up on the big screen behind him during concerts. Meanwhile, a whole bunch of men in suits turned up that night to watch the rehearsal. It seemed an odd formality to those who were there but presumably these were corporate clients who were AEG-related, coming to provide some kind of assessment which would have added further pressure on Michael.

Once Michael was finished in the video world, he went to his dressing room and got prepared for a full dress rehearsal, which he carried out without a hitch, it seems, before he left the Staples Center at just after midnight on 25 June. One of the last people to speak with him that evening said: 'Michael left looking forward to tomorrow. Apart from his obvious weight loss, there was no obvious sign of anything wrong those final two days and that was something his management, AEG and his inner circle would all agree on.' Michael told people he'd be in the next day to work on his vocals – the last thing he needed to tie up before the show was ready for London and the tour's new start date, 13 July. By then, he should have signed, sealed and delivered on his dream home in Vegas. I understand from people at rehearsals that after leaving the Staples Center, he was due to visit Tohme-Tohme to sign the papers. Tohme-Tohme was, apparently, holding the $15 million down-payment in a safe. I don't know whether Michael went there as intended or simply straight home, but it might explain why his ex-manager was at the hospital the next day. It shows that Michael's eyes were firmly on his future, should anyone suggest he was tempted to commit suicide.

When Michael got home, he struggled to sleep, with Dr Murray at his side. Within the next 12 hours, he would be dead. He was found on the left side of the bed, where Dr Murray says he tried to carry out CPR. On the floor, near one of the bed's feet, there was a tube of toothpaste and a string of wooden beads. His laptop and a pair of glasses were on the bedside table. There was also a urine sample in the room. Next to the bed, a tan sofa was, apparently, Dr Murray's seat.

One fact that has been established from preliminary hearings is that Dr Murray used his iPhone a lot through the early hours of that fateful day. One call was to a woman he'd recently met, logged at 11.51am, some 15 minutes before my brother apparently stopped breathing.

She said she was talking to him when she realised he wasn't listening any more but the line was still open and she heard 'a commotion – I heard coughing and mumbling' and she did not believe the coughing came from her doctor friend. She tried calling and texting him back, but received no reply.

The circumstances of Michael's death were rough enough without us learning about events in the run-up to 25 June. We're finding it impossible to accept Michael's inexplicable decline and that one company didn't spot that something was seriously wrong.

As a family, and for peace of mind, we would like to know who else – if anyone – entered and left the house on the night of Michael's death, but although the LAPD are treating his death as homicide, its investigators decided to retain only the four minutes of CCTV footage showing Dr Conrad Murray's expected arrival. Unless the authorities surprise us, it seems all other footage has been erased. It is hard for us to understand why such crucial footage could be wiped like that. It makes us wonder if every stone has been turned in the LAPD's investigation: it has so far concentrated on one doctor, and one night. I guess time will tell, but our only hope is that, ultimately, justice doesn't fail Michael, like everyone else seems to have done.

EPILOGUE

Smile

AS WE WERE ALWAYS TOLD, a song, story and a life need a beginning, a middle and an end. Now we had a life to honour: the life of a kid who started off, just like everyone else, with an impossible dream. But as Michael's death returned him to where he belonged, at No.1, I came to realise that Mr Gordy hadn't always been right: not every story has an end. Not Michael's, anyhow. He is, through his music – that which is past, and that which is yet to come – immortal. As he always wanted to be. His life, voice and message have a sense of continuation even in death and it's almost as if he's locked himself away in creative mode, writing songs up at Neverland. Sometimes that's what I tell myself.

So, when it came to planning his memorial service for the world, it wasn't about writing 'the end', it was about the send-off and honouring his legacy. We knew how close he had come to pulling off the comeback everyone had doubted: 'The most amazing show anyone will have ever seen,' as one of his inner circle said. And now we had to do our best, in limited time, to put on a memorial service to match no other. We had a family meeting and took our usual show of hands on the ambitious plans we threw around. Let's hold a service at the Washington Monument for one of America's greats. Let's do it at LA's Coliseum within its vast bowl. Let's hold a procession through the streets of LA. Let's drive his coffin from the city all the way to Neverland for one last trip home so the fans can line the streets and highways and throw flowers, just like they did with Gandhi and Princess Diana. But the ideas either didn't earn a majority vote or there were logistics to think about. The LAPD said it was expecting at least two million fans to pour into the city to commemorate him. 'We've never dealt with something on that scale before,' they said. All the police chiefs and sheriffs from different counties gathered in my living room to discuss street closures and security.

During the passionate discussions, I looked at Mother. She seemed, at first, uncomfortable with the size of our vision and we could tell that she was torn between her beliefs about praising only Jehovah and the need to give her son the global respect, love and remembrance that his star demanded. She was wondering if we were going a bit too far. Bless her. In her eyes, Michael was only ever one of her nine babies who had grown up and done well. She, like Michael, wasn't one for fuss when it came to private events and I think it was hard for her to reconcile a very private grief with an incredible public demand.

It was Janet who stood up and said respectfully that we were going large, regardless of what the people at the Kingdom Hall might think, because Michael belonged to his fans as much as he belonged to us. Mother – who had always told us that there would be no Jacksons without the fans – smiled. 'Okay, okay,' she said.

'And before the public memorial, we will hold a private viewing and family service in accordance with the Jehovah's Witness faith,' we reassured her.

'Okay, okay – I think that's what Michael would have wanted,' she said – and he would.

It was always going to be impossible to stage a memorial that was accessible for all Michael's fans so we had to settle for television to share the event with the world. When AEG stepped forward and offered the Staples Center – before we knew what had gone down at rehearsals – it seemed the most practical option at short notice and, as home to the Grammy Awards, this was a fitting venue.

We spent many of the days beforehand at Hayvenhurst, sorting out the plans and timetables, and often gathered in Michael's old theatre, where we had first watched with him the video for 'Thriller'. I guess it was the most confined room in the house. When we reached a consensus, many of us were exhausted by all the talking and planning. There was a moment when Mother and Joseph were just sitting together in the middle of those red velvet seats and Mother broke down. My father put both his arms around her and then we all joined them in a big family hug.

Eventually Joseph stood up. 'Stop it now! You all going to make me cry,' he said.

For the first time in our lives we saw our father show emotion: there were tears in his eyes. That was some moment. Joseph gets a hard time in the press, but Michael thought the world of him. People forget he's human, too: we're not a business, we're a family, and he is our father.

Those days in late June and early July passed so quickly – I have no idea how we got organised in time with AEG and all the friends, music and memories. But, come 7 July, we would stand backstage with Michael one last time, waiting to go on before a packed arena and a worldwide television audience: the brothers united, as it had been at the beginning.

BEFORE THE PUBLIC MEMORIAL, WE HELD a family-only service at Forest Lawn Cemetery, where we would later lay Michael to rest. I had always wanted Neverland to be his final resting place and I flew up there to scout for an appropriate plot. I found a site not far from the train station, near a paved area with the ranch logo – the boy in a crescent moon. It was, to me, the ideal location for a private mausoleum, but Mother didn't agree, probably because she had heard Michael talk so strongly about never going back there. Yet Neverland *is* Michael, his joy and his fairytale, and I will always maintain that that is where he should be.

On the morning of our private memorial, we left for Forest Lawn in Glendale, setting off from Hayvenhurst in a fleet of vehicles under police escort. From the air, the cortège must have looked as long as a presidential cavalcade. That was when I started to notice how many people had stopped in Ventura Boulevard out of respect. And when we reached the 101 freeway heading south it was shut down on both sides. There wasn't a car in sight in either direction, which, as anyone from LA will tell you, is as rare a sight as can be. *Wow, Michael, you've cleared the roads.*

At the service, Wendell Hawkins, our cousin and an elder at the Kingdom Hall, gave a eulogy that was positive and uplifting: he spoke of the spirit and eternal life. We ended the service with a request from Paris. She wanted to hear her daddy sing 'Gone Too Soon' and when Michael's voice came from the speakers, I understood that he was still with us in spirit, and always would be.

AT THE STAPLES CENTER FOR THE public memorial, every little detail mattered. The brothers wore matching suits, with white shirts, gold ties, and a red rose tucked into our top left pockets, accentuating the huge bouquet of roses on Michael's coffin. The coffin came from Indiana. We took up our positions, flanking him, each wearing one sequined glove. Pulling his coffin on its trolley into that arena would be our proudest, saddest, most surreal and yet most honourable moment. After everything that had been thrown at him and said about him, this was the dignity he deserved. I was facing Randy at the front of the coffin, with Jackie behind me, Marlon on the other side in the middle and Tito holding up the rear, with two pallbearers from the funeral director's. We then heard our cue: the gospel choir – standing beneath the projected image of church windows letting in shafts of sunlight – singing 'We Are Born To See The King'. As we began to walk, I looked ahead and saw our mark: a pool of light where we would let the coffin rest on a raised platform surrounded by flowers. I kept my eyes on it and, as we came into view, cheers and applause greeted our brother. Glinting flashbulbs popped across the floor, up in every tier, and from high up in the glassed-off suites.

Mr Gordy walked onstage to deliver the first eulogy and pay tribute to his 'consummate student' from Motown University. As so many friends and artists spoke, I think we all felt that Michael's spirit filled that vast space, but as everyone remembered 'Billie Jean', 'Thriller' and his Moonwalk, I smiled at the memory of the kid who had stuck a pencil through two Quaker Oats cartons and who sang 'Climb Ev'ry Mountain', bringing a school to its feet. Fame and fortune hadn't changed his soul, it had just changed how people treated him. He left behind so many great deeds, far bigger than the superstar he was, and he did what every one of us should do: he lived his truth, undeterred by what anyone said and, forever kind, trusted God. I heard Mother's voice from our childhood asking, 'Is Michael okay?' *Yes, Mother. Michael is okay now. He's more okay now than he's ever been.*

Before the 'This Is It' concerts began, Michael had planned to visit Vevey, Switzerland, to spend time with the family of Charlie Chaplin. He wanted to take Prince, Paris and 'Blanket' to show them everything about the legend who had inspired him. No one loved the song Chaplin wrote, 'Smile', better than Michael. The intention of our family was that none of us would perform at the memorial service, but Michael and I had visited Vevey at different times and we had both raved about the experience of being at the Chaplin home, so I told Mother, 'I know what's been agreed about not performing, but I have to do this ...'

'Baby, if there's anything you want to do for Michael, now is the time,' she said.

In rehearsal, I was strong. But when it came to going live, it didn't feel so easy, probably because the occasion was so loaded with emotion. But someone pointed out to me backstage that Michael's image would be projected behind me, his arms out wide and a smile on his face. I'd be singing in his shadow, standing before his coffin. I had to do him proud. I hate wearing 'in-ears' and usually avoid them during performances, but on that occasion I had them – so I knew something was off as I sang the first line: the music in my ears kept cutting out, like a cell-phone with a bad signal. That was why I looked to my side for a split-second and put a hand to my ear. I had no idea there was no music in the arena, just my voice – it was by accident that I started to sing a cappella, but then the band kicked in until the music tracking returned. I felt so emotional that I forgot part of the lyric but we'd been taught to keep going, of course, so I pulled myself together and finished the song. It was then, as the audience applauded and I threw my rose on to Michael's coffin, that the reality hit me: this was the last time we'd share a stage. In our Jackson 5 days, he always said he was used to looking to his left and seeing me there. Now, when the brothers and I sing our music or his, it is healing for us. It cannot fill the hole, but it keeps us close to him.

AFTER THE PUBLIC DUTIES AND THE private burial, Mother needed to feel close to Michael in her own way. She packed her bags and told us she was returning to Gary to spend some time at 2300 Jackson Street. None of us joined her; she wanted to be alone. When I checked in with her that first week, she sounded so calm. 'I've found comfort,' she explained. 'I can hear him running around the house playing when he was a kid; I can hear his laughter.' She stayed at the old house for more than a month, living among those memories. But she also expressed a slight worry: she had noticed, when she looked out of the front window into Jackson Street, that more and more people were stopping their cars outside to take pictures. 'I've got to get this place fixed up ... We can't have it looking like this if people are going to keep coming by,' she said. And guess what? She ensured it was given a lick of paint and made to look pristine again. I heard Michael's laughter, too, when she told me that.

I also had to smile when she told me that the stack of bricks was still in the backyard after all those years. I asked her to bring one back as a souvenir for me. If it hadn't been for those damn bricks, we wouldn't have turned into the perfectionists we were, I told her. Those bricks were a lesson for life. I have that memento to this day – and Michael's voice is always in the back of my head, saying, 'Remember the bricks?'

When Mother was back in LA, she came across a lost poem of Michael's, written some time in the nineties and rediscovered in 2011. It was as if he was pointing her to his own words, two years after he had died, to provide her with further comfort. This is what he wrote – in pencil, on yellow legal-pad paper – and she treasures his words:

The reflection of a Mother's heart
Is in the glimmer in her children's eyes
Her every emotion and feeling is somewhere in her
    children's character
Noble men are what this Mother made them
Why does my Mother cry?
Are these happy tears or sorrow?
Oh please God, let them be happy tears
All my success has been based on the fact
That I wanted to make Mother proud
To win her smile of approval.

IN JANUARY 2011, HALIMA AND I travelled to Senegal to visit some old friends. One day, we drove three hours away from the city to a village in the middle of a dusty nowhere, where a community lived in clay huts with no water, no electricity, no nothing. As we arrived, so did some guy on a wagon loaded with yellow canisters carrying the village's water supply. But the kids didn't chase that vehicle, they chased ours. Dozens of children ran alongside us, waving and laughing. That day I learned a lot: those people were happy and joyful without material possessions or expectations. Apparently they knew little about the outside world, but they had their community, each other and family, and that was all that mattered. As far as they were concerned, I was just another black man, but one dressed in smart clothes and visiting from America. My name was Jermaine and my wife was Halima. That was how we were introduced.

We were led into a hut, where we met the village sage: a 97-year-old man with skin wizened like leather and only patches of white hair left on his head. His name was Waleef and he moved real slow, but he was the head of the village and what he said went. We stepped into his tiny place: it had a concrete floor and one raised mattress on a wooden frame, with four poles in the corners and a mosquito net. The flies were coming in and out, yet that man and his two elderly friends were sitting down, untroubled. He took my hand and invited me to sit. He read my palm and told me I was going to have a long life, then said a prayer as he traced every line in my hand. He reached under his bed, took out a pan, mixed the contents of four plastic bottles with some oil and sand, then started to rub it into my face and hair. Now, nobody touches my hair – nobody – but this man was allowed to, because I felt nothing negative from him as he mumbled and closed his eyes. 'What is he saying?' I asked Kareem, our friend who had taken us there.

'He's blessing you, and wishing you a good and safe onward journey,' I was told.

Halima, out of random curiosity, then said, 'Ask Waleef if he's ever heard of Barack Obama.'

It drew a blank expression and our host was unmoved.

'Ask him if he's ever heard of Michael Jackson,' she said.

Kareem relayed the question in their native tongue and the man started nodding and talking. 'Yes! He knows Michael Jackson.'

'Wait,' I said. 'He's heard of my brother? Out here?'

The sage took his hands off my head, placed them together as in prayer and said two words of English: 'Michael … Jackson.'

The two men either side of him were nodding, and one asked Kareem a question.

'Yes!' he replied. 'This is Michael Jackson's brother.'

At that, a teenage boy who had been standing in the doorway rushed off. A few minutes later, I heard a gaggle of children getting giddy, jumping up and down. When I walked outside, there must have been 50 of them and more were coming out from behind the huts to swarm around me. They started to shout my brother's name: 'MICHAEL JACKSON! MICHAEL JACKSON! MICHAEL JACKSON!' How was it possible that they knew of him in a place so detached from the modern world, without television? Kareem explained they sat around the odd crackling radio.

My eyes filled with tears: this was innocence, purity – this was what Michael was all about, and he had penetrated the most primitive, most remote of places. It blew me away, because those people had no preconceived ideas that would have tainted him for them. They knew Michael only as an incredible human being, an entertainer – and that is how the world should remember him; that is what he deserves.

I sat down to write this book two weeks after that visit, because it is important to me that people the world over understand who Michael was, what his legacy is, and how his time on earth was spent. I couldn't have been more motivated to write after walking into that village, where I didn't need to explain who he was or defend him. Those African children already knew his name, and the sound of it lit up their faces.

Halima threw me a bag of candy and I stood in the middle of the mêlée to hand it out. It was amazing to see the excitement that a piece of candy could bring. I remembered Michael standing at our back fence in Gary giving candy to the kids in the neighbourhood who were less fortunate. And now here I was in an African community that perfectly illustrated what he had been about all his life, surrounded by his 'We Are The World' children, who had nothing but love to give and joy on their faces as they shouted, 'MICHAEL JACKSON! MICHAEL JACKSON!'

That is the power of what he achieved.

That is his legacy.

That's my brother.

ACKNOWLEDGEMENTS

THIS IS A PROJECT THAT WAS long ago in my head, but it has waited for the right moment and people to come along and make it a reality.

I reserve my first and foremost gratitude to ghostwriter Steve Dennis who has shared my determination to do justice to the memory of Michael. Over many months he helped me shape my beginning, middle and end. His name might be invisible but his craft is on every page.

I owe a huge debt of gratitude to Andrew Higgie and David Foster because it was these two gentleman who first believed in this project and steered me to agent Gordon Wise, from Curtis Brown, London. His faith and guidance kept me on track. He made this book happen, and introduced me to publishers who have been a joy to work with: Natalie Jerome at Harper Collins in the UK and Stacy Creamer at Simon & Schuster (Touchstone Books) in the US, both of whom embraced this project with a mutual passion.

In London, Natalie led a classy production, bringing a special touch to this project. In New York, Stacy brought her infectious energy and her direction has been invaluable. I can't thank enough their teams of people for working so tirelessly on this book. Special thanks to Hazel Orme, Graham Holmes, Monica Green, Carole Tonkinson, Georgina Atsiaris, Ruth Deary, Andrew Cunning, Kevin Cahill, Joshua Karpf and Cherlynne Li. Also Ali Qamber, Harrison Funk, Hazel Gordy, Joy Robson, Viraf Sarkari, Andre Timmens, Lori Shapiro, and the brothers and sisters I bothered with 'Do you remember whens?': Marlon, Randy, Tito, Janet and Rebbie. My biggest gratitude in this regard, though, goes to Mother who greeted my endless questions about the past with patience and a memory that never falters.

Other people I would like to acknowledge are: Mr Berry Gordy, Clive Davis, Bobby Taylor, Suzanne de Passe, David Ritz, Deysha Britt, Janice Smith, Joel Katz, Allan J Freidman, Al Sharpton, Larry King, Brett Livingstone-Strong, Jillian Branco, Robert Sebree, Simmie Williams, Christophe Charlot, Maarten Mulder and my mother-in-law Laila Rashid whose fine cuisine provided sustenance during those endless nights of writing. There are also anonymous people who I cannot name for their assistance. You know who you are and my gratitude to each of you is immense.

The fondest memories I hold dear are those times as brothers. Sometimes, we don't express it enough to one another but Jackie, Tito, Marlon, Randy – and Michael – I am proud to call each one of you my brother, and remain proud of what we all built and achieved. Love and thanks also to Rebbie, La Toya, and Janet. Of course my gratitude to Mother and Joseph is immeasurable for the life, love and dreams you made happen.

As for my own children – Jermaine junior, Autumn, Jeremy, Jamie, Jourdyn, Jaafar and Jermajesty – you each make me proud as a father in your own different ways. I love you all.

And then my wife, Halima, for giving me the love and the strength over the years we've been together. It is your belief in me – and force for good – that always keeps me going. I love you.

Finally, to Michael whose spirit is with me every day. I never got the chance to properly express my gratitude before you left us, but I hope this book does some justice to the love, life and memories we shared. The world misses you.

JERMAINE JACKSON, September 2011